Southerners, Too?

Essays on the Black South
1733–1990

Alton Hornsby, Jr.

University Press of America,® Inc.
Dallas · Lanham · Boulder · New York · Oxford

Copyright © 2004 by
University Press of America,® Inc.
4501 Forbes Boulevard
Suite 200
Lanham, Maryland 20706
UPA Acquisitions Department (301) 459-3366

PO Box 317
Oxford
OX2 9RU, UK

Library of Congress Control Number: 2004102176
ISBN 0-7618-2872-9 (paperback: alk. ppr.)
ISBN 0-7618-2871-0 (hardcover: alk. ppr.)

⊖™ The paper used in this publication meets the minimum
requirements of American National Standard for Information
Sciences—Permanence of Paper for Printed Library Materials,
ANSI Z39.48—1984

To all those black southerners who bore their burdens
in the heat of the day

Contents

Preface

In the fall of 2001, as I prepared to retire from the position of editor of the *Journal of Negro History* after 25 years of service, colleagues who were preparing a dinner program in my honor asked that I compile a list of my publications and other scholarly activities. During this process, I, also, had an opportunity to revisit many unpublished essays, lectures, and other related materials. I discovered that most of these related, in one way or the other, to the Black South, particularly to Texas, a southwestern state (where I did my graduate work) and to Georgia, a southeastern state (where I was born and have spent most of my professional career). The geographical distinctions alone suggested the value of some of the case studies. But, the recent reemergence of the debate and controversy over the flying and display of the Confederate flag, particularly as it relates to race and "Southern heritage" suggested still another use for much of this material.

In much of the public as well as scholarly debate on the Confederate flag matter, "Southern heritage" has been seen in the context of the White South. Although we have a few published works on the black southerner, in the debate and in some of the literature, African-Americans are either invisible or appear in an ambivalent manner. Hence, the intent of this work is to contribute to, and encourage, a new focus on the Black South.

Several persons have assisted in the production of this book, and I wish here to express my deep appreciation. My graduate research assistants were J. Shaun King and Dedric Bonds. Angela Hornsby did extensive proofreading and Bettye Spicer and Natalie Dukes typed the various drafts of the manuscript. Mr. Bonds, Ms. Spicer and Ms. Dukes also provided technical assistance.

Introduction

One of the major bi-products of the Modern Civil Rights Movement was the rise of Neo-Confederate attitudes and practices among many white southerners. As a part of the backlash against school desegregation, desegregation of public accommodations, affirmative action and other civil rights initiatives, many of these white southerners took to the streets in protest. Others used the media, legislative and executive offices as well as the pulpit to voice their opposition to racial and other changes in the "New South." Most of these people were outside of the fanatical fringes of the often violent Ku Klux Klan, but they frequently shared a common symbol — the St. Andrews Cross or Confederate battle flag.

South Carolina had a long history of flying the Confederate banner alongside its state flag above its capitol building in Columbia. Mississippi and Georgia had incorporated the St. Andrews Cross in newer editions of their flags in 1897 and 1956, respectively. Georgia's inclusion, in 1956, coincided with the rise of the "massive resistance" to the school desegregation movement in the South.[1]

Although only three states had officially adopted the St. Andrews Cross in their state banners by the end of the twentieth century, the state imposed nature of these adoptions, together with the widespread use of the Confederate flag in anti-civil rights protests disturbed and angered many blacks as well as other Americans, including some southern whites. Typically, these individuals and groups charged that the banner was a symbol of slavery, racism, and oppression. Some even labeled the Confederate flag an emblem of "treason," in that the Confederates had waged an illegal rebellion against the United States between 1861 and 1865.

In a suit which he filed against the states of Georgia and Mississippi and the United States government in 1994, a black Atlantan, James Coleman, argued that these states' flying of the Confederate banner was "not only offensive to most African-Americans" but it also taught "that it's okay to try to overthrow the U.S. government." Although the federal courts, including the U.S. Supreme Court, dismissed Coleman's plea, arguing that the flag issue was a state matter, both the U.S. Court for the Northern District of Georgia and the Eleventh U.S. Circuit Court of Appeals agreed that the Confederate flag was "a symbol which creates controversy and discontent in the minds of many" and offended many Georgians. The Appeals Court, however, also recognized that "to some it honors those who fought in the Civil War."[2]

The leading organization supporting the use of the St. Andrews Cross as a legitimate state symbol, the Sons of the Confederate Veterans (SCV), founded in 1896, argues that it is "Southern heritage" including honoring the Confederate war effort and the Confederate dead, which is at the heart of the proponents' arguments. They deny that their advocacy is rooted in slavery and racism. They purport to deplore the use of the banner by violent-prone, racist groups, like the Klan, and suggest that many blacks are also descendants of Confederate veterans and are not offended by the St. Andrews Cross banner.[3]

The virulent supporters of the Confederate banner, "the flaggers," are a diverse group. Although the SCV is comprised of males, mostly white southerners, it includes blue collar as well as white-collar members, barely literate persons as well as highly educated individuals. Within and outside of the SCV are other individuals and organizations, including journalists, ministers, and scholars, who argue that "the Old South" was characterized by a unique culture that included chivalry, valor," love of family, respect, duty, and religious understanding." These values contrasted sharply with the morally corrupt Yankee society of the North, which placed economic gain and collectivism above all else. In large measure, they argue the Civil War was about turning back the attempt of the North to impose its industrial and commercial economy and collective values on a rugged individualistic, agricultural South, dominated by values and mores, which were imbedded in agrarianism, Christianity, and "the American Creed."[4]

The attack on the Confederate flag, then, in the view of the "flaggers," is really a continuation of an age-old struggle between those who would Yankeenize the South and those who would preserve the vaulted southern heritage. Nevertheless, some "flaggers" do admit that the movement for school desegregation and civil rights, while part of

"Yankee aggression," was also an effort to place blacks in places where many white southerners believed they should not be. Hence, at least, in this view, white supremacy and exclusivism play a pivotal role in the Neo-Confederate struggle.

The depth and the strength of Neo-Confederate feelings were most recently displayed in Georgia, which had won widespread national and international praise for diminishing the size of the Confederate banner on the new flag that it adopted in 2001. The "flaggers" movement immediately set out to overthrow the decision by political retribution on its political supporters, particularly Governor Roy Barnes, who engineered the flag change. Largely on the strength of Neo-Confederate, rural white votes, several of the state legislators who had supported the flag change, and Governor Barnes, were turned out of office in the November 2002 general elections. State Senator Sonny Perdue, who had voted against the flag change and who had supported a state referendum, such as the one held in Mississippi in 2001 (in which the Confederate symbol won overwhelming approval), was elected governor. The "flaggers," rejoicing, shouted, "Hell, no-we'll not fergit" and claimed a victory for their "Southern heritage."[5]

Racism or "Southern heritage"? Whose "Southern heritage"? Has the South been, and does it remain, a unique region in the United States? Is it the United States' Quebec?

Many scholars and other learned observers have believed that the South has been identified as a distinct region of the United States since the earliest periods of United States history. Although Charles Pinckney's declaration in 1787, "When I say Southern, I mean Maryland, and the states to the southward of her," was concerned principally with geographical boundaries, his implications for the future were clear. Pinckney anticipated what the next generation of Americans on both sides of the Mason-Dixon line came to believe: "that the South as a section possessed a separate and unique identity."[6]

Many visitors to the South during the first half of the nineteenth century also saw the "region as distinct, and they both influenced and were influenced by those who stressed the South's Uniqueness. Alexis de Tocqueville, Frederick Law Olmsted, Frances Kemble, and others wrote many pages describing or reflecting upon this region which appeared to be out of the mainstream of the American experience." The questions of when the South "developed its distinctive characteristics and, more important, how a consciousness of the region's separateness evolved" remain the subjects of considerable scholarly debate. Historian John R. Alden has written "the South's awareness of itself first appeared with the discovery of nationalism during the American Revolution, although most historians elaborating the identity theme date the development of the region's self-consciousness from the sectional controversies of the 1820s and subsequent years." John G. Van Deusen found that southern sectionalism emerged from the depression following the Panic of 1819; Glover Moore saw sectional animosities growing out of the 1820 debates on slavery and territorial expansion. Joseph C. Roberts believed that "the peculiarly Southern attitudes resulted from Nat Turner's revolt and its implications."[7]

Most observers seem to believe that "regardless of when the political, economic, societal, and attitudinal differences between the South and the remainder of the nation began, they were clearly evident by 1861 and they combined to play a part in bringing on a bloody conflict." While the Civil War held the Union together, the impact of the war and the Reconstruction Era "sustained sectional feeling, particularly in the former confederate states. Northern attempts to reconcile the South with the Union were unsuccessful . . . ."[8]

Following the Civil War, scholars and other observers, northerners, as well as southerners, and some foreigners, increased their fascination with "the mystery of the South." Many of these concluded that the presence of the Negro gave the South "distinctiveness." The pioneer proponent of this idea was the Southern-born historian, Ulrich B. Phillips. In an essay, first published in 1928, Phillips argued that southern whites "have resolved that above all else the South must remain a white man's country." According to Phillips, the South developed this doctrine of white supremacy "as soon as Negroes became numerous enough to create a problem of race control." He further contended "that the concept of the South would refer to a geographical region of the United States only if white supremacy were somehow overcome, but he assumed that white supremacy would remain forever with Southerners." Several years after Phillips first wrote on the subject, another southern historian, Francis B. Simkins continued the theme that white racism constituted "the one facet of the South" which made "the region different from the remainder of the nation." Although he conceded that racism was not peculiar to southerners, he held "that the particular set of events which [occurred] during and following Reconstruction gave Southern racism a special quality not found elsewhere." Also, like Phillips, Simkins believed "that an end to the doctrine of white supremacy would destroy the reality of Southernism" and he could not "conceive of a time when white supremacy will not exist in the South."[9]

More recently, other scholars have continued to point to the

significance of the Phillips thesis in explaining southern distinctiveness. Thomas D. Clark has argued that, "the Negro and his relationship with the white Southerner have constituted the distinguishing features of the Southern way of life." He states that the "old patterns of race relations," based largely on paternalism, eroded at "mid-century as well as the Southerner's resistance to the recent advances of the Negro." Implicit in his discussion is "a changing if not vanishing South." Historian George B. Tindall also saw a diminishing role for race in Southern identification. A "preoccupation with race," he thought, was no longer "a necessary feature of Southern life." Although, "an identifiable South will remain for years to come," Tindall thought, "that the region's future [was] related to much more than a system of segregation and proscription."[10]

In a somewhat different vein, Arkansas journalist Harry S. Ashmore saw the essentials of "modern Southernism as the institution of share tenancy, one partyism, and segregation of the races which developed with the abolition of slavery after the Civil War." Share tenancy, he thought

> provided an outlet for the former slave's labor; one-party politics controlled the Negro's political power; and Jim Crow practices circumscribed the social contact of the two races. In recent years these institutions have been profoundly altered: sharecropping declined after 1930; a viable two party system was in its infancy in the South by 1900; and events after World War II indicated the forming of irreparable cracks in the color wall. These internal changes were aided by powerful external forces that coalesced to diminish the South's separateness which, in turn led to a sharp reaction against the victorious North. The development of the myth of an idealized ante-bellum civilization, the glorification of the war, economic doldrums, and the determination to maintain white supremacy by saddling the freed Negro with second-class status kept alive in the late nineteenth and early twentieth centuries the belief that Dixie was a land unto itself.[11]

As suggested earlier, "the presence of the Negro" thesis has never been universally accepted, even among some southerners. Others have argued "that the presence of an aristocracy was more crucial to the region's identity," while another group saw the influence of a bellicose attitude on the part of southerners as a prime determinant in the region's character. Still others turned to the South's agrarianism and the ideals of an "agrarian society," "the inner nature of the region," and the South's "regional, cultural, and intellectual traditions."[12]

Louis B. Wright, for example, has described the development and growth of a "tight little aristocracy" in Colonial Virginia "which patterned its ways after the English ruling class." This "politically and economically powerful land gentry affected all of Southern colonial society." Other scholars have suggested, "the prevalence of the country gentleman ideal — a pattern of society borrowed from the English, justified by French physiocrats, and taking root naturally in the agricultural South — best explains the entire region." They argue "the ideal of the country gentleman was carried by emigrating Virginians and Carolinians to all corners of the South."[13]

Until recent times, the South has been a predominantly rural area, producing food for the table and staple crops for others. The southern-born historian, Charles W. Ramsdell believed that "the region's overriding attention to agriculture, particularly cotton, tobacco, and sugar, constitutes 'the most constant factor — thus the central theme — in the South's history.' This preoccupation with the cultivation of the soil has given the South's agricultural classes a crucial role in determining the conditions of Southern life and the patterns of its thinking." Although Ramsdell admitted "that poverty, the race problem, the consciousness of the South as a sectional minority, and the development of industry were additional components in the regional equation," he argued, "none of these factors was as significant a determinant as agriculture." He did, however, recognize that "as industry developed in the South, the region's devotion to agriculture began to weaken."[14]

When 12 Southern scholars and students, writing in 1930, looked at the "benefits of industrialization," they saw "the South gradually bartering away its tranquil agricultural ways for the gaudy." They, then "raised their voices against the trend, elaborating their objections in a book of essays entitled *I'll Take MY Stand*. These agrarians did not want the South to surrender its unique agricultural tradition and culture for dubious material gain. They sought to defend the Southern way of life against the American way, and they agreed that the phrase "Agrarian versus Industrial" best represented that distinction.[15]

The 12 southerners based their study and "manifesto" mainly on the ante-bellum South, while John Crowe Ransom carried "the concept of the agrarian South" into the period after the Civil War, arguing anew "that the values and ways of the agrarian South set it apart from the North." He, too, issued "a call to all Southerners to resist growing industrialism in their region in order to maintain a traditional agrarian philosophy."[16]

Thirty years after the agrarian manifesto was published, historian

David M. Potter saw

> the nation being overpowered by a pervasive urban-industrial
> culture. He found the South's past and future bound up in the
> survival of a meaningful folk culture rather than in its agricultural
> traditions. Potter does not argue that this folk culture, which
> survived into the age of the bulldozer, is ideal or utopian, although
> he does state that it has a relatedness and meaning not found in the
> materialistic mass culture. He [was] convinced that it is the key to
> an understanding of the South.[17]

On the other hand, the noted black historian John Hope Franklin
believed that militancy and violence could best characterize the Old
South. Southern society, he argued

> was afflicted with a martial spirit brought about by the glorification
> of war, by Southerners' long careers as frontiersmen and Indian
> fighters, by the region's deficient political system, and by the
> organization and discipline Southern whites effected to maintain
> the institution of slavery. Violence was inextricably woven into
> the fabric of Southern society, and it constituted an important
> element in the total experience of Southerners.[18]

Other observers have linked trends and patterns evident in the ante-
bellum South to more modern times and have seen extremism and
conservatism as major distinctive features of the region. Frank E.
Vandiver, for example, has suggested that:

> The most constant theme in the Southern experience has been
> response to challenge. [He explained] the Southerner's extremism
> in the nineteenth and twentieth centuries not only in terms of his
> past environment but also in terms of forces outside the South.
> Southerners' extreme reactions have been triggered by 'aggravated
> provocation,' and Northern, federal, and Negro pressures have set
> off the 'offensive-defensive mechanism' of militant Southerners,
> bringing bloodshed and death in the twentieth century as well as
> the nineteenth.

About the same time, historian Clement Eaton concluded
that there had been "little of . . . liberalism" in an Old South
"marked by extreme conservatism; a spirit of intolerance; a
powerful religious orthodoxy; an intense attachment . . . to
local community"; and "a powerful race feeling."[19]

The Southern journalist James Jackson Kilpatrick, looking at the modern South, saw

> A basically conservative regional civilization and culture based
> upon a reverence for tradition and good manners, the desire for
> liberty [not to say equality], and the attempt to resist industrialism
> by upholding old agrarian ideals and ways. Above all [this
> conservatism was related] to states' rights, and he use[d] that
> concept as a justification for many of the South's actions in recent
> years, especially regarding race relations. He contends that the
> Southern states collectively represent the final hope for the
> continued existence of a conservative philosophy in the United
> States.[20]

The most extreme example of southern extremism and
conservatism, James Silver believed, was in modern-day Mississippi
where a "closed society organized for the defense of white supremacy
and capable of vast quantities of self-deception" existed. In committing
itself to the defense of the bi-racial system, Mississippi, he felt, had a
totalitarian society.[21]

One of the premier historians of the South, C. Vann Woodward has
suggested that the region's distinctiveness lies in its history, that is, in
"the collective experience" of the Southern people. He points out that
Americans, generally have known abundance, while Southerners have
known poverty; that the United States has experienced success,
whereas the South has known frustration, failure, and defeat, including
not only military defeat in the Civil War but also the frustration of
Reconstruction and long decades of failure in economic, social, and
political life; that Americans have known innocence, even as the South
has felt guilt; that Americans were "born free," yet southerners were
not, since they had and have the problems of the slave and Negro.
Thus, Woodward concludes, "the South has had a tragic history and
that this has helped unify the section and contribute to its
uniqueness."[22]

Some scholars have argued, the South's distinctiveness lay not in
any single factor, but in several aspects of its history. For example, the
aristocratic and chivalrous traditions, William R. Taylor believes are
embodied in "Cavalier myths," which have ante-bellum origins. He
suggested that:

> During the first four decades of the nineteenth century, Southern
> fiction tended to be a means of self-admonition and reconciliation
> rather than the militant advocacy of a Southern cause against all
> corners. The Southern gentleman was indeed "synthetic" and

embraced by Southerners not so much because they believed in him but because they needed him so badly. Moreover, the Cavalier was the invention of both Northerners and Southerners to fill the common need for codes and creeds that were not bound to the bustling, acquisitive materialism of nineteenth-century American society.[23]

As the previous discussion has demonstrated, for a long time, most scholars and other observers of the South, regardless of regional or ethnic origins, tended to agree, although for differing reasons, that the South has been (and some would suggest remains) a distinctive region — "a nation within a nation." But, increasingly, particularly since the Second World War, these views of a collective South have come under increasing scrutiny.

Diversity in the region and the "Americaness" of southerners was seen even in the ante-bellum period. "In several Southern states during the 1850s politicians came to power who represented the common white man. Conceptions of 'Jacksonian democracy' vary, but by definition, Southerners were participants. Ameliorative and moral reforms such as poor relief, school drives, temperance campaigns and moral improvement societies also existed in Southern states."[24]

Dewey W. Grantham, Jr. has cautioned that the image of a monolithic and conservative South completely given over to political reaction and racial demagoguery must be tempered by the reality of a liberal tradition. He argued

> that every reform movement affected the South, and that Wilson's New Freedom and Roosevelt's New Deal had strong Southern support and local manifestations. Even the Dixie demagogues who flourished so dramatically in the era between the two world wars represented something more than violent Negrophobia and surrender to large property interests — Hoke Smith of Georgia and Huey Long of Louisiana, and others had sponsored authentic reform programs for white citizens.[25]

Carl Degler and other scholars have also presented persuasive evidence that there has always been "The Other South." From the ante-bellum period through the early days of the Civil Rights Movement, southern whites have appeared who have raised voices of dissent against prevailing and monolithic views. Although, for the most part, they were part of a losing cause, when reforms did occur, they were in the forefront of them.[26]

And by the 1960s, scholars such as Howard Zinn were arguing that "the Southern mystique" had always been more myth than reality. Zinn conceded that the South was indeed "racist, violent, hypocritically pious, xenophobic, false in its elevation of women, nationalistic, conservative and [harbored] extreme poverty in the midst of ostentatious wealth." But, an examination of the histories of the North and West also showed "the United States as a civilization embodies all of these same qualities" and that the South was merely a mirror of the Republic which reflected national images more vividly and sharply." Zinn further suggested "the tendency of Americans to be overawed by history acted as a barrier to the social change which must come in the future." In the end, Zinn concluded, "we created the mystery of the South, and we can dissolve it."[27]

Interestingly and ironically, almost all of the studies and observations that have been made about southerners and 'Southerness' involve whites (and, in many cases, only white men). Even when observers admit that blacks, too, were (and are) southerners, they develop their theories and theses around whites only — in most cases seeing blacks as "victims" only; persons acted upon, rather than playing leading roles in the determination of the region's cultural philosophies and practices. Among the first major deviants from this norm was the black scholar Lawrence D. Reddick. For the Negro, Reddick suggested, "identification has always been a problem." Inescapably he has found himself to be a "Southerner."

> He may not have preferred the term, but the objective fact could not be denied. As everyone knows, the majority of Negroes, historically and currently, have been born in the South and lived out their lives there. By way of residence and experience, the region has set its mark upon all of its people.

> Likewise the Negro has set his mark upon the South. It is difficult to imagine that part of the country without colored people — their presence, their labor, their music and humor, and their challenge. What would be left of Southern literature, for example, if we took away the black man as subject and creator?

> Negro and white Southerners are reluctant to admit their kinship, not merely at times when it is biological, but more generally when it is regional. They tend to stress their differences, while in fact they are in so many ways brothers under the skin. Their similarities are remarkable especially in speech, gait, food habits, and orientation toward life. Often, when the person we just heard

over the telephone appears before us, we are surprised to find his skin color different from what we expected. One perceptive white Southerner, sensitized to this by his residence in the North, has 'noted again and again how often we laugh at the same things, how often we pronounce the same words the same way to the amusement of our hearers, judge character in the same frame of reference, mist up at the same kind of music.' 'All men, to be sure, are kin,' concludes Charles L. Black, 'but Southern whites and Negroes are bound in a special bond. In a peculiar way, they are the same kind of people . . . . [Even] their strife is fratricidal.'

Southerners — black and white — tend to exhibit an open, sprawling friendliness, yet strongly emphasize family ties and personal loyalties. To them it is the man that counts, rather than the idea he represents. Talk runs to conversation, not discussion. Orators are everywhere. Church going is habitual and regular, manifesting a religion that is active and demonstrative. The womenfolk move about the home, but the menfolk take to the woods and rivers. Perhaps not quite so well armed as the mythical American Westerner, the Southerner is, nevertheless, notably quick with his fists. In a word, the people of Dixie are still relatively rural and folkish, encouraged in this by the open country, blue skies, and warm weather. This is true for blacks as well as whites and is fairly obvious to any observer who can see beyond skin color.[28]

In *Redefining Southern Culture: Mind and Identity in the Modern South*, James C. Cobb has provided one of the latest syntheses of southern identity that also underscores the notion of African-Americans as southerners. He concluded that by the 1990s blacks were increasingly embracing a southern identity that includes a regional lifestyle, "dialects and dietary preferences."[29]

In the selections that follow, I, too, will show that blacks have been an indispensable part of the history and culture of the South, both in its distinctive as well as national features. The essays will re-enforce the notion that the cultural experiences of Africans and Africans in the Diaspora have been intertwined with Euro-Americans and others to help define the heritage of the South and the nation.

Notes

[1] David Firestone, "The New South: Old Times They Are Not Forgotten", *New York Times*, January 28, 2001, sec. 4.4., Steve Lopez, et al., "Ghosts of the

South," *Time Atlantic*, 157, No. 17; Michael Schaffer, "The New Battle for the States," *U.S. News and World Report*, February 12, 2001, 130, No.6.

[2] *Atlanta Journal-Constitution*, December 25, 1998.

[3] Department of the Army of Northern Virginia," Defending the Colors... Advancing the Colors," *Sons of Confederate Veterans*, October 11, 2002, http://www.scv.org/education.

[4] *Ibid.*

[5] *Atlanta Journal-Constitution,* June 10, 2001; Lopez, et. al., "Ghosts of the South"; Schaffer, "New Battle of the States," *Atlanta Journal-Constitution*, November 6, 2002.

[6] Monroe L. Billington, ed., *The South: A Central Theme?* (New York, 1969), p.1.

[7] *Ibid.*

[8] *Ibid.*

[9] For a full text of the Phillips thesis, see *American Historical Review*, XXXIV (1928), pp. 30-43; Francis B. Simkins, "Unchanging White Supremacy," *Current History*, XXXV (November, 1956), pp. 282-286; Billington, *Ibid.*, pp. 3, 8-13.

[10] George B. Tindall, "The Central Theme Revisited," in Charles Grier Sellers, Jr., *The Southerner as American* (Chapel Hill, 1960); *Ibid.*, pp. 3, 14-23.

[11] *Ibid.*, pp. 3, 36-40.

[12] *Ibid.*, p. 4.; Charles Crowe, ed., *The Age of Civil War and Reconstruction, 1830-1900: A Book of Interpretative Essays* (Homewood, Il, 1966), pp. 44-52.

[13] *Ibid.*, pp. 4, 41-46.

[14] *Ibid.*, pp. 5, 77-90.

[15] Billington, pp. 5, 6, 91-96; Crowe, *The Age of Civil War and Reconstruction*, pp. 44-52.

[16] Billington, *The South: A Central Theme?*, pp. 6, 93-96.

[17] *Ibid.*, pp. 6, 97-101.

[18] Billington, *Ibid.*; Crowe, *The Age of Civil War and Reconstruction*, pp. 75-80.

[19] Billington, *Ibid.*, pp. 6, 69-76.

[20] *Ibid.*, pp. 6., 111-118.

[21] Charles Crowe, *Slavery, Race and American Scholarship: Explorations in Historiography* (Needham Heights, MA), p. 125.

[22] Billington, ed., *The South: A Central Theme?*, pp. 6, 102-109; Crowe, *The Age of Civil War and Reconstruction*, pp. 139-144.

[23] Crowe, *Ibid.*, pp. 108-116.

[24] *Ibid.*

[25] See also Charles Grier Sellers, Jr., *The Southerner as American*, (Chapel Hill, 1960).

[26] See Carl N. Degler, *The Other South: Southern Dissenters in the Nineteenth Century*, (Tallahassee, FL, 1974).

[27] Crowe, *The Age of Civil War and Reconstruction*, pp. 127-139.

[28] See Sellers, ed., *The Southerner As American*, pp. 130-147; Historical treatments of black Southerners include Arnold H. Taylor, *Travail and Triumph: Black Life and Culture in the South* (Westport, CT, 1977) and John B. Boles, *Black Southerners, 1619-1869* (Lexington, KY, 1984).

[29] See James C. Cobb, *Redefining Southern Culture: Mind and Identity in the Modern South* (Athens, GA, 1999).

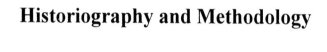

Historiography and Methodology

Chapter 1
The Changing Vicissitudes
of Black Historiography

Many years ago, a young black child asked an eminent historian: Why is it that black people are not represented in our history books? Why, don't you know, the scholar answered, the Negro race, both in Africa and America, has no history.

The response of this historian was, in fact, typical of the view held by most whites at the time that Africans were enslaved in the Americas. Both scholars and laypersons allowed their own racism to color their study, analysis, and understanding of the African race. These attitudes persisted into the nineteenth and early twentieth centuries. Except for such black historians as George Washington Williams, William Wells Brown, W. E. B. DuBois, and Carter G. Woodson, the prevailing scholarship viewed blacks as universally inferior, happy, docile, child-like, and dependent upon others who were morally and intellectually superior. These historians took an extremely negative view of African as well as African-American culture. They argued, for example, that all slaves had been mentally retarded and irresponsible; that black families had been matriarchal, dysfunctional, and pathological. These families, they said, were characterized by incompetent, shiftless fathers, and parents, generally, who were unconcerned about their children's welfare. African and African-American cultures, then, were seen as

Presented at Southern University at Baton Rouge, Louisiana, February 14, 1982

virtually non-existent, except in the crude and primitive ways that blacks expressed the most basic and base human needs.

One of the first prominent white historians to set the negative tone in American historiography was Albert Bushnell Hart. In 1906, in his work, *Slavery and Abolition*, Hart wrote that the majority of blacks were "course and unattractive in appearance. Women were clumsy, awkward, gross, elephantine in all their movements . . . sly, sensual, and shameless in all their expressions and demeanor." Furthermore, blacks were not to be trusted since they were prone to lying and stealing. At best they were . . . big children, pleased with trifles and easily forgetful of penalties and pain." In his view, blacks made no cultural contribution to American life because they came from retarded cultural backgrounds. He continued: blacks felt little or no obligation to their spouses and parent-child relationships were weak because of the "casual sensuality" that was so characteristic of African culture.

Twelve years after Hart wrote, U. B. Phillips published his so-called classic, *American Negro Slavery*. For Phillips, there was no doubt that the slaves were inferior people, victims of a weak, unstable African environment and weak, biological genes. The African climate, he said, discouraged "mental effort of a severe or sustained character, and the Negroes have submitted to that prohibition through countless generations, with excellent grace." Again, adult blacks were little more than big children, devoid of any significant cultural heritage, completely dependent upon the benevolent influence of their white enslavers and far better off in American slavery than they had ever been in the wilds of Africa. Nevertheless, they exhibited an eagerness for "music and merriment, a fondness for display whether of person, dress, vocabulary, or emotion." They had "a receptiveness toward any religion whose exercises were exhilarating, a proneness to superstition [and] a courteous acceptance of subordination." Their African heritage, he concluded, had made them all well suited for a life of control and supervision. White planters, then, ought to be praised for providing them with the benevolent, benign, and paternalistic life which they enjoyed in American slavery.

Because of his academic credentials as well as his long and painstaking research, U. B. Phillips influenced nearly two generations of white American historians. His conclusions on the economic operations of the plantation and the general economics of slavery are still respected by some modern scholars, like Eugene Geneovese. But his methodological approach and his obvious racism gradually fell into disfavor.

First, we should understand that many, perhaps most, blacks never accepted the positions of men like Hart and Phillips. Even as early as the ante-bellum period, intelligent blacks like Benjamin Lewis, J. W. C. Pennington, and William C. Nell had rejected the racist historical scholarship, and placed blacks in a much better light. Lewis wrote *Light and Truth: Containing the Universal History of the Colored and Indian Races, From the Creation of the World to the Present Time* in 1836; Pennington authored *A Textbook of the Origin and History of the Colored People* in 1847; and Nell wrote *The Colored Patriots of the American Revolution with Sketches of Several Distinguished Colored Persons to Which is Added a Brief Survey of the Conditions and Prospects of Colored Americans* in 1852. Because of Nell's verbosity, most of us simply call his work *The Colored Patriots of the American Revolution*. Although, these men were untrained as historians, they sought to identify and document the significant contributions which blacks had made to the world and to American civilization.

But the valiant efforts of the pioneer black chroniclers of the African and African-American past were only read by a few whites and blacks. Whites, whom it was hoped would be forced to recognize the sins of their degradation of blacks, while at the same time seeing the race as one of producers rather than dependents, of equals rather than inferiors, rarely saw the publications. Even when they did peruse them, they criticized the scholarship as unscientific and primitive. The authors had not done sufficient research and they had not subjected their materials to critical analysis. Blacks, it had been hoped, would see the severity of their oppression, but at the same time learn of others who had succeeded and contributed despite their adversities. But, only the relatively small group of literate, free blacks could be exposed to these messages.

By the time, however, that George Washington Williams published his *History of the Negro Race in America from 1619 to 1880* in 1883, there was a wider readership among whites, and, especially, the newly freed blacks. Nevertheless, although Williams' work is often cited as the first scientific history of American blacks by an African-American, and Williams, himself, is sometimes called the Father of Black History, the book, too, was attacked for containing too many embellishments and speculations. Whatever the flaws in Williams' work, it was, perhaps, just as scientific as the so-called scientific works of white scholars of the period, and, more importantly, it offered a basic framework of scholarly research upon which later scholars could build. One such person was W. E. B. DuBois who began his career as an historian with the publication of *The Suppression of the African Slave*

Trade to America, 1638-1870 in 1896.

As important as the efforts of men like Williams and DuBois were, they still made little inroads between both the white and black populations. Even the impeccable scholarship of DuBois in *The Suppression of the African Slave Trade* and his article on Reconstruction in the prestigious *American Historical Review* in 1910 received only scattered favored comments among whites and generally failed to reach the black masses.

But, by the time of the First World War, a new group of black historians had arisen to record and assess the black experience, particularly in the United States. Foremost among the growing cadre of professionally trained scholars was probably Carter G. Woodson. Woodson, most commonly known as the Father of Black History, revolutionized the discipline. He not only met most of the criteria for scientific studies of his subjects, but he extended the history of African peoples much further than any of his predecessors. Through the Association for the Study of Negro Life and History, founded in 1915, Woodson first published the venerable *Journal of Negro History* in 1916. This important periodical was shortly followed by the establishment of the associated publishers, to publish books by and about blacks, and *The Negro History Bulletin*, which was designed to take black historical scholarship into the elementary and secondary schools as well as public libraries and the home. But, it was, perhaps, his founding of Negro History Week in 1926 that did the most to introduce the masses of black Americans, particularly, to their long and rich history.

Woodson's approach to black history was basically the same as that of the earlier generation of popular African-American historians. He, and his disciples, sought, on one hand, to tell the truth about black conditions and accomplishments, to motivate and inspire African-Americans; and, on the other, to promote "harmony between the races by acquainting the one with the other." While, again, this approach was not new, the significance of the Woodson group was that they were generally better trained than their predecessors, they were more prolific, and their message reached a far greater audience than ever before.

The Woodson group also realized to a greater extent than earlier popular writers that their treatments of the African-American experience had to relate to the African backgrounds of most American blacks. But, here they were hindered by the relative inaccessibility of original documents on the African experience. After all, the prevailing scholarship had maintained that Africans had no history, or, at least, none worth recognizing. So while George Washington Williams and W. E. B. DuBois, but particularly Carter G. Woodson in the *African Background Outlined* in 1936, were countering the racist consensus, another black scholar, E. Franklin Frazier, in 1939, gave some considerable comfort to it.

Frazier believed that African slaves had no cultural background: the horrors of the middle passage, the dispersal of blacks throughout the South, and the mixing of recent African arrivals with native African-Americans had all so diluted the African heritage until it had absolutely no influence on black culture in America. According to Frazier, "African traditions and practices did not take root and survive in the United States . . . probably never before in history has a people been so nearly completely stripped of its social heritage as the Negroes who were brought to America." "As regards Negro family life," Frazier wrote, in *the Negro Family in the United States*, "There is no reliable evidence that African culture has had any influence on its development. The black family was at the mercy of the American environment, and it deteriorated badly." For Frazier, slave marriages were most often the result of basic or base sexual desires and were easily dissolved once those desires were satisfied or disappeared. Only when the blacks modeled their values after those of whites did their marriages show any maturity or stability. Spousal relationships and the bond between parents and children were very weak, thus making black society very different from white society. And so, he concluded, most black people were fundamentally different from whites.

Frazier was particularly harsh in his criticisms of black men. They, he said, had been emasculated of any patriarchal authority by the power of the white man. They became weak and culturally impotent, and, thus, the black family took on a distinctly maternal flavor. With our hindsight, perhaps the only good things that one can admire about Frazier are that he, himself, opposed slavery and blamed white masters, not black genes, for the slave's alleged pathologies. Otherwise, however, his ignorance of the African past and his narrow methodology placed him in the same school of historiography, or in the same boat, with U. B. Phillips.

Meanwhile, a few white scholars had joined blacks like Woodson and DuBois in producing studies which exposed the deficiencies of the racist school of African-American historiography. Among these were, Richard Hofstadter, Gunnar Myrdal, and Melville Herskovitz. Hofstadter, in an article in *The Journal of Negro History* in 1944, attacked Phillips' concentration on the larger plantations, where only about half of the slaves worked and his ignoring of black sources. He also pointed to Phillips' ignorance of African history and culture and his apparent narrow racial attitudes.

Three years earlier, as part of his study of black life and democracy in the United States, Gunnar Myrdal had commissioned the anthropologist Melville J. Herskovitz to study the roots of black culture. Herskovitz went further, and in 1941, published the classic, *The Myth of the Negro Past*. According to Herskovitz, much of the earlier work on blacks by historians had been misleading and erroneous. He rejected the notion of an absence of a black past as well as the child-like, docile personality which had been ascribed to African slaves. Instead he found a people who had consistently resisted slavery both through subtle and non-violent means, as well as open, violent protest. And they had not been robbed of, nor forgotten, their African past. Indeed, "African traditions, attitudes, and institutions had survived the middle passage and the other horrors of slavery. These included techniques for cooking, birthing and rearing children, and health care. Although the slaves adopted fundamental Protestantism, they injected into it an African emotional spirit — in musical rhythms, dance, and the decoration of graves." Although the slaves assumed the English language, they placed English words in a grammatical context which was both English and African in origin. So, Herskovitz concluded that, as other immigrants to the United States retained their culture, so did Africans.

Yet, amazingly, despite the works of prominent black scholars as well as white ones like Hofstadter, Herskovitz, and Herbert Aptheker, the white scholarly establishment continued to ignore the vast, often unique, features and contributions of African peoples to world civilization, generally, and American society, particularly. It was not until the 1950s and 1960s, spurred by the Civil Rights Era and the reawakening of black consciousness, particularly on the nation's college campuses, that the contents and issues introduced by the earlier scholars found wide acceptance in the American academy and in American public opinion. Much of the credit for these developments is rightfully attributed to individuals, mainly black scholars and students, who called themselves or came to be known as Afro-Centrists. The Afro-Centrists were really both Infusionists and Centrists. They urged, even demanded, that black culture, particularly black history, be added to the curricula of schools and colleges and be inserted, in a much larger way than had hitherto been the case, into textbooks and monographs. They then argued that black history could best be understood by beginning with the African background of black

Americans and, then, placing the African and African-American culture as the central focus of the enterprise.

Interestingly and ironically, although some railed against Infusionism and Afro-Centrism as illegitimate academic endeavors, based more on emotion than sound scholarship, others plowed into the new efforts with reckless abandon — and most of these were white scholars. Out of the emergence of this new emphasis came what was called the New Black History, which, of course, was not new at all. We simply now had some of the most prominent white scholars in America conceding that the African race, both on the continent and in the Diaspora, did have a history. And so while Malcolm X, among others, still cried that it was a shame the lie that had been told to black men and white men alike . . . that the black race had no history, Malcolm could also say, "The truth is coming out of the bag now."

By all measurements, one of the most significant studies to emerge from this period was Herbert Gutman's, *The Black Family in Slavery and Freedom, 1750-1925* in 1976. Gutman, unlike the racist school of historiography and E. Franklin Frazier, saw the black family as the essence of black culture. He said that "African religious, folk, family, and cultural practices came across the Atlantic with the slaves, but by 1800, when American-born blacks outnumbered Africans, a new Afro-American culture had emerged." Many men and women, though, remained together as a family unit throughout slavery and after emancipation, and the black family "developed into the foundation of black culture." Gutman also argued, as others before him, that the two-parent patriarchal family was the norm and that the extended family was a curative, stabilizing influence for nuclear families separated by forced sales and other dislocations. The appearance of Gutman's work was not only a rebuttal to the white racist school of historiography and Frazier, but also to contemporary Neo-Frazerites, like Professor and Presidential Advisor Donald Monyihan. It firmly established, through the research and writings of a major, contemporary white scholar, the image of an ancestral black family which was "proud and emotionally healthy" and which "nurtured feelings of self-worth for men, women, and children."

Still, in the reactionary atmosphere created in the country during the administration of President Richard M. Nixon, there was far from full acceptance of the new black history. Black scholars and activists, particularly, came under attack for "sugar-coating" their history and other distortions, designed to raise black self-esteem. To be sure, some of the Afro-Centrists had, as the contributionists before them, raised certain figures, like Crispus Attucks and Phyllis Wheatley to statures that they probably did not deserve, but these did not illegitimize the whole movement. Others, including some young, mobile black scholars, decried the Afro-Centricity for ignoring the more central place of class, or even gender, in the black historical experience. And they argued that it was inaccurate and misleading to place African-Americans and their African background as the principal focus of these historical works. And so there was, even on some historically black college campuses, a waning of interest in Afro-Centric studies.

Then after the interlude of the moderate presidential administration of Jimmy Carter and the return to Republican reactionism under Ronald Reagan, there arose new cries of discontent in Black America which, again, attacked the traditional black agenda of established black leaders and organizations as partially responsible for the continued pathologies among African-Americans. Nevertheless, the new Afro or more correctly Afri-Centrists, espoused the infusion of African and African-American culture into western-centered or euro-centric curricula, books and other materials, with Africanism as the central focus, as critical to fostering black self-esteem and countering white racist stereotypes and actions. The African heritage received new prominence through not only the resurrection of the great black dynasties of Egypt and the legendary kingdoms of the western Sudan, but even in the discarding of the American suffix to refer to African peoples in America. The more rabid Afri-Centrists, then, became simply Africans. At the same time, past heroes, including Richard Allen, Mary McCleod Bethune, W. E. B. DuBois, and, even Martin Luther King, Jr. lost some of their halo, as Angela Davis, and, particularly Malcolm X, emerged as more relevant models for the new Afri-Centrism. For the new Afri-Centrism tended to disdain the politics and integrationism of the traditional black agenda and endorsed black nation-building, even separatism. It also rejected Kingsian non-violence in favor of "by any means necessary."

The new Afri-Centrism not only raised fears, then, among many whites, but also many blacks as well. And there emerged renewed attacks on the academic credibility of both Infusionism and Afri-Centrism emphases. The noble Western canon of scholarship was being unfairly assailed, critics claimed, in favor of a politically correct curriculum. The new Afri-Centrists, some railed, with its focuses on Africa, Nationalism, and Separatism, was little more than black racism. They failed to concede that, in the first place, separatists and racists, even among the new Afri-Centrists, did not constitute the core of theoretical underpinnings or actual adherents. Basic Afri-Centrism simply stipulated that African and the experiences of African peoples in the Diaspora should be placed at the center of their reality; for it was in these cultures that such individuals usually had the essence of their beings. In this sense, Afri-Centrism was no different from any of the other ethnic, religious, or regional focuses, which have constituted the melting pot out of which American history emerges. And the opponents also fail to take into account that any philosophy or practice which claims a cultural or material dominance of the contributions to civilization is not only racist and ethno-exclusivist, but is politically incorrect.

Indeed Afri-Centrism, even in the earliest writings of blacks on their history, is a central theme. For, as early as those days when hope unborn had died, the centrality of black life was not in the big house among white enslavers, but in the fields and quarters, among bondsmen and bondswomen. And the essence of black life, then as now, has not been in "the rockets' red glare [where] our flag was still there," but more so in "we have come over a way that with tears has been watered, we have come treading our paths through the blood of the slaughtered."

Chapter 2
Drum Major on the Mountaintop: Martin Luther King, Jr. and the Great Man Theory Of History

As you know, for several years now both the Georgia legislature and the National Congress have been debating the proposition of this day, January 15th, the birthday of Martin Luther King, Jr., as a state and national holiday. Proponents have argued that Dr. King was, indeed, a great Georgian and a great American, and like most other such greats, deserves singular recognition by observing a day of rest and commemoration in his honor. The more reasoned opponents of the idea argue, among other things, that Dr. King's true greatness, his proper role in history, has not yet been established. They plead for additional time and for the judgment of history before bestowing greatness and before establishing a holiday.

While it is true that most historians prefer the passage of several decades before ascribing greatness to any single individual, there are other criteria, which come to bear which may shorten the time necessary for a judicious assessment. Thomas Carlyle and other proponents of the "Great Man Theory" of history believe that certain almost super-human characters do appear on the globe from time to time who dominate an era, an epoch, or an age and, thus, rightfully can be called great men and women. They would cite the Alexanders, the Napoleons, the Lincolns, perhaps the Cleopatras, the Elizabeths, the

Presented at Paine College (Augusta, GA), January 15, 1983

Washingtons, and Jeffersons as examples of such personalities. Most would assert that such individuals must possess charisma and a degree of genius and must, somehow, largely through their own ideas and/or leadership, alter the course of history. In other words, if one assumes that time and history are on a steady continuum, these exceptional individuals help to forge a mutation in that continuum or in the normal flow of events. Such a feat, all admit, is very rare and must involve the overcoming of powerful social forces, like religion, nationalism, racism, and economic determinism, which may be arrayed against the individual.

I would suggest that, even today, we can, with great influence and certain plausibility, assert that Martin Luther King, Jr., was a charismatic individual. He possessed outstanding oratory; he had the ability to inspire loyalty; and he had the ability to influence legions of others to follow in the paths he trod.

King's genius did not lie solely in his I.Q., which his several books and essays, particularly his "Letter From The Birmingham Jail" and his orations, particularly his "I Have a Dream Speech," indicate was considerable, but also, and perhaps, more importantly, in his powers of discernment, that is, in the ability to perceive significant situations or events and to plot appropriate strategies. While critics may argue, perhaps correctly, that King did not wisely perceive and plan his campaigns at St. Augustine, Albany, and Chicago, it may also be countered that he was not fully in control of the events at those places. For example, at Albany (and one hesitates to raise the name of that city after I was almost run out of town a couple of years ago for even mentioning the possibility that King suffered a defeat there); nevertheless, at Albany, the local leadership was divided and at Christmas in 1961 changed strategies while Dr. King was in jail and unaware. Specifically, they bailed King out of jail before the holiday, depriving him of the opportunity to dramatize the spending of Jesus' birthday behind bars. When, at the same time, Albany police adopted a policy, which they described as civil toward the demonstrators, King had to leave Albany without being able to mount the dramatic confrontation and achieve the notable settlements that became associated with his name. Thus some suggest that King encountered a major defeat, at Waterloo, at Albany. But this criticism ignores the fact that Albanians had called King into the city to increase the momentum of their Movement, recognizing, as they did, the power of his oratory — of his charisma — and the success of his leadership elsewhere. And, it cannot be denied that King, while in Albany, to use his own words, helped blacks to straighten up their backs. Once this happened, the campaign had already been won, although there were, to be sure, individual setbacks from time to time.

Also at Chicago, local leaders apparently were divided and apparently did not appropriately prepare the city or properly prepare Dr. King, himself, for the campaign there. Hence, the demonstrations in Chicago were not as fervent as those in the South. They were also more prone to violence. Additionally, Chicago's political leaders accustomed to dealing with blacks through ward and precinct patronage, furnished little confrontation on their own and sought to provide protection against racist hecklers. While King may be properly criticized for lacking the foresight to appreciate that Southern-style demonstrations would be received lukewarmly in the North, he did not incorrectly gauge the degree of racism in that section of the country. But, perhaps, as even Southerners are now learning, he should have also known that the contours of subtle and overt racism are different and should be attacked in varying ways. Yet, one must credit to King's great charisma the fact that a Southern preacher was allowed to take command in Chicago in the first place and inspired at least hundreds to join him in the streets. And, there remains an outstanding legacy of the King campaign in Chicago, even today, in Operation Push, led by one of his lieutenants, Jesse Jackson.

While many raise questions about King's genius, while probably conceding his charisma, at Albany and Chicago, almost all would agree that he showed both genius and charisma at Birmingham and Selma and, indeed, achieved historical mutations in these places.

Following the setback at Albany, King and his lieutenants carefully planned for Birmingham. They, importantly, worked closely with local leaders, like the Reverend Fred Shuttlesworth. Local leaders handled the advance preparations. To be sure, King had a willing symbol for confrontation in Birmingham's Police Commissioner Eugene Bull Connor and his legion of Klansmen on and off the police force, but the orchestration of the confrontation was directed by King. The highlight of the drama may well have been the march on Good Friday in 1963, when King and his followers brought reminders of Christ's pilgrimage to Calvary. Fortunately they, unlike he, did not have to pay the supreme sacrifice on that occasion, but the day was, indeed, a dangerous one and King, as he had wished, spent Easter Day in jail.

As you know, while in jail, King penned the famous "Letter from a Birmingham Jail," in which he gave legal, moral, and intellectual justification for non-violent, direct resistance to segregation.

Meanwhile, the Birmingham campaign continued in the streets. The vivid pictures of black women being mauled by white policemen, of vicious dogs snipping at the pants and dresses of demonstrators, and of high powered water hoses knocking down children telecast and printed, as they were, around the world, not only led to an end to segregation in Birmingham, but further propelled the civil and human rights struggle of blacks in America into a national, even international issue. No longer could any ambassador, any president, any congressman, any preacher, or teacher ignore or downplay the realities of American white racism, and for segregation and discrimination in the public sectors of American life the bell had been tolled.

The March on Washington in August 1963 was, I suggest, a national affirmation that the outrages in law and in practice against black Americans, symbolized at Birmingham, must end. The Civil Rights Act of 1964 was the legal pronouncement of the nation that the outrages were an anathema to the American creed and its perpetrators were outlaws. Civil rights were then a phenomena whose time had come. A manipulation and modification of the course of history had occurred.

All of this is not to say that King did not receive, and continues to receive, criticisms for his Birmingham campaign. Some complain about the use of children in the demonstrations. Others say he did not go far enough in that radical social reform was not achieved. But, of course, King did not originate the idea of children participating in civil rights demonstrations. Children had been active in Louisville and Albany before Birmingham and they set out on their own, at least on one occasion, later at Memphis. And, was it not true that children also suffered from the degradations of segregation and discrimination and would ultimately be the principal beneficiaries of their eradication? That the Birmingham drive, or any other of King's campaigns did not achieve radical reform is a correct accusation. But, then, King never sought radical reform. He only sought to have America live up to the creed that it already professed. He was, undoubtedly, wise enough to know that those who seek radical reform in America also seek suicide. And despite the alleged attempts of J. Edgar Hoover's FBI to encourage him in that direction, King was not suicidal.

After Birmingham and after the March on Washington and the Civil Rights Act of 1964, the naïve might have concluded that the millennium was at hand, for an enforcement of that act, together with previous civil and voting rights acts and the Brown school desegregation decision, should have meant full civil freedom, equality, and justice for black Americans. But the fallacy and naiveté in such reasoning were that (1) such rapid reforms would have required blanket and massive enforcement and (2) that such rapid reforms would have implied a substantial obliteration or lessening of white racism. Moderate white Americans, while supporting the reforms, would not countenance blanket or massive enforcements, arguing that the American Constitutional system required individual and specific proof of guilt to adjudications. Conservative white Americans took the position that the decisions and laws were ill-advised, if not illegal, and, hence, resisted reform. And so the struggle continued, and for Martin Luther King, Jr., it was on to Selma.

The ingredients at Selma were very similar to those at Birmingham — entrenched white supremacists willing to confront, and a rather well prepared local black leadership. Critics charged that Martin Luther King, Jr. should have led the first Selma to Montgomery March on March 7, 1964, which ended in blood on the Edmund Pettus Bridge just outside the Selma city limits. This, they say, would have been a fitting climax to the organization and the solidarity he had helped build in the city. But King bowed to the concern and the advice of federal officials, lieutenants, friends, and family and declined to risk his life on that fateful Sunday. One may not necessarily choose where he obtains his martyrdom, but it is clear that the goals at Selma were achieved and a national consensus for unfettered voting developed without Martin Luther King, Jr. dying on the Edmund Pettus Bridge. Without the federal protection, which developed after March 7, King would have been no safer on March 7th than any other marcher and there were no guarantees that his presence would have brought protection on that day. Yet, here again, it was the charisma, often the genius, and often the leadership of King, himself, that helped spell success at Selma.

These examples, I suggest, are sufficient to determine King's greatness, at least according to Carlyle and other traditional theses. One does not have to wait 20, 50, or 100 additional years for the judgment of history (as a matter of fact, history makes no judgments; historians do, and these are subject to all of the biases and influences of race, sex, and class as any other judgments). Posterity, including historians, may see King somewhat in a different light than contemporaries. That is to be expected! Times change and issues and outlooks change! But if Martin Luther King, Jr. is measured by the standards of one who possesses charisma, a certain degree of genius and whose ideas and leadership modified the prevailing historical contours, then he has already achieved greatness and it will be accorded to him forever and ever.

Interestingly and ironically, however, King, himself, never desired greatness in a Carlylian sense or to be placed in the company of the Napoleons and the Alexanders. These men had been given greatness largely because of their desire to rule the world. They were personifications of an egotistical phenomenon that is sometimes called the "Drum Major Instinct," that craving of men and nations to be superior, to have hegemony, to be the leader of the band. King, instead, chose a new norm for greatness — the ability to serve his fellow man and chose as his example, the poor carpenter who preached from Bethlehem to Jerusalem. If, then, he were to be a great man, it was because he did give his life serving humanity. If he were to be a Drum Major, he preferred not to be a conqueror of nations, but a Drum Major for righteousness, a Drum Major for peace, and a Drum Major for justice.

If we follow the life of Martin Luther King, Jr. from Montgomery to Memphis, we will, indeed, see a man who qualifies for Carlylian greatness, but also who qualified for Judaeo-Christian Greatness. Most of us fail to achieve either one of these; Martin Luther King, Jr. achieved both. I think it is for that reason that we are gathered here today and that there are similar gatherings all over the world. Rarely do men and women come among us with such qualities, and leave with such an impact as Martin Luther King, Jr. and so, I think, we owe it to those who labored in an era when hope unborn had died, and to those who tread their paths through the blood of the slaughtered, and to Martin Luther King, Jr., himself, to remember and study his dream, his life, and his works, and to build upon these for our nation, ourselves, and our posterity.

Chapter 3
The Central Theme Revisited—Again

In 1928, the Southern-born historian Ulrich Bonnell Phillips wrote that the unifying principle of Southern history was "a common resolve" maintained by the white people that the South "shall be and remain a white man's country." "The consciousness of a function in these premises" he said, "whether expressed with the frenzy of a demagogue or maintained with a patrician's quietude, is the cardinal test of a Southerner and the central theme of southern history."

In the years after 1928, many scholars, Northerners as well as Southerners, readily, adopted Phillips' thesis as the best explanation for the "uniqueness" of the South as a region in the United States. Just as Marx defined the economic motive as the determinant for all cultural endeavors, the exponents of Southernism applied Phillips' central theme sweepingly to all aspects of Southern life. Whether the issue be political, economic, social, or religious, in the South it could best be explained in terms of race or more specifically in terms of white supremacy. And so it was for many years, Phillips' views on race relations were as unchallenged as his monumental studies on slavery, first published in 1918.

As late as the 1950s, prominent scholars were still contending that the South was a unique region in the United States and that the distinctive quality of Southern life was still "white supremacy." But the vast international and national changes, which had occurred in the

Presented at the Annual Black History Month Program, Texas Southern University, Houston, Texas, February, 1980

ways of life of almost all people since World War II had begun to profoundly affect the scholarship on race in this country and the role of the South in American history. Gunnar Myrdal's classical study, *An American Dilemma*, was the most prominent of many post-war studies, which sought to place race in America in its national context. There were many others, including my own *In the Cage*, which even explored the international aspects of racism.

Typical of the works arguing for unchanging white supremacy in the South was an article by the Southern historian, Francis B. Simkins, which appeared in *Current History* in November 1958. Simkins granted that there had been considerable racial desegregation in the schools and in public accommodations in the previous decade. The federal courts and the Justice Department, he said, had "made dents in the sectional armor. The Army makes white and colored boys drill together and sleep together in the same barracks. Many Southern church conventions have pronounced against segregation, and some Southern universities admit a few Negroes to their halls." Yet, Simkins believed, "this attempt by official pressure to destroy the color line has made it tighter." No longer was there, as in ante-bellum times, "the close cohabitation and association of black and white"; no longer, he said, do "appreciable numbers" of white men indulge in miscegenation; no longer, as in ante-bellum days, "do the two races worship together." In fact, according to Simkins, "in the newer sections of the cities residential segregation is so complete that it is possible for a white person to pass years without contact with a single Negro."

Simkins contended that the only Southerners he knew who advocated racial equality were a few college professors and ministers. They were able to do this only because they were "the two elements of the white population who are most rigidly separated from the blacks by nature of their occupations." Simkins wondered, however, how these learned men would act if, like policemen and doctors, they had regular physical contact with blacks. "Not one of them, despite their advocacy of equality, had ever gone out of his way to meet a Negro in fraternal accord." "It is not fair," Simkins said, "to expect them to do this. It would mean social and occupational suicide."

Continuing his indictment of white professors, Simkins recalled that there was a university in the South where "much eloquence" was "spent in history and sociology classes advocating racial equality. A new professor could not get a position in that institution if he denied the innate equality of the races. But it never occurs to anyone on the campus to implement these sentiments. Distinctions of caste are accepted as unconsciously as rain or sunshine . . ." U .B. Phillips' central theme, then, still was very much alive in 1958, according to Francis Butler Simkins.

Two years later, another distinguished Southern historian took pointed exception, without specifically referring to his work, to Simkins' views. George Bell Tindall in an essay entitled "The Central Theme Revisited," challenged the Phillips thesis both in its historical and contemporary applications. Tindall admitted "a preoccupation with the issue of race, its mythology and its symbolism has been one of the major themes of southern history." But "to speak of a preoccupation with issues of race is not to say that there is or ever has been a monolithic unity in the thought or practice of Southern whites on the subject." Particularly, in recent years, Tindall believed, dramatic changes had occurred in the attitudes of white Southerners. Whereas, for example, "in 1940 a Gallop poll showed that about half of the white Southerners frankly opposed 'equal' education for Negroes. Today even the segregationist leadership avows equality as its goal and has taken important steps toward it." Tindall concluded "present perspectives suggest, indeed, that the 'credo of the South with reference to the Negro' can no longer be regarded as the indispensable key to Southern distinctiveness."

Phillips' central theme also came under attack, but from a different perspective in 1960. Howard Zinn, a Northern-born historian, who taught for several years at Atlanta's Spelman College and was an active participant in the civil rights movement in Georgia, wrote a work called *The Southern Mystique*. Zinn argued that the South, "far from being utterly different, is really the essence of the nation." Racism, Zinn believed, was an American, not simply a Southern, phenomenon. Building upon the important work of Leon Litwack, *North of Slavery*, Zinn demonstrated how blacks faced segregation and discrimination in the North and West, even in Colonial times. He further argued that Northern white supremacist attitudes have prevailed ever since, becoming less subtle, perhaps, as the black population increased in the periods of the World Wars. In other words, Zinn contended that the South's long history of overt racism was but a mirror of the national attitude. "That the South possesses them with more intensity simply makes it easier for the nation to pass off its characteristics to the South, leaving itself innocent and righteous."

It is, of course, now clear to all that the South has never possessed a monopoly on white supremacist attitudes and that the North has been far from "innocent," although perhaps "righteous." Many recent works, including Winthrop Jordan's *White Over Black* and Hornsby's, *In the*

Cage, have bolstered the arguments of Myrdal, Litwack, Zinn, and others as to the universality of white racism. For example, General Samuel Armstrong, although a son of a missionary to the Sandwich Islands, a distinguished Union soldier in the Civil War, and a founder of Hampton Institute for blacks, could say in 1868 that "the blacks are certainly inferior to the whites in intellect." He also thought "one-third of the negroes are decidedly good; one-third may be made good by good management; and one-third are bad." In like manner, Albert Bushnell Hart, the distinguished Harvard historian, could say in 1908 that "the people of mixed blood are more intelligent and prosperous (than the darker blacks), and more interested in their children's future." And, even Lord James Bryce, after several visits to the South prior to World War I, expressed serious doubt about the Negro's intellect. In fact, he saw "something pathetic in the eagerness of the negroes... to obtain instruction. They seem to think that the want of it is what keeps them below the whites . . ." Northern Americans, Englishmen and other Europeans who observed blacks first-hand in this country continued to express racist attitudes toward them even down to present times.

Interestingly enough, as the nation came to accept the universality of its racism, particularly after the Northern urban riots of 1964-1967 and the Kerner Commission Report documented it, there was increased speculation that the South, for so long the villain in America racism, would lead the nation in the quest for equality.

Variations of the arguments were that the South understood blacks best; the South had lived longer and closer with the problem than had the North and, thus, could solve it more readily; growing black political influence in the South would speed equality in the region; the South's patriotism and piousness would help her show the nation the way to brotherhood, and so on. Very often, exponents of these views cited the city of Atlanta, Georgia "an oasis of tolerance", and "the city too busy to hate", as an example of what could be done and would be done in the South.

Atlanta, in fact, had impressive credentials as a showplace for good race relations. Since 1948, a group of elite black professional people, using the large black vote as their principal agent, had bargained with the city's political leadership for a favorable climate of race relations. Unlike in Birmingham and elsewhere, the white business community, which had close ties to the city administration, endorsed racial tolerance as good for profits. Between 1948 and 1969, by every yardstick Atlanta was a leader, not only in the South, but, in the nation, in the conditions under which blacks lived. For example, it had one of the nation's most articulate and affluent black middle classes; it had pioneered, among Georgia cities, in the use of black policemen; its mayor, Ivan Allen, was the only prominent Southern politician to endorse the Civil Rights Bill of 1964 before the United States Congress; it had won national approval for the orderly way in which it was desegregating its schools and colleges; and it had a major daily newspaper whose editors and leading columnists championed the cause of equal justice. Yes, Atlanta was an "oasis of tolerance" in matters of race and no persons were prouder to boast of this fact than Atlantans, black and white, themselves.

Mayor Ivan Allen, Jr. later admitted what many could not see amidst the hoopla about Atlanta's exemplary race relations. Allen confirmed that, in reality, blacks had been unequal partners in the much heralded Atlanta coalition of black voters and upper income whites — this coalition had elected Atlanta mayors since 1949 and was the foundation of the Atlanta style of race relations. Although, as Allen said, blacks were consulted on many policy matters; on many they were not, even on issues affecting blacks. And, as Mayor Allen, himself, demonstrated, in a clear black versus white issue, such as black encroachment into all-white neighborhoods, the administration sided squarely with the whites. As early as 1955, Floyd Hunter, in his classic study, *Community Power Structure*, had emphasized the unevenness of the Atlanta coalition.

He had argued that in fact blacks who were perceived as "powerful" by the black community were in fact "powerless." At that time, the idea was to show some deference to the black businessman and the black Atlanta University Center professors, but clearly Atlanta was to be, to paraphrase Phillips, a white man's town.

Whatever the realities of the moment, Atlantans, black and white, continued to delude themselves as to the true nature of white racial attitudes in the city. It was, of course, easy to be mesmerized. Even more so after 1969, when, thanks to the strength of the black vote, a young, racially tolerant Jewish mayor was elected; a young, racially assertive black vice mayor was elected; and blacks moved toward parity on the Board of Aldermen (City Council) and Board of Education. The euphoria was heightened by the election of venerable black educator Benjamin E. Mays to the presidency of the school board. The nation's media again stood up and took notice in January 1970 as Atlanta inaugurated what was called a government of brotherhood. Few, if any cities in America could duplicate the feat.

Soon after the inauguration, however, the new mayor, Sam

Massell, crushed a strike of mostly black garbage workers. Thereafter, despite significant appointments of blacks to high positions and an endorsement of 50 percent black employment in city government, Massell was not entirely welcome in the black community. Late in his first term, faced with a measurable degree of black hostility, a decreasing white population and voting percentage, and an increasing black population and voter registration, Massell became extremely concerned about his own political future. Citing the declining city revenues caused by the white exodus from the city, he urged blacks to forego any thoughts of political dominance of the city and to support a plan of annexation of surrounding white suburbs. The plan would make Atlanta a whiter city and a richer city, but blacks, at about 407,000 would retain substantial influence. The mayor told the blacks that he spoke as a long-time friend, one who had urged whites to "think black" as he espoused racial equality; now he was asking blacks to "think white" as they considered his proposal. Black Atlanta gave the idea little or no hearing at all but, instead, responded with a thundering "no." The "think white" speech, perhaps more than anything else, helped make Sam Massell a one-term Atlanta mayor. Ironically enough, however, it was that alleged atypical Atlantan of the 1960s, arch-segregationist Lester Maddox who all but sealed Massell's fate. Maddox, as Lieutenant-Governor of Georgia, was angered by some of the procedural ploys of his Senate colleagues and refused to call up an Atlanta annexation bill in the closing days of the 1973 session of the Georgia General Assembly. With the Atlanta municipal elections scheduled for the fall and with a majority black population and a near majority of black voter registrants, the political future of Sam Massell was, indeed, cloudy.

In the General Election of 1973, Massell, himself, killed what slim chance he had of winning re-election over black vice-mayor, Maynard H. Jackson. After having run a poor second to Jackson in the primary, Massell panicked. He abandoned any hope of securing a substantial number of black votes and instead appealed for a white bloc vote, stopping just short of employing open racist appeals. His tactics were too low even for some moderate to conservative whites. The *Atlanta Constitution*, for example, no friend of candidate Jackson, urged Massell to stop his racist campaign and reluctantly endorsed the black vice mayor. After Massell's predictable defeat, Atlanta inaugurated in January of 1974, the first black dominated city administration in the modern South. The *New York Times* proclaimed "Jubilee in Atlanta."

It was indeed, a black jubilee, not only for Atlanta but, for Black America, as was witnessed by the bus loads that came in from far away

places to see the swearing-in ceremonies. Not only had a black mayor been elected, but, blacks had gained control of the School Board and parity on the new City Council. Jubilee!! But, for the first time in the history of the South's gate city, the white population was without political power. Many tried to make the most of it, hoping for the best. In other white quarters, however, there was great fear. The *Atlanta Constitution* cautiously expressed these fears. Would Jackson, in fact, give all the spoils of office to blacks? Would he recklessly ignore the experienced white leadership? Did he, in fact, have the administrative skill and sound judgment to maintain Atlanta as the premiere city of the South? The *Constitution* hoped so, but it had its doubts. After all, wasn't this the same man who, as Vice Mayor, had "shot off his mouth" protesting every instance of "alleged police brutality" in the city and who had tried to remove police officials who allegedly participated in or sanctioned the "alleged brutality?" Jackson, in fact, was a Negrophile whose policies would reflect prejudice against the now white minority.

In truth, the white community had not voted for Maynard Jackson for mayor (estimates are that he got 20 to 30% of the white vote) and it would be hard for that community to accept him. After all, Cleveland whites had not really accepted Carl Stokes, Newark whites held grave reservations about Gibson, and there was great hostility among Gary's whites to Hatcher. But these were Northern cities, Atlanta was the gateway of the South and the South, particularly Atlanta, was supposed to be showing the nation the way to racial harmony. Regrettably, however, the facts were showing that Atlanta was in no position to lead anyone; new racist attitudes had surfaced in the city. Although they had all the subtleties of the "innocent and righteous," North, Atlanta, during the administrations of Mayor Maynard Jackson was a city seriously divided by race.

The roots of recent white supremacist attitudes in Atlanta are directly traceable to events after 1961. The evidence is apparent in several areas, only a few of which can be mentioned here. First, residential segregation; Atlanta is a city divided by race in housing. The whites generally live on the north side, the blacks live to the south. Northern suburbs are almost lily white; southern suburbs are becoming jet black. The last mayor's effort to stabilize desegregated neighborhoods failed more than a decade ago when whites refused to share plush Cascade Heights with black doctors, lawyers, and college professors. The contention that whites move because of class was shown to hold about as much water as a leaking bucket. The issue was clearly race, compounded by increasing efforts for school desegregation.

Secondly the Supreme Court's new school decision in October 1969 which decreed "integration now," as opposed to "all deliberate speed" and its subsequent decisions sanctioning some cross-town busing revealed Atlanta's racism. The "white flight" to the Northern suburbs, which had begun in the wake of black residential encroachment, now proceeded apace. As it became apparent that the schools in the southern part of the city were remaining all-black or re-segregating and northern and suburban schools were becoming principally white, court-ordered busing became a great concern to Atlanta parents. In Federal Court hearings on the question of further desegregation of Atlanta schools in 1972 and 1973, a number of black parents and organizations opposed the concept of busing because of time, safety, and other factors, but a majority showed a willingness to comply if necessary to achieve further desegregation. White parents and organizations, although de-emphasizing the question of race, generally opposed any court ordered busing. The result of the whole controversy was the famous or infamous "Atlanta Compromise Plan" of 1973, in which a handful of the black elites met with influential whites to decide the course of future school desegregation in the Atlanta area. The black leadership agreed to abandon demands for further desegregation, including mandatory cross-town and cross-suburban busing, in exchange for black control of the administration of the school system. All parties knew that, given present conditions, there could be no meaningful desegregation of Atlanta schools without large-scale busing. Obviously, large segments of White Atlanta, including the media, applauded the "compromise" because of racial bias; and large segments of Black Atlanta agreed, expressing its feeling, perhaps, in the phrase: "We're tired of chasing white folks around to sit next to them in a schoolroom."

The role of the media in the retreat from school desegregation in Atlanta was symptomatic of the new racism in the city. Under Ralph McGill and Eugene Patterson, the *Atlanta Constitution*, for example, had achieved an international reputation as a beacon of Southern journalism. In fact, the Atlanta media's calls for tolerance during numerous racial crises had helped earn Atlanta's reputation as "a city too busy to hate." But, the *Atlanta Constitution* lost its great champions of racial justice Ralph McGill and Eugene Patterson through death and resignation respectively and, after 1970, the newspaper became increasingly moderate in its approach to black conditions. As the *Atlanta Constitution* went, so went its blood sisters the *Atlanta*

Journal and the Cox Broadcasting radio and television stations. Opposition to mandatory busing to achieve school desegregation was followed by attacks on the "mal-administration" of Mayor Maynard Jackson. The mayor had not been in office a year before the Atlanta newspapers declared that Atlanta was "a city in crisis," and suggested that much of it was caused by the black administration at City Hall. Eventually, the mayor, himself, joined the black chorus of protest and suggested that racial considerations had prompted the criticisms. After 1974, the black government and the white business community, including the media, achieved an uneasy detente, but this was shattered by the alleged police cheating scandal of 1977-78. Here again, although many tried to de-emphasize race, most of the support for the black police administration came from the black community and most of the critics were white. The role of the media in this matter and in previous matters of race became of such concern to some blacks and whites, by 1978, that more than 100 professors and administrators in the Atlanta University Center signed a plea in which they said they perceived racial bias on the part of the Atlanta media.

Clearly, then, recent events have shown that Atlanta, while still possessing many admirable qualities in its race relations, is not presently equipped to lead the nation away from racism. Instead, the city appears to be in step with a central theme of the nation — a nation of two societies, one white, one black, separate and unequal. U. B. Phillips might have called the theme white supremacy. Francis Butler Simkins might have called it "unchanging white supremacy." No matter what phrase one uses, the end result seems to be continued racial tensions and continued delay in achieving the great American ideals of equality and justice for all.

REFERENCES

Ivan Allen, Jr. (with Paul Hemphill), "Mayor Notes on the Sixties" (New York, 1971)

Atlanta Constitution November 21, 1974; February 20, March 24, March 29, April 3, 1975

Atlanta Daily World July 10, 17, 23, 1947; November 26, December 2, 1947; January 7-9, 23, February 26, 1948

C. A. Bacote, "The Negro in Atlanta Politics," *Phylon* 16, 1950, pp. 333-350

Jack Bass and Walter DeVries, *The Transformation of Southern Politics* (New York, 1976)

Monroe L. Billington, ed., *The South: A Central Theme?* (New York, 1969)

Charles Crowe, *Slavery, Race and American Scholarship: Explorations in Historiography* (Needham Heights, MA), p. 125

Helen Fuller, "Atlanta is Different," *The New Republic*, CXI (February 2, 1959), pp. 8-11

Alton Hornsby, Jr., "The Negro in Atlanta Politics, 1961-1973, *Atlanta Historical Bulletin*, 21 (Spring 1977), pp. 7-33

Alton Hornsby, Jr., *In the Cage: Eyewitness Accounts of the Freed Negro in Southern Society* (Chicago, 1971)

Floyd Hunter, *Community Power Structure* (Chapel Hill, 1953)

Winthrop Jordan, *White Over Black: American Attitudes Toward the Negro, 1550-1812* (Pelican Books edition, Baltimore, 1967)

National Advisory Commission on Civil Disobedience ("The Kerner Report"), ___, pp. 52-55

"Mayor Hartsfield Uses the Light Touch", *Readers Digest*, LXXII (June, 1958), p. 205

Francis B. Simkins, "Unchanging White Supremacy," *Current History*, XXXV (November, 1958), pp. 282-286

George B. Tindall, "The Central Theme Revisited" in Charles Grier Sellers, Jr., ed., *The Southerner as American* (Chapel Hill, 1960)

Jack Walker, "Negro Voting in Atlanta, 1953-1961" *Phylon*, XXIV (Winter, 1963)

See also "Not Eaves Please", "Race, Class and Atlanta's First Public Safety Commission" in Chapter 5 Politics and Civil Rights below

Chapter 4
European Intellectuals and
Southern Negroes, 1877–1901

The American Civil War and the ensuing Reconstruction aroused substantial interest in Europe, especially in Great Britain. The Civil War, as is well known, was, for a time, a major diplomatic topic in European capitals.[1]

But European intellectuals were also keenly interested in the sectional conflict and the efforts at reconciliation in America, so much so that several of them traveled across the seas to witness and write about the developments.[2]

The status of the Negro, first as a slave during the Civil War and then as a freedman in the Reconstruction Era, attracted much attention. Yet, despite the number of European scholars who came to America and studied the scene, many more were obviously dissuaded from making trips because of the unsettled conditions during the war and Reconstruction. It is not surprising, then, that travel to the United States on the part of intellectuals and others increased markedly in the post-Reconstruction Era.

The condition of the newly freed blacks remained a major attraction for European scholars. Some had speculated on their status from afar and some had written generally about the African race, but

Portions of this essay were based upon Alton Hornsby, Jr., ed. with intro., In the Cage: Eyewitness Accounts of the Freed Negro in Southern Society, 1877-1929 (Chicago, 1971).

few had made prolonged serious observations of the race in the American South. The visits to the South in the post-Reconstruction Era then afforded most of them their first real opportunity to see and to record impressions of the recently enslaved race. The South was, of course, the best place to begin any study of the American Negro, for the overwhelming majority of the black population resided there until the middle of the present century. In 1870 nearly four and one-half million of the 4,880,009 American blacks were residents of the late slave states and of Washington, D.C.; in 1900, 7,823,786 of 8,833,994 lived in those places. To observe the Southern Negro during these decades was tantamount to seeing the American Negro.[3]

In the period 1877-1901 the newly reunited United States was reaping fully the fruits of an industrial and technical revolution and setting its feet upon the world stage. For blacks, however, this period was what Rayford Logan and other historians have called "The Nadir." The Republican Party had abandoned the blacks to the "benevolent" hands of former masters and their descendants. Segregation, discrimination, disfranchisement, anti-Negro violence, and economic exploitation were increasing. Yet, out of this "nadir" rose two major spokesmen for black ambitions and strategies. Booker T. Washington, following his "Atlanta Compromise" address in 1895, became the leading apostle of a program of educational and economic self-help, while eschewing social and political equality. W. E. B. DuBois, recently arrived from the North in 1896, took the leadership of those black intellectuals clamoring for racial equality in all aspects of American life.[4]

What picture, then, do European intellectuals present of the condition of the Southern blacks during the period of the "nadir?" These men and women, with better than average facilities for observation, reflection, and recording, and detached from the everyday scene, can undoubtedly add much to our knowledge of the complexity of life for Southern blacks. In this study I have focused on their views of the Negroes' physical appearance, their economic pursuits, and their religion, and I have given some attention to black educability and education and the matter of crime and punishment. From these observations, we learn much of the existence, outlook, and potentials of the blacks and that we should not overlook the lessons these accounts give us concerning the limitations of outsiders' views.[5]

For many of the scholars who visited the South following Reconstruction the very sight of the Negro, especially in large numbers, was a source of amazement. Except in the very large cities, and fairly recent, the Negro has been an almost non-existent element in the

European population. The same was largely true, as the census reports show, for the Northern United States until the twentieth century.

The physical appearances of a few Virginia Negroes encountered by Arthur Granville Bradley, English author and traveller was striking though seemingly not representative. One was a man barely five feet, who "had a head upon him the size of a Missouri pumpkin." He wore upon his "dark seamed face a perennial frown." Bradley felt that his "front view was hideous," but "his reverse side was much the funniest in the whole county." Another Virginia Negro had a "bad stammer, with terrific facial contortions," a condition that Bradley thought rare among the Negro race. The stammer in this case gave a "quizzical appearance," which added to the Negro's "round, smooth, beardless," and oily black face, made laughter "irresistible" for the onlooker.[6]

Three-fourths of the Negro school children seen in Virginia by William Saunders, an English journalist and politician, were more or less white. Indeed, "many are quite fair, and some have red or golden hair, which would prevent them from being regarded as mulattoes in any place where their parentage was unknown."[7]

Beauty was found among the mulattoes and quadroons of Louisiana by the noted traveler George Augustus Sala, on a second visit to the South in 1879-1880. He saw mulattoes and quadroons, very handsome individuals, sitting in the state legislature in New Orleans. He could not say the same for the "full-blooded" blacks.[8]

Fair-complexioned mulattoes drew the attention also of Sir George Campbell, a Scot, whose *White and Black* became one of the most widely used travel books about the South. After a long service in India, this British M.P. visited the United States in 1878 specifically to observe the Negro and to compare his condition with that of the Indian. Remaining through part of 1879, he toured Georgia, North Carolina, South Carolina, and Virginia. Campbell saw "some extremely fair children — sometimes fairer than the average of white children — among the ebony, woolly-headed Negroes." One mulatto, in particular, "who would have been very fair for a European, was placed among the blacks, many of whom are very black and hideous." These latter Negroes led him to reflect that he "hardly knew before what an ugly race some of the blacks are."[9]

The allusion to hideous blacks by Campbell is mild in comparison with the statements of Charles Boissevain, a Dutch journalist. To him the Negroes were wild and savage in appearance, no different from their forefathers "on the shores of the Congo."[10]

Black deck workers on a cargo boat sailing south from St. Louis, men who were black and flat-nosed but proud, presented a picturesque sight that Ernst Von Hesse-Wartegg thought all artists and all philanthropists would understand, however sorrowfully. Hesse-Wartegg, a German privy councilor and consul-general repeatedly in the United States, noted that many of the young mulatto women he saw on a boat trip through the Louisiana sugar district were of a different variety from the black deck workers. One of them, *eine schwarze Schonheite* (a black beauty) with a scanty corset, fascinated the German. Her name was Calypso, and she spoke only French. She had big, sparkling eyes, a full, half-opened mouth with "an odd, but delightful appearance," and a certain radiance.[11]

The contrast between white linen and the color of the skin of black waiters struck the eye of the Italian diplomat, Carlo Gardini, whose Southern travels, in the 1880s took him to Alabama, Louisiana, Missouri, Tennessee and Virginia. The skin color ran through all gradations "from ebony black to the lightest shade of coffee."[12]

The comparison between the physical features of Negroes and American Indians was attempted by only a few outsiders. One of these was Edward Augustus Freeman, the English historian, yet what he had to say was not very enlightening. Such Indians as he saw impressed him as being "less ugly than the Negroes. But then they lacked the grotesque air, which often make the Negro's ugliness less repulsive."[13]

The "absolutely bestial aspect" of some blacks, especially those who begged in the streets, led a French royalist and author, Gabriel Paul Le Vicomte D'Haussonville to adopt the "Darwinian theories and to understand why all acquaintance" between a white woman and a black man "should be regarded as the final degree of perversity and degradation." D'Haussonville arrived in America in 1882 "completely a Negrophile" and convinced that there was no difference between Negro and Caucasian except color of skin. It took only a short stay at Richmond, however, to change his thinking to the point that he had to overcome a certain physical repugnance in order to accustom himself to the black hands which made his bed and served his bread.[14]

The bestial appearance of the Negro also struck Iza Duffus Hardy, an Englishwoman who was in Florida, mainly around Orlando, in 1885-1886. She employed an old black maid with a "good-natured black, monkey face and frizz of wool" reminding Miss Hardy of "one of those dark shiny bronze statuettes of the typical Negress, come to life." She was, however, "the proprietress of three cottages," and in addition, she and her husband had "three thousand dollars in the bank."[15]

Blacks exhibiting "cheerful," "open" faces and appearing glad to be alive were seen by Leon Paul Blouet ("Max O'Rell") at Jacksonville and Saint Augustine. He had difficulty in distinguishing between Negroes, for to him they, like French gendarmes, all looked alike at a glance. Generally, they had great dark eyes and rolled the whites thereof "in their own droll fashion." They swayed when they walked with heads thrown back and toes turned out. White teeth, "framed in thick retrousse' lips," were constantly displayed. Black voices were musical, "sweet but sonorous," "so pleasing compared to the horrible twang of the lower-class people of the North." Obviously a romantic, Blouet found blacks so picturesque that he forgot their color and fell to admiring them, especially the "Negresses," who were "good, merry-looking creatures with buxom faces and forms, supple, light, graceful gait and slender waists," often "quite pretty."[16] No other European observer saw blacks in such a favorable light.

Paul Bourget, another Frenchman, a writer, who visited Florida and Georgia, in the spring of 1894, saw the typical, black, thick-lipped Negro, but took more interest in a yellow-faced man, "nearer neighbor of white blood than the Negro's," whose straight hair and "aquiline" nose led Bourget to recall that he was said to be the son of a prominent white man. Bourget had heard that Southern whites greeted the idea of race mixture with utter disdain, but now saw clear evidence of this hypocrisy.[17]

The Civil War destroyed the slave economy, but agricultural pursuits continued as a way of life in the post-Reconstruction South, and, despite the coming of industry, most blacks remained tillers of the soil. Numbers of them had, of course, become self-sufficient farmers owning their property and sometimes employing fellow blacks to work sizeable acreages. The great majority, however, were tenants, croppers, or wage or day laborers. Often they worked on cotton or other plantations as they had in the ante-bellum period.[18] European intellectuals, some of them students of agriculture, observed and assessed the status of the freed black farmers.

The Sea Islands of South Carolina were inhabited mainly by blacks who formed "independent and self-supporting rural communities." The Islands' blacks labored under great disadvantages in that long staple cotton and rice had declined and their land was not suitable for short staple cotton. Sir George Campbell observed that many of them supplemented their income by occasional labor at the ports and in the phosphate industry. They were fortunate in having the assistance of "Northern and other whites who would do for them those things which they cannot do for themselves." Northern dealers ginned and bought their cotton, and white storekeepers maintained a "wholesome system of ready-money payment" that was better for the blacks than the crop-lien system under which landlord or merchant advanced supplies and took control of the crop.

In the South generally black farm hands or wage laborers, particularly those who were "on small farms" under the immediate supervision of their employers, worked "exceedingly well," Campbell thought. Inept black workers might be found on the larger farms, where supervision was insufficient, but this fact was not a reflection on the Negro race; under like conditions "most such races" would be guilty of the same inefficiency. Farm hands earned about 50 cents a day, "six or eight times the wages of a coolie in India." This wage coupled with cheap food, inexpensive shelter (croppers, and sometimes day laborers, were often provided with homes by landlords), and a climate requiring little for fuel, meant that the Negro farm worker was, in truth, "very well off."[19]

Negro earnings as sharecroppers were meager, often below subsistence level, in the "Yazooland" of Mississippi and in the Alabama cotton fields, according to Hesse-Wartegg. Most of the blacks he saw were cultivating very small patches of land, and few owned livestock.

On the Louisiana sugar and rice plantations Hesse-Wartegg found the economic condition and morale of the Negro more encouraging. At Governor H. C. Warmoth's "Magnolia," "the greatest sugar plantation in Louisiana," the blacks were grouped and counted each morning, as under slavery, and marched onto the fields by the white overseers. Baskets on heads and tools on shoulders, they were gay and vivacious, singing and dancing as they moved to work. All of this deeply impressed Hesse-Wartegg, who commented that, "the Negro generally shows in his daily performance a certain 'Tournure', a burlesque elegance, which contrasts sharply with the sullen rude ways of the white plantation workers."

The usual ration of labor to land on sugar plantations was one black worker to every seven acres. Black men might expect $18 dollars per month and free living quarters, considerably more than the $12 to $16 dollars a month generally paid to cotton laborers. Black women did the same work for only 50 cents a day. For work at night, or in excess of eight and one-half hours per day, black men were paid 50 cents per hour.

In Plaquemines Parish, Louisiana, Hesse-Wartegg visited a rice plantation whereon the workers were mainly black women, 'Guinea wives'; with thick lips, stupid faces and bulky figures." They marched onto the fields with their aprons draping to their knees. Seeds were carried in these aprons or in little baskets and sowed by hand in the

furrow. The crop was harvested by blacks of both sexes who cut the stalks with "rice hooks" and then bundled them. For Hesse-Wartegg the harvesting was, like most other things connected with the Negro, "a picturesque sight."[20]

Though hardly outstanding as a student of Negro affairs, the most famous foreign analyst, James Bryce of the American scene in the late nineteenth century, did notice that in the rural areas of the South the "immense majority" of blacks were either hired laborers or tenants of small farms. He observed that the tenants were more numerous the further south one went, especially in the "hot and malarias regions, where the white man is less disposed to work on his own land." Some of the tenants were "both active and thrifty," but others were content with "getting from the soil enough food to keep their families; and this is more especially the case in the lower lands along the coast, where the population is almost wholly black, and little affected by the influences either of commerce or of the white race." All of the tenants, Bryce noted, cultivated "upon a system of crop-sharing, like that of the metayers in France."[21]

Though most blacks in the late nineteenth century were tillers of the soil, a good many were found in other occupations, sometimes in the country, more commonly in the towns. In Virginia, Arthur Bradley remarked, with some nostalgia and much inaccuracy that by 1880 most of the black labor had disappeared from the rural districts and flocked into the big cities for factory or domestic work. "Agriculture of a large and careless sort is almost dead, killed by its own futility."[22]

South Carolina blacks might find jobs in mining phosphates, which were processed into fertilizers. Pay was $1.75 a day, or ton."[23] Sir George Campbell reported that many of the Sea Islands farmers made "ends meet" by occasional labor on the "great phosphate beds, which have become a large source of industry and wealth to that part of the country."[24] As a recent scholar puts it, "Negroes struggling to retain their small farms on the Sea Islands during the hard years following emancipation must have viewed the rise of the phosphate industry as providential."[25]

At Greensboro, North Carolina, and at Richmond, Virginia, William Saunders saw large numbers of blacks working successfully. The Greensboro blacks were making wooden handles, presumably for tools, and earned from "two shillings to three shillings" (about 50 to 75 cents) per day, approximately the going rate for farm labor. Saunders saw nothing to criticize in this, but felt rather that the abundance of this cheap labor should be an encouragement to industry in the South. A large flour mill at Richmond employed many blacks. The proprietor said that they were more regular in attendance than white men and he therefore gave them preference.[26]

In Virginia, evidently in Richmond, George Campbell visited a factory that produced chewing tobacco wherein blacks did by far the greater part of the work. "Tobacco seems to be specially their vocation." (This had been true in the ante-bellum period also.)[27] "Most of the foremen are white and some of the work is done by white and black men mixed." Campbell saw no mixture of white and black women, and assumed that it was not allowed. Cigars were not made by blacks, that being "one of the skilled things they do not do." (Sir George was perhaps unaware that the manufacture of cigars received little attention in the Virginia-Carolina area.) Wages at the factory were "about a dollar a day for moderately skilled work, and sometimes more," but employment was not very regular, averaging perhaps four days a week. All informants agreed that the black workers were fond of amusements, including fishing or other excursions. Though Nannie Tilley questions the extent of "melodious singing" among black tobacco workers, those at Richmond, especially the women, were set to sing for Sir George's benefit, "and they certainly do that very well."[28]

In iron foundries Boissevain saw black and white laborers working together, but in textile mills he saw no Negroes. Like Campbell, he observed that the preparation of tobacco was entrusted almost exclusively to the blacks; unlike Campbell, he asserted that they also made cigars.[29]

Black children, as well as men and women, were observed performing such operations as sorting and rolling up leaves in a Virginia tobacco factory visited by W. H. Russell as one of a party headed by the Duke of Sutherland and the Marquis of Stafford in 1881. "A happier looking people could not be seen, and at times their feelings of contentment burst out into a song." Their "half comic, half religious . . . extraordinary melodies" were sung with "a great sweetness."[30]

James Bryce also noticed the Negro's role in tobacco manufacture, presumably in Virginia. Blacks handled tobacco better than the whites and appeared to monopolize the less skilled departments of the industry. They were not good in textile mills, where the whirr of the machinery was said to daze them or put them to sleep. Many blacks were working in the mines and iron foundries of southeastern Tennessee and northern Alabama. Although generally poor, they seemed to be getting along well, and some belonged to the trade unions.[31]

In terms of numbers employed, the various forms of personal service remained much more important as black occupations than was industry. By far the largest economic group outside agriculture was in such service. Theodor Kirchoff, a German writer in the United States about 1875-1877, noted with obvious inaccuracy that in restaurants North and South the waiters were invariably black. Their efficiency left much to be desired, a loud voice being required in most instances to summon them. Leon Blouet, at Jacksonville, complained of the black waiters. One who was "extremely obliging" once allegedly brought him a glass of water containing a snake. When Blouet protested, he was assured that the reptile was dead. When he further protested that the snake might have left eggs, the Negro re-examined the glass and announced that the snake was a male. Blouet also observed that the black waiters working in almost all of the hotels south of Washington were extremely slow — it was the guest who did the waiting. On the other hand, Carlo Gardini received acceptable service, as did James Fullarton Muirhead, who was in the South first in 1888 and again from 1890-1893. The black waiters seen by Muirhead displayed an "expansive geniality" in contrast to the "supercilious indifference, if not positive rudeness of his pale colleague." The blacks were "indefatigable" in ministering to one's wants, and dressed more neatly than the "greasy" European waiter.[32]

The old black servants who surrounded Arthur Granville Bradley in Virginia "were for general purposes as reliable and trustworthy as good English farm servants." Their families had generally "got out of hand, but the older darkies were often the very models of honesty."[33]

The fact that most blacks outside agriculture not only worked in servile occupations but also seemed to enjoy doing so disgusted and angered D'Haussonville, who came to the South a Negrophile, and left almost a Negrophobe. Reflection led him to suppose that the Negroes' servility stemmed from the oppression of slavery, and that the newer generation might change. Yet "the Negro population will remain inferior to the whites; it will become for the South the same as the immigrants, Irish, and others, were for the North, agents of work and thus of progress."[34]

Black servants were, in the experience of Iza Duffy Hardy, often very satisfactory, the better ones being preferable to whites. Unfortunately, there was a shortage of the industrious and an abundance of the "slow, indolent, shiftless, untidy, and extravagant" ones. Black workers in Florida generally "get good wages and find plenty of employment; indeed the demand for labour is chronically greater than the supply, especially in the line of domestic help."[35]

The economic status of the better-situated black servants was adjudged favorably also by Blouet. Black train porters, pretty much a class unto themselves, often made ten to 12 dollars a day in tips, some amassing $2,500 to $3,000 a year independent of their regular salary. Their politeness was universally acknowledged by outside observers though Blouet sensed, no doubt correctly, that much of it was feigned for the sake of the financial reward. Black maids, though they were often too noisy (an opinion shared by Muirhead), did rather well from tips, and so did bellhops.[36]

Blacks were employed to a very limited extent in public service as policemen and clerks. George Sala saw a good many policemen on duty near the White House and the Capitol in Washington. Hesse-Wartegg first observed black public employees at Memphis, mainly policemen. In Petersburg, Virginia, Sir George Campbell remarked: "I notice that generally most of the United States employee's [sic] are blacks, while the State and Municipal employee's [sic] are whites." Even the street-sweepers were white in Petersburg. At Columbia, South Carolina, Campbell encountered a black "Trial Justice" and "a Coloured man, apparently connected with the city water works," who seemed very sensible and intelligent, at least on political matters.[37]

European intellectuals apparently took little interest in the black business and professional class, and in Negro property holding. Perhaps, some were as unenlightened as Sir George Campbell who claimed that he had "not been able to hear of a successful Negro merchant — the shopkeeping business in the most Negro districts is almost entirely in the hands of whites." He had "scarcely found a Negro who had risen in the mercantile world higher than an apple-stall in a market."[38]

George Sala, however, stayed in a black-owned hotel, Wormley's in Washington, which he described as "one of the quietest most elegant, and most comfortable hotels in the Federal capitol." Sala met Mr. Wormley, a man "of gentle manners and great administrative abilities." He was typical of the "better" Washington Negroes, who were not only "invariably civil and obliging, but in many cases [also] very bright and intelligent."[39]

On the subject of property holding, William Saunders did observe that a large number of Richmond blacks owned the property they occupied and that in Alabama the assessed value of black property, about 1878, was seven million dollars. When Saunders asked some of the more prosperous, intelligent blacks how they were getting along as compared with former times, a typical reply would be:

Well, sir, most of us are doing better, but some are doing worse. Those who can't take care of themselves are going to the bad faster than before; but if a man can take care of himself, he now has the chance.[40]

American whites had been prone to look upon the Negro's simple and emotional religion as very different from theirs (although there were, to be sure, more similarities than differences, particularly in the South), so much so that they, especially Southerners, often made special visits to black churches to observe the rites. This being so, it is no surprise that Europeans also exhibited a great curiosity about the Negro's religion. Black church services, especially in North Carolina, were attended by Sir George Campbell, who also witnessed a convention of black Baptist ministers. The oratory of Negro preachers tended to "exaggerate the American style," which itself exaggerated the British; but Campbell felt on the whole "considerably edified" by the performances. "They come to the point in a way that is refreshing after some sermons that one has heard." The churches were thoroughly democratic, and were independent of all white guidance and control, affording the blacks a significant experience of self-government. While Campbell did not witness the excessive emotion attributed to black worshippers — the few hearty responses to sermons that he heard were not irreverent — he understood it to be an expression of direct communion with God, which was not without merit. Because of this desire for direct communion Campbell predicted that Roman Catholicism would never enjoy much success among blacks.

The convention of Baptist ministers that Sir George attended was held in a rural church, and proved "a pleasant sight." Campbell understood that black preachers were chosen because they were leaders, rather than the other way around. This group did not, however, deliberate in seclusion. The "whole country-side seemed to have come in to assist, both men and women, and they seemed to be making a time of it, camped about for the day."[41]

Black preaching, and congregational reaction to it, were never heard by William Saunders, to his regret, for each time he visited a black service a white man preached. The sermons were among the best he heard in America, for white preachers seemed to speak "plainly" to black congregations. On one occasion the blacks even mistook Saunders for a preacher; when he protested his lack of calling, they suspected him of being a detective.[42]

The black practice of "lining out" their hymns, i.e., to read a stanza of a song, then sing it, was necessary, as William Aubrey noted, because few of the congregation could read. The "lining out" was done by any literate preacher, deacon, or sister the congregation happened to possess. Aubrey was especially critical of the discourses of the preachers. "Even charity cannot condone the absurdity, the ignorance, and the irreverent parodies of sermons by unlearned but fluent and conceited preachers, of whom there are far too many."[43]

Edward Freeman, the English historian, attended black services at a Methodist church in Baltimore after shying away from attendance in Virginia because "the undertaking seemed somewhat wild and perilous." Even at Baltimore the services struck him as "strange." The black minister made a number of errors, including the assertion that the will of Herod the Great had been "taken to Rome to be probated by Augustus." On the other hand, the services at the city's black Episcopal Church, "with tendencies to what is called an 'advanced ritual,'" were probably more akin to those of the "better" white churches.[44]

A more favorable sampling of black ministers and their sermons was made by the Reverend John Kerr Campbell, a Presbyterian minister from Scotland, who attended black worship at Paris, Kentucky, just northeast of Lexington. He was asked to preach, but declined on account of a later engagement. The black pastor in discussing the creation, fall, and redemption of man began by exploring various prevailing theories of man's creation, including the agnostic, Darwinian, and speculative ones, then dismissed them all in favor of Genesis. (The preacher's audience in rural Kentucky must have been severely taxed if he actually discussed these matters in a learned manner.) The world was, he said, too mutable to be regarded as external. His second topic, the fall, he depicted in vivid terms, and at this point brought the audience into the act. As the minister cried "oh, brethren! What shall we do?" his auditors "began to sway to and fro on their seats and some of them groaned." With each, "Oh, what shall we do?" the groaning grew louder. The sermon ended with a calm discussion of man's redemption. The lung power of the preacher Campbell found a little strong for his appreciation, but otherwise he was impressed with the sermon. It did credit to the minister and his teachers. Only when he spoke rapidly and excitedly did he err in his pronunciations; then he uttered such sounds as "fadder," "mudder," and "Republican sinner." Negro spirituals baffled the Reverend Mr. Campbell. To him they were in an unknown tongue, though later he heard from blacks and understood such familiar tunes as "Nearer, My God to Thee."[45]

Black ministers at Savannah exhibited considerable ability in the opinion of the Reverend Timothy Harley, a Methodist minister from Great Britain. Even the older ones, though "lamentably ignorant," possessed a "natural eloquence" more effective than argument in dealing with the "emotional hearers whom they have to address." One of the black worshippers stole a goose on Saturday and yet took communion on Sunday, apparently seeing nothing incongruous in the fact. Harley feared that the black churches encouraged this type of behavior, and he denounced as dangerous that theology "which talks of 'mere morality.'"[46]

Blacks were much more devout in their worship than whites, Dean Hole of Rochester observed. Hole was particularly interested in the hymns heard in a Richmond Church, "strange... and unsound in doctrine, quaint... in their language and in their association with common things," yet "stirring, pathetic, and harmonious." For example:

"De Gospel Train
"De Gospel Train's a-coming,
I hear it just at hand,
I hear dem car wheels movin',
And a rumblin' through the land . . .

Chorus ---
"Get on board, children; get on board, children;
Get on board children, for dere's room
for many more . . ."[47]

Not all blacks worshipped formally in churches, or were exclusively devoted to the Christian God. There were other spiritual and emotional forces at work among a large segment of the race, including many dutiful church members. For convenience's sake one may call these forces superstitions and fears, though these labels do not really explain the wide variety of phenomena of a religious character prevalent among Southern blacks of the late nineteenth century. Such names as voodoism, conjuration, and spooks are closer to the point. To some European observers, these matters were as interesting, or more interesting, than the Negro's practice of Christianity.

Voodoism greatly intrigued the Irish-Greek journalist Lafcadio Hearn. The story of his association with a mulatto called Marie Laveau, reputedly a Voodoo Queen, is told by his biographer, Edward L. Tinker. Marie was about 50 years of age in 1879, although she looked younger. She had been free before the war and had started life as a "coiffeuse." An early leader of the voodoo cult in New Orleans, she gained considerable control over superstitious blacks; indeed many whites became her "victims."

On one occasion Marie took advantage of the Negro's fascination with death. She had a man pose as dead and requested money to bury him. Blacks by the score came to view the "body" and contributed. Marie sold charms for "good luck" in love, politics, or business, and amulets, such as snakeskin or teeth, to ward off "evil spirits." Many a black who discovered some voodoo sign on his doorstep, placed there obviously by Marie, would rush to her New Orleans residence to buy an antidote. Such a sign, unless nullified by amulet, meant "bad luck" or even death.

Marie's principal activity was voodooism. She conducted her meetings mainly at midnight, in a swamp near one of the cottages she owned. To the traditional worship of a serpent, the sacrifice of a white cock or a goat, the drinking of "tafia," and orgiastic dancing, Marie added certain new features, and she sought to make the rites acceptable to Roman Catholics, of whom there were a good many among New Orleans Negroes. She introduced the adoration of the Virgin Mary side by side with the worship of the serpent. Thus many Christian Negroes joined the "pagans" in wild, drunken dancing, sometimes going into convulsions. Marie's practices so captured Hearn's "peculiar imagination" that the frequency of his visits to her gave rise to "disagreeable gossip which has persisted to this day."[48]

Hearn was also acquainted with Jean Montanet, another noted New Orleans voodoo leader. Montanet's practices differed little from those of Marie, but his ideas were more extreme: He had apparently been exposed to voodooism in Africa and his "ideas of religion were primitive in the extreme." He always subordinated the Christian influences to the African. When Montanet died in August 1885, aged nearly 100, "New Orleans lost . . . the most extraordinary African character that ever gained celebrity within her limits" and "the last of the voodoos." Later, at the end of 1886, Hearn could even say that, "as a religion — an imported faith — Voodooism in Louisiana is really dead; the rites of its serpent worship are forgotten. What was left was not an African cult, but a curious class of Negro practices, some possibly derived from it, and others which bear resemblance to the magic of the Middle Ages."[49]

Voodoo rites were seen by Johannes Baumgarten during the Mardi Gras of 1880. The German writer managed, however, to get participation in Mardi Gras confused with the voodoo worship, and concluded that all the black celebrants were worshipping the "Voodoo Queen," Marie, whom he also designated their Mardi Gras Queen. The blacks were dancing, clowning, screaming, and crying around a big fire. At the midnight hour many jumped into a pool of water, reemerged shortly thereafter, and continued dancing. Baumgartner was displeased with what he saw, and surprised that these practices of "fetishism," unlike their counterparts in Haiti, were not secretive in their behavior.[50] James Bryce also noted disapprovingly that in parts of Louisiana the blacks had "relapsed into the Obeah rites and serpent worship of African heathendom. How far this has gone no one can say." Similarly, the English Naval historian W. Laird Clowes said in 1891 that voodooism certainly existed in the South, "and especially in Louisiana." Whether either of them actually saw voodoo rites is doubtful.[51]

"Scientific studies" of Negro capacity before and during the nineteenth century had raised serious doubts as to the educability of the black race. Yet the Freedmen's Bureau and Northern missionary groups had since the Civil War undertaken the task of giving the Southern Negro "book learning." European intellectuals were keenly interested in how the blacks were doing in school.

The Oxford historian, Edward Freeman, even after seeing blacks in school, remained pessimistic concerning their ability to grasp knowledge. "Education cannot wipe out the eternal distinction that has been drawn by the hand of nature. No teaching can turn a black man into a white one." Dean Hole of Rochester was similarly convinced, after his short tour of the South, that there was no hope that the Negro's intellectual capacity could be substantially improved on any level.[52]

A majority of the students in a black school in Virginia visited by William Saunders, the English journalist, were more or less white; "the nearer the mulattoes are to white the brighter as children they seem to be." Teachers at Atlanta, however, insisted that black children equaled whites in intellectual capacity. It was too early in 1880, George Sala thought, to say whether "full-blooded" Negroes could meet the demands of academic training. Undoubtedly the "mixed-bloods" could become as intellectually distinguished as Alexander Dumas. A certain number of the black youngsters at Richmond impressed the French politician D'Haussonville as being "very precocious and. intelligent." They seemed to learn faster than white children, but he understood that their learning stopped toward the age of 12 and they remained children for the rest of their lives. Even so, D'Haussonville hoped that the influences of education would prevent the total degradation of the race.[53]

The blacks' eagerness for knowledge evoked mixed feelings among observers. Saunders admired the Negroes' perseverance in sending their children to school even when the family could "ill afford to lose their services." Sir George Campbell also found zeal for education on all levels and felt that as much had "been done as could be expected under the circumstances." George Sala noted that blacks were grasping the opportunities for education at New Orleans in 1880. But James Bryce felt that there was something pathetic about the zeal for knowledge because "book learning" would not necessarily raise the blacks "in the industrial scale."[54]

Important as the grammar schools were, it was the fledgling Negro colleges that constituted the core of the black educational system. Many expected that they would someway, somehow, work miracles; that they would take the recently emancipated race and from it produce immediately scientific farmers, skilled craftsmen, teachers, doctors, nurses, and lawyers. European scholars were eager to see how this Herculean task was being performed.[55]

The "big five" among Southern Negro colleges prior to 1900 were Hampton Institute, Tuskegee Institute, Howard University, Fisk University, and Atlanta University. Hampton and Tuskegee were the principal representatives of the agricultural-industrial tradition in Negro education, while Atlanta University, especially since the arrival of W. E. B DuBois as a teacher in 1896, was primarily associated with the academic or liberal education. It was upon them, then, that the attention of most observers was focused.

Sir George Campbell found Hampton Institute to be principally a teacher-training institution instead of the major agricultural and industrial school he had expected. Several trades were taught there, however, and he understood, probably erroneously, that it was the only place "in the Southern States where black printers are educated." Campbell himself was more interested in the Western American Indians sent to Hampton by the United States government than he was in the Negroes there. The Indians were yellow rather than red, not "unlike some of the Indo-Chinese tribes to the east of Bengal." General Samuel Armstrong, the white head of Hampton, thought both whites and Indians stronger than blacks in intellect, but the blacks were improvable, and the Indians "much more difficult to manage." James Bryce visited Hampton as well as the newly founded Tuskegee Institute and praised their work, though they were, like other black colleges, on "a comparatively humble scale and . . . might rather be called secondary schools than colleges."[56] When Bryce returned to Tuskegee in 1908, he was to be more lavish in his praise of the institution, which by then had become famous.

A visit to Atlanta University convinced the Reverend Timothy Harley that the "coloured student is capable of liberal education and that the white Southerner is as ready as any man to acknowledge and rejoice in it." Harley asked one of the professors whether or not he had detected any considerable difference of intellectual capacity between the "pure" Negro and the mulatto. The teacher reported that no great differences existed. Harley was not wholly convinced on this point, however.[57]

White control of black colleges and their dependence upon white support, both almost universal in the South between 1877 and 1901, were denounced by some blacks, while approved by many more. William Aubrey, the English writer, applauded the support of black colleges by whites (usually Northern ones). Yet he felt their aid was insufficient to meet the blacks' pressing need for education. Federal assistance was as essential in the area of higher learning as in primary and secondary education.[58]

In the matter of crime and punishment the foreign observers had an opportunity to witness and react to one of the most critical areas of black life and Southern race relations. Almost universally they testified to, and deplored, the black's proneness to petty theft, much of which went unpunished. Crimes of a more serious nature often drew heavy penalties.

Blacks had "brought from slavery times a sort of childish want of respect for property in certain things," Sir George Campbell admitted. But he was inclined to think that petty thievery which resembled a child's "taking a spoonful of jam" was a "misconduct" rather than a crime. Sir George placed Negroes above most other races in that they were "not much given to violent, and… vicious crimes" (he was probably unaware of the rather large number of homicides attributed yearly to them). A much harder justice seemed to be dealt to the blacks than to whites. Blacks were disproportionately represented in the prison population, a fact, which Sir George attributed, probably correctly, to harder justice and to the absence of blacks on juries. He detected also "a strictness in penal management," as far as blacks were concerned, a strictness which needed watching considering "how much of the administration of justice is now in the hands of whites." The most shocking thing to him was the continued existence of lynching, particularly in cases of alleged assault by blacks on white women. "The blacks are popularly said to be prone to that kind of crime; with what justice I cannot say."[59]

Although it was "extremely hard to ascertain the truth" about lynchings, James Bryce concluded that there was no doubt that all over the South blacks accused of "outraging" white women had been "frequently seized by white mobs and summarily killed; that occasionally, though probably most often, an innocent man perishes, and that the killing, is sometimes accompanied by circumstances of revolting cruelty." Bryce believed that in "a thinly peopled and un-policed country" white women did stand in serious risk, but that the practice of lynching had a pernicious effect on the whites themselves, "accustoming them to cruelty, and fostering a spirit of lawlessness which tells for evil on every branch of government and public life." Yet, on the other hand, were it not for the fact that the blacks were "cowed by the superior strength and numbers of the whites," reprisals, "now rare, would be more frequent."[60]

In Florida, Paul Bourget witnessed the search for a mulatto, once the servant of Bourget's host, a Southern "Colonel," now suspected of robbery and murder. The "Colonel," as a member of the search party, refused to shoot the Negro, and the black fugitive passed up an opportunity to fire on him. When two other whites wounded the black suspect, the "Colonel" attended his wounds and gave him a cigar and whiskey. Later, while the Negro awaited execution, the "Colonel" secured permission for him to drink a bottle of whiskey in prison. Bourget understood that the "Colonel" was the Negro's father, but the caste system in the South precluded his trying to prevent the execution.[61]

From a study of the rising homicide rate in the United States, "the founder of the science of criminology," Cesare Lombroso, concluded that it was the black population which kept homicide from being "almost as rare" in the United States as in "the most civilized countries of Europe." Professor Lombroso recognized that in the South much prejudice against blacks persisted; that they faced severe racial discrimination; and that they were careless about concealing crimes and more prone than whites to confess them whether guilty or not. Lombroso also thought that a warm climate was "prone to engender violence." Yet the Negro's tendency to crime arose mainly from "natural," i.e., inherent, causes; he had "latent within him the primitive instincts of the savage." Lacking the sentiment of pity, he regarded "homicide as a mere incident, and as glorious in case it is the outcome of revenge." The abolition of slavery had produced "a ferment in the minds of the colored people" and exposure to social problems with which they could not cope. This ferment and exposure adversely affected morals and helped increase criminality.[62]

The European scholars who toured the South during the black, "nadir" and wrote about Negro life there were, of course, a select class,[63] a group which, because of its intellectual status, might be expected, moreover, to have formed preconceptions and prejudices about the South and its people before arriving there. Most were sure to be strongly influenced by contemporary scholarship, especially as to race. Indeed, some contributed to such scholarship themselves.[64]

Preconceived notions help to explain how some intellectuals of international stature could arrive at unscientific and contradictory assessments, while others seemed to stretch the truth in an opposite direction in conveying their admiration of many Negro traits. Despite their stature and their preconceptions and biases, we do get certain useful impressions of Negro life from the European scholars who roamed the South following the close of Reconstruction.

Ethnic studies dating as far back as the fifteenth century appear to have affected the observers' comments on the Negro's physical appearance.[65] The European scholars looked at the Negro and, in most cases, immediately saw a mental if not a physical inferior, a being closer to beast than to man. Some gave especial attention to the mulatto and other "mixed" Negroes. While not all were willing to grant even these full status as men, there was a general belief that the whiter the Negroes the greater their intelligence and the more "beautiful" their physical features.

The gravest challenge that had faced the newly emancipated blacks had been the need to make a living. The testimony of the observers would confirm that the challenge was, up to a point, successfully met, for black economic activities after 1877 belied ante-bellum fears or contentions that black labor must always be slave labor. Since most blacks remained tillers of the soil, and many even continued to work under rules and authority reminiscent of slavery, some observers saw little difference between the blacks' labor as slaves and as freemen, and thought that the greater the white supervision the more successful the blacks' labor.

The urban blacks who came under the eyes of European scholars were working mainly as domestic and personal servants (waiters, porters, shoe-shine boys, etc.) or factory workers. In the tobacco factories blacks worked well and sang even better. But in the mills, particularly the textile mills, their performances were not adjudged satisfactory. The work of black domestic servants was represented as generally poor and marred by proneness to petty thievery. Blacks in other service occupations, such as waiters and bellhops, were not much better thought of as a rule, though the ever-smiling Pullman porter was a delight to all.

The masses of blacks were locked into the manual or menial occupations of farm laborers, tenancy or sharecropping, factory laborers, and personal servants. They were in the eyes of the travelers, fair-to-good workers who made fair-to-poor wages, but appeared to subsist all right. Considering from whence they had come, the sum of the scholars' views seem to be that economically the blacks had not reached the pinnacles of wealth, but they were not at their nadir.

Efforts to educate Southern blacks after the Civil War attracted wide attention. Many doubted whether such an "inferior race" could learn. Others thought Negro education feasible, and the Freedmen's Bureau and Northern missionary groups plunged energetically into the task. Not only grammar schools but also colleges and universities were established for blacks at many places throughout the South. European intellectuals were, obviously, particularly curious to see the work of all these institutions. Their assessment of the Negro's educability often depended, it would seem, not upon what they actually saw in the schools — most did not see enough to make a judgment — but rather upon preconceptions derived from contemporary ethnology and psychology, and upon what they were told by teachers and others.

The general verdict was that blacks lacked capacity equal to that of whites, even though mulattoes and other "mixed bloods" might closely approach the white level.[66]   Two distinguished historians, Edward Freeman and James Bryce, even saw something pathetic in the blacks' zeal for learning, considering that its procurement would hardly advance their status.

Unlike the lower schools, some black colleges, particularly Hampton and Tuskegee, although the former as an industrial school was somewhat of a disappointment to Sir George Campbell, possessed adequate plants and equipment. For this reason, and because of the work of such men as Washington and Carver at Tuskegee, Armstrong at Hampton, and DuBois at Atlanta, some observers saw significant advances in black higher education. Yet while approving what Hampton and Tuskegee did, James Bryce probably reflected the general attitude of the scholars when he described them as being on "a rather humble scale."

Contemporary ethnological and psychological studies, and the tales of Southern whites, probably led the distinguished Italian criminologist Cesare Lombroso to exaggerate immorality and crime among blacks. On the other hand, Sir George Campbell was disposed to under-estimate the extent of "vicious" crimes by blacks. In any case the disproportionate number of blacks in Southern prisons would suggest either that the race furnished a disproportionate number of criminals or that convictions of blacks were disproportionately large. Both explanations would encompass the views of the European scholars who visited the South. In the area of crime and punishment, especially when one includes lynching as a common form of punishment in the post-Reconstruction South, the contemporary views confirm that this was, indeed, a nadir in Negro life.

The black church in the South was the most important of Negro social institutions. It afforded blacks an opportunity to exercise independent leadership, indeed, to develop politically when such privilege was denied them outside the church. Most of all, the black church was a tool for survival — the one place where blacks could preach, pray, sing, or shout about their daily oppression and frustrations. These larger roles of the black churches were only dimly seen by one or two observers, notably Sir George Campbell. Others tended to criticize black preachers for distorting theology in their simple, fiery sermons and the shouts of the congregations were deemed nothing short of fanatical; and even the revered Negro spirituals were "strange" and "unsound" to the eminent Dean Hole of Rochester. Interestingly enough, however, European theologians tended to be more complimentary to black preachers than the laymen observers, granting to the ministers, even when illiterate, a certain eloquence. The observers unanimously agreed, however, that religion, whether practiced in a Baptist church or a "voodoo house" thoroughly affected the blacks.

In the end, how are we to evaluate these views of the Southern Negro — observations through the eyes of some of Europe's most distinguished scholars at the close of the nineteenth century and the opening of the present one? American blacks, to be sure, have not, on the whole, shown themselves to outsiders or natives as they are. Except in the matter of physical appearance, three centuries of slavery and oppression have obscured the real Negro. His economic, social and cultural capacities have always been stifled, and his personality so conditioned that it was in a sense enslaved even though the body was emancipated by 1865. Many blacks have acted and reacted as they were supposed to, or thought they were supposed to, to meet white expectations. The real personality has often been submerged, or in many cases, lost, as a result of the conditioning process.[67] European intellectuals who allowed preconceptions stemming from racist attitudes and scholarship to influence their assessments of black conditions and character and who failed to consider the dominating role of racial oppression in Southern Negro life actually tell us little about the complexity of life for blacks during the nadir. The judicious observer, the true scholar, who combined a keen eye for observation with an open, penetrating mind, geared to assessing the facts, adds to our knowledge of the rich black past. Most of the sampling of European intellectuals included in this study, of course, fall into the former, rather than the latter category. While this is unfortunate in that it indicates a great deal about the shortcomings of observer sources, the universality of racist attitudes, and the poor state of scholarship on the subject of race in the recent past; these samplings also might tell us how far we have come in these areas and how much further we still have to go.

Notes

[1] See Samuel Flagg Bemis and Grace C. Griffin, *Guide to the Diplomatic History of the United States, 1775-1921* (1935); Donalson Jordan and Edwin J. Pratt, *Europe and the American Civil War* (1931); James M. Callahan, *Diplomatic History of the Southern Confederacy* (1901); Frank L. Owsley, *King Cotton Diplomacy* (1931); Belle B. Sideman and Lillian Friedman, *Europe Looks at the Civil War* (1960); and Ephraim D. Adams, *Great Britain and the American Civil War* (2 vols., 1925).

[2] See, for example, Arthur J. L. Fremantle, *Three Months in the Southern States: April-June, 1863* (New York, 1864); Edward Dicey, *Six Months in the Federal States* (2 vols., London, 1863); Rev. William W. Malet, *An Errand to the South in the Summer of 1862* (London, 1863); Fitzgerald Ross, *A Visit to the Cities and Camps of the Confederate States* (Edinburgh, 1865); Justus Scheibert, *Sieben Monate in den Rebellen-Statten wahrend der Nordamerikanischen Krieges, 1863* (Steltin, 1868); John H. Kennaway, *On Sherman's Track; or, The South After the War* (London, 1867); Robert Somers, *The Southern States Since the War* (London, 1871); and George Clemenceau, *American Reconstruction, 1865-1870* (1928).

[3] U.S. Bureau of the Census, *Negro Population, 1790-1815* (Washington, 1918), p. 43.

[4] See Rayford W. Logan, *The Negro in American Life and Thought: The Nadir, 1877-1901* (New York, 1954), ix-x, 11, *Passim*; C. Vann Woodward, *Origins of the New South, 1877-1913* (Baton Rouge, 1951), pp. 205-235, *Passim*; Arthur F. Raper, *The Tragedy of Lynching* (Chapel Hill, 1933); Paul Lewinson, *Race, Class, and Party: A History of Negro Suffrage and White Politics in the South* (New York, 1932); and C. Vann Woodward, *The Strange Career of Jim Crow* (3rd. ed., New York, 1966).

[5] For a good discussion of the question of observer bias see John Dollard, *Caste and Class in a Southern Town* (3rd. ed., New York, 1957), pp. 32, 40.

[6] Arthur Granville Bradley, *Other Days: Recollections of Rural England and Old Virginia, 1860-1880* (London, 1913), title page; Arthur G. Bradley, *Sketches From Old Virginia* (London, 1897), pp. 249, 250, 253, 254. Bradley was the son of a dean of Westminister. Educated at Trinity College, Cambridge, he wrote for *MacMillan's* and other magazines. His published works include *Life of Wolfe*, 1895 and *Owen Glyndur*, 1901. Especially fond of

Virginia, Bradley was there much of the time period between 1860 and 1890 and spent many hours listening to reminiscences, including those of blacks.
[7] William Saunders, *Through the Light Continent* (2nd. ed., London, 1879), pp. 78-80. Saunders (1823-1895), son of a businessman of Bath, started the Plymouth *Western Morning News* in 1864 and founded the Central News Agency. He was in the U.S. in 1877-1878, his itinerary included Virginia, North Carolina, Louisiana and Georgia. Well known in the politics of his day, he entered Parliament in 1885, and gradually became extremely socialistic in his views.

[8] George Augustus Sala, *America Revisited* (New York, 1880), p. 190. Sala (1828-1895), born of slaveholding parentage in the West Indies, "an ardent sympathizer with the South," when he visited the United States in 1863-1864, declared in 1880 "my heart is still in the South." Sala first wrote of his experiences in letters to the London *Daily Telegraph.*

[9] George Campbell, *White and Black: The Outcome of a Visit to the United States* (New York, 1879), pp. 196, 284. Campbell first went to India in 1842 and was in and out of the country for some 30 years as a magistrate, district commissioner, and finally lieutenant-governor. He had a reputation for working in the best interest of the Indians. Campbell wrote a multi-volume *Ethnology of India* (1864-1865).

[10] Oscar Handlin, ed., *This Was America* (Cambridge, Mass., 1949), pp. 333, 334. Boissevain (1842-1927) came to the United States in 1880 as correspondent of the Amsterdam *Algemmen Handelsblad*, which as editor he subsequently made one of the most distinguished liberal journals on the continent of Europe. His survey of economic and social conditions in the United States included Louisiana and other parts of the South.

[11] Ernst Von Hesse-Wartegg, *Mississippi-Fahrten: Reisebilder aus dem Amerikanischen Suden (879-1880)* (Leipzig, 1881), pp. 22, 23, 256. Quotations are the present author's translations. Hesse-Wartegg (1854-1918), born in Vienna, was an author and world-traveler as well as a diplomat. In 1909 he published another book about the United States, *America als neueste Weltmacht der Industrie.* He spent much of his latter years in London.

[12] Handlin, ed., *This Was America*, pp. 343-348. Gardini, author of the popular *Gli Stati Uniti* (1891), had many contacts with the United States prior to his visit. For a time he was actually an American consular agent in Bologna.

[13] Edward A. Freeman, *Some Impressions of the United States* (London, 1901), pp. 1, 150. Freeman (1823-1892), who became reguis professor of modern history at Oxford, published some 40 books. He was described as a liberal humanitarian, but especially critical and impatient, and tending to be hasty, cocksure, and dramatic.

[14] Gabriel Paul D'Haussonville, *A Travers, Les Etats-Unis: Notes et Impressions* (Paris, 1883), p. 152. D'Haussonville (1843-1924), the son of a conservative French deputy and historian, was himself a leader of the Orleanist party in 1891-1894. His published works include *Socialisme et Charite'* (1895) and *Ombres Francaises et Visions Anglaises* (1914).

[15] Iza Duffus Hardy, *Oranges and Alligators: Sketches of South Florida Life* (London, 1886), pp. 101, 102. Iza Duffus Hardy, novelist, was the only daughter of Sir Thomas Duffus Hardy, deputy keeper of the Record Office, 1861-1878, and editor of medieval documents. Most of her own time was spent traveling and writing under such titles as *A New Othello, Love in Idleness and A Butterfly.*

[16] Max O'Rell and Jack Allyn, *Jonathan and his Continent: Rambles Through American Society*, trans. Madame Paul Blouet (New York, 1889), pp. 300, 303. Blouet (1848-1903), born at Brittany, was an officer in the Franco-Prussian War. In 1873, he went to England as a newspaper correspondent. He taught at Saint Paul's School and the University of London (1876-1884), but gave up teaching with the success of his first book, *John Bull and His Island* (1883). Blouet lectured in the United States in 1887 and 1890. He spent much of the winter and spring of 1889 in Florida.

[17] Paul Bourget, *Outre-Mer: Impressions of America* (London, 1895), pp. 387, 396. Paul Charles Joseph Bourget (1825-1935), son of an eminent mathematician, was himself a Catholic conservative who wrote novels, short stories, plays, poetry, criticism, and travel books. His dogmatism has been regarded as disastrous to his creative writing.

[18] Even though his works reflect the racism of the time, U. B. Phillips' *American Negro Slavery* (1918) and *Life and Labor in the Old South* (1929) remain classic studies of the nineteenth century plantation. Useful studies after the war include M. B. Hammond, *The Cotton Industry* (1897), E. M. Banks, *Economics of Land Tenure in Georgia* (1905), Robert Preston Brooks, *The Agrarian Revolution in Georgia, 1865-1912* (1914), and Fred A. Shannon, *The Farmer's Last Frontier* (1945).

[19] Campbell, *White and Black*, pp. 142-144, 155-157.

[20] Hesse-Wartegg, *Mississippi-Fahrten*, pp. 77, 78, 148, 173, 264, 268-270, 284, 296.

[21] James Bryce, *The American Commonwealth* (2nd. Rev. ed., 2 vols., New York, 1918), II, pp. 514, 515. Bryce (1838-1922) won the Arnold Prize at Oxford in 1863 for his essay on the Holy Roman Empire. He taught civil law there from 1870 until 1893. First elected to the House of Commons in 1880, he was a member of Gladstone's cabinet in 1892; president of the Board of Trade under Lord Rosebury in 1894; administrator in Ireland until 1907; ambassador to the United States, 1907-1913. He was the author of numerous works including *The Relations of the Advanced and Backward Races of Mankind* (1902).

[22] Bradley, *Other Days*, p. 396.

[23] Joel Williamson, *After Slavery: The Negro in South Carolina During Reconstruction, 1861-1877* (Chapel Hill, 1965), p. 161.

[24] Campbell, *White and Black*, pp. 155-157.

[25] Williamson, *After Slavery*, p. 161.

[26] Saunders, *Through the Light Continent*, pp. 75, 76.

[27] Joseph Clarke Robert, *The Tobacco Kingdom: Plantation, Market, and*

Factory in Virginia and North Carolina, 1800-1860 (1937; reprint, Gloucester, Mass., 1965), pp. 197-208.

[28] Campbell, *White and Black*, p. 285. Cf. Nannie May Tilley, *The Bright-Tobacco Industry, 1860-1929* (Chapel Hill, 1948), pp. 318, 319, 490. Taking up where Robert left off, Tilley gives a good survey of the industry down to the Great Depression.

[29] Handlin, ed., *This Was America*, p. 336.

[30] W.H. Russell, *Hesperothen: Notes from the West*, (2 vols., London, 1882), I, p. 97. Educated at Trinity College, Dublin, Russell became famous as a war correspondent of the London *Times*. His *My Diary North and South* (1863) has been widely used by American historians.

[31] Bryce, *The American Commonwealth*, II, pp. 514, 515.

[32] Johannes Baumgarten, compl. *Amerika: Eine ethnographische Rundreise durch den Kontinent und die Antillen* (Stuttgart, 1882), pp. 316-3221; O'Rell, *Jonathan and His Continent*, 287, 288; Handlin, ed., *This Was America*, p. 348; James Fullarton Muirhead, *America The Land of Contrasts* (London, 1898), pp. 39, 40, 253, 254. Muirhead (1853-1934), educated at Edinburgh University, was most noted for editing the English editions of *Baedeker's Handbooks*, a job he held for over 35 years. He married the great-granddaughter of Josiah Quincy.

[33] Bradley, *Other Days*, p. 382.

[34] D'Haussonville, *A Travers, Les Etats-Unis*, p. 153.

[35] Hardy, *Oranges and Alligators*, pp. 100, 101, 109, 110.

[36] O'Rell, *Jonathan and His Continent*, pp. 276, 282.

[37] Campbell, *White and Black*, pp. 217, 218, 281, 327.

[38] *Ibid.*, p. 137.

[39] Sala, *America Revisited*, p. 165.

[40] Saunders, *Through the Light Continent*, pp. 76, 77.

[41] Campbell, *White and Black*, pp. 132, 133, 307.

[42] Saunders, *Through the Light Continent*, pp. 76, 77.

[43] W. H. S. Aubrey, "Social Problems in America," *Fortnightly Review*, n.s., XLIII, (1880), p. 861. William Hickman Smith Aubrey (b. 1848), edited a number of English newspapers and magazines, including *Capital and Labour* (1874-1882), and was an unsuccessful Liberal candidate for the Parliament in 1886 and 1892. He visited Kentucky and other parts of the South in 1888.

[44] Freeman, *Some Impressions of the United States*, pp. 170, 171.

[45] John Kerr Campbell, *Through the United States and Canada: Being a Record of Holiday Rambles and Experiences* (London 1886) pp. 151-154. Campbell, a fellow of the Royal Physical Society, Edinburgh, published an account of his "rambles" in the Middle East, entitled *Through Egypt, Palestine and Syria.* Campbell was in the South in the fall of 1885.

[46] Timothy Harley, *Southward Ho! Notes of a Tour To and Through the State of Georgia, in the Winter of 1885-1886* (London, 1886), p. 77. Harley, fellow of the Royal Astronomical Society, and author of *Moon Lore*, toured the

South, mostly Georgia, during the winter of 1885-1886. He stopped at several places between Atlanta and Savannah.
        [47] Samuel Reynolds Hole, *A Little Tour in America* (London, 1895), p. 298. Dean Hole (1819-1904), a moderate high-churchman educated at Oxford, became very popular as a preacher and speaker. Besides books he wrote several hymns including "Father, Forgive," which sold nearly 30,000 copies.
        [48] Edward Larocque Tinker, *Lafcadio Hearn's American Days* (2nd. Ed., New York, 1925), pp. 132-135. Hearn was born in 1850 on the Greek Isle of Santa Maura. His father was surgeon-major of a British infantry regiment stationed there. His mother was Greek. Hearn came to the United States in 1869 and by 1877 was a newspaperman in New Orleans. He achieved some fame as an editorial writer and actually much more as an author. Hearn left the United States in 1887 for the French West Indies and finally Japan.
        [49] Lafcadio Hearn, *Miscellanies* (2 vols., London, 1824) I, pp. 201, 202, 206, 209.
        [50] Baumgarten, compl., *Amerika*, pp. 314-326.
        [51] Bryce, *American Commonwealth*, II, p. 521; W. Laird Clowes, *Black America: Study of the Ex-Slave and His Late Master* (London, 1891), p. 114. William Laird Clowes (b. 1856), chiefly remembered as a Naval historian was educated at King's College, London. He prepared for the bar, but never practiced. Beginning newspaper work in 1885 as special correspondent for the *Standard* he was with the *Times* of London 1890-1895. He wrote *The Navy and the Empire* (1892) and *The Royal Navy* (7 vols., 1897-1903).
        [52] Freeman, *Some Impressions of the United States*, p. 286; Hole, *A Little Tour in America*, p. 286.
        [53] Saunders, *Through the Light Continent*, pp. 79, 83-85; Sala, *America Revisited*, p. 191; D'Haussonville, *A Travers, Les Etats-Unis*, p. 158.
        [54] Saunders, *Ibid.*; Campbell, *White and Black*, p. 131; Sala, *America Revisited*, p. 191; Bryce, *American Commonwealth*, p. 521.
        [55] One should not allow the designations "college" and "university" to obscure the fact that most black institutions attempted to offer work on the "secondary level" and almost all had "normal" departments.
        [56] Campbell, *White and Black*, 275, 276; Bryce, *American Commonwealth*, II, p. 519.
        [57] Harley, *Southward Ho!*, p. 130.
        [58] Aubrey, *Fortnightly Review*, XLIII, n.s., p. 861. See also James M. McPherson, "White Liberals and Black Power in Negro Education, 1865-1915," *American Historical Review*, LXXV (June, 1970), pp. 1357-1379.
        [59] Campbell, *White and Black*, pp. 169-171.
        [60] Bryce, *American Commonwealth*, II, pp. 526-528.
        [61] Bourget, *Outre-Mer*, pp. 396-401.
        [62] Casare Lombroso, "Why Homicide Has Increased in the United States," Part I, *North American Review*, CLXV (December, 1897), pp. 647, 648. Lombroso (1836-1909), an Italian Jew, became widely known through his investigations of the abnormal human being, and spent much time in minute

measurements of criminal types. He looked on criminality as marking a reversion to an earlier type and as largely the product of nervous disease. Lombroso does not seem to have gone any further south than Virginia.

[63] Those represented in this study are, of course, only a representative sampling of their class.

[64] See, for instance Sir George Campbell's *Ethnology of India* (1864-1865) and James Bryce's *The Relations of the Advanced and Backward Races of Mankind* (1902). Bryce's racist assessment of Brazilian Negroes and his comparison of their condition with that of American blacks can be seen in his *South America: Observations and Impressions* (New York, 1914), pp. 404, 405, 414, 415.

[65] Adequate summaries of learned views prior to 1890 on the Negro's physical, mental, and social traits can be found, among other places, conveniently in Daniel G. Brinton, *Races and Peoples: Lectures on the Science of Ethnography* (New York, 1890), in John C. Greene, *The Death of Adam: Evolution and Its Impact on Western Thought* (New York, 1961), and in Mark Hughlin Haller, *American Eugenics: Heredity and Social Thought, 1870-1930* (Ann Arbor, 1959). For the period 1890 to the First World War, see in addition to Haller, George Oscar Ferguson, Jr. "The Psychology of the Negro: An Experimental Study," *Archives of Psychology*, V (1916), No. 36, and Thomas F. Gossett, *Race: The History of an Idea in America* (Dallas, 1963).

[66] Contemporary scholarship concerning race taught that mulattoes and other "mixed bloods" were superior in intellect to "pure blooded" blacks and that the Negro mind often stopped grasping facts at the age of 12.

[67] Novelists, historians, sociologists, psychiatrists, and psychologists have treated the effects of racial oppression on Negro character. Among the more prominent works are: Kenneth B. Clark and Mamie Phipps Clark, "The Emergence of Racial Identification and Preference in Negro Children," in E. E. Maccoby, T. M. Newcomb, and E. I. Hartley, *Readings in Social Psychology* (3rd. ed., New York, 1958), Ralph Ellison, *The Invisible Man* (New York, 1947), Charles S. Silberman, *Crisis in Black and White* (New York, 1964), Abram Kardiner and Lionel Ovesey, *The Mark of Oppression* (New York, 1959), and Price M. Cobb and William H. Grier, *Black Rage* (New York, 1968).

STATE AND LOCAL STUDIES

Chapter 5
A Brief History of African Americans
in Georgia, 1733–1868

Negro Slavery Enters Georgia

When the colony of Georgia was established in 1733 the intention of the charter was to provide a place for poor persons who were unable to subsist for themselves in England and to establish a frontier for South Carolina, which because of its small number of white inhabitants, was very much exposed to hostile Indians and Spaniards. The sponsors of the colony felt that it was unlikely that the poor people who would be sent from England as well as any poor person who would enter the colony voluntarily to escape religious persecution or for other reasons would be able to purchase slaves or to maintain them even if they were furnished free of cost. At the time the average cost of a black slave was $150. This was enough money to pay for the passage from England to Georgia of a white man, supply him with tools and other necessities and take care of him for a year. The strength of the colony, the trustees thought, lay not in populating it with black slaves, but with able-bodied free white men.

The trustees' desire to prohibit slavery in Georgia soon, however, came under strong attack. Faced with mounting expenses for military

Prepared to help commemorate the unveiling of the sculpture, "Expelled Because of their Color," a project of the Black Caucus in the Georgia Legislature in 1976.

protection against the Spaniards and a decline in private contributions for the aid of the colony, the Georgians were, by 1738, short on military supplies and even food. On December 9, 1738, a group of 121 white males met at Savannah and drew up a petition to the trustees on the economic crisis. In the petition, they said that their poor condition could partially be alleviated by the use of slaves "with proper limitations." The trustees, however, refused to allow slavery to enter the colony at this time.

If the fervor of the pro-slavery movement was diminished, the movement did not die. Some prominent voices continued to be raised in support of black servile labor in the colony. Among these was the evangelist George Whitefield. Whitefield had become convinced that the lack of slaves was one of the principal causes of the poor condition of the colony. Nevertheless, the trustees remained firm in their stand against slavery.

In the face of the trustees' position, some Georgians felt they had no recourse other than to evade the law and move toward the use of black slaves. They said that the colony was facing an acute shortage of labor, which would further exacerbate the poor economic conditions, so they devised a scheme to introduce slavery into the colony. They proposed to hire blacks from their masters in South Carolina with the understanding that if colonial authorities attempted to enforce the law against the use of slaves, then the owner in South Carolina would be promptly notified so that he might come to return his slaves to the adjoining colony. After having encountered little or no resistance to these evasive tactics, the Georgians adopted a new and firmer procedure. Slaves were hired for a period of 100 years or for life. The owners were paid fully in advance with the understanding that they should intervene and claim the blacks in the event the authorities in Georgia chose to enforce the prohibition against slavery.

The success of the pro-slavery forces bred further bold action. Soon blacks were being openly purchased from slave traders in the city of Savannah and were being employed in such visible institutions as orphan homes. The local authorities generally ignored the violations of the law. When news of these evasions and laxity of enforcement of the law reached the trustees, they told the local authorities to end the illegal activities. But the pro-slavery steamroller could not be stopped. In January 1749 a new petition was sent to the trustees asking for immediate authorization to use black slaves in Georgia. The trustees could resist no longer. They promptly announced their intention to seek the king's approval for "a repeal of the act prohibiting the importation and use of black slaves within the province of Georgia."

In their capitulation, the trustees warned of the inherent danger in the use of black slaves and reminded the Georgians of the ease with which their slaves might escape to Florida. They also suggested certain restrictive regulations for the institution in the colony. Among these was a requirement that every slaveholder should keep one indentured white male servant, aged between 20 and 55, for every four black slaves above the age of 14. To protect the health of the colony, ships transporting blacks were to be quarantined until such time as a certificate of health could be obtained. Masters were encouraged to permit "or oblige" their slave to attend church on Sundays and no work was to be required of the blacks "on the Lord's Day." The trustees decreed "corporal punishment" for any interracial sexual cohabitation and declared interracial marriages illegal. Finally, the trustees declared that masters should not exercise "an unlimited power" over their blacks, and suggested, for the maintenance of public works, that each slave trader and each slave holder be required to pay an annual tax on each slave.

Prominent representatives of the Georgians quickly agreed with the trustees' stipulations and the way was clear in the fall of 1749 for the introduction of Negro slavery into Georgia. For 16 years, Georgia had stood alone among the Southern colonies as an English province where only free men could legally live and work. Because of physical, diplomatic and economic dangers, the prohibition against slavery had, at first, received widespread and favorable support. But for 16 years, another group insisted vehemently that economic necessities outweighed all of the dangers and that the survival of the colony required the use of black slaves. In the fall of 1749, this group — the pro-slavery forces — won a triumphant victory.

The regulations of slavery adopted by the trustees in 1749, with minor modifications, constituted the body of laws governing the institution in Georgia for the next six years. However, when the first Colonial General Assembly met at Savannah on January 7, 1755, immediate attention was given to the question of adopting new, Georgia grown, slave codes.

The new laws were contained in an "act for the better ordering and governing of Negroes and other slaves," and they covered the treatment, management, trial and punishment, sale and recovery, and the privileges and disabilities of black slaves in Georgia. According to the code, all offsprings of "negroes, mulattoes and mestizoes" who were slaves at the time of the act (1755) were to be assigned to slavery forever.

The statute prevented cruel and unusual treatment of slaves, but subjected murderers of slaves to the full penalty of the law only on second offenses. Those convicted of manslaughtering slaves were subject to be fined.

Slaves could not, without a permit, sell fishes, vegetables and produce, or be employed as a fisherman or porter. No slave could keep a boat or canoe; or breed or own any horse or raise cattle.

The law forbade the selling of liquor to slaves. Slaves could not lease any house plantation, store or room. They could not be taught to write.

Slaves could be worked up to 16 hours out of a 24-hour day. Owners exceeding this limit were subject to be fined. No slave could be forced to work on Sundays.

Severe penalties were provided for crimes committed by slaves. Offenses carrying the death penalty included arson, malicious mischief, certain categories of theft, and murder of a white person.

Cases involving capital punishment were to be tried by a court, comprised of two justices of the peace and three to five property owners of the district where the felony occurred. The testimony of slaves was admissible only for or against another slave. A slave could not testify against a white person.

Many of the regulations for the control of slaves also were applied later to the so-called free Negroes — that small class of blacks who were not legally in bondage. The Georgia regulations were also very similar to those adopted by other colonies, North as well as South.

With the slave codes serving as an inhibition to most economic and social pursuits, the average slave in Georgia, as elsewhere in the South, was a tiller of the soil with a circumscribed social life. The cultivation of rice and silk was the first major occupation for Georgia blacks. Later, however, the production of the cotton crop became their principal task.

Aside from religious activities, often in the company of whites and other times autonomous, the slave's social activities were limited to occasional recreational activities with the master and his own late night, weekend, or holiday entertainment — singing, storytelling, etc. On the Fourth of July or other holidays, the slaves might be treated to a barbecue or fish fry. On Christmas, the holiday of holidays for slaves, there might be a new suit of clothes or even a bottle of whiskey. These ameliorations, however, could not lessen the overall impact of the degrading system of human bondage. Thus, many slaves often longed for the Promised Land — whether that land be heavenly or the free states of the North or Canada.[1]

Georgia Blacks In The American Revolution

At the outbreak of the American Revolution, it was general and official policy in most American colonies to exclude blacks from the colonial militias, but military necessities often made these rules invalid. Thus, by 1775, blacks were serving in the militias of several colonies. At the national level, General George Washington and the Continental Congress vacillated on the use of blacks as soldiers — first approving, then disapproving, then approving again, but only free blacks.

By 1778, manpower shortages and the worsening military situation on the American side suggested the recruitment of soldiers wherever they could be found. Several New England colonies and New York soon authorized the use of slaves. Most of these colonies promised the slaves their freedom after the war if they served faithfully.

In the summer of 1780, Maryland took the lead among Southern colonies in authorizing the use of slaves as soldiers. Many white Georgians believed that the army would become a refuge for runaway slaves and that slaves would be taken from their work for long periods. There was also a general fear of a Negro with a gun. Georgia law, in fact, prohibited slaves from carrying firearms for any purpose.

At the national level, the Continental Congress had, since the spring of 1779, been recommending the employment of slaves as soldiers. After the British had occupied Savannah and opened a second campaign to subdue the South, the Congress sent a specific request to Georgia and South Carolina to enlist slaves. The Congress requested 3,000 able-bodied blacks from these colonies. These were to be formed into separate battalions with white officers. Owners of the slaves were to be paid $1,000 for each able bodied man under 35 years of age. The slave was not to receive any salary, but those who served "well and faithfully" to the end of the war were to be freed and given the sum of $59. Despite the perils and despite the pleas and offers of the Congress, both South Carolina and Georgia refused to employ slaves as soldiers.

Although Georgia never authorized the use of slaves as soldiers, the colony at a very early stage in the war used blacks in non-combat roles. In November 1775, the authorities ordered that 100 blacks be impressed to help General Charles Lee enclose the military storehouse at Savannah. In June 1776, blacks were hired to build entrenchments around Sunbury. And in June 1778, blacks were hired to repair the roads between the Ogechee and the Altamaha rivers.

The Georgia officials ordered the use of blacks, even though in many cases their masters were opposed. The masters were particularly concerned about their property loss if an impressed slave escaped, took ill, or died. To help soothe the owner's concerns, they were told that sick or wounded slaves would be taken to a proper hospital and given the necessary "sustenance, medicine, and attendance."

The British, also like the Americans, employed a number of blacks as laborers, guides, scouts, and spies. In the fall of 1779, for example, the British commander General Augustine Prevost was trying to decide whether or not he should surrender to the Americans and their French allies. During the 24-hour period in which he had to make up his mind, he was re-enforced by a friendly detachment under the command of Colonel John Maitland. Success in reaching Savannah to rescue Prevost was attributed to his black guides. At the Dawfuskie River, enroute from Beaufort, South Carolina, Maitland was blocked by French forces. Some blacks in the area volunteered to lead him around the enemy. The British force used obscure, winding waterways, swamps, and marshes and the covering of a dense fog to reach Savannah undetected. The route had never been used before except by "bears, wolves and runaway Negroes." The American commanders were later to observe that Maitland's success, with the aid of the blacks, caused their operation to fail.

Georgia did not exhibit the same attitude toward free blacks as soldiers as it did toward slaves. Free blacks were probably fighting in Georgia as early as 1775. But because of the very small number of free blacks, only about 300, living in the state during the Revolutionary Era, this class was destined to be an almost negligible factor as combatants.

The most notable black arms-bearer for the Patriots in Georgia was an artilleryman, Austin Dabney. Dabney's master, Richard Aycock, brought him to Wilkes County, Georgia from North Carolina shortly after the beginning of the Revolutionary War. After Aycock was called to serve in the Georgia militia, he used the rule of substitution, whereby persons who could furnish able-bodied substitutes could be exempted from military service, to ask that young Dabney be permitted to take his place. Aycock swore that the young boy, allegedly the son of a Virginia white woman and a black father, was indeed a free person of color, since the law forbade slaves from bearing arms for any reason.

As a soldier, Dabney was probably the only black person to participate in the fierce battle of Kettle Creek in 1779. Two years later he was wounded in the thigh at Augusta — the wound crippled him for life and ended a brief, but distinguished military adventure.

In recognition of Dabney's distinguished service, the Georgia legislature in 1786 freed him by statute, perhaps to prevent the former master's heirs from seizing him as a slave and reaping benefits from the young soldier's military fame. Then in 1821, although several white Georgians objected, the Legislature passed a special act granting Dabney a farm of 112 acres in Walton County.

As combatants and non-combatants, Georgia blacks, then, aided both Americans and the British in their respective causes during the Revolutionary War. Only in a few cases, however, such as that of Austin Dabney, did the blacks reap the benefits of their labor. Most, particularly on the American side, saw their masters win freedom from the British, but they, themselves, remained in slavery.[2]

Free Blacks in Ante-Bellum Georgia

The so-called free blacks in ante-bellum Georgia, i.e., before the Civil War, never comprised more than one percent of the total population of the colony. The census of 1790, for example, listed only 398 of these persons. Yet despite their small number, these people were the object of a great deal of attention from the white community. The dominant group sought to control the free black population in a manner similar to that of slaves (hence the term so-called free or quasi-free blacks) through social restrictions and legal enactments. The great fear was that the existence of even this small number of persons had a disturbing influence on the larger system of slavery. The free black population clearly demonstrated to the slave that there was an alternative condition for black people in Georgia.

In order to keep the free black class small, the Georgia Legislature in an act of 1818 forbade the freeing of slaves by will and testament. Since, heretofore, most slaves freed in Georgia had achieved their manumission in this way, the law had the effect of stifling the growth of the free black population. According to a judge of the Superior Court of Georgia, the law was designed "to prevent a horde of free persons of color from ravaging the morals and corrupting the feelings of our slaves."

The precise legal status of the free blacks in Georgia was made clear in an opinion by Chief Justice Joseph H. Lumpkin of the State Supreme Court in 1853. Judge Lumpkin said:

> The status of the African in Georgia, whether bond or free is such that he has no civil, social, or political rights whatever, except such as are bestowed on him by statute; that he can neither contract, nor

be contracted with; that the free Negro can act only by and through his guardian; and that he is in a condition of perpetual pupilage or wardship; and that this condition he can never change by his own volition.   It can only be done by Legislation ...The act of manumission confers no other right but that of freedom from the dominion of the master and the limited liberty of locomotion ...To be civilly and politically free, to be the peer and equal of the white man, to enjoy the offices, trusts, and privileges our institutions confer on the white man, is not now, never has been, and never will be, the condition of this degraded race.

The free blacks found almost all of their social associations within their own group, as they were almost totally cut off from the slave community and interacted with the white community only under specified arrangements. Much of this interracial interaction was on the same basis as that of slaves and white persons as servants and laborers of one kind or another for whites. Nevertheless, in Georgia, as elsewhere a number of free blacks, despite the caste system, achieved notable successes. The military career of Austin Dabney has already been mentioned. But, in later years, Dabney became a rather prosperous landowner and sportsman in Pike County, Georgia. He became very attached to a white family, the Giles Harrises, who had befriended him during his war-time convalescence. He was also on intimate terms with several other prominent white Georgians and when he died about 1830, he was, in the words of the black historian Carter G. Woodson, "mourned by all."

Other affluent blacks in the pre-Civil War Era included Andrew Marshall, a free Negro drayman of Savannah who was worth $5,000 in 1850, James Oliver of Savannah and Jeffrey Moore of Augusta. All of these blacks owned either gigs and/or carriages. As Professor Edward Sweat put it, "certainly the possession of such means of conveyance represented not only a measure of economic stability, but social distinction as an approach in the direction of social equality . . . ." Understandably then, the city of Atlanta passed an ordinance in 1853 which made it illegal "to hire, bind, or deliver" to any free black a "gig, sulky, buggy, or carriage..."[3]

Also in the Revolutionary period, two blacks, George Leile and Andrew Bryan organized at Savannah, Georgia what was probably the first stable black Baptist Church in the American colonies. In 1773, the church, founded by the ex-slaves, opened its doors to a small congregation. Both men had only a modest amount of education and began preaching at very young ages. At the time there were no black denominations. Although the men preached without pay, Leile supported himself after being freed by his religious master by hiring out his labor.

Opposition to black worship, to be sure, was as strong in Savannah as elsewhere in the colonies. Hence, during the Revolutionary War, Leile fled with the British soldiers to Jamaica where he served two years as an indentured servant. After completing his service, he resumed preaching and soon founded the only Baptist Church on the island. Bryan's master, on the other hand, defended him against other whites who were alarmed over the growth of the black church. In gratitude for his master's defense, Bryan did not purchase his own freedom until after his master's death. He did, however, earlier purchase the freedom of his wife. In 1783 Bryan was certified as the minister of the Ethiopian Church of Jesus Christ (a predecessor to the First African Church), which by 1800 had reached a membership of 700 persons.

The founding of independent black churches was a monumental development in the history of black Georgians. The church became not only a place to worship freely, but it also became the race's most important social institution.[4]

In addition to Austin Dabney, the Reverends Bryan and Leile, the best known of Georgia's free blacks before the Civil War were Anthony Odingsells and Solomon Humphries. Odingsells, who was perhaps the son of his master, was freed in 1809. He soon came into possession of several items of property, including land, slaves, and an island. Even in 1860, he retained much of his valuable holdings. Solomon Humphries of Macon, on the contrary, gained his wealth by "probity, industry, and gentle manners." In an unusual circumstance for a black person, he owned property in the city and was a successful merchant and cotton broker.

While the founding of independent black churches and the attaining of affluence on the part of a few blacks were of the utmost significance, it would, in the end, require real freedom, such as that made possible by the post-Civil War's 13th, 14th, and 15th Amendments to the U.S. Constitution, to give blacks an opportunity for major progress.[5]

Emancipation And Reconstruction

On September 22, 1862, President Abraham Lincoln issued a proclamation which in effect declared that all persons held as slaves in any state that was in rebellion against the United States as of January 1,

1863, would be "then, thenceforward, and forever free." As a matter of fact, the proclamation was virtually groundless. Slaves could be freed only where the Union Army was in control and the Union controlled very little Southern soil on New Year's Day, 1863.

Real freedom for Georgia's slaves, as well as most others elsewhere, came clearly with the end of the Civil War and the subsequent passage of the 13th Amendment to the Constitution. That Amendment forbade slavery or involuntary servitude throughout the land, except as punishment for a crime. Yet, in a sense, even now real freedom had not come. As President Lincoln and the Congress debated whether or not blacks should be allowed to remain in the country, whether or not they should be extended political and civil rights, and whether or not they should be given an economic start-up in terms of 40 acres of land and a mule, some blacks wandered helplessly from the old plantations and farms, while others remained where they were to await further and, hopefully, better developments.

President Lincoln, for his own part, was not at all sure that whites and blacks could live together in peace in the United States. One of his first thoughts was to colonize the freedmen in other lands outside of the United States. He found Africa and the Caribbean particularly appealing. After a group of blacks sent to one of the Caribbean islands began to die "like flies," the President reconsidered his actions. Meanwhile, black leaders, including Frederick Douglass, had counseled the President against his colonization scheme and advised him that large numbers of blacks would not leave the country voluntarily.

After abandoning colonization, Lincoln embraced the idea of helping blacks to survive where they were. Congress and the President established a Freedmen's Bureau which sought to insure to blacks the necessities of life; to help them find employment and to prevent their exploitation on the job; and to give to some an education.

The social customs of the period after the death of Lincoln and the assumption of the presidency by Andrew Johnson of Tennessee, in 1865, dictated that blacks should show the proper deference to whites. If, for example, a white person passed a black on the street, he could show his proper respect by doffing his hat or stepping aside until the white person passed. Rather than run the risk of being accused of making an "amorous glance" toward white women, he could bow his head in the presence of such women. Violations of the caste system could bring swift and certain punishment, but only in the courts. Sometimes full-fledged race riots, such as the ones in Memphis and New Orleans in 1866, would break out.

Fortunately for blacks, there was a sizeable element of the

Republican majority in Congress who opposed Andrew Johnson's program for the reconstruction of the South — the program that allowed such repressions of blacks. Some of these congressmen, like Charles Sumner and Thaddeus Stevens, combined a genuine humanitarian interest in the welfare of blacks with a more practical desire to see a viable Republic Party in the South, based upon black votes. After the Congressional elections of 1866, when several other legislators of this persuasion were elected, the Congress was able to overthrow President Johnson's program for the South and institute a new plan — one which provided for full black participation in government for the first time in American history.

The Congressional or "Radical" Reconstruction program was based on the Reconstruction Acts of 1867, which called for new governments founded upon new constitutions to be established in the South, and the 14th and 15th Amendments to the U.S. Constitution which assured the civil and political rights of "all persons born or naturalized in the United States."

In 1867, there were 465,000 blacks and 591,000 whites residing in Georgia. After the pollsters completed their registration of voters under the Reconstruction Acts of 1867, it was found that 95,000 blacks and 96,000 whites were eligible to cast ballots. In the ensuing elections for delegates to the Constitutional Convention and representatives to the first legislature, 33 blacks and 137 whites were elected to the Convention, while 32 blacks and 214 whites were sent to the General Assembly. Clearly, the blacks had not exercised a proportionate degree of their newly won political influence in the election of members of their own race to office.

The explanation for the failure of black voters to vote black or, more precisely, not to vote at all lies in several areas. First, despite the presence of federal troops in the South (under the terms of the Reconstruction Acts of 1867), anti-Negro violence, reminiscent of the Johnson era, continued. Much of this violence was directed at would-be black voters. Secondly, since blacks had failed to receive even the economic security that "40 acres and a mule" could have provided, they were ripe for economic intimidation at the hands of their white employers. Much of this intimidation was directed at would-be voters. Finally, black apathy played a large role in the elections. Much of this apathy was apparently occasioned by the novelty of black candidates for office. Many blacks seemed unconvinced that this was the time to place fellow blacks in public office.

Although the proportion of blacks who were elected to the

Constitutional Convention of 1867 was far below what it could have been and only 19 percent of the total, the blacks did not become an invisible segment of the delegation which met at Atlanta City Hall during the winter of 1867-1868. Among the most notable of the 33 blacks were Aaron A. Bradley, Tunis G. Campbell, James T. Costin, and Henry McNeal Turner. Bradley became the Convention's most notorious black member while Turner was without doubt its most outstanding one.

Aaron Alpeorra Bradley, who was a former resident of the North, attacked both his Republican and Democratic colleagues vociferously for misleading him and other black delegates on issues important to freedmen and for not pushing vigorously ahead on these issues themselves — things like relief, the suffrage, and office holding. As an example of white duplicity, Bradley learned that he and other blacks were led to vote to strike out a section of the new Constitution that would have guaranteed blacks the right to hold office. It was represented to the Negroes, that they were eligible to hold office without such a distinct clause, when all knew that they would encounter serious difficulties qualifying without such a clause in the most prejudiced areas of the state. Bradley was also the sponsor of an ordinance prohibiting racial discrimination on public carriers. Apparently because of such attitudes and practices, Bradley attained a reputation as a delegate "who has made himself quite conspicuous in the convention by the advocacy of extreme measures, and a somewhat turbulent opposition to moderate counsels."

White delegates felt that Bradley was so "extreme and turbulent" that they soon expelled him from the Convention. The specific charges against him, however, were that his name had been removed from the roll of lawyers in Massachusetts for contempt of court and that he had been convicted and sentenced to two years in prison in New York for seducing a woman. To the charge of seduction, Bradley replied that his white colleagues were undoubtedly guilty of the same thing. If one had to be innocent of seduction in order to sit in the Convention, he charged, the Convention would be unable to meet for lack of a quorum. As Lerone Bennett put it, such a black man — "defiant, daring, unchastened" — surely, in the view of the white delegates, had no place in the Georgia Constitutional Convention.

Henry McNeal Turner, a native of Abbeyville, South Carolina, was probably no less militant than Bradley, but was probably less seductive. Turner, an African Methodist Episcopal minister, came to Georgia in 1865 as an agent of the Freedmen's Bureau. Previously, during the Civil War, he had served as the first black chaplain in the United States

＊

Army.

Turner supported a number of measures in the Convention designed to enhance the economic, educational, and judicial status of the state. For example, he introduced an ordinance to prevent the sale of property on which owners were unable to pay taxes. He also introduced a measure to provide relief to banks in an effort to restore prosperity. Both of these measures were approved by the delegates.

In the Convention, Turner also opposed a measure to collect taxes to defray the expenses of the body; supported a resolution declaring that all civil offices of the state were vacant; a measure giving the legislature or the governor the power to appoint judges of the Superior and Supreme Court; and the pardon of Confederate President Jefferson Davis. He also called for the hiring of a black porter for the legislative body. In the end, Turner was seen in the Convention as a man who was "more interesting than polite, a man who thinks for himself, speaks as he feels, and who fears only God."

Because of his wide popularity among both blacks and whites, it was not surprising that Turner, in April 1868 became one of the first blacks elected to the Georgia Legislature in the state's history. Turner was elected from Bibb County. Along with Turner, three blacks were elected to the State Senate and 29 others to the House of Representatives. The senators were: Aaron A. Bradley, Tunis G. Campbell, and George Wallace. Three of the representatives were from Burke County; two each from Chatham, Clarke, and Hancock Counties. Other counties represented by blacks were: Jasper, Richmond, Wilkes, McIntosh, Monroe, Greene, Talbot, Morgan, Warren, Liberty, Bryan, Laurens, Columbia, Baldwin, Muscogee, Jefferson, and Harris.

During the elections of 1868, many white Democrats, including former Governor Joseph E. Brown, contended that the new state Constitution did not specifically authorize blacks to hold office and hence they could not do so. Shortly after the new legislature opened, a resolution was introduced in the Senate to "inquire into the eligibility of the several persons of color holding seats as Senators . . . ." The proponents of the resolution cited the fact that even "one of the ablest lawyers of the Republic party of Georgia," Governor Brown, "'as well as persons distinguished for their knowledge of Constitutional law" had held that blacks were not entitled to hold office.

While the general question of black eligibility to serve in the Senate was being debated in Committee, the Senate expelled Aaron A. Bradley on the ground that he had earlier been convicted of seduction in New York.

In the House of Representatives, moves were also underway to challenge the eligibility of the 30 black members. The House moved with even quicker dispatch than the Senate. The resolution challenging the seats the black members held was introduced on August 26 and by a vote of 83-23, the black members were expelled on September 3rd.

The issue of black exclusion was more prolonged and more heatedly debated in the Senate, but that body soon also concluded that "persons of color" were ineligible to hold elective office in Georgia. Consequently by a vote of 24-11 the two remaining black senators, Tunis G. Campbell and George Wallace, were removed.

Several white leaders, including Governor Rufus Bullock, joined blacks in asserting that the expulsions were unconstitutional, but the white, mostly Democratic, legislators stuck to their decision. Conservative white Democrats then moved in to claim the seats of the ousted blacks.[6]

On the part of blacks, the protest against the legislative action was led by the venerable Henry McNeal Turner. Following the vote to expel, Turner took the House floor and in a memorable address declared:

> Cases may be found where men have been deprived of their rights for crimes and misdemeanors; but it has remained for the State of Georgia in the very heart of the Nineteenth Century to call a man before the bar and there charge him with an act for which he is no more responsible than for the head which he carries upon his shoulders. The Anglo-Saxon race, Sir, is a most surprising one. No man has ever been more deceived in that race than I have been for the last three weeks. I was not aware that there was in the character of the race so much cowardice, or so much pusillanimity . . . It is very strange, if a white man can occupy on this floor a seat created by colored votes, and a black man cannot do it. Why, Gentlemen, it is the most short-sighted reasoning in the world . . . . If Congress has simply given me merely sufficient civil and political rights and made me a mere political slave for Democrats, or anybody else — giving them the opportunity of jumping on my back in order to leap into political power — I do not thank Congress for it. Never, so help me God, shall I be a political slave . . . . You have all the elements of superiority upon your side; you have our money and your own; you have our education and your own; you have our land and your own too. We, who number hundreds of thousands in Georgia, including our wives and families, with not a foot of land to call our own — strangers in the land of our birth; without money, without education, without aid,

without a roof to cover us when we die! It is extraordinary that a race such as yours, professing gallantry, chivalry, education, and superiority, living in a land where ringing chimes call child and sire to the Church of God — a land where Bibles are read and Gospel truths are spoken, and where courts of justice are presumed to exist; it is extraordinary, I say that with all these advantages on your side, you can make war upon the poor defenseless black man.[7]

After this memorable oration, Turner helped attract national attention to the expulsions through mass meetings in the state and speeches around the country. The matter was quickly appealed to the United States Congress. The Congress responded by refusing to seat the new congressmen recently elected from Georgia and ordered a new reconstruction program for the state under military rule. Under these circumstances, the Georgians gave way and the black legislators were re-admitted in 1870. Interestingly enough, the new military government then expelled all of the white members who would not take an oath of allegiance under the new Constitution or who were found ineligible for other reasons.

As the black lawmakers reclaimed their seats it was, again, Henry McNeal Turner who stood out among them. He introduced several bills, including ones designed to strengthen the executive branch of government by allowing the governor to appoint judges and by creating the office of lieutenant governor. Ironically, he also devoted much effort pleading for a pardon for former Confederate President Jefferson Davis.

With the return of the black legislators, conservative white Georgians had suffered a setback, but not a defeat. Violence and intimidation still kept many black voters from the polls, and following the elections of 1870 and the new withdrawal of military rule, white supremacy again reigned supreme. Only two blacks were elected to the Georgia Senate until Leroy Johnson accomplished the feat in 1964. The last black to serve in either house of the legislature prior to the election of Johnson was W. H. Rogers of McIntosh County who retired in 1907.

After 1900 Georgia, like most Southern states, severely restricted black political participation through such extra-legal devices as literacy and understanding tests, poll taxes, and white-only primary elections. With these measures added to violence and intimidation, blacks were destined to remain for nearly a half century a negligible factor in the political life of the state. Nevertheless, the few years of political participation in the Reconstruction Era, highlighted by the election of William Finch to the Atlanta City Council, Jefferson Long to the U.S. House of Representatives, and 35 blacks to the Georgia House of Representatives were important milestones in the transition of Georgia blacks from slavery to freedom. Real political emancipation, however, would come only after the U.S. Supreme Court in 1946 struck down the Georgia white primary, thus removing a major extra-legal obstacle to black voting and office holding.[8]

After nearly a half century of disfranchisement, Georgia blacks after 1946 were eager to claim their new political opportunities and, in later years, the results could be most clearly seen in the presence of two blacks in the Georgia Senate and 21 in the Georgia House — more blacks than any other state in the Union. Under the leadership of Representative Ben Brown of Atlanta, an effective "Black Caucus," composed of all of the blacks, was developed. Although, unfortunately, Henry McNeal Turner could not see it, by 1977 black men were again occupying many legislative seats in Georgia *"created by colored voters."*

NOTES

[1] Asa H. Gordon, *The Georgia Negro* (Ann Arbor, Michigan, 1937), pp. 1-23, 27-39; John Hope Franklin and Alfred A. Moss, Jr., *From Slavery to Freedom: A History of Negro Americans* (6th ed., New York, 1988), pp. 58-59, 66, 70-71; Alton Hornsby, Jr., *The Negro in Revolutionary Georgia* (Atlanta, 1977), pp. 3-4.

[2] Franklin and Moss, *From Slavery to Freedom*, p. 23; Hornsby, *The Negro in Revolutionary Georgia*, pp. 6-13.

[3] Franklin and Moss, *Ibid.*, pp. 139-141, 153; Hornsby, *Ibid.*, pp. 5-6, 9-10.

[4] Gordon, *The Georgia Negro*, pp. 110-112; Franklin and Moss, *Ibid.*, p. 93; Hornsby, *Ibid.*, p. 5.

[5] Franklin and Moss, *Ibid.*, pp. 93, 139-141, 153; Gordon, *Ibid.*, pp. 110-112; Hornsby, *Ibid.*, pp. 5-13.

[6] Franklin and Moss, *Ibid.*, pp. 219, 227; Gordon, *Ibid.*, pp. 41-68; Lerone Bennett, Jr., *Black Power U.S.A.: The Human Side of Reconstruction, 1867-1877* (Baltimore, 1969), p. 306.

[7] Bennett, *Black Power U.S.A.*, pp. 323-324.

[8] Bennett, *Ibid.*, pp. 301, 323-324; Franklin and Moss, *From Slavery to Freedom*, pp. 219, 227; Gordon, *The Georgia Negro*, pp. 41-68.

A Selected Bibliography

Acts of the General Assembly of the Colony of Georgia, 1775-1774. Wormalee, 1781.

Acts of the General Assembly of the State of Georgia passed at Milledgeville, at an Extra Session in April and May, 1821.

Allen, James S. *Reconstruction: The Battle for Democracy, 1865-1876.* New York, 1937.

An Account Showing the Progress of the Colony of Georgia in America from its First Establishment. London, 1741.

Bennett, Lerone. *Black Power U.S.A.: The Human Side of Reconstruction. 1867-1877.* Baltimore, 1969.

Candler, Allen D., comp., *The Colonial Records of the State of Georgia.* 26 vols. Atlanta, 1904-1916. Vols. XVIII, XVX.

Candler, Allen D., ed. *Revolutionary Records of Georgia*, three volumes. Atlanta, 1908.

Clayton, Augustus S., comp., *A Compilation of the Laws of the State of Georgia*, Augusta, 1821.

Cobb, Thomas R., ed., *A Digest of the Statute Laws of the State of Georgia, In Force Prior to the Session of the General. Assembly of 1851.* Athens, 1851.

Coleman, Kenneth. *The American Revolution in Georgia, 1763-1789.* Athens, 1958.

Collections of the Georgia Historical Society, five vols. Savannah, 1873-1901.

Conway, Alan. *The Reconstruction of Georgia.* Minneapolis, 1966.

Dawson, William G., ed., *A Compilation of the Laws of the State of Georgia, 1819-1929.* Milledgeville, 1831.

Donald, David. *Lincoln Reconsidered.* New York, 1956.

Donald, Davis. *The Politics of Reconstruction, 1863-1867.* Baton Rouge, 1965.

DuBois, W. E. B. *Black Reconstruction in America, 1860-1880.* New York, 1935.

Dudley, G. M. *Reports of Decisions Made by the Judges of the Superior Courts of Law and Chancery of the State of Georgia.* New York, 1837.

Flanders, Ralph B. *Plantation Slavery in Georgia.* Chapel Hill, 1933.

Flanders, Ralph B. "The Free Negro in Antebellum Georgia," *The North Carolina Historical Review*, IX (July, 1932), pp. 250-72.

Ford, Worthington C., ed. *Journals of the Continental Congress, 1774-1789*, XXVIII. Washington, 1904-1937.

Franklin John Hope. *Reconstruction After the Civil War.* Chicago, 1961.

Fuller, Chet. "Black Georgians in History," A Savannah Branch NAACP Bicentennial Publication. Savannah, 1976.

Gilmer, George W. *Sketches of the First Settlers of Upper Georgia.* New York, 1855.

Hornsby, Alton, Jr. *The Black Almanac*, fourth edition. Woodbury, New York, 1977.

_____. "Austin Dabney," *Dictionary of American Negro Biography.* 1977.

Hornsby, Alton, Jr., ed. *In the Cage Eyewitness Accounts of the Freed Negro in Southern Society, 1877-1929.* Chicago, 1971.

Hough, F. D. *The Siege of Savannah.* Albany, New York, 1866.

Jones, Charles C., *The History of Georgia.* two vols. Boston, 1883.

_____. *The Life and Services of the Honorable Major General Samuel Elbert.* Cambridge, 1887.

Knight, Lucian Lamar. *Georgia's Roster of the Revolution.* Atlanta, 1920.

Lamar, Lucius Q., comp., *A Compilation of the Laws of the State of Georgia, 1800-1810.* Augusta, 1813.

Lawrence, Alexander A. *Storm Over Savannah.* Athens, Georgia, 1951.

McCall's History of Georgia, I. Savannah, 1811.

Marbury, Horatio and W. W. Crawford, eds., *A Digest of the Laws of the State of Georgia, 1755-1800.* Savannah, 1802.

Quarles, Benjamin. *The Negro in the American Revolution.* Chapel Hill, 1961.

Rogers, McDowell. "Free Negro Legislation in Georgia Before 1865," *Georgia Historical Quarterly*, XVI (March, 1932).

Stevens, William B. *A History of Georgia.* two vols. II. New York, 1847-59.

Sweat, Edward F. "Social Status of the Free Negro in Antebellum Georgia," *Negro History Bulletin*, 21, 1958.

Sweat, Edward F. "Free Blacks and the Law in Antebellum Georgia," Southern Center for Studies in Public Policy. Atlanta, 1976.

Chapter 6
The Albany Movement within the Context
of Local and Georgian History

As many of you know, historians and other scholars, for some time now, have recognized the value of regional, state, and local case studies in trying to better understand broad and general international and national developments and movements. This approach has become increasingly relevant and increasingly employed as we seek to explain the Civil Rights Movement of the 1960s. Commendably, articles and books are appearing on the Movement in Chapel Hill, in Greensboro, in Jackson, in Selma, in Atlanta, and in Albany. These studies are tending to confirm that the national Civil Rights Movement was in large part a series of indigenous efforts, which varied in strategy, approach, and momentum from place to place and from time to time. At any rate, they suggest that very few of the occurrences were directed from central organizational headquarters in New York or Atlanta, but that most emerged as spontaneous outcries from local people confronting local oppression.

In the context of state and local, and even regional, history, the Albany Movement was a part of the history of the New South. When we speak of the New South here, we are not talking about the post-Reconstruction South of Henry Grady or of C. Vann Woodward or of George B. Tindall, but the South after 1960. This is the South of

Prepared for presentation at the 20th Anniversary Celebration of the Albany Movement at Albany State College, Albany, Georgia on August 7, 1981

Martin Luther King, Jr., Mary Young, Charles Sherrod, and of Vincent Harding and Howard Zinn — the South where blacks ceased to be invisible and where, like in Albany, as Martin Luther King, Jr. once said, "they straightened their backs up," and hence modified the course of Southern history.

The emergence of Albany from a major center of cotton production before the Civil War to a peanut capital and industrial city in the 1960s is a story very different, in many ways, from that of the emergence of Savannah as a major port city or of Columbus as an important military center or of Atlanta as a regional transportation and commercial metropolis.

Similarly the history of the black communities in these cities offer interesting comparisons and contrasts. One cannot, for example, understand the Movement in Albany in the context of what happened in Atlanta or Savannah during the 1960s. While one can find parallels in the existence of black institutions of higher education and of a sizeable black middle class, there are even differences in the natures and structures of these commonalities. For example, Albany State and Savannah State were publicly supported institutions. This fact placed their faculty and students in much greater jeopardy as they participated in the Movement of the 1960s than was the case with their counterparts in the private black colleges of Atlanta. This is not to say, as some of you here know, that Atlanta demonstrators did not face difficulties with conservative administrators in their schools, but the net effect was much less than in state supported institutions. Also, organized political activity and an organized, protest tradition among blacks in Savannah and Atlanta was much older than in Albany or Columbus or Fort Valley. On the other hand, black protest against oppression and the boll weevil in the form of migration reached its greatest peak in the entire state of Georgia in the Albany area during World War I. From mid-1916 until mid-1917 alone, over 4,500 blacks left this area for the so-called "Promised Land" of the North. The drain of black man and woman power was so severe that thousands of acres of land were abandoned and small towns were deserted. Early in 1917, the Southwest Georgia Conference of the A.M.E. Church expressed its own concern for the exodus, noting that within only a few months a thousand of its best paying members had migrated to the North.

In terms of patterns of wealth, by 1960 Atlanta blacks had outstripped all others in the state in the value of real property and in the value of business enterprises. This, of course, had not always been the case. In the ante-bellum and immediate post-bellum periods, sizeable chunks of black wealth were concentrated in Savannah and Augusta and there were large black property holdings in the Albany vicinity. In 1900, for example, a prosperous black in Dougherty County, Deal Jackson, owned 2,000 acres of land worth $50,000. Another black, Bartow Powell, owned several farms, a cotton gin, and a store in Dougherty and Baker counties. And in 1902, M. U. Lee opened the Artesian Drug Store in Albany, which operated successfully for several years.

To be sure, the existence of black institutions of higher education, of black businesses, and of black wealth and social status were not the norm for the race in Atlanta or Albany or Savannah or anywhere else in the South prior to 1960. The masses remained as always, un or under-employed, ill-fed, ill-clothed, and ill-housed. Poor education, poor health, and a continued environment of crime and violence were additional general characteristics of the black communities. Among the middle and upper classes, even the nature of black religion was changing, although the church remained the most important social institution for the race.

For rich as well as poor, literate and semi-literate, skilled and unskilled, the one common constant among Southern blacks in 1960 was still the pervasive influence of white racism and its tangible expressions in segregation and discrimination. Racial oppression in the Old, New South prior to 1960 was just as much a fact of life in Atlanta as in Albany, in Savannah as in Americus. For example, in 1903, the Atlanta City Council barred blacks from playing in city parks. Blacks were excluded from the city's Carnegie Library and from the zoo. Black prisoners were segregated and black witnesses in Court swore on separate Bibles. In this same period, blacks in Augusta and Savannah organized some of the South's first protests against Jim Crow streetcars. Housing segregation spread rapidly in the cities, although no Georgia town matched the "ingenuity" of Albany where a line was drawn through the center of town dividing most of the blacks from most of the white population.

Wealth and education were also no guarantees of immunity from racist inspired physical assaults in the segregation era. For example, Bartow Powell, the successful black landowner in Dougherty County was killed by an unknown person in Albany while driving his carriage through the city. Local blacks believed that jealous whites killed him. And, in Atlanta, Bishop J. W. E. Bowen, President of Gammon Theological Seminary, was one of several prominent blacks beaten during the infamous Atlanta Race Riot in 1906.

Whereas in the Reconstruction Era, some blacks could effectively lift the burden of Jim Crowism through voting and office-holding, this leverage was lost in Georgia by 1910. Poll taxes, the white primary, and literacy requirements drove almost all blacks from the voting booth and from elective office. When the white primary was declared illegal by the U.S. Supreme Court in 1946, the ballot was legally unshackled in Georgia. However, only in Atlanta was there to be effective political participation by blacks until the 1960s. Elsewhere, illegal and extra-legal devices were often combined with economic and physical intimidation to keep blacks away from the polls. Such was the case in the Albany area and most of the Black Belt of Georgia where blacks constituted more than 60 percent of the population.

So then by 1960, if one studied local and state history in Georgia, he or she found a story of mass deprivation, disadvantage, and discrimination among almost one-third of the citizens, those who were black. In every section there were a few prosperous persons who lived a life of social and economic security, but who like their poorer fellows, suffered racial oppression through segregation and discrimination and even, in many cases, political disfranchisement. Also, no matter what the social or economic status of the person might be, he could, at the whim of any white man, from a street bum to a streetcar operator to a policeman, be the victim of physical assault, which most often went unpunished. It was into this milieu, that the Civil Rights Movement came to Georgia in the 1960s.

As you know, 1960 was one of the most dramatic years of the Black Revolution. The sit-ins at Greensboro in February represented one of the most stirring direct action campaigns on the part of blacks since the Montgomery bus boycott of 1955-1956. The momentum of the sit-ins rekindled the Movement and sparked its expansion into new and unchartered areas. In Georgia, prior to 1960, direct action had been confined mainly to Atlanta where attacks had been made on busses, golf courses, and a few restaurants. There were also school desegregation suits, involving lower and higher institutions. But, even these could not be called "mass movements," as they generally involved only a handful of black ministers, teachers, and other members of the middle class.

Then in 1960, following the Greensboro sit-ins, 200 black students demonstrated at restaurants in downtown Atlanta and a sit-in siege, which was to last for more than six months, hit the city. Later, the U.S. Justice Department sued to insure black voting rights in several counties in southwest Georgia. At about the same time, the U.S. Supreme Court ruled unanimously that the right of blacks to register and vote in Terrell County must be upheld. This case was the first filed under the 1957 Civil Rights Act and the first in which the Justice Department had asked for the appointment of a voting referee under the 1960 Civil Rights Act.

As significant as these acts were, they were to be later overshadowed by the desegregation of the University of Georgia in the winter and the desegregation of the Atlanta public schools in the fall of 1961. The former event paved the way for the latter and both signaled the end of legalized segregation in Georgia and the dawn of a new era in the state. Significantly, this new era would not only be characterized by expanding desegregation in all areas of public life, but also by a new and fierce determination on the part of blacks to demand justice and fair treatment for themselves.

While, at the time, it might have been hard to imagine that a new year, 1961, could match the drama of the national events of 1960, CORE did furnish such an impetus with its Freedom Rides. The Freedom Riders carried direct action into places in the South which had previously been untouched by the Movement and, in most places, they drew both covert and overt local support. In Georgia, the riders used Atlanta as a staging area as they moved throughout the region. Within the state, they also stopped at Savannah, Thomasville, and at Albany. The visits to Albany were to set the stage for one of the most famous mass movements of the era, one that we are reliving and commemorating here this week.

In the context of local and state history, the Albany Movement began at a time when Freedom Riders were passing through several other localities in the state; when the Columbus airport was being desegregated; when the University of Georgia and Atlanta public schools opened their doors to blacks; when Atlanta restaurants and lunch counters were serving blacks for the first time; when Catholic schools in the state began voluntary desegregation and when Georgia Tech also voluntarily admitted its first black students.

While the arrests of demonstrators at Albany bus and train terminals in November and December 1961 may be conventionally labeled the beginning of the Albany Movement, the groundwork had, as you know, been laid many months in advance by local petitions to the city commissioners which asked for better public services, especially in Lincoln Heights, and for desegregation of public facilities; and by the work of the local NAACP Youth Council and organizers from the Student Nonviolent Coordinating Committee (SNCC). To be sure, however, it was the events in mid-December, including the jailing of 736 blacks and Martin Luther King, Jr., and the suspension of the demonstrations in the controversial agreement of December 18, which focused national attention on Albany.

Why Albany in 1961-1962? Why did the Movement proceed here as it did? Historians must seek the answers to these questions in the history of the city and its surrounding areas and more specifically in the history of the internal structure of the black communities. As we mentioned earlier, Albany had been a cotton capital in the ante-bellum South and as such was a center of slavery in the state. In contrast, Savannah, and especially Atlanta, had not nurtured large slave plantations and both cities, particularly Savannah, had a noticeable free black community. But, as DuBois said in *Souls of Black Folk*, Albany was "the heart of the Black Belt." Within a hundred miles of the city lay great fertile lands and rich forests. By the time DuBois, himself, arrived in the city at the turn of the century, Albany had already become a "typical Southern country town." It was the center of social and economic life for the more than 10,000 blacks who then lived in the area. Nevertheless, in contrast to the major cities of the world, and even to Atlanta and Savannah, Albany was, to use a DuBosian phrase "dull and humdrum." The establishment of Albany State College in 1903 and the attraction which it gave to black professionals offered an alternative, and, perhaps, more exciting lifestyle for a few, but only a few.

As Howard Zinn has suggested, civil rights activists of the 1960s were largely attracted to Albany because of its history — its tradition of plantation slavery and of segregation, discrimination, and disfranchisement. Inherent in all this was a system of economic intimidation, harassment, and brutality. Yet in 1961-1962, as even the civil rights activists might well have noted, Albany was no longer a country town of 10,000 blacks, it was a thriving industrial city – a prime example of the "Old New South" and soon to be a leader in the New South, 1960s style. The Albany of 1961-1962 was the commercial and industrial center of southwest Georgia, with the peanut industry preeminent, but also containing textiles, clothing, furniture, and pharmaceutical plants. An Air Force base and a Marine Corps supply depot were already there and rubber and beer were not far behind.

Fifty-six thousand people, more than one-third of them black, lived in the new Albany. The city's whites solicited and welcomed the new industries and the growing economic prosperity. Blacks also welcomed these developments, but as Claude Sitton, a *New York Times* correspondent, pointed out, "their share of the new wealth [was] modest indeed." Sitton also agreed that the modernization of Albany, as could be seen through its new industry and wealth, led to rising expectations among blacks and helped set the stage for the Albany Movement. Conversely, the Albany white power structure became increasingly sensitive to the adverse effect of racial violence on the growth of local industry. Atlanta, as "the city too busy to hate," had provided the positive example. Little Rock and others had shown the negative. Thus, as the Movement hit Albany, the town fathers would adopt a policy of "killing them with kindness." This local strategy, as has been seen, combined with some miscommunication among Albany's blacks, many scholars now contend, perplexed Martin Luther King, Jr. and gave him one of his first, major defeats.

Perhaps, King, SNCC, SCLC, and others had not read their local history carefully enough. A closer reading might have shown that Albany was not Montgomery or even Savannah or Atlanta for that matter. Blacks in the Albany area had lived in a climate of fear far greater than that experienced in most urban areas of Georgia. The violent attacks upon civil rights activists and local leaders in the area during the summer of 1962 were more typical of the prevailing atmosphere than the "kindness" of December 1961. This atmosphere made the expression of open, militant leadership extremely dangerous. Whites knew this to be true and blacks lived daily with the dreaded knowledge. Thus, the Albany black leadership in 1961-1962 might be described as perhaps, understandably, a little afraid, perhaps a bit inexperienced in directing mass movements, but nevertheless, very proud. Hence, when the whites appealed for local people to sit down and draw up local solutions, there was a welcome response among many, some of whom wanted to show "the Atlanta boys" that local people really could organize and control a movement. Of course, it should be said that local chauvinism was not confined to Albany. Atlanta blacks, for example, had pointedly told Martin Luther King, Jr. to stay out of their movement until students brought him in, in 1960. King, also, learned anew the value of local hegemony at Albany and visibly used it at Birmingham.

Those studying Albany would also want to note the role of the local press in the Movement. Few places in the South had a more rabid anti-black voice than that of the Gray family's Albany *Herald*. It served the not too useful purposes of promoting fear and intra-movement divisions. It was a stark contrast to the reasoned influence of the Atlanta *Constitution*, especially under Ralph McGill and Eugene Patterson.

There is also now very strong circumstantial evidence that the FBI was used for the first time at Albany to undermine the leadership of Martin Luther King, Jr. Certainly, they cooperated with Albany police at the time of the Movement and did very little to protect the constitutional rights of local, black citizens. While we do not now know enough about the FBI's role in Albany to make sweeping definitive judgments, the beginning of the war against King here may have been an additional divisive force.

Finally, I think historians of the Albany Movement should consider the role of the black bourgeoisie spawned and nurtured by Albany State College in analyzing the causes and effects of the protests. Unlike at Montgomery, Birmingham, and Atlanta, the Albany protests were more largely mass oriented. Some activists, at the time, and many scholars since, have contended that the teachers and students of Albany State abdicated, for the most part, their leadership roles. As one contemporary activist put it, the campus was separated from the community by more than "a river, dump yard and a cemetery." There also seemed to be great ideological, social, and economic differences. If these charges against Albany State are true, the historian will seek their causes in the fear of jobs, scholarships, and careers. He might also explore the more elevated position of the black bourgeoisie in a smaller town with only one college, as in contrast, for example, to Atlanta with a historically broader middle class and with several colleges. Having said this, however, one must also consider the facts that bourgeoisie hesitancy was not confined to Albany — almost every city in Georgia had a sizeable share of it — and that it is perhaps just as well for the black bourgeoisie to be led as to lead. A related matter, which should be studied, is the church affiliations of Albany's black bourgeoisie. In other studies of indigenous civil rights movements, churches with large middle class memberships or with a thorough mix of the classes have been seen in the forefront of the local movement. I do not know, for example, whether or not the Albany State faculty and students were concentrated in churches apart from the black masses. In most cases in Georgia where there was widespread social separation among blacks, the greatest integration was in the churches. If the converse was true in Albany, we have discovered another rather unique feature in the city's history.

To sum up, I think we have tried to suggest that an understanding of the Civil Rights Movement in this country can be greatly aided by studying what happened in Albany in 1961 and 1962 as an indigenous phenomenon. To do so, it would be helpful to look at the Albany Movement in the context of local and state history. So we have tried to say something about the historical evolution of Georgia blacks in general, and Albany blacks in particular. Such an examination, even as brief as the one we have given tonight, shows useful similarities as well as pointed differences in the environments in which blacks lived. One, then, cannot understand Albany in 1961-1962 by studying the history of Albany, New York, or for that matter Biloxi, Mississippi, or even Savannah or Atlanta. In the end, the contrasts may be a matter of degrees — degrees in economic development, in social status, in educational development, in racial oppression, in disfranchisement, and in traditions of protest. The importance of these degrees, however, is what makes Albany, Georgia, a different species from its namesake at the north and its state capital to the north. It was these degrees that enabled Albany to become what many scholars call "a turning point" in the black struggle for freedom.

REFERENCES

Forman, James, *The Making of Black Revolutionaries*, 1972

King, Slater, "The Bloody Ground of Albany," *Freedomways*, (Winter, 1964)

King, Slater, "Our Main Battle in Albany," *Freedomways* (Summer, 1965)

Kunstler, William, *Deep in My Heart*, 1966

National Committee for the Albany Defendants, *The Albany Cases*

Watters, Pat, *Down to Now, Reflections on the Southern Civil Rights Movement*, 1971

Watters, Pat, *The South and the Nation*, 1978

Zinn, Howard, *Albany* (Southern Regional Council Report, 1962)

Zinn, Howard, *Albany: A Study in National Responsibility* (Southern Regional Council Booklet, 1962)

Zinn, Howard, *SNCC, The New Abolitionists*, 1964

Zinn, Howard, *The Southern Mystique*, 1972

RELIGION

Chapter 7
Religious Practices of Blacks
in Atlanta, Georgia, 1865–1990

The Black Church in America has been historically more than an "opiate" for an oppressed people, it has been the race's most important social institution, and, at times, the bulwark of their economic and political lives. In 1960, six Bishops, including leaders of the African Methodist, Colored Methodist, African Methodist Episcopal Zion, and Church of God, were residents of the city. By 1970 there were more than 500 black churches in Atlanta, enrolling about 50,000 members, with an average Sunday attendance of about 70,000.[1]

Big Bethel African Methodist Church claims the title of "the oldest predominately African-American congregation" in the city, dating its origins from 1843 in the old city of Terminus (later Marthasville, then Atlanta in 1847). Friendship Baptist Church, founded in 1862, one year before the Emancipation Proclamation and three years before the end of the Civil War, laid claim to the title of "the oldest independent congregation of blacks in Atlanta." It was organized under the leadership of the Reverend Frank Quarles, with 25 members, when they separated from the First Baptist Church of Atlanta. The Reverend Quarles served as pastor of Friendship from its founding in 1862 until his death in 1881. During his pastorate the church membership was significantly increased from 25 to 1,750 members. The church first

Reprinted from Alton Hornsby, Jr., A Short History of Black Atlanta, 1847-1990 (Atlanta, 2003), with the permission of the author.

held services in a freight boxcar that had been donated by the Ninth Street Baptist Church of Cincinnati, Ohio. By 1870 a house of worship had been constructed at the corner of Haynes and Markham Streets near downtown Atlanta; however, as the congregation increased in number, the Haynes Street site was inadequate and a new building was needed. In 1871 the Atlanta Baptist Home Mission provided a loan for the construction of a new building at the present location on Mitchell Street, also near downtown Atlanta.[2]

During the economic depression and political upheaval of the post-Civil War Era, Friendship Baptist Church was an "oasis of knowledge" for black people. The Church played a unique role in the development of institutions for the education of blacks. In 1865, Atlanta University was founded in the boxcar that had served as the first church for Friendship. The Church's second building became the E. A. Ware Elementary School in 1879. The Atlanta Baptist Seminary, now Morehouse College, held its first classes in the basement of Friendship when it moved to Atlanta from Augusta, Georgia in 1867. In 1881, two women from the Women's American Baptist Home Mission Society of New England founded the Atlanta Baptist Female Seminary, later Spelman College, in the basement of the Friendship Church. Friendship has continued to maintain close ties with these institutions.[3]

The Reverend Edward Randolph Carter succeeded the Reverend Quarles as pastor of Friendship in 1881 and served the church for 62 years, the longest tenure of any minister at this time. Under Dr. Carter's leadership, the church membership was increased to 2,000 persons and a home for the aged was built. Dr. Carter was a nationally and internationally recognized leader; in 1885 he preached before the World Baptist Alliance and he was the recipient of honorary degrees from Morehouse College, Howard University, and Gaudalope College.[4]

Dr. Maynard Holbrook Jackson succeeded Dr. Carter as pastor of Friendship in 1945. Dr. Jackson was active in civic affairs and established a health center for children in the community. He enjoyed a relatively brief, but fruitful tenure as pastor before his death in 1953. The Reverend Samuel W. Williams became the fourth pastor of Friendship in 1954. The Reverend Williams was also Professor of Philosophy and Religion at Morehouse College, as well as a scholar and social activist. Under the leadership of Dr. Williams, Friendship continued its tradition of social, political and economic involvement. The Reverend John Thomas Porter, a student in the Morehouse School of Religion, and Dr. Williams were successful plaintiffs in a federal suit to desegregate the public transportation system in Atlanta in 1959. In 1967, the church sponsored the construction of 208 low-cost housing units in southwest Atlanta, near the church site. These units have provided "comfortable" low-cost housing for members of the community. In 1970, following the death of Dr. Williams, the Reverend William Vincent Guy became the fifth and current pastor of Friendship. At the 123rd anniversary of the church on April 28, 1985, Dr. Guy issued a renewed challenge to his flock: "The challenge of Friendship today remains the challenge of Friendship yesterday; to proclaim the Gospel to all, to serve those in need, and to work for justice and peace in our time. As we commemorate our past, let us also rededicate ourselves to the Christian tasks of the future."[5]

In southeast Atlanta, four years after the founding of Friendship Baptist Church, Clark Chapel (later Central United Methodist Church) was established on Frazier Street in the Summerhill neighborhood. Davis W. Clark organized a group of black Methodist ministers during the Annual Conference of the Methodist Church in 1864. Dr. James W. Lee, who later became the fourth president of Clark College, was chosen as the first pastor of the church.[6]

The Clark Chapel Church, the first black Methodist Episcopal Church in the city, remained in the Summerhill community for about ten years before moving to a new site at Hunter and Lloyd Streets in downtown Atlanta. After purchasing the predominantly white Lloyd Street Church, Clark Chapel then "relinquished its name" and became the Lloyd Street Methodist Episcopal Church. The church, subsequently, became "one of the most prominent black churches in Atlanta." In 1901 when the name of Lloyd Street was changed to Central Avenue, the church also changed its name to Central Avenue Methodist Episcopal Church.[7]

Among the prominent African-Americans in Atlanta who were associated with the early development of the Central Avenue Methodist Episcopal were Dr. M. C. Mason, the Corresponding Secretary of the Freedmen Aid Society, who had a reputation as "a great orator"; Bishop Lorenzo King, who served as Editor of the *Southwestern Christian Advocate*, the first black Methodist periodical; The Reverend L. S. Allen who was an Editor of the *Central Christian Advocate* and later a bishop: Miss Ann E. Hall, who became a missionary to Liberia, and the sisters, Dorothy and Ellen Barnette, who were missionaries to India and Africa.[8]

In 1928, Central Avenue Methodist Church moved from the old Lloyd Street site to its present location on Martin Luther King Jr. Drive near Morris Brown College and the "Avenue" was deleted from the church's name. The merger of the Methodist Church and the

Evangelical United Brethren in 1968 resulted in the current name - Central United Methodist Church.   Also in 1968, Dr. Joseph E. Lowery, the noted civil rights leader, became pastor of the Central United Methodist Church.   Under Lowery's leadership, the congregation grew steadily and continued to attract some of the more prominent black Methodists in the city. Lowery also began a television ministry, which he used to preach a "political gospel." After 18 years at Central, Lowery was transferred, over the objection of many of his parishioners to the Cascade United Methodist Church. Cascade had its origins in the home of a white family on Beecher Street in the Cascade Heights subdivision in 1926. As blacks began to move into the area in the 1960s, the church, for a time, had a bi-racial congregation. But, with accelerated "white flight" from the area, particularly after more and more blacks moved into the area and the city's schools were desegregated, the congregation eventually became mostly black and acquired black pastors. Although he had a less historic congregation at Cascade than at Central, Lowery used his leadership skills, combined with his charisma, to add more than 1,000 new members to the church's rolls by 1990. In these efforts, he had built upon the success of the Reverend Walter L. Kimbrough, a "dynamic" young, black minister. Kimbrough, who had "proven expertise in transitional church ministry," including the Ben Hill United Methodist Church (also in southwest Atlanta) brought more than 100 new members into the church during the first year of his ministry. The congregation grew so rapidly that two morning worship services had to be held and television monitors had to be installed "in order to accommodate a growing membership." Indeed, Cascade's congregation, under Kimbrough and Lowery's leadership had, by 1990, reached almost 3,000 members. Thus, in the fall of 1990, the church "broke ground" for a new "Cathedral" at Cascade Road and Childress Drive. The projected cost of the structure was $4 million.[9]

The African Methodist Episcopal (A.M.E.) Church was another major black denomination, which took early roots in Atlanta. In 1787, Richard Allen and a group of black Methodists who withdrew from the St. George Methodist Episcopal Church in Philadelphia as a protest against segregation in the congregation founded the A.M.E. Church. From these beginnings, the A.M.E. Church grew and expanded throughout the Northern states, into Canada, and even to Africa, itself. After the Civil War the A.M.E. Church spread into the South. Henry McNeal Turner, an ex-bondsman and the first black Chaplain in the U.S. Army, was appointed by the South Carolina Conference, which met in Savannah, Georgia in 1866 to "plant and train mission churches."

One of the first A.M.E. churches established in Atlanta was the Big Bethel A.M.E. Church, which traces its origins to a congregation in pre-Atlanta Terminus and Marthasville in the early 1840s. Following the Civil War, the congregation, variously known as Old Bethel, Bethel, the African Methodist Episcopal Tabernacle and finally Big Bethel, affiliated with the A.M.E. Church. The national Church sent the Reverend James Lynch to help organize A.M.E. churches throughout the South. Lynch later endorsed the appointment of the Reverend Joseph Woods, a member of Bethel Tabernacle, as the first pastor of the Big Bethel A.M.E Church. Big Bethel grew rapidly, both as a congregation and as "a center of the community" in northeast Atlanta. One of Atlanta's first schools for African-Americans, The Gate City School, was founded in the Big Bethel basement and Morris Brown College, founded in 1881, held some of its first classes there. This edifice, however, was destroyed by fire in 1920. Although, the church's insurance had lapsed, the congregation was able to rebuild at its present site on Auburn Avenue and Butler Street. The Romanesque structure was distinguished by an impressive steeple, proclaiming "Jesus Saves." After 1930, the church achieved national distinction for its annual drama of a wicked Satan clashing with Saints, known as "Heaven Bound." And, during the 1960s, it was further distinguished for its support of the Civil Rights Movement, under the leadership of Reverend (later Bishop) Harold I. (H. I.) Bearden. Bearden, using a weekly radio broadcast, came down equally hard on white segregationists and black accommodationists. The Reverend McKinley Young, who became pastor of Big Bethel in 1980, continued the activist ministry exemplified by Bishop Bearden. He encouraged the church to support community outreach and involvement ("without excuses"). Another of the A.M.E Mission Churches established in the post-bellum period was the Allen Temple A.M.E. Church.

After the Emancipation, many ex-slaves settled in the Summerhill section of southeast Atlanta and they sought to organize an A.M.E. Church. In the spring of 1866, Elder J. A. Wood was authorized to organize the first church in the area. A bush arbor was constructed at the corner of Martin and Crumbley Streets and several services were held at this site, before the congregation purchased a lot at the corner of Martin Street and Hammock Place, where the first church building was erected. The church was named Wood's Chapel in honor of its first pastor, the Reverend Wood, who served the congregation until 1869. Other ministers who served as pastors of Wood's Chapel included the

Reverends A. G. Gonickey, George Washington, and Lazarus Gardner, until Wood returned for a second term. Later the Reverend John Yeiser of Rhode Island became pastor of the church and led the construction of a new building, which was called Allen Temple in honor of Bishop Richard Allen, the founder of the A.M.E. Church.[10]

After Yeiser left the Allen Temple pulpit, the church was served by several ministers including "the great revivalist," Reverend A. S. Jackson; the Reverend Mister Downs, who expanded the church and purchased its first organ; "the singer, poet and scholar," Reverend A. A. Whitman; and the Reverend W. H. Heard, who organized the Allen Christian Endeavor League. The expansion of the church was continued under the Reverend William Alfred Fountain, who later became Bishop of the Georgia Conference. During Fountain's tenure, additional property was purchased, the church building was renovated "and more than 300 young people were baptized." The Reverend H. D. Canady who succeeded the Reverend Fountain "was known as a great gospel preacher" and organized the young women of the church into an auxiliary. Several pastors followed Canady, but, perhaps, the most notable was the Reverend W. R. Wilkes. Wilkes served the congregation for nearly 14 years. During that period the church underwent renovation and purchased "the Howard Home." Other property was purchased on Frazier Street and a church annex was built. When Wilkes was elevated to the Bishopric in 1948, the Reverend R. H. Porter, who died suddenly only a few years after becoming pastor of Allen Temple, succeeded him. In 1954, the Reverend John A. Middleton became Allen Temple's next pastor. During his tenure, "a major relocation and building program was initiated." A parsonage and educational center were constructed and "ground was broken for the construction of the Allen Temple Homes," a housing project for low to middle income tenants. The Reverend A. D. Powell succeeded Middleton, who later became president of Morris Brown College, in 1965. The next year, 1966, the church celebrated its centennial anniversary. During this period Allen Temple apartments, valued at $6,000,000 were completed. Reverend Powell resigned as pastor in 1972 because of "failing health." Between 1972 and 1982, three other men, the Reverends Daniel Jacobs, A.R. Smith, and Benjamin Gray served as pastors of the church and maintained its position as one of the premier African-American churches in the city.[11]

On Atlanta's northeast side, members of the American Missionary Association (AMA), which was made up largely of New England Congregationalists, founded the First Congregational Church of Atlanta in 1867. Among these were two former Yale University students,

Edmund Asa Ware and Erastus M. Cravath. Both of whom were instrumental in the founding of the First Congregational Church along with the Reverend Frederick Ayer, Charles H. Morgan and others. Edmund Ware was also a founder of Atlanta University. The church and the university maintained a close association during that period. Ware and Cravath traveled throughout Georgia visiting plantations and promoting the new educational centers in Atlanta. Many former slaves moved to Atlanta from the rural areas and some of them became associated with the Storrs School on Houston Street, which was established by Ware, Cravath and other members of the American Missionary Association. The Storrs School became a major center in the black communities for education and religious training, and in 1867 the former slaves expressed a wish to form a church. The first service for the new church was conducted by Erastus Cravath on May 26, 1867. The Storrs School Chapel served as the worship site for the First Congregational Church until 1877 when a building was constructed at the corner of Courtland and Houston Streets. Students from Atlanta University provided much of the labor to erect the church building. During the period from 1867 to 1894 a number of ministers provided by the AMA served as pastors of the First Congregational Church. These included the Reverend Frederick Ayer, the Reverend Charles M. Southgate, the Reverend Evarts E. Kent, the Reverend Simon S. Ashley, the Reverend Samuel H. Robinson and others.[12]

The year 1894 initiated a significant era in the history of the First Congregational Church when the Reverend Henry Hugh Proctor began his ministry there. The Reverend Proctor, a graduate of Fisk University, was one of a number of young black men that had been sent to various colleges founded by the AMA "for training to assume leadership in churches of the South." Proctor, who also attended Yale Divinity School, was invited by Booker T. Washington of Tuskegee Institute to become a part of the "new colored leadership." Washington was present at the groundbreaking service for the new church edifice in May 1908. Dedication and dynamic leadership characterized the ministry of the Reverend Proctor; during his tenure as pastor a number of new programs were established, including the neighborhood missions. The missions were the Carrie Steele Orphanage on Fair Street in southwest Atlanta, the Decatur Street Mission, the Irvin Street Mission (all near the church, itself), and the Prison Mission that held services at the Federal Penitentiary and the Fulton County Jail. The church maintained a library, kindergarten, and a gymnasium, and conducted classes in business education and domestic science. Dr.

Proctor was also one of the leaders who helped restore order following the Atlanta Race Riot of 1906. He helped restore self-confidence in the black community and devoted considerable time to that effort. In 1919, Dr. Proctor resigned as pastor and accepted a position at Nazarene Congregational Church in Brooklyn, New York.[13]

The Reverend Russell S. Brown succeeded Dr. Proctor as pastor of the First Congregational Church. The Reverend Brown organized "service circles" in order to raise the funds required to maintain the church during the period of social and economic upheaval that followed World War I. The next pastor of the church was the Reverend William J. Faulkner who was "an outstanding preacher" and later became College Minister at Fisk University. The Reverend John C. Wright who was pastor of the church for ten years succeeded the Reverend Faulkner. In 1947, the church called the Reverend Homer C. McEwen as pastor. Under the leadership of the Reverend McEwen, the First Congregational Church continued its pioneer work in social commitment to the community, which was begun during the pastorate of the Reverend Henry H. Proctor. During the 1960s the church was the site of mass meetings, which resulted in the appointment of more blacks to the Atlanta Police Force. The church also supported the 1961 black boycott of downtown Atlanta and provided leadership for the fight against a "welfare freeze" which was a threat to many poor people.[14]

Also in northeast Atlanta was the Wheat Street Baptist Church, which was founded in 1870, and was one of the nine churches organized by Friendship Baptist Church in the Atlanta area. Thus both Friendship and Wheat Street recognized the Reverend Frank Quarles as the first pastor of their respective congregations. With the Reverend Quarles' consent, members of Friendship organized a second mission near their homes. The Reverend Andrew Jackson became the pastor of the new church and worship services were held in the pastor's yard on Howell Street. During the Reverend Jackson's pastorate the church membership increased to almost 100 individuals. In 1875, the Reverend William Henry Tillman succeeded the Reverend Jackson as pastor of Wheat Street and served the church until 1897. After Wheat Street grew to a membership of more than a thousand, the church moved to a new site at Fort and Old Wheat Streets near Auburn Avenue. The Reverend Peter James Bryant was called as pastor in 1898.[15] The Reverend Bryant was "a dynamic leader and under his evangelism" more than 3,000 persons were added to the membership. Fire destroyed the church in 1917 and services were temporarily held in an Auburn Avenue theater. A new church site was then selected at

Yonge Street and Auburn Avenue.[16]

Following the death of Dr. Bryant, the Reverend Lewis Foster, Sr. and the Reverend Lewis Foster, Jr. were co-pastors of Wheat Street for ten months. The Reverend J. Raymond Henderson succeeded the Fosters as pastor of the church and served from 1930 to 1937. The church debt that accumulated during the Depression was retired during the pastorate of Reverend Henderson; he then moved to another position.[17]

The Reverend William Holmes Borders followed the Reverend Henderson as pastor of Wheat Street in 1937. The Reverend Borders earned many distinctions both as a pastor and as a civil rights leader. As pastor of Wheat Street, Dr. Borders completed the construction of the church, which had remained incomplete for 17 years and the church's indebtedness of $127,000 was paid off in three and one half years. Under Borders, 29 new church auxiliaries were established and the Wheat Street Gardens, a housing project, was constructed. As a civil rights leader, Borders led the movement for desegregation of public transportation in Atlanta and the hiring of black bus drivers. He also served as a leader of a committee that helped to desegregate Atlanta restaurants, lunch counters and hotels. Borders' other contributions included leadership of black voter registration drives; fundraising for Phyllis Wheatley YWCA; support for the 1945 strike of workers at the Scripto Pencil Factory; and overall chairman of the Community Chest Drive in Black Atlanta. Borders also became noted for "the poetic statement of the triumph of black people," " I Am Somebody," which summarized the accomplishments of the past and the hope for the future of black Americans.[18]

The Zion Hill Baptist Church, like Wheat Street, also grew out of Friendship Baptist Church on Mitchell Street, near downtown Atlanta. In 1872, several members of Friendship, "who found it difficult to attend services at the Mitchell Street site," organized a church at the corner of Glenn and Humphries Streets in southwest Atlanta. As was the case with a number of other black churches established in the post-bellum era, the first services for Zion Hill were held in a bush arbor until a building was donated. The Reverend Robert Grant, who organized the church, along with seven members, was the first pastor of Zion Hill. Shortly thereafter the Reverend Grant and the Reverend M. C. McGuire conducted a ten-week revival service, which significantly increased the church's membership. But after only "a brief service," the Reverend Grant resigned as pastor. Several other men followed him until 1899 when the Reverend W. W. Floyd took over as pastor.

Floyd "restored unity to the church," which then "grew and prospered during the 17 years of his pastorate." The sixth pastor of Zion Hill was the Reverend Claud H. Robinson who served the church from 1916 to 1926. The major achievement during his tenure was the building of "a church house" for Zion Hill. In 1926 the Reverend J. T. Johnson became the seventh pastor of Zion Hill and led the church during the difficult period of the Depression. The eighth pastor, the Reverend Levi M. Terrill, Sr., "restored a spirit of prosperity to the church" during his 28 years of service. During Terrill's tenure the church's membership grew significantly, a weekly radio program was begun, and a nursery school was established. The Reverend Terrill was also president of the black State Baptist Convention. The Reverend Larry H. Williams succeeded Terrill in 1971. In 1976 the present church site was purchased on Lynhurst Drive in southwest Atlanta and Zion Hill moved to that location. During this period "more than 1,000 new members were added to the church."[19]

In 1877 four residents of the Marietta and Wallace Street area, in northwest Atlanta, organized a prayer group that later became the Antioch Baptist Church. The prayer group soon expanded from 20 to 30, and shortly thereafter became the Bethel Baptist Church. Later, the group changed the church name to Antioch. One of the church's major leaders during this formative period was Robert Lee Craddock who insisted that the church's ministers should be trained and experienced as well as "called" to the ministry. Early pastors, who generally met Craddock's requirements, included the Reverends Jerry Davis, B. T. Harvey, and Alfred C. Williams. In 1921 the church purchased property on Gray Street, also in northwest Atlanta for construction of a new sanctuary. In 1922 the Reverend Timothy S. Saine became pastor of Antioch. He was "very successful" in his work with the youth of the church through reorganization of the Sunday School and establishment of a Baptist Young People's Union (BYP). The Reverend Saine also organized a youth division in order to get more young men and women involved in church work. The new church building was also completed during the tenure of the Reverend Saine and he achieved a reputation "as a great leader and administrator." Saine was succeeded by the Reverend Timothy George, described as a "prudent and pragmatic leader," who helped the church survive the Depression of the 1930s. The "dynamic and emotionally charged" preaching of the Reverend George gained many new members for the Antioch congregation. During the 1940s the church site was moved from Gray Street to Lambert Street in order to allow for construction of public housing in the community. Timothy George's successor was his son, the

Reverend Dormitory T. (D. T.) George. The new young minister "began his tenure as pastor by seeking to improve the organization of the church, as well as familiarizing himself with the needs of the congregation and improving his own skills as a spiritual leader." He married Carrie Leigh who became his "confidant and chief advisor," as well as a leader in church activities. A possessor of a divinity degree from Gammon Theological Seminary, Mrs. George served as Director of Christian Education for the Antioch Church and was later ordained as a minister, herself. The Reverend D. T. George was forced to retire as pastor of Antioch in 1963 "because of failing health." Because of her strong qualifications and leadership abilities, some at Antioch considered the possibility of offering the pastorate of the church to the Reverend Mrs. Carrie L. George "in order to continue the leadership and family tradition of the George Family." However, in 1963 "the congregation as a whole was not yet ready for such a bold move as to name a woman pastor." Thus, the Reverend W. Marcus Williams succeeded the Reverend D. T. George as pastor of Antioch. Since, Antioch was "in such a sound fiscal condition," Williams could "concentrate his attention on social welfare programs that would benefit the church membership." He led the organization of a credit union, which provided loans for members of the congregation at low interest rates. He also established a day care center at the church, "which was the first of its kind in the nation," representing a joint venture project with the federal government through Economic Opportunity Atlanta (EOA). But, in 1969 the Reverend Williams resigned as pastor of Antioch "to accept another position."[20]

After the pastorate of Reverend George and the resignation of Reverend Williams, Antioch faced a certain amount of disunity. Then in August 1963, the Reverend Cameron Madison Alexander was installed as the church's pastor. He moved quickly "to reunite the church and foster a new and positive morale," by "initiating a basic training program of 'Christian Spiritual Confidence.'" During his tenure, Antioch grew from a relatively small membership to more than 1,800 regular members. Alexander also instituted a number of innovative programs to "increase participation in Christian works." These included a food and clothing bank "for people in need"; a scholarship fund to encourage "non-traditional students to seek training beyond high school"; a "'Family Night' to encourage neighborhood families to come to church in an informal manner"; a weekly tutorial program "to assist individuals in strengthening basic academic skills"; and "a cultural enrichment guild for artistic expression in the performing arts." As Alexander's membership and programs at Antioch expanded, so did his reputation for effective leadership. He was subsequently elected President of the General Missionary Baptist Convention of Georgia and Vice President of the National Baptist Convention. The Morehouse School of Religion elected him to serve on its Board of Trustees; Atlanta Mayor Maynard Jackson appointed him a co-chairman and presiding officer of the Atlanta Religious Mobilization Against Crime and President Jimmy Carter appointed him to the National Advisory Board for the 1980 Census.[21]

The Bethlehem Baptist Church was founded in 1879 on Frazier Street in the Summerhill community. The Reverends Messrs. Hall and Smith were the first pastors of Bethlehem serving between 1879 and 1911. The third pastor of Bethlehem was the Reverend Paul Scruggs who served until 1921. In 1922, the Reverend Nathanial T. Thompson was called as pastor. He established a second Sunday service and organized "the Ward System for financial improvement of the church." In 1935, the Reverend William Jackson was elected pastor of Bethlehem. Jackson expanded "the Ward System" "to accommodate the growth of the church." Under Jackson's leadership new usher boards, including a Junior Usher Board, were added, and a "Junior Church" was established. In the 1940s, additional property was purchased for the church at Clark and Frazier Streets, which allowed for remodeling and expansion. The loan for this project was repaid in two years through an organization, with a unique capital funds program, known as, "the May and November Rallies." These rallies, then, became institutionalized and continued as a part of the church's traditions. When the Reverend William Jackson died in August 1970, his son, the Reverend Roswell Francis Jackson served Bethlehem briefly as his successor. In February 1972, the Reverend William Boyd was installed as the new pastor of the church. During Boyd's tenure, the church purchased the property of the formerly white Hillside Baptist Church, on Hogan Road in northwest Atlanta, for $320,000. But, this edifice was damaged by fire in 1973, which forced the congregation to return to the old Frazier Street building, while repairs were being made to the Hillside facility. When these repairs were completed the next year, the congregation returned to its new edifice with "a fervent determination to do God's will." Four years later, Bethlehem called the Reverend Carl H. Moncrief, Sr. as its new pastor. During Moncrief's tenure, church membership rose sharply; "a nomination committee" was established to identify able leaders for church organizations, and a constitution committee was organized. In 1980 a church constitution was adopted and ratified by the congregation.[22]

Meanwhile, the Reverend William Jackson's son, the Reverend Roswell F. Jackson had taken a small congregation in the Rockdale community of southeast Atlanta, moved the church to a new edifice on Fairburn Road in northwest Atlanta, substantially increased memberships and developed several innovative programs.[23]

In 1881 what became the West Hunter Street Baptist Church was organized by a small group of African-Americans in the Raymond Street community of northwest Atlanta. The Reverend Alex Allen was called as the first pastor and the church was named the Mount Calvary Baptist Church. The Reverend Joe Wilson, the second pastor of the church led the congregation in constructing its first building. Over the next several years, the church moved forward under the leadership "of several distinguished ministers." The eighth pastor, the Reverend A. W. Bryant, actually fostered the purchase of the land on Hunter Street, near Morris Brown College, for the construction of a new edifice. The name of the church became the West Hunter Street Baptist Church "in anticipation of the move to the new site." However, the actual construction of the new church on Hunter Street did not occur until the pastorate of the Reverend Robert R. Smith, who came to the church in 1906. Under the Reverend Smith's leadership the senior choir, trustee board, and missionary society were organized, and the general church membership was significantly increased. Reverends J. A. Johnson, S. J. Wooden, and W. F. Paschal succeeded the Reverend Smith, respectively. The Reverend Paschal became known as "an excellent organizer and financier." He led the church out of debt and made periodic improvements in the church building. The 13th pastor of the West Hunter Baptist Church was the Reverend J. R. Bowen. Bowen was recognized as one of the more "dynamic leader[s] and pastor[s] of his time." In 1935, he was succeeded by Reverend Samuel Patterson Pettegrue. Pettegrue organized a number of auxiliaries and achieved notoriety for his leadership in "paying off the debt and burning the mortgage" on the Hunter Street building. In July 1948, the Reverend A. Franklin Fisher became pastor of West Hunter. He was a well-known theologian who achieved a reputation as a counselor and "friend to all." Under Dr. Fisher's leadership, West Hunter's membership continued to increase and a new church building was constructed. Fisher also organized a new "ward system" for the church, as well as a number of additional auxiliaries, including the A. Franklin Fisher Choir, a Youth Choir, two Usher Boards, a Vacation Bible School and a Board of Christian Education. After Fisher's death in 1960, Martin

Luther King Jr.'s chief aide, the Reverend Ralph David Abernathy was called as pastor of West Hunter Baptist Church in 1961. His first sermon as pastor of West Hunter, "Give Me This Mountain," "set the stage for the dynamic leadership which characterized his tenure as pastor." More than 1,300 persons joined the West Hunter congregation after Dr. Abernathy became pastor. The church's financial operations were reorganized and systematized and new church properties were acquired. The major acquisition was at 1040 Gordon Street in the West End section of the city. The West Hunter congregation moved into the large edifice, formerly occupied by whites, in November of 1973. In 1985, the Abernathy Towers, a housing project on Oglethorpe Street, near the church, was begun. While pastoring at West Hunter, Abernathy continued to serve as president of the Southern Christian Leadership Conference (SCLC), a position he inherited after the assassination of Martin Luther King, Jr. in 1968.[24]

The Reverend W. R. Clement organized the Mount Olive Baptist Church in 1885 and a committee was formed to select a site for worship. The first church was located at the corner of Harris and Butler Streets, in northeast Atlanta. From 1887 to 1938 the Mount Olive congregation was served by a number of men, including the Reverend C. H. Lyons, Dr. E. J. Fisher, the Reverend A. P. Dunbar, the Reverend C. H. Young, and the Reverend T. L. Ballon. The Reverend James M. Nabrit became pastor in 1921 and served until 1938. While pastor of Mount Olive, Nabrit was also President of the Georgia Baptist Convention and Secretary of the National Baptist Convention, Incorporated. Nabrit's successor was the Reverend Dr. W. W. Weatherspool. Shortly after his installation, Weatherspool presented a 50-point program that served as a guide for the development of the church for the early years of his tenure as pastor. Under Weatherspool's leadership, the church burned two mortgages, including the one for the new church constructed in southwest Atlanta during the 1960s.[25]

The Ebenezer Baptist Church was founded in 1886, just two decades following the Civil War. The selection of the name of Ebenezer, "Stone of Help" (I Samuel 7:12), was "profoundly prophetic," for this church attained a unique history "in the struggle for freedom of all oppressed people." The Reverend Dr. Martin Luther King, Jr. was born into and nurtured by the Ebenezer Baptist Church.[26]

Its first pastor, the Reverend John A. Parker, served from 1886 to 1894. The church occupied four different structures during its early history and moved to the present Auburn Avenue site in 1914. The Reverend Adam Daniel Williams, who assumed the leadership of

Ebenezer in 1894, was the second pastor of the church. During Reverend Williams' pastorate, the construction of the present church building was completed in 1922, and mortgages were paid off on property acquired during Reverend Parker's tenure as pastor.[27]

The Reverend Martin Luther King, Sr. (Williams' son-in-law), who had served as assistant pastor from 1927 to 1930, became the third pastor of Ebenezer upon the death of the Reverend Williams in 1931. In order to increase the membership of the church, the Reverend King initiated a series of revivals as one of his first acts as the new pastor. A pipe organ was purchased and a second choir was organized. In the early years of his leadership, King improved the physical facilities of the church and reorganized the financial system and the Sunday School grew from one assembly group to an organization with seven departments. By the 15th anniversary of King's pastorate of Ebenezer, in 1947, there had been a tremendous increase in the membership and auxiliaries. In 1956 the Christian Education Building and renovations to the church sanctuary, itself, were completed.[28]

The Reverend Dr. Martin Luther King, Jr. became co-pastor of Ebenezer with his father in 1960. Among the many accomplishments of the father and son team were: publication of an Annual Church Report, revision of the worship service, establishment of a monthly Fellowship Hour, and the naming of a Mission Station in Africa for Ebenezer; and it was during this period that Ebenezer gained its "ecumenical and international stature."

Following the assassination of Dr. Martin Luther King, Jr. in 1968, the Reverend Alfred Daniel Williams King, Sr. became co-pastor of Ebenezer with his father. During his tenure as co-pastor a televised Sunday Morning worship service was initiated and a "benevolent committee" to provide for the needy was organized. The Reverend Otis Moss succeeded the deceased Reverend A. D. King as co-pastor in 1971, but served only briefly in that position. The Reverend Martin Luther King, Sr. retired as pastor of Ebenezer in 1975 after 45 years of "outstanding and dedicated service to the church."[29]

The Reverend Joseph Lawrence Roberts succeeded King, Sr. as the fourth pastor of Ebenezer. Under his leadership more than 1,700 new members were added to the church and financial contributions significantly increased. The church was organized into committees, one of which assumed responsibility for a community outreach project. There were several improvements in the physical plant and a new organ and piano were purchased. Another innovative program initiated under Roberts was "A Watch Care Program for Students." In this program a student or young person from another city was assigned to a family in Ebenezer that provides a "Home Away From Home." Ebenezer has also been involved in the Atlanta Ministry to International Students as well as the Ebenezer Day Rehabilitation Center, an outreach service, which provided medical and recreational daycare to senior citizens. Then, in 1984, Roberts established the "team ministry" concept and invited the Reverend Sharon Genise Austin and the Reverend Edward Spencer Reynolds as part-time assistant pastors. Through increased membership, the team ministry concept was expanded. Under Roberts' leadership "the church continued to fulfill its historical destiny as Samuel's 'Ebenezer' and the 'Stone of Help' for oppressed people."[30]

The famous secession of blacks from the Methodist Church in Philadelphia, under the leadership of Richard Allen and Absalom Jones, in 1787, was followed by similar actions in New York City. Peter Williams, Sr. and other blacks in New York organized the Zion Church out of which developed the African Methodist Episcopal Zion Church. The first A.M.E. Zion Church was organized in Atlanta in the early 1890s in the old Badger Hall on Piedmont Avenue near Ellis Street, in the northeastern quadrant of the city. Bishop M. R. Franklin was assigned as overseer of the new church in 1891. In that year, the first church building was erected near Boulevard and Irvin Streets in the same area. The church was then named Franklin Memorial Institutional A.M.E. Zion Church in honor of Bishop Franklin, who died before construction of the church was completed. The name of the church was changed several times before the current name of Shaw Temple A.M.E. Zion was established in honor of Bishop B. G. Shaw. The church remained at the Boulevard site for more than 40 years and several different men served as pastor during that period. Among those were the Reverend Godwin, "a builder who urged and inspired" the church to construct its first brick structure in the 1920s. The Reverend Goodwin raised funds from the community in order to meet the mortgage payments to the black-owned Standard Federal Bank. During the 1930s Bishop Shaw and the Reverend Mr. Fattis helped to reunite the church "following a brief split." Another minister, the Reverend George W. McMurray launched a membership campaign in the 1940s and established the Progressive Club. He also formed a gospel chorus and an intra-church Thanksgiving Fellowship. In 1949 the Reverend William A. Potter became pastor of Shaw Temple. During his tenure the church was host for the First National Meeting of the C.M.E., A.M.E. Zion and A.M.E. churches on church union. In 1959 the church site was moved from Auburn Avenue, in northeast Atlanta, to Hightower Road, in the northwestern part of the city, and a new parsonage was built.   Shortly thereafter, the sitting minister, the Reverend Mr. Potter resigned as Senior Pastor and became Presiding Elder.   During the 1960s, the Reverends Cameron W. Jackson and Walter E. Beamon served as pastors of the church and were instrumental in making many improvements to the physical plant of the institution.   In 1975 the Reverend Beamon resigned as pastor to become an Air Force Chaplain.   The Reverend Raymond C. Hart was, then, appointed pastor of Shaw Temple.   Under Hart, a radio ministry was established, Bible Studies were instituted, a Senior Citizens Center was founded, and a Christian Education Department was begun.   The church's membership also grew under the Reverend Mr. Hart.   Hart's successor was the Reverend Dr. George Oforriatta-Thomas, who maintained the church's tradition "of spiritual growth and development," started a credit union, opened a food and clothing bank, and organized a Youth Usher Board.   Like many other black Atlanta churches, pastors at Shaw Temple have gone on to higher positions in regional and national church organizations.   For example the Reverends Messrs. J. Blakeley and F. J. Baptiste became a General Officer on the Staff of the A.M.E. Zion Publishing House; the Reverend George W. McMurray became pastor of the mother A.M.E. Zion Church in New York City; and the Reverends Felix Anderson and C. C. Coleman became Bishops of the A.M.E. Zion Church.[31]

One of the first African-American churches founded in Atlanta in the early part of the twentieth century was the Mount Vernon Baptist Church.   The church evolved from the efforts of three former members of the Mount Carmel Baptist Church.   The first pastor of Mount Vernon was the Reverend E. D. Florence.   The first worship services were held at 55 Markham Street, in northwest Atlanta, with 35 persons in attendance.   Under the leadership of the Reverend Florence, the church grew quickly and a Sunday School and other auxiliaries were organized.   By 1918 the first church edifice, valued at $50,000, was purchased at the corner of Mangum and Hunter streets.   Over the next four years, the church mortgage was paid off, the membership increased to over 700, and two choirs were organized.   When the Reverend Florence resigned as pastor of Mount Vernon Baptist Church in 1929, he was succeeded by the Reverend C. H. Pickett.   Under Pickett a "Junior Church" was organized and the Sunday School expanded to include four additional classes.   In 1932, the Reverend Pickett resigned as pastor and the Reverend W. G. Bivins assumed the pastorate of Mount Vernon.   The Reverend Bivins' early tenure was characterized by the establishment of "special recognition services."   In

1933 the first Woman's Day Program was held and "Harvest Day" and Youth Day services were initiated. Membership rose to more than 1,000 persons, and "the church was cleared of all indebtedness." Attendance at Sunday School increased to such an extent that the program was organized into four departments. Reverend Bivins died on January 17, 1945, while still sitting as pastor of Mount Vernon. The fourth pastor of the Mount Vernon Baptist Church was the Reverend E. M. Johnson. During Johnson's tenure a new church annex was constructed and other property was purchased for the institution; a church library was established and the membership increased to 2,000, making Mount Vernon Baptist one of the largest black churches in Atlanta at the time. Also during this period, Mount Vernon hosted the General Missionary Baptist Convention of Georgia. The Reverend Johnson died in 1952 and the Reverend J. R. Lovett was called to the Mount Vernon pulpit. Shortly thereafter, the church building was remodeled and other property was purchased. A number of new auxiliaries were organized, including several "financial aid clubs" and the J. R. Lovett Gospel Chorus was established. In 1955 the church was informed that it had to relocate because of the imposition of *imminent domain* in the area in which it was located. Property on Northside Drive and Hunter Street in northwest Atlanta was purchased for the construction of a new church edifice. However, in 1960, before a new building could be constructed, the Mount Vernon membership was forced to leave the church site at Mangum and Hunter Streets. For nearly three years Mount Vernon shared the facilities of the nearby Saint Stephens Missionary Baptist Church. Then, in May 1961 ground was broken for the construction of a one-half million dollar structure and the Reverend Marcus Williams of Antioch Baptist Church "delivered the sermon on that significant day in the church's history." But, the Reverend Lovett died in 1962 before the new church was completed. The significance of the move to the new edifice, particularly under the circumstances of Lovett's recent death, inspired one of the church's historians to write:

> With voices raised in praise, thanks, and glory to God, they marched singing 'We are Marching to Zion.' The line of march proceeded to the church and stopped at the steps. Reverend Ernest Wilkerson offered a prayer of thanks. Following the prayer, Mrs. J. R. Lovett cut the ribbon . . . . In order that the entire structure and all its parts be dedicated to God, a full week was given to dedicational services.

Mount Vernon was without a pastor for nearly a year, which resulted in a rather significant decrease in membership. Then, in November 1963, the Reverend S. A. Baker was called to pastor the church. Baker immediately began a comprehensive membership drive and revamped the financial operations of the church. Auxiliaries were reorganized and new ones were established. A nursery and kindergarten were opened with "state of the art" equipment. In 1973, a private, church sponsored school, The Mount Vernon Academy was founded.[32]

The Union Baptist Church was organized in 1916, under the leadership of the Reverend C. H. Sharpe, with five members. Sharpe served as pastor of the church for eight years, during which the first Sunday School, Baptist Training Union (BTU) and choir were established. Between 1925 and 1946, several men, including the Reverends H. M. Smith, S. M. Bryant, J. Cox, M. Jackson, and Herman Stone served as ministers at Union Baptist. Stone, who became pastor in 1940, succeeded in adding many new members, paid off the church debt, and oversaw the remodeling of the church building. In August 1946, the Reverend J. A. Wilborn became Union Baptist's pastor. Wilborn "brought new life and vigor" to the church. He spearheaded the purchase of new property for the growing congregation. But this land, on Mozley Drive and West Lake Avenue in northwest Atlanta, was never used because of the imposition of *imminent domain* for new highway construction in the area. Hence new property was acquired at Hightower and Simpson Roads, farther to the north and west. In November 1962 the congregation moved into a new facility. Even in its larger building, the congregation soon found itself crowded, as membership grew to more than 1,200 persons. By 1980, Union had gained a high prominence among Black Atlanta churches and developed a motto as "a church, which cares for and serves the community."[33]

The Flipper Temple A.M.E. Church was organized under the leadership of the Reverend C. D. Thornton in 1919. With the assistance of Bishop Joseph S. Flipper and Presiding Elder L. A. Townsley, the Reverend Thornton built the first church edifice on Fair Street, near the Atlanta University Center in southwest Atlanta. The Reverend J. G. Brown succeeded the Reverend Thornton as pastor in 1922 and continued the construction of the edifice, but unfortunately the building was completely destroyed by fire. Under the Reverend Brown's leadership a new church building was erected at the same location. The church was renovated and expanded under the leadership of the Reverend J. F. Moses, who was appointed to succeed the Reverend Mr. Brown. Reverend Moses also reduced the church debt. The next two pastors of Flipper Temple continued to reduce the debt and finally the Reverend David Norris liquidated the indebtedness of the church. The Reverend Norris established a building fund for the construction of a new church, which was begun during the pastorate of the Reverend Lutrell G. Long who came to Flipper Temple in 1951. The Reverend Long, who was described as an "exciting preacher," significantly increased the church membership. The Reverend Mr. Bussey followed the Reverend Long as pastor of Flipper Temple. He guided the church to the financial stability required for the expansion and the completion of the church building program. The next pastor of Flipper Temple, the Reverend Julius C. Williams, succeeded in completing the building program, as well as liquidating the mortgage. In addition, there were many other improvements to the church and the purchase of considerable property. The Reverend Mr. Williams was praised for his openness to visiting ministers and "his untiring efforts to serve the congregation."[34]

Another church which had its beginning in the Rockdale community is the Zion Hill Missionary Baptist Church, founded in 1924 under the leadership of the Reverend Tom Davis. After four years the Reverend A. L. Butler succeeded the Reverend Davis as pastor. During the Reverend Butler's tenure a lot was purchased and a church was built at the corner of Lively and Taft Streets. In 1933, under the leadership of the Reverend B. R. Matthews, the congregation grew and a larger church building was constructed to accommodate the membership and visitors. After the brief pastorates of the Reverend Moses Biggs and the Reverend Thomas H. Hurley, the Reverend R. H. Gresham became pastor of Zion Hill in 1940. During his 12 years as pastor, a number of purchases were made including a piano and new pews, and "the church prospered." The Reverend Gresham was succeeded by the Reverend C. H. Tigne in 1952, followed by the Reverend A. D. Tucker in 1956. The Reverend Hilton J. Taylor was elected pastor of Zion Hill in April 1957. The Reverend Taylor provided the leadership for the purchase of new property at the corner of Boulder Park Drive and Fairburn Road, in northwest Atlanta, and the construction of another structure, in 1966. An organ and church furniture were purchased, and other improvements were made. Also during Taylor's tenure, numerous auxiliaries were organized, including the Young Men's and Young Women's Usher Boards, the Sunbeam Choir, the Pastor's Aid Club, the Young Adult Choir and the Courtesy Guild. In 1980 and 1981, a radio broadcast program began as an outreach ministry and the Board of Christian Education was organized. During the early 1980s an Educational Building was also constructed and other improvements were made to the church facilities. Expansion in the church's ministry and service resulted in more than 17 auxiliaries and support groups, and Zion Hill "continued to grow and prosper."[35]

One of the more recent churches to develop out of "the spiritual needs of a growing community" was the Dixie Hills First Baptist Church. In 1932 a small group of persons organized a Bible Class in the Dixie Hills community of northwest Atlanta. After several meetings in different homes in the community each week, the group decided that a church was needed in the area which was located some distance from downtown Atlanta and other Baptist congregations. On the first Sunday in May 1933, Dixie Hills First Baptist Church was organized in the home of the Reverend B. D. Howard at 285 Spelman Street. The Reverend Howard and the charter members of the church began missionary work immediately; 47 were baptized and 43 were accepted "by Christian experience." In 1936 land was purchased and a small frame church edifice was erected. Several pastors followed the Reverend Howard, including the Reverend T. J. Ball, the Reverend I. S. Mack, and the Reverend A. G. Davis. The Reverend R. D. Sutton was called as pastor in 1945.[36]

When the Reverend Sutton accepted the pastorate of the Dixie Hills First Baptist Church, the membership had declined to 45 individuals. Under Reverend Sutton's leadership the church's enrollment soon increased to over 600 members. After four years, the cornerstone for the new church on Morehouse Drive, in the same area, was laid on May 29, 1949. The new church building and facilities were completed in 1953. During the 1950s a number of improvements in the church occurred, including decoration of the interior, "the fellowship and spiritual life of the church was enhanced and the worship service enriched." Attendance at church services increased and additional auxiliaries were organized. Noteworthy among the new auxiliaries was a well-organized youth department. Each auxiliary of the church had a well-planned program, which not only provided financial support to the church, but "also provided moral and spiritual support to the Dixie Hills community at large." "This emphasis on service to the community, through the spiritual commitment of the church, characterized the Reverend R. D. Sutton's tenure as pastor of Dixie Hills First Baptist Church." Sutton and the church were greatly assisted by the work of his wife, Victoria. Mrs. Sutton was "a devoted church worker" as well as a teacher at the Henry McNeal Turner High

School, which served the Dixie Hills area. She and her husband were known in the community as a couple who loved people, whatever their station in life. After Sutton's death, the Reverend R. B. Sutton succeeded his father as pastor of the Dixie Hills First Baptist Church and "continued the tradition of service to the church and the community."[37]

As has been seen, the evangelical Baptist and Methodist Churches attracted the majority of African-American worshipers in Atlanta. But other sects of evangelicals, variously known as Pentecostal and "holy rollers" also enrolled large numbers of blacks. Most notable among these was The Church of God in Christ. That denomination, "in which the word of God is preached, ordinances are administered and the doctrine of sanctification or holiness is emphasized, as being essential to the salvation of mankind," had its origins in rural Mississippi in 1866 and was officially organized as The Church of God in Christ in 1897 by Elder Charles Harrison Mason. In 1925 the church completed its national tabernacle, and subsequent headquarters, in Memphis, Tennessee. By the 1970s, the Church had an international membership of more than three million and by the 1990s it had almost eight million members.[38]

Churches of God in Christ in Atlanta tended to be found in the southwest and northwest quadrants of the city. In the pre-Civil Rights Era, the larger churches included the Hinsley Temple Church in southwest and the Jones Avenue church in northwest Atlanta. The former was led for more than a quarter of a century by Bishop James J. Hinsley; the latter became identified with the ministry of George Briley. Both had radio ministries.

In the post-Civil Rights period, one of the largest Church of God congregations was the Cathedral of Faith in southwest Atlanta, led by Bishop Jonathan Greer. Greer attracted a large number of young worshipers who were drawn, at least partially, by his Afri-Centric messages and dress. He also had a popular television ministry. In northwest Atlanta, on the fringes of a white Buckhead residential area, was the Lynwood Park Church of God in Christ, pastored by Bishop Marshall Carter. Carter also had a television ministry.[39]

Although much of Black Atlanta, like most of Black America, worshiped in the evangelical churches, principally Baptists and Methodists, the city, because of the diversity of its African-American population, was also the home of a number of non-evangelical denominations. Within a few years after the Civil War, St. Mark, the first Lutheran church for blacks in Atlanta and in Georgia, was established. The Atonement Lutheran Church was dedicated in

October 1959 and the St. Mark Lutherans indicated a willingness to consolidate with the new mission because of a decline in their membership. At the 1964 Florida-Georgia District Convention, the Atonement Church became a member of the Lutheran Church-Missouri Synod. Pastor William Jones, the first minister for Atonement, resigned in 1968. The next year, Vernon Schultheis was assigned to pastor Atonement. During his tenure, evangelism and other new innovations in worship were introduced. In 1974, Leslie Weber became the new pastor at Atonement. The next year, the Charles B. Hart, Jr. Memorial Scholarship Fund was established to support members of the congregation for study of the Lutheran ministry. Then, the congregation voted to leave the Lutheran Church-Missouri Synod and affiliated with the Association of Evangelical Lutheran Churches. A joint youth program, the YEA, Inc. was begun with the Emmanuel Lutheran Church in 1981. The first evening Vacation Bible School was conducted and a joint picnic was also held with the Emmanuel Church at this time. In the 1980s Atonement gained new notoriety when it hosted the "Congregation of the Southern Region" in a weekend convention. And Atonement continued to symbolize "the desire for unification within the Lutheran Church."[40]

The first African-American Catholic parish established in Atlanta was located in the northeast section of the city on Boulevard near Auburn Avenue. The Our Lady of Lourdes Church was founded following a visit to Atlanta in 1911 by Father Ignatius Lissner of the Society of African Missions. Lissner observed that the large, diverse black population in the city was fertile ground for a Catholic parish. Outraged whites, however, thwarted the first effort to purchase church property, near a largely white neighborhood. The Boulevard property was purchased in 1912 with the aid of J. J. Spalding, a prominent Catholic from the Sacred Heart parish. Major financial support for the purchase came from Mother Mary Katherine Drexel, founder of the Sisters of the Blessed Sacrament, an order that she had established in 1891 to serve blacks and Native Americans.[41]

The parish, "the only non-territorial one" in Atlanta is located within the boundary of the Sacred Heart parish. Its earliest members came from the Auburn Avenue area, but by 1990, parishioners came from as far away as Stone Mountain and other areas of Dekalb County. Members included "upward mobile families" as well as persons, most of them elderly, from the nearby public housing projects. In 1990, there were about 500 parishioners in 220 family units, including six white families and a half-dozen Vietnamese families. The parish school which was founded in 1913, enrolled Catholics, Protestants, and unaffiliated children. More than two dozen children from the nearby public housing projects attended on "scholarships." The church's auxiliaries included a social action committee, which provided food for the homeless, as well as the needy in nearby neighborhoods; turkeys were added to the food boxes during Thanksgiving and Christmas. The church has been pastored by several white priests, including Father Frank Giusta and Father Joseph Cavallo.[42]

In November 1954, a formal announcement was made in Our Lady of Lourdes Church that a new African-American parish was being established in northwest Atlanta. This announcement reflected the growth of Catholicism among black Atlantans and the continuing expansion of the black population into the far west side of the city. In January 1915, a temporary parish rectory was occupied at 29 West Lake Avenue in northwest Atlanta. On January 20, the first mass was celebrated in the rectory basement. In October 1960, the church's present sanctuary on Harwell Road, also in northwest Atlanta, was formally dedicated. Its mostly black middle-class parishioners have included Charlayne Hunter Gault, one of the first two blacks to desegregate the University of Georgia and a prominent national journalist; Michael Gaines, the first black youth from Georgia to be accepted at the U.S. Military Academy at West Point; and Emmut Jones, a 1982 graduate of West Point. A parish school was opened in 1958. It consisted of five grades and was staffed by five nuns from the Sisters of St. Joseph of Baden, Pennsylvania. The last eighth grade class graduated from St. Paul of the Cross School in 1989 and the school later closed, because of financial exigency. The parish has been served mainly by white priests, beginning with Father Emauel Trainor in 1955.[43]

Like other Catholic parishes in Black Atlanta, St. Paul has always had a few white parishioners and a mostly white leadership for the church and school. This was, perhaps, the motivation for a series of hate incidents at the church. As late as 1988 a dummy with a black face was found tied to the parish mailbox. A rope around the neck of the dummy held a sign reading, "White Power."[44]

When the St. Anthony's Church was founded in the West End section of southwest Atlanta in 1903, by a group which included Mrs. Joel Chandler Harris, wife of the famed author of the Uncle Remus tales, the community and the parish were all white. The present church was dedicated in January 1924. After West End was transitioned from white to black in the 1960s, white flight also turned St. Anthony's into a largely black parish, which, by 1990, was served by black priests.

The most prominent of these has been Father Bruce Wilkinson. Under Wilkinson's leadership, the church's outreach ministry operated a lunch program for the homeless and needy as well as a program for the elderly, addressed traffic problems in the neighborhood, advocated better maintenance of nearby Howell Park, and participated in an "affordable housing" program. In the housing program, the parish joined with the Atlanta Mortgage Consortium (AMC) of the Community Home Buyers Education Program to offer a free five-week course on home ownership. The topics of the course included budgets, credits, taxes, "understanding home mortgages," "planning for home ownership," "closing the loan," and "avoiding default." A certificate of completion was issued at the end of the course, which was a requirement to qualify for an AMC mortgage. By the fall of 1990, about 550 homes had been purchased under the program. A homeless shelter for men, which was begun in 1983, was discontinued in 1988. By 1990, the church enrolled more than 550 families.[45]

The newest of the black Catholic Churches is Most Blessed Sacrament, which was founded as a diocesan parish in November 1960 as Ben Hill Mission, out of St. Anthony's Church. It was turned over to the Missionaries of LaSalette in June 1975. The Sisters of Saint Joseph of Carondelet operated a parish school there from 1965 to 1976. In October 1989, the church moved to its present site on the property that once housed the Village of St. Joseph on Butner Road in the Ben Hill section of southwest Atlanta. Twelve priests have served the parish in its brief history. The founding pastor was Father Walter Donovan; the pastor in 1990 was an African-American, Father Bruce Wilkinson. It has generally maintained a membership of about 200 families, including military personnel and their families from nearby Fort McPherson. Parish organizations include the Lay Congress, a Sunshine Club, which sends birthday cards and get well greetings to parishioners, a youth ministry, an "Assistance to the Needy Committee," the Knights of Columbus, and an AIDS Task Force. The school of religion includes classes and ministries for young people and children and an Adult Spiritual Enrichment Program. Most parishioners agree that the small mission survives largely because of the dynamic and creative leadership of Father Wilkinson. He is "the water that draws people here and keeps them here," according to Robert Warren, one of the church's oldest members.

The importance of black Catholicism in Atlanta was recognized internationally in 1988, when the Most Reverend Eugene A. Marino was appointed Archbishop of Atlanta, the first African-American to hold such a position in "the New South." But, two years later Marino resigned amid rumors of sexual misconduct and "misuse of funds." An audit later cleared the diocese of the latter accusation.[46]

Prior to the beginning of the Civil War, there were a rather large number of black Episcopalians in South Carolina and Georgia. But, by 1880, there had been "a mass exodus" of the formerly enslaved members of the church. Yet, during this same period, a group of blacks organized an Episcopalian Sunday School in Atlanta. Shortly thereafter, this small group was granted the status of a mission by the Diocese. The mission became the St. Paul's Episcopal Church.[47]

The earliest services of St. Paul's Church were held upstairs over a drug store at the corner of Lee and Gordon Streets in the West End section of the city. Subsequently the church moved to facilities in the Pryor Hall at Peachtree Street and Auburn Avenue in northeast Atlanta and Butler Street in the same area. During this early period, laypersons directed the services. In 1895, the Reverend William A. Green was named "Minister-in-Charge" of St. Paul's. Shortly after his appointment, Green led the congregation into a new building on Auburn Avenue "in the heart of the Black community." These moves were accompanied by continuous growth of the church's membership. Subsequently, a second black mission, St. Matthias was established on Lawshe Street in southwest Atlanta, near the black colleges.[48]

Of the early rectors of St. Paul's, "the most energetic and dedicated" was the Reverend A. Eustace Day. Day oversaw the purchase of new land for the church and organized its first parochial school. He was also one of the ministers who helped to "reestablish racial harmony" in the wake of the infamous Atlanta Riot of 1906. Eleven years after the riot, a devastating fire forced St. Paul to hold services in theatres, storefronts, homes or wherever it could. Within a year, however, the white Cathedral of St. Philip provided its Sunday school building to St. Paul's. The building was then placed on the site of the former, burned out, edifice.[49]

A new era of progress for St. Paul's dawned with the appointment of the Reverend Henry J. C. Bowden as "priest-in-charge" in 1934 and rector in 1935. Bowden led a successful drive to build a parish house/rectory. In 1941, Bowden left his position to become a Chaplain in the United States Army. Then, in 1952, St. Paul's long quest to become a "full fledged" parish was granted by the Diocese. In 1958 the parish was incorporated with a board of trustees and other officers. During this period, the parish was ably led by the Reverend Samuel C. Usher. Usher's successor was the Reverend Robert Boyd Hunter, who came to the parish in 1964. Hunter, who "immersed himself deeply in community activities and had an avid interest in social action, political and community issues and involvement," led the congregation out of its cramped quarters on the near west side of Atlanta into a new, modern facility in northwest Atlanta in 1969. The handsome building on Peyton Road in a fashionable black subdivision continued as the site of the church. But, by the 1980s, it was becoming too small for the growing congregation. The plans for expansion and renovation were given a major boost in 1988 when a parishioner bequeathed $133,000 to the church. These developments occurred under the rectorship of the Reverend Edward L. Warner, who came to St. Paul's in 1977.[50]

Warner's tenure as rector of St. Paul's has been characterized not only by the church's human and physical growth, but also by the development of "lay ministries," and increased roles for women in the congregation, including altar girls, lay readers and Eucharist ministers. Warner also brought increased visibility to the church through his involvement in the city's political and civic affairs.[51]

For most of the history of the Black Church in Atlanta, the more "unorthodox" of the denominations were Catholics and Episcopalians. But, during the Civil Rights and post-Civil Rights Eras new forms of African-American worship entered the city, which were neither Protestant nor Catholic. These included non-denominational "mega churches" as well as non-Christian and unorthodox Christian sects. One such institution was the Hillside Chapel and Truth Center in southwest Atlanta. Hillside was founded in 1971 in the home of the Reverend Barbara Lewis King, a Chicago native, with about a dozen adherents of an "ecumenical international ministry." By 1990, the church had grown to more than 4,000 members and occupied a campus of several acres. Many well educated older blacks as well as students subscribed to the Hillside creed of a "positive approach to life, seeking to accept the good in all of life." "God is seen as having many attributes, but most important God is LOVE." Hillside stressed that God was not "a physical man in the sky," but was "Spirit — everywhere present; the one and only Spirit behind, in and through all things, visible and invisible." The most prominent of the non-Christian and the unorthodox Christian sects were the Nation of Islam and the Shrine of the Black Madonna. Interestingly enough, the Nation of Islam (NOI, which became known as the Black Muslims) was founded by one of Georgia's own black sons, who had migrated to the North. Elijah Poole, the son of a Baptist minister, succeeded W. D. Fard as leader of the Black Muslims in 1934, and took the name Elijah Muhammad. After its origins in Detroit, the Nation of Islam was largely relegated to such Northern cities as Chicago, Detroit and New York. But with the coming of the Civil Rights Movement and the beginning of a "reverse migration" movement to the South, about the same time, Elijah Muhammad authorized a "Southern thrust" for the Nation. Thus, a mosque was opened in Richmond, Virginia, as well as Mosque No. 15 in Atlanta.[52]

The Atlanta Mosque, which opened in 1957, originally found most of its adherents among young, urban blacks and economically disadvantaged African-Americans. These groups were particularly drawn to the teachings and the style of the most prominent Black Muslim minister of the period, Malcolm X. But the preaching of Elijah Muhammad and, particularly of the charismatic Malcolm X, frightened many white Americans. They saw in them their most dreaded fears of the consequence of Black Nationalism, Black Separatism and the Black Power Movement. But, many blacks, including members of the religious and political communities in Atlanta, also came to oppose the teachings and the presence of the NOI. Most of these people were Protestants or Catholics and hence unsympathetic to Islam, generally; and they also felt that separatist and nationalist teachings and preaching of "hate" were inimical to the aims, philosophies, and actions of the Civil Rights Movement. The aggressive proselytizing by the Black Muslims, including the attempts to sell their weekly newspaper, "The Messenger," on the streets of Atlanta, alarmed and angered many Atlantans, both white and black. In the 1970s, clashes between NOI proselytizers and the Atlanta Police Department increased. One of the most serious events occurred in June 1973 on one of the principal streets in the downtown shopping district. During the melee, a white police officer and a Black Muslim were killed. Six members of the NOI were charged in connection with the incident. But, an Atlanta Grand Jury failed to indict them the next month.[53]

Meanwhile, with the death of Elijah Muhammad (in 1975) and the assassination of Malcolm X (in 1965), the national tenor of the NOI on racial matters was tempered. Picking up on themes from the last days of Malcolm X, the group became more internationalist and more inclusive. Following a major Black Power Conference in the Atlanta University Center in the early 1970s, the NOI became increasingly involved in traditional politics in Atlanta and even joined with Christian leaders in promoting social causes to benefit blacks. Perhaps, the most notable example of the cooperation of the NOI and traditional black leaders in Atlanta was during "the Murdered and Missing Children's Crisis" of the early 1980s. The NOI participated in the searches for the missing youth and offered protection to other young blacks.[54]

The NOI in Atlanta, as elsewhere, also sought to become an economic force in the city. In addition to selling *Muhammad Speaks* on the streets, Black Muslims also sold fruit and other items. They opened small grocery stores, fish markets, and restaurants (selling mostly fish and vegetarian items). But these businesses, like most small black owned businesses in the city, were only marginally profitable and many closed shortly after their openings.[55]

The Shrine of the Black Madonna of the Pan African Orthodox Christian Church (PAOCC), also known as the Black Christian Nationalist Church, was founded in Detroit by Albert Cleage in 1972. Unlike the NOI, the Shrine was a direct product of the Civil Rights Movement, particularly the Black Power phase of it. It was nationalist and Afri-centric. Cleage, for example, soon took the name Abebe Agyeman.[56]

Like the NOI, the Shrine soon saw a need to expand into the South, where much of "the action" of the period was occurring. In the spring of 1975 black college students in Atlanta helped adherents from Detroit establish the Southern Region Shrine of the Black Madonna. The importance of this development was underscored when the Church held a national convention in Atlanta. Atlanta's new black mayor, Maynard Jackson and other traditional black political leaders welcomed the delegates to the city. Jackson called Cleage, whose daughter took up residence in the city, "a master teacher."[57]

Although, many of Atlanta's African-American political and religious leaders frowned upon the Shrine's nationalistic teachings, they did not see the organization as "hate filled"; and, after all, it was Christian. Thus, by the 1980s the Shrine had forged direct political and other relationships with other Atlanta organizations, including a number of Black Atlanta's religious institutions, to address pressing community problems. It also began to issue a "Black Slate," which promoted certain black candidates for political office.

The Shrine's Alkebulan Academy Kua Educational Center, Community Service Center and Bookstore provided educational and social services for its congregation as well as the surrounding communities, including the Atlanta University Center. Indeed, the Shrine of the Madonna Bookstore became one of the most important institutions in Black Atlanta. It drew nationally and internationally known authors for book signings and was the scene of various lectures, presentations and other events, which addressed issues of significance to the African World.[58]

While thousands of black Atlantans worshipped, mostly on Sundays, in large churches and mosques, hundreds more met their spiritual needs in homes, store-front edifices and in outdoor tents throughout the city. Many of the churches, large and small, in addition to broad out-reach programs provided "soup kitchens" and other daily services to the homeless and the poor. Oft-times, they also organized into larger units for social and political action. Prior to the 1970s, such action could be seen in groups like the Atlanta Baptist Ministers Union. More recently, the Concerned Black Clergy has been a major advocacy group for black social and political causes.

The Black Church, in Atlanta as elsewhere, has been often maligned as irrelevant in an Age of Hip Hop Culture, and as too "otherworldness." Others have decried its political activism as flaunting the line of demarcation between church and state. But, in the end, as this chapter has demonstrated, through social outreach, economic investments, and political activities, the Church has remained a bulwark for the salvation of the souls as well as the hearts and minds of black Americans.

Notes

[1] Trezzevant V. Anderson, "The Atlanta Story," *The Pittsburgh Courier*, July 15, 1961, p. 2.

[2] Roswell F. Jackson and Rosalyn M. Patterson, "A History of Selected Black Churches in Atlanta, Georgia," *Journal of Negro History*, p. 33.

[3] *Ibid.*

[4] *Ibid.*

[5] *Ibid.*, pp. 33, 34.

[6] *Ibid.*, p. 34.

[7] *Ibid.*, p. 34.

[8] *Ibid.*, p. 34.

[9] *Ibid.*, p. 34.

[10] *Ibid.*, p. 35.

[11] *Ibid.*, pp.35, 36.

[12] *Ibid.*, pp. 36, 39.; Grant, *The Way It Was*, pp. 208, 215, 271, 308

[13] Jackson and Patterson, *Ibid.*, p. 39: Grant, *Ibid;* Henry Hugh Proctor, *Between Black and White; Autobiographical Sketches* (Boston, 1925). See also H. C. McEwen, Sr., "First Congregational Church, Atlanta : 'For the Good of Man and the Glory of God,'" *The Atlanta Historical Bulletin*, XXI, No. 1, Spring, 1977, pp. 129-142 and Lester J. Rodney, "Henry Hugh Proctor: The Atlanta Years, 1894-1920. Thesis (D.A.), Clark Atlanta University, 1992

[14] Jackson and Patterson, *Ibid*; Grant, *Ibid.*

[15] *Ibid.*, pp. 36, 37.

[16] *Ibid.*, pp. 37, 38.

[17] *Ibid.*, p. 38.; See also "45th pastoral anniversary: Rev. William Holmes Borders, 1937-1982, Wheat Street Baptist Church, Atlanta, Georgia" (Atlanta, 1982).

[18] *Ibid.*, p. 38.

[19] *Ibid.*, pp. 38, 39.

[20] *Ibid.*, pp. 39, 40.

[21] *Ibid.*, p. 40.

[22] *Ibid.*, p. 41.

[23] *Ibid.*, p. 41.

[24] *Ibid.*, pp. 41, 42.

[25] *Ibid.*, p. 42.

[26] Jackson and Patterson, *Ibid.*, p. 42; Grant, *TheWay It Was*, pp. 270, 391, 421, 430.

[27] Jackson and Patterson, *Ibid.*

[28] Jackson and Patterson, *Ibid.*, pp. 42, 43; Grant, *The Way It Was*, pp. 270, 391, 421, 430.

[29] Jackson and Patterson, *Ibid.*, p. 43:Grant, *Ibid.*

[30] *Ibid.*, pp. 42, 43.

[31] *Ibid.*, p. 44.

[32] *Ibid.*, pp. 45-47.

[33] *Ibid.*, p. 47.

[34] *Ibid.*, pp. 47, 48.

[35] *Ibid.*, p. 48.

[36] *Ibid.*, p. 48, 49.

[37] *Ibid.*, p. 49.

[38] www.cogic.org

[39] http://ma/aco/gospel/greer/main.html; http://netministries.org/see/churches/ch04989; www.co7cogic.org

[40] elcanewberrynet;com/sc-AtlantaGir-Emmanuel; Jackson and Patterson, *A Brief History of Selected Black Churches*, pp. 49, 50.

[41] www.archatl.com/gabulletin/1998/98cl 22d.html; www.archatl.com/gabulletin/ 1989/871105@html.

[42] *Ibid.*; http://www.archatl.com/gabulletin/1968/680502b.html; http://www.archatl.com/ gabulletin/1980/800207d.html; www.archatl.com/gabulletin/1995/951602a.html.

[43] http://www.archatl.com/gabulletin/1968/680502b.html; http://www.archatl.com/gabulletin/1980/80020fd.html; http://www.archatl.com/gabulletin/1995/951102a.html.

[44] *Ibid.*

[45] http://www.archatl.com/gabulletin/1971/710701b.html; http://www,archatl.com/gabulletin/1978/780622a.html; http://www.archatl.com/ gabulletin1990/900913d.html.

[46] http://www.archatl.com/gabulletin/1989/890921b.html;
http://www.archatl.com/oooo525a.html; http://www.archatl.com/000525a.html;
http//www.archatl.com/archbishops/marino;atgen.com/bishop_marion.html.

[47] http://www.stpaulsatlanta.org; http://www.stpaulsatlanta.org/
historic_st.html.

[48] *Ibid.*

[49] *Ibid.*

[50] http://www.episcopalatlanta.org; http://www.stpaulsatlanta.org/
historic_st.html.

[51] *Ibid.* all.

[52] http://www.hillsidechapel.org.html. See also Karl Evanzz, *The Messenger: The Rise and Fall of Elijah Muhammad* (New York, 1999).

[53] *Atlanta Constitution*, June 20, 1973; July 14, 1995.

[54] See Evanzz, *The Messenger.*

[55] *Ibid.*

[56] See Albert Cleage, *Black Christian Nationalism* (New York, 1972).

[57] Atlanta *Daily World*, April 4, 1975; See also Cleage, *Black Christian Nationalism.*

[58] Atlanta *Daily World*, April 3, 4, 1975; See also Cleage, *Black Christian Nationalism.*

EDUCATION

Chapter 8
The Freedmen's Bureau Schools
in Texas, 1865–1870

The end of the Civil War not only brought an era of Southern history to a close, but it also ushered in a new time of strife. While the rebellious states had struggled through many difficult problems brought on by the rigors of war, peace brought not relief but fresh concerns. Among the most pressing was the plight of the approximately 4,000,000 newly freed blacks. If they were to survive and ultimately assume their rightful role among other Americans, immediate steps had to be taken to provide them with food, clothing, shelter, jobs, and particularly education. Humanitarians and political leaders took note of the conditions and needs of the near-helpless freedmen and began preparations to offer aid and assistance even before Lee's surrender at Appomattox.

On March 3, 1865, Congress established within the War Department a Bureau of Refugees, Freedmen, and Abandoned Lands.[1] The Freedmen's Bureau, despite many shortcomings, helped thousands of blacks survive by providing them with food, clothing, shelter, and medical attention. It sought also to promote economic stability among them by trying to oversee relations with their employers in order to prevent exploitation. Some of the Bureau's most important and lasting

Reprinted from The Southwestern Historical Quarterly, Vol. LXXXVI, No. 4, April 1973, pp. 397-417, with the permission of the Texas State Historical Association.

work, however, was in the field of education.

By legislative action in July 1866, Congress provided a legal basis for the schools already established by the Bureau for blacks throughout the South. The act provided:

> that the commissioner shall have power to seize, hold, use, lease, or sell all buildings and tenements, and any lands appertaining to the same, or otherwise, formerly held under color of title by the late so-called confederate states, and not heretofore disposed of by the United States, and any buildings or lands held in trust for the same by any person . . . and to use the same or appropriate the proceeds derived there from to the education of the freedpeople.[2]

To institute organized Negro education, however, the Bureau needed more than Congressional action.

Several factors militated against the concept and the reality of education for the freedmen. In the state of Texas, as well as in the rest of the South, massive Negro illiteracy contributed largely to the problem. Of the more than 180,000 Negroes in Texas in 1860 — nearly one-fourth of the total population — only 11 free blacks out of a total of 355 are recorded as having attended any school in that year, and none of the slaves are recorded as having attended. No real "public school" system existed even for whites — more than 18,000 white adults were reported as illiterate in 1860 — and attempts to institute any form of Negro education were bound to encounter widespread opposition from the white population.[3]

The white people of Texas, like those in most of the South, largely opposed Negro education because they feared education would exacerbate the difficulty of "keeping the nigger in his place." Education, many of them reasoned, would make the Negro arrogant, stubborn, and resentful of what they thought his rightful place of social and political inferiority in Southern society. Whites also were afraid that school attendance would interfere with the freedmen's work habits. Furthermore, was it not true that the Negro was "uneducable?" Had it not been "proven" that he was "inherently" an intellectual inferior to the white man? Was it not correct that Negro civilization, both in Africa and America, had failed, at least by Anglo-Saxon standards, to produce anything of cultural or technical significance? Many whites, Northerners as well as Southerners, pondered these questions and "facts" and came to the conclusion that Negro education was an impossibility.[4]

Although Texas' black population was smaller than most of the other Southern states, she was at a disadvantage in obtaining teachers because of the region's geographic position in relation to the North whence most of the teachers for black schools would come. This disadvantage only served to compound the problem of Negro education in Texas. During 1865, however, the Freedmen's Bureau, with the aid of various mission groups, stepped into this forbidding situation and opened 16 schools for Negroes. After only five years of work, characterized literally by a series of "ups and downs," the federal government terminated the Bureau's schools, but the agency left behind a legacy which included more than 20,000 literate blacks in the state and, perhaps more important, a sound foundation for Negro education in Texas.[5]

General Oliver O. Howard, Commissioner of the Freedmen's Bureau, with the advice and consent of Brevet Major General Edgar M. Gregory, commander of United States military forces in Texas,[6] and John W. Alvord, general superintendent of the Freedmen's Bureau Schools, in 1865 appointed Edwin M. Wheelock, a Northern-born author, lecturer, and chaplain, as the first superintendent of the Freedmen's Schools in Texas.[7] At the close of 1865 Wheelock reported to Superintendent Alvord that 16 schools had been established in the state — ten day and six night schools — with 1,041 pupils, many of them adults, and ten teachers. Thirty new teachers had been procured and would arrive in the state very soon. The curriculum consisted of the alphabet, simple and advanced reading, geography, simple arithmetic and "higher" mathematics, and writing. Classes usually began between eight and nine a.m. and ended at various hours beginning at noon. At least one day of each week was devoted to rhetorical exercises, singing, and Bible study. New schools were to be organized as soon as books were available. Wheelock called the schools "self-sustaining."[8]

The first comprehensive statistics issued relating to Freedmen's Bureau schools covered the period from their beginning late in 1865 to July 1, 1866. The report showed Texas leading in the number of Bureau schools with 90, although almost half of these were Sunday schools and night schools. The number of students was, however, far from impressive, for of an estimated Negro school-age population of 74,000, only 4,590 were reported in school in 1866. Yet these figures compared favorably with other Southern states, Arkansas — with a school-age population of 44,418 — had only 30 schools and 1,584 pupils, and Louisiana had just 73 schools with 3,389 pupils, even though she had a Negro school-age population of more than 185,000. Virginia and North and South Carolina with their massive Negro populations led in the number of blacks in school.[9]

During their first year of operation the Texas schools remained largely self-sustaining. Many of the freedmen were still working on the old plantations, making relatively good wages, and were able to contribute substantially to the support of the schools. The institutions did, however, receive some assistance from the North, especially in obtaining teachers. Superintendent Alvord reported that the Negroes of Texas were exhibiting high interest in the schools, as was shown by their financial support for them, and praised the management of Wheelock. The state had gained a number of experienced teachers from Louisiana, where the schools were broken up for a short time during this period. Alvord praised the Texas planters for beginning to concede that a certain amount of education must be given their laborers. He also commented favorably on the number of night schools in the state, which indicated that many adults were securing some sort of education. The superintendent closed his semi-annual report on Texas with remarks, however, that were not altogether flattering.

> These are interesting facts in regard to that far-off state; the more so, when we consider that a large portion of its white population is uncultivated, and has been disloyal and turbulent. And yet, while there are many warm friends of the Government and of the freedmen in Texas, it is the opinion of the state Commissioner that their schools could not go on at all without the presence of military authority. Especially would this be true in the rural districts.[10]

Later events were to substantiate, in some degree, the superintendent's fears. Yet the Texas report for 1865-1866 was one of the most impressive from the South, "a gain of more than four-fold over the report made on the first January last. No other state can show so rapid an increase."[11]

United States Army officers stationed in Texas were also asked to comment on the conditions of Negro education in the state. Major General David S. Stanley appeared before the Congressional Joint Committee on Reconstruction early in 1866 and was asked: "Can you tell what views the people have there as to the education of the blacks . . . ?" Stanley answered:

> No, sir; I cannot. They had no schools started when I left Texas. They were about starting [sic] a colored school at San Antonio. I heard no conversation about it, but any proposition about educating the colored people is received by a great portion of the residents there with a sneer.[12]

During the next academic year the schools slowly moved into new areas and expanded their offerings, their teaching staffs, and their facilities. Some native whites continued to give at least tacit support to the schools. Many planters offered school buildings and applied for teachers. At Gonzales, Seguin, Liberty, and other places, they made donations of land. On the other hand, opposition to the schools began to solidify, and many thoughtful persons feared that there would be outbreaks of violence, particularly in the rural areas of the southern and eastern parts of the state.[13]

General J. B. Kiddoo, General Gregory's successor as assistant commissioner of the Freedmen's Bureau of Texas, remarked in a report to Superintendent Alvord that many white people in Texas violently resented the presence of Northern white teachers, many of them women, simply because they were Yankee intruders. The general believed that while Texans of this persuasion would not themselves instruct the Negroes, they would be "willing and anxious to have them taught" by other Negroes. He accordingly acted to provide as many black teachers as possible. This project would, he hoped, serve a two-fold purpose: provide a source of emulation for the freedmen and disarm the white population of one cause of their opposition to the work of the Bureau. The problem of the Northern teachers in Negro schools, however, was still far from solved. Some of the Negroes employed to teach in various places in the state were of local background and had obtained a degree of elementary knowledge; a few were included among the "Yankee teachers" sent down by Northern missionary societies.[14]

Many of the blacks continued to support the Bureau schools through the use of their own funds. A majority of them were employed in "the great cotton-raising counties of southern Texas, between the Neches and Guadalupe rivers and on the Red River in the northeastern sections" and were still making fairly good wages.[15] But the strain of supporting the schools began to show more and more, and the Bureau and agencies from the North had to supplement the local contributions. General Kiddoo made arrangements with the American Missionary Association to furnish and pay teachers during the 1867 term at a rate of $15 per month. The Bureau's policy was to pay only what was needed after the freedmen had done their best with their own contributions. "This free-school system, as it is called, is not designed to relieve the Negroes from doing all they can themselves," a report explained, but "their means will be added to the ... public help, and thus greatly enlarge, as well as perfect [,] the general plan for their education."[16]

The good results of this cooperative financial arrangement had already been seen in Galveston and Houston where even the poorest blacks had been brought into the schools.

At this time some 50 noncommissioned Negro officers from the black regiments stationed at Brownsville attended the Bureau's local school. The general superintendent praised this venture and said that efforts would be made to induce these Negroes to remain in Texas as teachers after their discharge from military service.[17]   During an appearance before the Joint Committee on Reconstruction, Lieutenant Wilson Miller, commander of colored troops, praised the educational efforts exhibited by both military and civilian blacks. He stated:

> I have found among the Negroes, whether in or out of the army, that there has always been a disposition and a capacity to learn and improve themselves. In all our regiments whose internal arrangements I have known anything about, the most acceptable present you could make to a Negro soldier would be a spelling-book. Last winter I was instrumental in furnishing a large portion of the regiment with which I connected with schoolbooks of various kinds. I have generally found the disposition to learn stronger among the freed Negroes than among those born free.[18]

Despite some hopeful signs, however, the Texas report to the federal superintendent for the period ending in 1866 reflected the transitory nature of many of the Negro schools. Owing mainly to a cholera epidemic in the fall of 1866, the number of schools had dropped from 90 to 34, the number of teachers, from 43 to 34, of whom 23 were white and 11 black. Enrollment fell from 4,590 as of July 1, 1866, to only 1,366 as of January 1, 1867. On the favorable side was the fact that freedmen were themselves sustaining all of their schools, having actually purchased 19 of them, and had contributed more than $1,400 of the $1,780 needed to run them during the period.[19]

Of the total children enrolled as of January 1867, the average daily attendance numbered 1,059, or more than 70 percent. The students were evidently progressing about as well as could be expected academically, for 520 had moved to advanced reading classes, and 777 were taking arithmetic, although only one had reached the "higher branches" of mathematics. The intensity of the Negroes' interest in education was evidenced by the fact that some 40 schools operated throughout all the summer months of 1866. An estimated 10,000 blacks had become literate within the year.[20]

The Freedmen's Bureau announced a series of new policies in late 1866 and early 1867 to become effective beginning with the 1867-1868 school year. Military officers were given a more direct part in the operations of the schools. The agency instructed officers to make their reports on new forms designed to increase efficiency and to encourage schools and solicit donations throughout the state. (This new policy, however, probably resulted in decreased effectiveness because the new commanders were less interested in the schools and devoted less time to educational affairs.) One of General Kiddoo's orders specifically required each sub-assistant commissioner and agent in the state to make a special report to the superintendent of schools indicating the number of schools for freedmen already in operation in his district, the number of schools that could be organized ("stating explicitly their location, whether on plantations or in towns"), and what buildings might be obtained for school houses. The order also asked for the names of teachers, and whether "white or colored, etc.," what boarding places could be obtained for teachers, and any "general information on the subject of Education," in each district, "such as the views of the people with regard to Colored Schools, the wishes of the Negroes, and the necessity of military protection." The order instructed the sub-assistant commissioner "to make the organization of Freedmen's Schools an essential and paramount part of his labors," and to "organize them whenever practicable, protect them when organized, and . . . exercise *official supervision* over all schools within his jurisdiction."[21]

The Bureau also on January 1, 1867, ordered each employer to pay for the "examining and approving" of all contracts, at the rate of one dollar for the employer and 25 cents for each freedman employed. The agency assigned the money collected to the support of freedmen schools in the state. This order was revoked on January 29, 1867, however, when General Charles Griffin became assistant commissioner of the Freedmen's Bureau in Texas.[22]

Griffin set tuition rates for students attending the schools. His order required the payment of 50 cents per month "when but one pupil from a family attends school" and one dollar for all when the number exceeded two. Orphans and the children of widows were to be admitted to school privileges without charge. To become effective on March 1, 1867, the order further stated that "in addition to the income thus derived from tuition, those teachers now employed by the Bureau, and not receiving aid from any Benevolent Society" should be paid $40 per months.[23]

Disaster struck the system in the summer of 1867, when a yellow fever epidemic swept Texas, and many of the inhabitants, including some of the Northern teachers, fell victims. Superintendent Alvord related the tragic story in his report for January 1868. The schools in Texas, he said, had gone on "prosperously until about the end of June, and many of the teachers would have remained through the summer, but the fatal epidemic which prevailed brought the schools to a close in all the larger places of the State." Alvord optimistically predicted a gradual return to the former level of attendance.[24]

Despite the epidemic, 34 schools were reported for the 1867-1868 term, with a total enrollment of 1,133 students. The Negroes now owned only 11 schools and paid just $464 in tuition (in Arkansas freedmen paid $1,470; in Louisiana, $28,000).[25] Average daily attendance dropped to 688.[26] The freedmen were supporting only seven schools owned by the Bureau. The Fifth Semi-Annual Report had a bright side, however; 19 white and 13 black teachers were active; 34 students were still doing work in "higher" academic subjects; and ten whites and 14 "free" Negroes (i.e., Negroes free before the war) had entered the schools. But obviously the epidemic dealt the quest for Negro education in Texas a severe setback. To be successful the venture now needed to recover lost ground as well as gain new territory.[27]

After the death of General Griffin, a victim of the epidemic, Brevet Major General J. J. Reynolds took over as head of the Bureau's affairs in Texas. Commenting on Griffin's death, Alvord remarked: "one of the highest tributes to his memory is the record of what he actually accomplished in the educational interests of Texas." The tribute was obviously a perfunctory one, since Griffin's year in Texas was marked by declining fortunes for the freedmen's schools.[28]

Following the dismal report submitted by Texas officials for January 1868, the commissioner at Washington sent a dispatch, dated February 29, to General Reynolds asking for more detailed information with regard to the sharp decrease in school attendance. Reynolds, after repeating the story of the epidemic, adduced as other causes the exhaustion of the fund for the payment of teachers, the reduced income of the freedmen owing to the low yield of the cotton crop, and the withdrawal of many pupils for financial and other reasons. He predicted that the worst had passed and that succeeding months would show a "marked and rapid school growth."[29]

Joseph Welch, Wheelock's successor, gave his permission of the condition of the state's schools in a June message to the national offices. The schools, except those in Houston, he expected to remain open through the summer without vacation. Welch predicted that attendance would probably drop again in the fall, "as the crops are very promising and many of the pupils will be called upon to aid in gathering them." The greatest difficulty was procuring "a supply of competent teachers; as, owing to our distance from missionary societies and the disturbed and uncertain conditions of the State, I have not felt warranted in applying for teachers from the North."[30]

Welch also noted the increased proportion of black teachers, and he reported on the conditions of the schools that he had observed. He found the situation particularly distressing in East Texas — an area with a heavy concentration of Negroes. Most of the whites were ill-disposed toward black schools, and, even in the few localities where they were tolerated, the poverty of the Negroes was so great as to render it virtually impossible to secure scholars enough to support a teacher.[31]

The semi-annual school report for the period ending July 1, 1868, listed small increases in the number of both schools and teachers in Texas — 41 schools and 37 teachers (25 white and 12 black) — and a marked increase both in number of pupils and in average daily attendance. Pupils enrolled increased from 1,133 to 1,718, and average daily attendance rose from approximately 688 to 1,476. The freedmen also made new gains financially, for they now owned 17 schools and paid over $1,600 in tuition. Students doing "higher" academic work totaled 160, and while this was substantially above Arkansas's 47, it was considerably below the 237 in Mississippi — whose average daily attendance was only slightly above Texas. Agents throughout the state concluded that, "either the government or benevolent societies must continue the care of the education of the freedmen in Texas, at least until provision shall be made for them by the State."[32]

"The freedmen's schools [of Texas] do not compare favorably with those of many other Southern States," Commissioner Howard noted in his report to Congress in October 1868. Just two years previously a similar report praised the progress of Negro education in Texas and asserted that Texas was in this respect ahead of the other Southern states; but since then epidemics, crop failures, and natural disasters had caused great difficulties for the schools. Hostility displayed by many white Texans, especially as expressed through acts of violence, however, constituted the most serious and persistent problem confronting the Bureau's schools in the state. By the fall of 1868 Texas had been relegated to an inferior position in the Freedmen's Bureau venture in Negro instruction.[33]

Growing violence of the Ku Klux Klan variety occupied the major part of the reports coming from Texas in late 1868 and early 1869. This violence, coupled with intimidation and discrimination, was listed repeatedly as the major factor hampering Negro education. General Reynolds reported in the fall of 1868 that juries in Texas were beginning to exhibit flagrant examples of racial discrimination in their evaluation of testimony and in their verdicts. Ku Klux Klansmen "practiced barbarous cruelties upon the freedmen," and Negro morale was at its lowest point since the war. Reynolds said that the Klansmen were "most numerous, bold, and aggressive east of the Trinity River. ...The murder of Negroes is so common as to render it impossible to keep accurate account of them."[34]

In June 1868, Superintendent Welch reported that a new teacher was needed at Georgetown because the former teacher, a white woman, had to leave due to her inability to find a place to board. He stated that she had also "received insulting letters from some of the citizens, and was compelled to apply for personal protection to the sub-assistant commissioner." At Circleville, a few miles from Georgetown, a female black teacher had escaped personal insults but her school was burned and she was forced to return to the North.[35] From these and other reports General Howard was led to conclude that "Owing to these causes and the lack of schools the freedmen of Texas do not compare favorably with those of the States east of the Mississippi River. They have not made the same progress, and are less thrifty and provident."[36]

Reynolds drew a similar picture for Superintendent Alvord. He again cited the "rude state of society" and the "unsettled civil condition" as the principal causes of the distress. Alvord, as always, remained optimistic and predicted that Texas schools would again rise to prosperity. One of the Bureau's school inspectors, General C. H. Howard, visited the area during this period of strife, spending some time in Austin, Galveston, Houston, and several other towns. At Galveston he visited three Bureau schools and found them in "miserable houses," two of which were also used for churches. If the buildings were to be continued as schoolhouses, they would have to be made comfortable. At Houston he found a board of Negro trustees holding a lot, but waiting for Bureau aid in building, which he promised to urge.[37]

In his report of December 31, 1868, Welch acknowledged the growing violence but was otherwise more optimistic than the Washington inspector and the Bureau commissioner about the fate of Texas' schools. He noted that a new school had been recently constructed in Austin, on a lot donated by the City Council, and reported that others had also been recently built by the freedmen with Bureau assistance. Welch concluded that the schools were generally prosperous, but there was inadequate support of teachers. This report announced that the state had 57 freedmen's schools by January 1, 1869, an increase of 21. Of the 1,871 pupils in the schools, including five white students, only 32 were now doing work on the "higher" levels. The freedmen had contributed more than $2,500 for the support of their schools. Average daily attendance climbed to 1,543 (with a percentage near the regional average). Statistics suggest the picture in Texas at the close of 1868 was not as gloomy as the reports emanating from some of the national officers indicated.[38]

The abuses suffered by the Northern teachers who manned many of the Negro schools remained a grievous matter. These teachers, who came south with their aims of compassion and mission, strove to educate the blacks under almost impossible circumstances. Most of the teachers in Texas were members of the American Missionary Association of the Congregational Church, the society which carried on the first and most notable work of the several missionary associations for the training of the Negro race in the Southern states.[39]

A perusal of the teachers' letters to the Association reveals their thoughts on the hostility displayed toward them and their general observations on the unique mission, which they conducted. Miss Hattie C. Daggett wrote from Houston in 1867 that the city had several schools, which were "large and flourishing beyond our expectations." The Negroes controlled some schools, but the white-controlled ones were functioning much better, she said, and expressed optimism about the future of Negro education in Houston.[40]

Another letter, written in March 1867, from a teacher in Hempstead, site of a heavy Negro population, praised the efforts made by the local schools, but cited the stubbornness of most pupils. They were not "vicious" but were often "heedless." This teacher, however, pointed out that students' mothers had advised her that the pupils would require whipping from time to time because they "wouldn't mind without the stick" and "were used to it." Most of the Negroes learned to read with very little effort or study, but found difficulty in learning to spell correctly. In addition, she said that:

> They love their school as white children do not. As I was dismissing the primary classes at eleven, one day, a bright little fellow looked up at me and said, "I don't want to go home, I like it here . . . . School is a jolly good place, miss." They will never go home before school is dismissed unless compelled.[41]

A very perceptive letter from a Galveston teacher was published in the *American Missionary* in May 1867. She, also, praised the work being done by her city's schools. She claimed that she "never knew a class of white children with the same advantages, make more rapid progress than one of the arithmetic classes has," and remarked, proudly, on the intent interest that the Negroes exhibited in education. Four day schools and three night schools were in operation. There were 17 teachers from the Association in the area, seven of them from Wisconsin. The willingness of German families to receive Northern teachers as boarders was warmly praised by this woman: "in almost any town of importance, at least, one family can be found who will take a 'Yankee teacher' in." By contrast she understood that at Hempstead when a "rebel son" came home and found his mother had taken in a "Yankee teacher," he promptly ordered the teacher out the house. In some places where Northerners and Southerners lived in the same boarding houses, they were required to eat at separate ends of the table.[42]

Like many other observers, the Galveston teacher testified to the Negroes' interest in the Bible:

> In one cabin I found an old "uncle" who, on seeing the Bibles in my hand, wished me to give him one. I said "Uncle you can't read it." He replied: "But I can get heaps of folks to read to me, and I likes hab one to hold." I could not refuse this appeal.

In Galveston she had witnessed the death of a Negro from stabbing by three soldiers. Murder was "a common thing" in the city. As far as her own safety was concerned, she had no fears, "but it is not a very pleasant feeling to know one is alone and unprotected" in such a place.[43]

In April 1867, the Association had about 20 teachers in Texas. Galveston and Matagorda listed eight each, and Houston was next with four. Of the teachers in Galveston, two were men, two were married women, and four were single women. Matagorda had three male teachers and five women, all the women being single. Houston's four teachers were all women, only one of them married. Galveston's teachers hailed from Michigan, Wisconsin, and Illinois; Matagorda's and Houston's came from Minnesota and Ohio as well as the aforementioned states.[44]

What is to be said of the Northern teachers and their role in Negro education in Texas? Many of the Northern teachers were probably zestful idealists unsuited for the hard, practical problems posed by the attempt to educate the Negro, but the purpose for which they came south was a worthy one and most of them strove in their defined duties with determination and courage. Their accomplishments, under seemingly impossible conditions, are well attested by the fact that Negro illiteracy among the school-age population dropped from approximately 75,000 in 1860 to approximately 55,000 in 1870; and whereas only 20 Negroes attended school in 1850, more than 4,000 were enrolled by 1870.[45]

It was inevitable both immediately following the war and again after Radical Reconstruction began that Northern teachers coming into the South should face widespread and even violent opposition. Texans, like other Southerners, resented the "Yankee intruders" moving in to establish themselves as teachers and benefactors of "their" Negroes, some of whom they had held (benevolently, they thought) in human bondage for decades. Now these "outside agitators" had come to give the Negro "book learning" and to engender him in thoughts of social equality, ideas which would seriously upset the pattern of race relations that had so long existed in the area. Yet the same Southerners who so ardently opposed Northerners instructing "their" Negroes refused, for the most part, to instruct the freedmen or to lend any encouragement to efforts by local people to provide training.[46]

The social relations between white teachers, most of them women, and black students and their parents was a source of constant irritation to the white population and posed, in the latter's views, perhaps the most serious obstacle in their quest "to keep the nigger in his place." The mere fact of unmarried white women alone in classes full of blacks was enough to provoke serious resentment; but it was the visits of white teachers into Negro homes and the social courtesies extended to one another by the representatives of the two races that particularly excited the fears of many Southern whites. They looked upon this as the beginning of "social mixing" and all the horrors which they supposed it would bring.[47]

To say that the efforts of the Northern teachers were universally opposed in Texas would be, of course, an obvious untruth. As already intimated, some white Southerners not only extended courtesies to the teachers, but also welcomed them into their homes and contributed effort and money to their cause. And, while it is correct that opposition was great and often violent, particularly in the eastern and southern rural parts of the state, it is also true that some of the reports of violence were obviously exaggerations. In the central and western parts of Texas, and more particularly in urban areas where the black population was substantially less than the white, widespread encouragement and praise were given to the teachers.[48] Superintendent Welch, in his report for July 1869, commented on the growing interest and tolerance toward the Negro schools. He cited a change in the attitude of the press, which "now utters partial commendation where once it was characterized by the vilest ephithets [sic] . . . the native whites appear to favor what hitherto they have violently opposed."[49] One central Texas newspaper, after announcing a scheduled examination for black students in a Negro church remarked that "Mrs. Robinson is an industrious teacher, and her pupils will doubtless show a degree of proficiency little to be expected of them at this time."[50] A Waco paper commented in May 1869:

> We are decidedly in favor of the black people educating their children when able to do so and not neglect their duties. But we do not approve their sending their children to school from a mere hifalutin idea of making them smart and like white folks . . . [51]

An Austin paper remarked in July of that year:

> The colored school examination closed last Friday night. We hear it was well attended and that the scholars acquitted themselves well. The next day, Saturday, they had a picnic. We see that the press of the State, in many places, are noticing with more favor the colored schools, and the evidences of improvement in these schools, coming from all points, are favorable in a remarkable degree. Go it young America, Sambo is after you![52]

In mid-1869 Inspector Howard of the Bureau's Washington office again visited Texas. He expressed disappointment at not finding a good school at Galveston, despite a large Negro population: "one [was] in a colored Baptist church and the other in a dilapidated hall, owned by freedmen, but without windows, desks, or even suitable benches." Concerning the social ostracism suffered by American Missionary Association teachers, Howard said that "the wife of Judge Foyle [of the district criminal court] is the only white lady of Houston who has called upon the missionary ladies during the two years of their labor there." In Austin, where he found a good school with ample room and good attendance, he was especially impressed. He described the teachers, as well as their black assistant, as competent and called the proficiency of the pupils the best in Texas. He noted that:

> The freemen generally in Texas seem to be possessed of more property than in any other State. Several own land in Austin and Houston . . . If the fifteenth amendment becomes part of the constitution, I have no doubt all the rights of the freedmen will soon be respected in Texas as elsewhere.[53]

Superintendent Alvord's mid-year report for 1869 listed 70 schools in Texas with nearly 3,000 students (nine of them white) exhibiting an average daily attendance of more than 2,300 (the highest percentage in the South) and having 65 teachers, 24 of whom were Negroes. Nearly half of all the Negro children were paying their own fees (totaling more than $2,700) and the freedmen owned 47 of their schools. Texas schools had 247 pupils doing "higher" academic work — a percentage equal to that of the other Southern states and in excess of that of Arkansas — and was one of seven states that had not established "industrial schools." Welch also announced that contracts had been granted for the construction of new schools at Galveston, Houston, Hallettsville, Brownsville, and Walnut Creek. The state's schools were registering their greatest period of progress and barring the unforeseen, seemed destined to continue their growth.[54]

On January 1, 1869, Congress passed legislation ending the work of the Freedmen's Bureau with the exception of its school work. This was ordered to be ended in 1870. When it passed out of existence in 1871, the Bureau's educational work was remanded to the philanthropic and church societies, which had cooperated with it. Many of these institutions were gradually closed, and some were turned over to the states to be maintained by taxation. What follows constitutes, then, the last full year of the operations of the Freedmen's Bureau Schools in Texas, a year marked, as all the others had been, by progress mixed with disappointments.[55]

Superintendent Welch's final report to the Bureau told of decreased activity due to a late opening (caused by a "sickly season"), and to the "picking season" (cotton picking in which large numbers of Negroes participated), and to the "great flood of last July." He added, however, that prosperity was slowly returning to the state and to the schools. New brick structures were reported at Galveston, Houston, and Brownsville, and frame ones at Hallettsville, Walnut Creek, and Wallisville, built at a total cost of $22,393.25. Repairs had been affected at Victoria, San Antonio, Webberville, and Galveston, and both teachers and students were said to be immensely pleased with them. Welch praised the city of San Antonio for providing support for the Bureau's teachers, the "only instance of a corporation or public authority supporting a school in the State." He proposed joint Bureau-American Missionary Association action to establish high schools at Galveston and Houston.[56]

The national statistics for January 1870 showed the changing patterns of school activity throughout the South. The large contributions previously made by Louisiana's Negroes for their education dropped to more reasonable figures,[57] and South Carolina and Georgia, ranking second and third respectively in total Negro population, began to take a decided lead in the number of Negroes enrolled in schools. Texas was listed as having 46 schools with 1,733 pupils at this time. The average daily attendance remained high — 1,278 — and the schools were now staffed by 52 teachers, almost equally divided between white and Negro (27 whites, 25 blacks). Only 119 students were now doing "higher" academic work and the number of white students and "free" Negro students had dropped to five and one, respectively.[58]

L. W. Stevenson, the new state superintendent, sent the final school report for Texas to Washington in July 1870. At the time of the filing of the report, the state legislature was dealing with the issue of establishing a statewide public school system and Stevenson noted these efforts in the report.

> The State system of education is not yet developed. The first act of the senate was to reject the governor's nominee for superintendent. This was done, as is supposed, partly on account of railroad influence and partly because he was understood to be in favor of mixed schools. No doubt that strong efforts will be made to establish a *separate* system, though it will be met with strenuous opposition. The colored members only ask that nothing shall be said in the law on the subject, though they justly regard a separate system as a violation of their constitutional rights, both national and State.[59]

He also gave the condition of the state's schools for the current period, then offered a brief but perceptive review of the work of the Freedmen's Bureau in Texas education. Stevenson reported that a Mr. Sealy of Barnham was recently employed by the Bureau to teach and thus became one of the first native whites to teach in Negro schools in the state. In addition, the state school head cited a $675 contribution from the city of San Antonio for teachers' salaries, and then reviewed the work of the Bureau:

> In reviewing the work of the past five years, the extent of the field with the small means at command to do with, we are satisfied that the general results will compare favorably with any State in the South.

> The burning of schoolhouses and maltreatment of teachers, so common at the commencement of the Bureau operations, have almost entirely ceased.

The Bureau has allayed prejudice, confronted and combated all difficulties, and paved the way for the quiet and peaceful establishment of a free school system by the State.[60]

When the Bureau discontinued its operations in Texas, the state had 66 schools; 3,248 students with an average daily attendance of 2,639; and 307 students doing "higher" academic work. Sixty-three teachers (36 whites and 27 blacks) worked in the schools. The freedmen owned 43 of the schools, and paid more than $6,000 in tuition. Thus, statistically, the Texas schools were enjoying one of their better periods when the Bureau ended its operations in the state.[61]

Commissioner Howard, in his final report, however, was highly pessimistic concerning the future of education in the South, particularly Negro education. After announcing the resignation of long-time General Superintendent J. W. Alvord, Howard commented:

The people of the Southern States have been too much occupied with material interests, the restoration of industrial order and political reconstruction, to give to the subject of education the attention, which its importance demands . . . Even for the white children no adequate provision is made.[62]

While Superintendent Stevenson's evaluation of the work of the Freedmen's Bureau Schools in Texas may have been overstated, it can hardly be termed inaccurate. Upon its entrance into Texas in 1865 the Bureau found a chaotic situation with respect to Negro education, but by 1870, it had, to a considerable degree, brought order out of chaos. It reduced Negro illiteracy considerably and increased Negro school attendance from 11 in 1860 to 5,122 ten years later, and while this might not appear striking today, at the time it was revolutionary.

Historians have taken varying views, largely dependent upon whether the writers were white or black, Northerners or Southerners, "redeemers" or "revisionists," on the work of the Freedmen's Bureau and its Southern schools. A fair examination of the Texas record indicates that the Bureau performed a great service to education, and paved the way for a smooth transition to state-supported schools for the Negro race.[63]

Notes

[1] *The Statutes at Large, Treaties, and Proclamations, of the United States of America from December, 1863 to December, 1865*, Vol. XIII (Boston, 1866), pp. 507, 508.

[2] *The Statutes at Large, Treaties, and Proclamations, of the United States of America from December, 1863, to March 1867*, Vol. XIV (Boston, 1868), p. 176.

[3] U.S. Census Office, *Eighth Census of the United States: 1860. Population* (Washington, 1864), pp. 476-483; Department of Commerce, Bureau of the Census, *Negro Population, 1790-1915* (Washington, 1918), p. 57.

[4] Claude H. Nolen, *The Negro's Image in the South: The Anatomy of White Supremacy* (Lexington, 1967), pp. 104-109; Alton Hornsby, Jr. (ed.). *In the Cage: Eyewitness Accounts of the Freed Negro in Southern Society, 1877-1929* (Chicago, 1971), pp. 10-16.

[5] Bureau of the Census, *Negro Population, 1790-1915*, p. 44.

[6] Gregory, the Bureau's assistant commissioner for Texas, had been in the state since September 1865. He remained as assistant commissioner until March 1866. Although Gregory attacked his job with sincerity and industriousness, the task seemed at times too much for him. When he left his post the Bureau affairs in the state were badly in need of reorganization. Gregory, "a radical Abolitionist," was also accused of being "too prejudiced in favor of the Negro." See John A. Carpenter, *Sword and Olive Branch: Oliver Otis Howard* (Pittsburgh, 1964), p. 98; William S. McFeely, *Yankee Stepfather: General O. O. Howard and the Freedmen* (New Haven, 1968), pp. 68-70; and Claude Elliott, "The Freedmen's Bureau in Texas," *Southwestern Historical Quarterly*, LVI (July 1952), pp. 2, 3, 10, 11. The first quote in this note is from McFeely, *Yankee Stepfather*, p. 68; the second quote is from Carpenter, *Sword and Olive Branch*, p. 98.

[7] Wheelock, a lieutenant with the United States colored troops, came to Austin just after the Civil War. He was appointed to the Board of Education for Freedmen in March 1864, and subsequently served as secretary. He wrote *The Human Soul* (Boston, 1858); "The New Birthday of the Soul," *The New Church Independent, and Monthly Review*, XXIV (February 1876), pp. 4-59 and other works. In the early 1890s Wheelock served as minister of the Unitarian Church in Austin. He became involved in a factional struggle between Congregationalists and Unitarians, which prompted demands for his dismissal as superintendent in Texas. An American Missionary Association agent in the state accused Wheelock of showing a lack of enthusiasm in his work and criticized him for being a Unitarian, who would necessarily, in the view of the Congregationalist, be unfit for his job. All sorts of charges and countercharges developed. Wheelock was called a "profane, indolent, scoffing" preacher whose record was "one continuous narrative of malfeasance

and misfeasance." The matter eventually reached the attention of General Howard who, in cooperation with Assistant Commissioner Charles Griffin in Texas, managed to settle the dispute amicably. Walter Prescott Webb and H. Bailey Carroll (eds.), *The Handbook of Texas*, (2 vols.; Austin, 1952), II, p. 892; Bell Irvin Wiley, *Southern Negroes 1861-1865* (New York, 1938), p. 266; Carpenter, *Sword and Olive Branch*, p. 163, 164; Elliott, "The Freedmen's Bureau in Texas," p. 7. The quotes are from Carpenter, *Sword and Olive Branch*, p. 163.

[8] U.S. Bureau of Refugees, Freedmen and Abandoned Lands, *First Semi-Annual Report on Schools for Freedom, January, 1866* (Washington, 1867), p. 11; *Ibid., Seventh Semi-Annual Report on Schools for Freedmen, January 1, 1869* (Washington, 1869), p. 37; Elliott "The Freedmen's Bureau in Texas," p. 7, 8. Hereafter all references to the Freedmen reports, after the first reference, will be cited as Freedmen's Bureau, --- *Semi-Annual Report on Schools.*

[9] U.S. Bureau of Refugees, Freedmen and Abandoned Lands, *Second Semi-Annual Report on Schools for Freedmen, July 1, 1866* (Washington, 1867), p. 3; Elliott, "The Freedmen's Bureau in Texas," pp. 8-10.

[10] Freedmen's Bureau, *Second Semi-Annual Report on Schools*, pp. 15, 16.

[11] *Ibid.*, p. 16.

[12] Report of the Joint Committee on Reconstruction," *House Reports, 39th Cong., lst Sess.* (Serial 1273), H.R. No. 1, Part 4, p. 40.

[13] U.S. Bureau of Refugees, Freedmen, and Abandoned Lands, *Third Semi-Annual Report on Schools for Freedmen, January 1, 1867* (Washington, 1867), p. 27.

[14] *Ibid.*

[15] Report of the Secretary of War," *House Executive Documents;* 40th Cong. 2nd Sess. (Serial 1324), Doc. No. 1, p. 683.

[16] Freedmen's Bureau, *Third Semi-Annual Report on Schools*, p. 27; Elliott, "The Freedmen's Bureau in Texas," p. 11-13. Quote is from the *Third Semi-Annual Report.*

[17] Freedmen's Bureau, *Third Semi-Annual Report on Schools*, p. 27.

[18] "Report of the Joint Committee on Reconstruction," p. 45.

[19] Freedmen's Bureau, *Third Semi-Annual Report on Schools*, p. 28.

[20] *Ibid.*

[21] U.S. Bureau of Refugees, Freedmen, and Abandoned Lands, *Circular, No. 20,* August 31, 1866 (Galveston, 1866), p. 1. For views of the internal affairs of the Freedmen's Bureau see George R. Bentley, *A History of the Freedmen's Bureau* (Philadelphia, 1955); Carpenter, *Sword and Olive Branch*; McFeely, *Yankee Stepfather*; and John and LaWanda Cox, "General O. O. Howard and the 'Misrepresented Bureau,'" *Journal of Southern History*, XIX (November 1953), pp. 427-456. For the workings of the Bureau in Texas, see Elliott, "The Freedmen's Bureau in Texas," pp. 1-24. For Freedmen's Bureau educational activities in other Southern states see U.S. Bureau in Alabama," *Journal of Southern History*, XIV (February 1948), pp. 49-92; Ira V. Brown,

"Lyman Abbott and Freedmen's Aid, 1865-1869," *Journal of Southern History*, XV (February 1949), pp. 22-38; Luther P. Jackson, "The Educational Efforts of the Freedmen's Bureau and Freemen's Aid Societies in South Carolina, 1862-1872," *Journal of Negro History*, VIII (January 1923), pp. 1-40; Martin Abbott, "The Freedmen's Bureau and Negro Schooling in South Carolina," *South Carolina Historical Magazine*, LVII (April 1956), pp. 65-81; William T. Alderson, Jr., "The Freedmen's Bureau and Negro Education in Virginia," *North Carolina Historical Review*, XXIX (January 1952), pp. 64-90; John Cornelius Engelsman, "The Freedmen's Bureau in Louisiana," *Louisiana Historical Quarterly*, XXXII (January 1949), pp. 145-224; and Henry Lee Swint (ed.), "Reports from Educational Agents of the Freemen's Bureau in Tennessee, 1865-1870," *Tennessee Historical Quarterly*, I (March 1942), pp. 50-80. Quotes are from U.S. Bureau of Refugees, Freedmen and Abandoned Lands, *Circular, No. 20*.

[22] U.S. Bureau of Refugees, Freedmen and Abandoned Lands, *General Orders, No. 1*, January 1, 1867 (Galveston, 1867), p. 1; *Ibid.*, *General Orders, No. 3*, January 29, 1867 (Galveston, 1867), p. 1.

[23] U.S. Bureau of Refugees, Freedmen and Abandoned Lands, *Circular, No. 2*, February 7, 1867 (Galveston, 1867), p. 1.

[24] U.S. Bureau of Refugees, Freedmen and Abandoned Lands, *Fifth Semi-Annual Report on Schools for Freedmen, January 1, 1868* (Washington, 1868), p. 38.

[25] The heavy contribution attributed to freedmen in Louisiana was probably due to the inclusion of many of the wealthy Creoles in the Negro group.

[26] This was the lowest attendance of any state. Arkansas was next with an average attendance of 771, Louisiana had an average attendance of 6,156 and South Carolina 5,345. Of course, both of these states had substantially larger Negro population than Texas. See Freedmen's Bureau, *Fifth Semi-Annual Report on Schools*, pp. 12, 13.

[27] Freedmen's Bureau, *Fifth Semi-Annual Report on Schools*, pp. 3, 12. The Bureau's school division estimated that only one of ten Negroes of school-age in Texas was in school in 1868. This was the lowest enrollment of any state with the exception of Mississippi which had one out of 15 enrolled. The District of Columbia area led with three out of seven and Louisiana had one out of seven. *Ibid.*, p. 47.

[28] Freedmen's Bureau, *Fifth Semi-Annual Report on Schools*, p. 38.

[29] U.S. Bureau of Refugees, Freedmen and Abandoned Lands, *Sixth Semi-Annual Report on Schools for Freedmen, July 1, 1868* (Washington, 1868), p. 41.

[30] *Ibid.*, p. 42.

[31] *Ibid.*

[32] Freedmen's Bureau, *Fifth Semi-Annual Report on Schools*, p. 3; *Ibid.*, *Sixth Semi-Annual Report on Schools*, pp. 7-43. Quote is from *Sixth Semi-*

Annual Report, p. 43. There is no indication as to whether or not the white children attended school with blacks. However, the inference seems to be that there was "token integration" of these schools.

[33] "Report of the Secretary of War," *House Executive Documents*, 40th Cong., 3rd Sess. (Serial 1367), Doc. No. 1, Part 1, p. 1,053.

[34] "Report of the Joint Select Committee to Inquire into the Condition of Affairs in the Late Insurrectionary States," *House Reports*, 42nd Cong., lst Sess. (Serial 1529), H.R. No. 22, Part 1, p. 19; Elliott, "The Freedmen's Bureau in Texas," p. 16; McFeely, *Yankee Stepfather*, p. 69; Carpenter, *Sword and Olive Branch*, p. 128.

[35] Freedmen's Bureau, *Sixth Semi-Annual Report on Schools*, p. 42.

[36] "Report of the Secretary of War," *House Executive Documents*, 40th Cong., 3rd Sess. (Serial 1367), Doc. No. 1, Part 1, p. 1,053.

[37] Freedmen's Bureau, *Seventh Semi-Annual Report on Schools*, pp. 35, 36.

[38] *Ibid.*, p. 30. None of the figures should be taken as absolutely correct because of some inefficiency in reporting by local officials to the Bureau.

[39] H. Paul Douglass, *Christian Reconstruction in the South*, (Boston, 1909), p. 209.

[40] Hattie C. Daggett to Editor, (n.d.), *The American Missionary*, X (March 1867), p. 57.

[41] L. S. D. to J. R. Shipherd, March 1867, *Ibid.* (June, 1867), p. 137.

[42] Unidentified teacher to Editor, March 29, 1867, *Ibid.* (May 1867), pp. 103-105. See Douglass, *Christian Reconstruction in the South*, and Henry Lee Swint, *The Northern Teacher in the South, 1862-1870* (Nashville, 1941), for more detailed accounts of the role of the Northern teachers during Reconstruction.

[43] *American Missionary,* X (May, 1867), p. 103.

[44] *Ibid.*

[45] U.S. Census Office, *Seventh Census of the United States: 1850* (Washington, 1853), p. 511; *Ibid., Eighth Census of the United States: 1870. Population* (Washington, 1872), pp. 394-397.

[46] Nolen, *The Negro's Image in the South*, 104-109.

[47] *Ibid.*

[48] Bexar County (San Antonio) had only 2,303 Negroes as compared with more than 13,000 whites in 1870; Harris County (Houston) had only 2,109 Negroes as compared with nearly 11,000 whites; and Travis County (Austin) registered some 4,600 Negroes along with some 8,500 whites in the same year. Washington County (in the southeastern part of the state) numbered more than 12,000 blacks to its 10,000 whites, and Fort Bend County (also in the same area) had more than 5,000 blacks and only 1,604 whites. U.S. Census Office, *Ninth Census of the United States: 1870, Population*, pp. 394-397.

[49] U.S. Bureau of Refugees, Freedmen and Abandoned Lands, *Eighth Semi-Annual Report on Schools of Freedmen, July 1, 1869* (Washington, 1869), p. 52.

[50] Austin *Record*, July 2, 1869. The same paper had declared in a June 18, 1869 editorial: "While the grown up men and women of the race do not expect, as a general thing, to acquire much in the way of book information, they are exhibiting a commendable spirit of rivalry in the education of their children. Considering their means, they are doing much in the matter of common school education and religious training. They are doing well, and deserve encouragement."

[51] Quoted in Freedmen's Bureau, *Eighth Semi-Annual Report on Schools*, p. 54.

[52] Austin *Record*, July 9, 1869.

[53] Freedmen's Bureau, *Eighth Semi-Annual Report on Schools*, pp. 55, 56.

[54] *Ibid.*, pp. 6, 7, 54.

[55] *The Statutes at Large, Treaties, and Proclamations of the United States of America from December 1867, to March 1869,* Vol. XV (Boston, 1869), pp. 193, 194; see also Charles William Dabney, *Universal Education in the South* (2 vols.; Chapel Hill, 1936), I.

[56] U.S. Bureau of Refugees, Freedmen and Abandoned Lands, *Ninth Semi-Annual Report on Schools for Freedmen, January 1, 1870* (Washington, 1870), pp. 43, 44.

[57] Louisiana's total dropped because since July 1, 1869, part of her territory was combined with northeastern Texas to form a new Bureau district. Probably the dropped rate was also affected by a distinction in classification between Negroes and Creoles and by a better system of evaluating and reporting parish returns.

[58] Freedmen's Bureau, *Ninth Semi-Annual Report on Schools*, p. 7.

[59] U.S. Bureau of Refugees, Freedmen and Abandoned Lands, *Tenth Semi-Annual Report on Schools for Freedmen, July 1, 1870* (Washington, 1870), p. 37.

[60] *Ibid.*, p. 38.

[61] *Ibid.*, 7. By July 1870, Arkansas had only 23 schools; Louisiana's total had dropped to 61, and Mississippi had 65.

[62] "Report of the Secretary of War," *House Executive Documents,* 41st Cong. 3rd Sess. (Serial 1446), Doc. No. 1, Part 2, p. 317.

[63] Brown, "Lyman Abbott and Freedmen's Aid, 1865-1869," pp. 36, 37; Elliott, "The Freedmen's Bureau in Texas," p. 24.

Chapter 9
The "Colored Branch University" Issue in Texas—Prelude to *Sweatt vs. Painter*

The Texas Constitution of 1876 provided that:

> The Legislature shall also, when deemed practicable establish and provide for the maintenance of a College or Branch University for the instruction of the colored youths of the State, to be located by a vote of the people; provided, that no tax shall be levied, and no money appropriated, out of the general revenue, either for this purpose or for the establishment, and erection of the buildings of the University of Texas.[1]

In establishing a college for blacks as well as for a University of Texas or a "university of the first class," the lawmakers probably sought to avoid the problem, which occurred in the state of South Carolina. In that state, the failure to make provisions for the separate higher education of blacks led to the integration of the University of South Carolina and the subsequent withdrawal of most of the white students and faculty members.

In spite of the Texas Constitutional requirement, however, for many years black and white citizens of the state had difficulty in determining just how the constitutional provision was to be

Reprinted from The Journal of Negro History, XLI, No. 1, 1976, pp. 51-60, with the permission of The Journal of Negro History

implemented. Some contended that the establishment of Prairie View College in 1878 had fulfilled the constitutional requirement.[2] Others held that Prairie View was only a "normal school" or, at best, an A & M College, and that the constitutional convention had intended that the black youths should have a "classical" university similar to the University of Texas. Some advocated the expansion of Prairie View so as to include a "classical division," while still others insisted that a new, separate university be constructed, like the University of Texas, at Austin. The controversy over the issue was to be one of the most heated in Texas educational and political history.

According to the Constitution of 1876, the "colored university" was to be located by "vote of the people." On May 5, 1982, the 17th Legislature approved a measure calling for the election. The act required that all localities put in nomination for the location of the colored branch of the State University shall be forwarded to the Governor at least 40 days before the holding of said election, and the Governor shall embrace in his proclamation ordering said election the names of said localities, provided that any citizens may vote for any locality not named in said proclamation.[3] The locality receiving the largest number of votes was to be selected as the location of "the branch of the University for the instruction of the colored youth of the State."[4] The election was held on November 7, 1882. Austin received 28,329 votes for the location of the branch university; Houston came in second with 14,000 votes. On December 19, Secretary of State T. H. Bowman declared that Austin had been selected "as the location of the State University for the instruction of colored youth."[5] However, no immediate action was taken to implement the constitutional provision, even after the election results were declared.

In 1884 the Republican Party renewed the agitation for the "colored branch university." In a resolution adopted at their annual convention in Dallas, the Texas Republicans declared they favored not only "the early completion of the University of Texas, but also of its colored branch."[6] By 1892, however, even though the University of Texas at Austin was open, construction had not begun on the school for black youths. So again, in 1892, the Republicans at Fort Worth demanded "that the legislature comply with the constitutional requirement and establish a branch of the State University for the colored people." Again, at Dallas two years later, the Republican platform favored "equal school accommodations for all races" and urged the state to "as early as practicable, take the necessary steps toward instituting the colored branch of the University, thus putting into effect the expressed will of the people."[7] The Democratic controlled legislature still made no effort to appropriate funds for the erection of the black university. The growing popularity of Prairie View was one of the factors which influenced the procrastination of the state's leaders. By 1896, things were going so well there that the President of the Board of Directors, Major Rose, could report that "this institution is gradually becoming more popular wherever its great advantages and usefulness are known." One indication of Prairie View's increasing popularity was the appearance of Booker T. Washington as commencement speaker in 1897.[8]

The most vocal group agitating for a separate branch university for blacks was the Colored State Teachers Association. Beginning in the spring of 1896, the black teachers organized a propaganda campaign aimed at achieving the black college. The Negro section of the *Texas School Journal* relayed the appeals for action across the state. In an editorial in May the black education leaders said:

> Now is the time to strike for a colored university. The iron is heating — the political iron — it will soon be red hot. We must prepare to strike. Every teacher who reads this is urged to get to work at once. Call your people together, organize a University club and send the name of the officers to the secretary of the central committee at Austin . . . . The entire state must be organized. Only by organized effort can we hope to accomplish our purpose. Every teacher and preacher in the State must see the importance and necessity of this school.

According to the editorial writer, "the best and ablest men of the race in Texas" were committed to the "colored university." Blacks were encouraged to draw up and circulate petitions to the legislature, asking for the establishment of the school. J. D. Pettigrew, an Austin minister, was to receive the petitions. The blacks were also urged to press all candidates for State Senator and State Representative, "of whatever party, who expects the support of Negro votes, to pledge that if elected he will support a bill for the establishment of a branch university for colored youth."[9]

Pressure from black leaders continued throughout the summer. In the editorial, June 1896, a Negro educator declared:

> The wise and patriotic men of the Constitutional Convention of 1876 thought the time would come when the colored youth would need higher training. These statesmen present a marvelous contrast to a few upstarts of today, who claim that the Negro needs no such training. According to these little fellows there is no need of well-

educated teachers, ministers and doctors in our race; no need of any literary talent of any higher order. If some Negroes had their way, all the schools would be closed and the Negro doomed to be an ignorant serf.[10]

Later, before the annual black teachers convention held at Corsicana in July 1896, President M. H. Broyles of the state association publicly expressed himself in favor of the "branch university for colored youth."[11]

Meanwhile, the state's white educational and political leaders, responding to the black pressure, were busily advocating the expansion of Prairie View as the best solution to the "colored university" issue. Governor Charles A. Culberson and Superintendent of Public Instruction James M. Carlisle said in a joint statement in the late summer of 1896 that Prairie View "had done more than any other single institution in the state for the colored schools and the colored people of Texas." They expressed the hope that "at least twice 50,000 acres of public lands" would be set aside for the proposed enlargement of the school and that an "additional number of scholarships" would also be provided.[12] The Democratic State Convention meeting at Fort Worth in August 1896, pledged to all races and classes "equal protection in the enjoyment of life, liberty, and the pursuit of happiness." The expansion of Prairie View would be one means of assuring these rights to blacks. To that end the party favored "setting apart immediately for the purpose 50,000 acres of the unappropriated public domain." The party suggested the addition of "industrial features" at the school and its gradual conversion into "a university for the colored people."[13]

The Prairie View Board of Directors in their report for 1896 called for the further development of Prairie View because they were confident that it would become the "colored branch university." The conversion of Prairie View, they felt, could be done "at comparatively little expense to the state by the addition of a few buildings and teachers, and by this means the colored race could obtain both an industrial and classical education. The former, all will admit, would be of untold advantage in connection with higher education, especially for the negro race." The directors said they were informed that the blacks throughout the state were practically unanimous in favor of "this university plan" and that it "would be a great saving to the State, and expedite the establishment of the colored university which has so long been asked for by the negro race."[14]

The Republicans, in the 1896 election year repeated their

insistence "that laws should be speedily enacted extending to our colored youths the opportunities of a university education."[15] Thus, the "colored university" question had become a major topic in the educational and political arenas of the state, engaging the attention of both political parties and educators of both races.

The Prairie View directors in their report for 1896 obviously exaggerated the extent of black commitment to the Prairie View expansion plan, for many black educators viewed with skepticism the suggestion, now sometimes, indeed, coming from among their own ranks, that Prairie View be made the Negro "branch university." E. L. Blackshear of Prairie View and H. A. Maxwell of Austin, writing in the October 1896 issue of the *School Journal*, asked the black teachers of Texas for clarification of their stand on "the Colored State University question." Blackshear and Maxwell were both disturbed by a portion of President Broyles' annual address before the State Colored Teachers Association. While Broyles had come out in favor of the black branch university, he had recommended that, for the present, blacks should request the A & M College board of directors to add some of the college branches or courses to Prairie View, and let it be a nucleus of a university in embryo. But Blackshear and Maxwell were of the opinion that if this were done "it would be the last of the 'University'; but, of course, we do not dare express this as the general opinion." Instead, they advocated striking "the iron" and keeping "it hot until we accomplish our purpose." "Their view was not to be interpreted as in any way hostile to Prairie View; as Texas teachers we could not be. We believe it to be one of inestimable value to Texas as a normal school, but we believe that we should have a university on a broader scale equipped with *first class* facilities, such as the grand old Texas is well able to afford her citizens of color. Texas is the richest state in this grand southland, and out of her abundant resources can easily afford to help the struggling negro in his attempt to gain a higher education."[16] Later Blackshear called for a conference of the state's educators to meet in Hempstead at the end of the year to discuss the problem.

In the black community, the movement for a separate branch university, other than Prairie View, received substantial impetus when Robert L. Smith, one of the wealthiest and most influential blacks in Texas, came out in favor of a new school for blacks. Smith was born in Charleston, South Carolina in 1861. He graduated from Atlanta University, and was for a short time afterwards editor of a paper in Charleston. In 1895 he was elected a member of the Texas legislature from Colorado County. He was a founder of the Farmers'

Improvement Association, which by 1912 owned more than 75,000 acres of land worth considerably over $1,000,000. In 1906 the association, under Smith, had founded a school at Ladonia, and in 1911 organized a bank at Waco. Smith was also a trustee of the Jeanes Fund[17] and an aide to Booker T. Washington.[18] At the opening of the 25th Texas Legislature in 1896, Representative Smith introduced a bill to appropriate 50,000 or more acres of the public domain for the establishment of the black state university at Austin. Smith's action was immediately applauded by black leaders, who took the occasion to chide those still insisting on Prairie View as the location for the school. They trusted that:

> the State Legislature will have judgment enough (and we believe it will) to ignore this, and locate the University at Austin where the popular vote has placed it. We think the people's interest ought to be served and not those of a few select political teachers, and the people [want] the University at Austin. It seems strange that some, who a year ago, were opposed to Prairie View as a place for its location, now think it just the place. We suppose they are now looking from a different direction."[19]

The lawmakers responded favorably to Smith's bill and enacted a law authorizing the Governor and the Commissioner of the General Land Office to have surveyed 50,000 acres to "be set apart and constitute a permanent endowment for a branch university for the colored people." The school was to be under the control of the Board of Regents for the University of Texas, "and held by the board in trust for the benefit of the said branch university for the colored people."[20]

The legislative action produced elation among black educators throughout the state. The editors of the Negro section of the *School Journal* stated that:

> The teachers of Texas and the friends of education, as well as the colored citizens of the State, owe a debt of gratitude to the 25th Legislature, for its generosity in appropriating 50,000 acres of the public domain toward the establishment and maintenance of a branch university for the colored race. All honor to the Solons, especially to the entire senate, who championed and favored our cause. We hope to see the matter pushed forward with all possible energy.[21]

The desires of the black educators and the good intentions of the Legislature were, however, handed a decisive set-back when the Texas Supreme Court in *Hogue vs. Baker*[22] nullified the action by prohibiting

Land Commissioner A. C. Baker from appropriating any more land for educational purposes. The court declared that the "one-half of the public domain appropriated for free school purposes had been so appropriated," and that the remaining half was not available for such purposes.

Yet the spirit of the black educators and their law-making friends remained undaunted. The legislators, after the Baker decision, reaffirmed their intention to act "in good faith." They adopted a concurrent resolution explicitly stating their intent to circumvent the court's ruling and to give the blacks their university,

> Whereas, the people of Texas are pledged by Constitutional provision to establish a university for the colored race whenever it is practicable; and
> Whereas, the democratic [sic] party has acknowledged the necessity for said university through its platform adopted at Fort Worth, 1896: and Whereas, the democratic [sic] party in the 25th Legislature carried out in good faith the demands of said Fort Worth platform by appropriating and setting apart 100,000 [actually 50,000] acres of the public domain for the establishment of said university for the colored race; and Whereas, the Supreme Court of Texas has nullified the action of the Legislature . . . by its decision in declaring that Texas had no public domain unappropriated; and . . .
> Whereas, the Legislature is prohibited by the Constitution (Article 7, Sec. 4) from levying any tax or making any appropriation out of the General revenue to establish said university; therefore be it resolved by the House of Representatives, the Senate concurring, that it is the duty of the state, as well as the expressed will of the democratic [sic] party, to faithfully carry our this obligation, which was voluntarily taken by our party in convention assembled.
> Resolved further, that as soon as the commission appointed to investigate and ascertain the exact status of the public domain and of the public free School lands of Texas shall make its report to the Governor [stating] the amount of said land belonging to the state, that steps shall he taken to establish said university for the colored race, either by appropriating public domain, if there is any public domain, or by appropriating lands regained to the state from railway corporations that have refused to comply with their charter grants or to obey the law of Texas.[23]

While the legislators were trying to figure a way to give the blacks their state university, the blacks themselves were still arguing about its location and character. As time passed, more and more influential black educators switched to the so-called Prairie View expansion plan. One black educator from Brenham, H. M. Tarver, stated emphatically that he opposed the establishment of any "colored university," unless it was an expanded Prairie View. E. L. Blackshear, Principal of Prairie View since 1985,[24] who had long been in the camp of the militant group agitating for a separate school at Austin, then announced that he heartily agreed "with the remarks," made by Professor Tarver. He claimed to believe that the "colored youth of Texas will be more benefited [sic] by the additional facilities which will be afforded by the [Prairie View expansion] plan . . . ."[25] The statements of Tarver, who had headed the committee of the State Colored Teachers Association campaigning for a separate university, and of Blackshear took most of the steam out of the blacks' drive for a separate school at Austin. At the same time, M. H. Broyles, a Prairie View mathematics teacher and one-time head of the black teachers' association, expressed the blacks' appreciation for the efforts of the Legislature to provide a black university, despite the unfavorable court ruling. He said the action showed that the "Democratic Party, in pledging the establishment of a branch university for colored youths in 1896 and in appropriating 100,000 [sic] acres of land during the session of the 25th Legislature, acted in good faith."[26]

Thus, with an unfavorable court decision blocking action and with growing Negro acquiescence in the so-called Prairie View expansion plan, the legislature set out to make Prairie View a "classical college." First in 1897, the state moved to increase the number of students eligible for admittance to Prairie View and to improve the administrative machinery of the school. The civil statutes relating to Prairie View were revised so that the school's board of directors could admit one student from each senatorial district appointed by the Senator representing that district, and one student from each representative district appointed by the legislator representing the district. The students could not be less than 16 years of age at the time of their admission. Under the new laws, Prairie View, heretofore a normal school or a school for black teachers was to be called and known as the "Prairie View State Normal and Industrial College." The Prairie View Board of Directors was reorganized so as to make it more independent of the Texas A & M board. It was given broad powers to appoint administrative officers and faculty members, to discipline faculty and students, and to take other appropriate action for the "benefit of the people of the State and the officers, teachers, students and employees of said school."[27]

Prairie View's Principal E. L. Blackshear praised the legislative action of 1897 and said it was "evidence of the growing interest taken by the State of Texas in the education of the negro population." The legislature then moved, in 1901, to make available at Prairie View work appropriate to a bonafide "classical" college. A sum of $2,500 was set apart for the first year and $1,800 for the second year for the "inauguration and maintenance of a four year college course of classical and scientific studies." Graduates of the normal course were to be admitted to the new program without examination, others were to be admitted "after having passed a satisfactory examination in the branches comprised in the normal course." The completion of the new program would entitle the holder of the diploma "without other or further examination to teach in any of the colored public free schools of the state." The faculty and staff were substantially increased and some evidences of academic quality slowly appeared.[28]

It was 1915 before the legislature took any new action on the black university question. During that year, the leaders sought through constitutional amendment to get around the prohibition against levying any tax or making any appropriation of "general revenues to establish or maintain the University of Texas or its branches," in order to assure new funds for black higher education. The proposed amendment provided for the allocation to the A & M College of Texas "600,800 acres of land from that set apart to the University Permanent Fund." Of this amount, 150,000 acres was to be allotted to Prairie View. The amendment was defeated at the polls on July 24, 1915 by a vote of 81,658 to 50,318. Four years later on March 18, 1919, House Joint Resolution 29 proposed an amendment to those sections of the state constitution dividing the "university Permanent Fund between the University and A & M [Texas A & M College] on a two to one basis." The proposal would have required the A & M board to apportion to Prairie View an equitable part of A & M's one-third. The amendment was defeated by a vote of 36,560 to 76,422.[29]

Although the voters would not approve the allotment of extensive new acreage for Prairie View expansion or new sources of revenue, the annual appropriations for the school climbed steadily. Whereas Prairie View received $6,000 under the first state grant in 1879, annual appropriations had by 1915 reached $136,000 — only Texas A & M with $469,200 and the University of Texas with $711,682 received larger amounts from the state. Two normal schools for whites, Sam Houston and North Texas, received $75,800 and $74,800 respectively.[30] Prairie View also benefited from the Smith-Hughes Act, Passed by Congress in 1917. A four-year course of agricultural education was established, and a home economics department was added.[31]

In the period between World War I and World War II, Prairie View continued to grow, doubling the size of its physical plant by adding six buildings at a cost of more than one-half million dollars and more than doubling its enrollment."

As the Second World War closed, two important developments occurred in the history of Negro higher education in Texas; one of these, in fact, had profound consequences for the entire nation. In 1945 Prairie View was made a "University." The university could offer, as the need arose, all courses offered at the University of Texas. Many state leaders viewed the granting of "university" status to Prairie View as a temporary arrangement until such time as a permanent black university could be "legally" established. Nevertheless, by the close of the Second World War, Prairie View remained the only state-supported institution for the higher education of blacks in Texas.[33]

In that same year, 1945, a Houston postal clerk, with a "yen to become a lawyer," applied for admission to the University of Texas Law School. Heman Marion Sweatt wanted to begin study at the opening of the 1946 term. When his application was denied, he filed a suit in the District Court of Travis County at Austin on May 16, 1946 to compel his admission. The NAACP attorneys representing Sweatt sought a writ of mandamus on the ground that the University of Texas Law School was the only such school maintained by the state and Sweatt, therefore, had a right to enter. In June, the state court ruled that Sweatt was entitled to relief under the equal protection clause of the 14th Amendment to the United States Constitution. The trial court, however, postponed the effective date of its order for six months so that the state might have time to supply facilities for Sweatt which were substantially equal to those offered white students at the University of Texas Law School.[34]

State officials moved quickly in a desperate effort to thwart the desegregation of the University of Texas. When the Sweatt trial reopened in December 1946 the state's attorney was prepared to present minutes of meetings of the Board of Regents of the Texas A & M College system that indicated that a law school for blacks, was to be established at Houston in February 1947. The new school would be a part of the Texas A & M system and would be supervised by officials at Prairie View.[35]

In January 1947 a new state administration took over at Austin. Following the inauguration of the new governor, Beauford Jestor, a Corsicana attorney, the legislature convened to hear the administration's plans for dealing with the law school crisis. The immediate problem was to get the law school opened in line with the promise the officials had made to the court. The February deadline was eased by the fact that Sweatt's attorneys had appealed the trial court's acceptance of the arrangements proposed by state officials. The state administration asked the legislature to approve the establishment of a completely separate university for blacks, offering instruction in all the branches of learning provided at the University of Texas. The plan also called for the immediate establishment of a separate law school which would eventually become a part of the new black university. The Texas Constitution, it will be recalled, prohibited taxing or appropriation of funds out of the general revenue for the establishment of such schools. A proposed constitutional amendment which would have provided additional funds for the support of black higher education had been defeated by the voters in 1919. These factors, plus the State Supreme Court's adverse decision in *Hogue vs. Baker* in 1897, figured prominently in the state's failure to provide a black university up to this time. Fortunately, the state had accrued an enormous balance in its surplus fund, an amount in excess of $120 million. The state administration was in a position to suggest that funds be appropriated from the surplus to establish the black university.[36]

While debating the administration's proposals to establish the new black university, the legislature, obviously in anticipation of favorable action, voted on February 27, 1947 to change the name of Prairie View University to Prairie View Agricultural and Mechanical College of Texas. During the debate in the Texas Senate, several senators announced opposition to the entire black university plan. They argued that any money spent on the venture would be wasteful since there was an ultimate possibility that the case might go up to the Supreme Court and, in view of the rulings in *Missouri ex rel Gaines*, 1938 , and *Sipuel vs. Oklahoma*, 1947, Sweatt might win. They felt that the rather enormous amount of money required to establish a separate university could be used to a better advantage on some of the state's internal improvement projects.[37] Another group, students at the University of Texas opposed the administration's proposals, insisting, instead, that Sweatt had a legal and moral right to attend the University at Austin.[38]

The demonstrating students and the frugal senators were an apparent minority, however, because the legislature approved the establishment of the separate black university on March 3, 1947. The new institution was to be known as the Texas State University for Negroes (later Texas Southern University). An initial appropriation of three million dollars was granted to execute the plans. Despite the results of the election of 1882, which had approved Austin as the site of any black university, the legislature chose Houston as the location of the new institution.[39] Houston was chosen because of its large black population and the fact that officials of teetering Houston College for Negroes, a municipal college, agreed to cede the land, buildings and equipment of the institution to the state for use as a nucleus for the new black university. This cession included 53 acres of land, two permanent buildings, and several temporary structures. The state authorized the immediate construction of an additional building at a cost of two million dollars.[40]

Meanwhile, in Austin, a three-room building was leased to house the temporary black law school and an appropriation of $100,000 was made for the purchase of a law library. Pending the arrival of the books, the students were granted permission to use the state library in the capitol building, since the black law school was located near the capitol. Instruction was to be provided by teachers from the University of Texas law school.[41]

In 1947, black Texans, then, were to have "separate-but-equal" higher educational facilities for the first time — an A & M College, like Texas A & M at College Station, and a "classical" university with a law school, like the University of Texas at Austin. Ironically, the state had managed to establish the "branch university for colored youth" in a matter of a few months, having been unable to do so for the previous 70 years.

This long delay, in the end, would prove to be tragic for the supporters of racially segregated schools in Texas. Heman Sweatt refused to attend the three-room make-shift law school in Austin on the grounds that it was not equal to that at the University of Texas. Although the state courts sided with the University of Texas, Sweatt took his plea to the United States Supreme Court which was to rule in 1950, in the historic case of *Sweatt vs. Painter*, that the black law school (which had by now been expanded and moved to Houston) was, indeed, not equal to the one at the University of Texas, and so the doors of "the university of the first-class" — the University of Texas — would have to be opened to all qualified students, black as well as white.[42]

Notes

[1] Texas *Constitution* (1876), Art. 7, Sec. 7.

[2] The Texas Legislature authorized the establishment of Prairie View in 1876. The school was first called the Alta Vista Agricultural College, for it was constructed upon the ruins of the old slave plantation of Colonel Jared Ellison Kirby, CSA — Alta Vista — in Waller County, east of Hempstead. The three-man commission of J. H. Raymond, Dr. Ashbel Smith and J. D. Giddings appointed to supervise the establishment of the school spent in excess of $115,000 in purchasing the land and buildings and making necessary repairs.

The president of the A & M College at College Station was designated as the chief executive of the school. During the early stages of the school's development, it was also general policy to have a supervisor over the nominal black head of the institution who was, for the next 70 years, called "the principal". The first principal of the black school was L. W. Minor, a heavy, dark-complexioned Negro from Mississippi, who was selected at the urging of his friend, Thomas S. Gathright, the first president at College Station.

The school's first students — eight black boys — were enrolled on March 11, 1878 by "Professor" Minor. They represented the first blacks in history to attend a state-supported college in Texas. The tuition was set by the Board at $130 for nine months of instruction, board and uniform.

It was the original intent of the state to organize an agricultural college for the blacks (which would have made the school eligible for federal grants under the Morrill Act), but the state's blacks were largely opposed to such schools, as they saw in them an effort to hinder their intellectual and social progress. Thus, owing to the lack of students, the school failed completely. In 1879 Governor Roberts proposed that the institution be converted into a normal school for the training of teachers for black children. The legislature approved the suggestion and appropriated $6,000 for the school's operation. It was, then, accordingly reestablished as the Prairie View Normal School. It was placed under the control of the board of regents of the A and M College." See Frederick Eby, *The Development of Education in Texas* (New York, 1925), pp. 271, 274 and Texas *Acts* (1879), Chap. 159, Secs. 1, 2, 3, p. 48.

[3] Texas *Acts* (1882), Chap. 19, Secs. 2-3, p. 285.

[4] *Ibid.*

[5] Texas Secretary of State, *Report*, 1882 (Austin, 1882), p. 5.

[6] Ernest W. Winkler, *Platform of Political Parties in Texas* (Austin: The University of Texas, 1916), p. 332.

[7] *Ibid.*, p. 329.

[8] Prairie View A & M College, *Annual Report, 1895-1896*, p. 9; Texas *School Journal*, XV (July 1897), 75; Galveston News, June 4, 1897; George R. Woolfolk, *Prairie View: A Study in Public Conscience, 1878-1946* (New York, 1962), pp. 125, 126.

[9] *Texas School Journal*, XIV (May 1896), p. 191.

[10] *Ibid.*, p. 193.

[11] *Ibid.*, XIV (July 1896), p. 266.

[12] Texas State Board of Education, *Report*, 1894/96, pp. LIV, LV.

[13] Winkler, *Platforms of Political Parties in Texas*, p. 388.

[14] Prairie View A and M College, *Annual Report*, 1896, pp. 8, 9.

[15] Winkler, *Platforms of Political Parties in Texas*, p. 427.

[16] Texas *School Journal*, XIV (October 1896), p. 398.

[17] The Jeanes Fund was founded in 1900 by a Philadelphia Quaker, Anna T. Jeanes. The Fund was the first to deal only with rural public schools for blacks. It provided black teachers and "Jeanes Supervisors" for the schools. Its expenditures for this work in 12 Southern states from 1915 to 1920 alone totaled $246,500. Other trustees of the Fund were President Taft, Andrew Carnegie, George Foster Peabody, Booker T. Washington, and Robert Russa Moton. (See Anna T. Jeanes Foundaton, *The Negro Rural School Fund* (New York: The Anna T. Jeanes Foundation, 1907, 1933), pp. 7-9; William R. Davis, *The Development and Present Status of Negro Education in East Texas* (New York; Columbia University Bureau of Publications, 1934), pp. 78, 79; Lance G. E. Jones, *The Jeanes Teacher in the United States, 1908-1933* (Chapel Hill, 1937); and Alton Hornsby, Jr., ed., *In the Cage: Eyewitness Accounts of the Freed Negro in Southern Society, 1877-1929* (Chicago, 1971), pp. 79-82.

[18] Tuskegee Institute, *Negro Year Book 1912*, p. 168; *Negro Year Book 1914-15*, pp. 165-168.

[19] Texas *School Journal*, XV (February, 1897), p. 75.

[20] Texas *Acts* (1897) Chapter 109, Secs. 1, 3, p. 1202

[21] Texas *School Journal*, XV (May, 1897), p. 204.

[22] 92Texas 58, 1898; 45 SW 1004.

[23] Texas House Concurrent Resolution No. 26 (1897), p. 336.

[24] Blackshear, a native of Iowa and a product of the public schools of Bastrop and Austin, Texas and of an Iowa college, served as principal for 20 fruitful years. Possessor of a Bachelors degree, Blackshear became an ardent disciple of Booker T. Washington.

[25] Texas *School Journal*, XVII (February, 1899), p. 490.

[26] *Ibid.*, XVII (March, 1899), p. 531.

[27] Texas *Acts* (1897) Chapter 185, Sec., p. 325.

[28] Texas *Acts* (1901) Chapter 30, Sec. 1, p. 35; Texas *School Journal*, XVII (December, 1899), p. 21.

[29] Texas Legislative Council, *Staff Monograph on Higher Education for Negroes in Texas* (Austin, 1951), p. 8.

[30] Texas *Acts* (1915) General Appropriations, pp. 99-107.

[31] Texas State Board of Education, *Report*, 1916/18, pp. 246, 249-260.

[32] Prairie View A & M College, *Annual Catalogue*, 1966-67, p. 10.

[33] *Ibid.*

[34] Loren Miller, *The Petitioners: The Story of the Supreme Court of the United States and the Negro* (Cleveland, 1967), pp. 338-341; Ozie H. Johnson, *Price of Freedom* (n.p., 1954), pp. 2, 3; Henry Allen Bullock, *A History of Negro Education in the South* (Cambridge, 1967), p. 229; M. M. Chambers, *The Colleges and the Courts*, 1946-50 (New York, 1952), pp. 21-23.

[35] Miller, *The Petitioners*, 338-341; Bullock, *A History of Negro Education in the South*, 229.

[36] Johnson, *Price of Freedom*, 4; Miller, *The Petitioners*, 338-340; Bullock, *A History of Negro Education in the South*, 229; Chambers, *The Colleges and the Courts*, 21-23.

[37] 305 U.S. 337; U.S. 631.

[38] Prairie View A & M College, *Annual Catalogue*, 1966-67, 10; Johnson, *Price of Freedom*, pp. 3, 7.

[39] A black dental student filed a suit to compel the Regents of the University to establish the "branch university for colored youth" at Austin as the vote of 1882 had dictated. The Texas Court of Appeals ruled that he section of the Constitution of 1876 calling for the establishment of the black university, "to be located by a vote of the people," was not self executing, and thus was not a mandate to the Board of Regents (See *Givens et al. vs. Woodward et al.* 207 S. W. 2d. 234 and 208 S. W. 2d. 363).

[40] Johnson, *Price of Freedom*, pp. 4-5.

[41] Ibid. See also Bullock, *A History of Negro Education in the South*, p. 229; Miller, *The Petitioners*, pp. 338-339.

[42] In the Sweatt decision, the Supreme Court undermined and discredited the separate-but-equal doctrine, but did not go so far as to overturn the *Plessy vs. Ferguson* precedent of 1896. But the Court showed that it was ready to inquire into specific situations to determine whether or not the separate-but-equal rule was applicable to the facts of a particular case. For segregated education, the Sweatt case demonstrated that the handwriting was on the wall. 339 U.S. 629; Miller, *The Petitioners*, 338-339; Bullock, *A History of Negro Education in the South*, p. 229.; Johnson, *Price of Freedom*, 167; Chambers, *The Colleges and the Courts*, pp. 21-23.

Chapter 10
Black Public Education in Atlanta, Georgia, 1954–1973: From Segregation to Segregation

On August 30, 1961, nine black children entered four previously all-white high schools in Atlanta, Georgia. Atlanta police watched nervously, as did an entire city, but at the end of the day the first public school desegregation in Georgia below the college level had been achieved without violence.[1] The peaceful desegregation of Atlanta's schools marked a turning point in the heretofore tumultuous annual fall ritual of trying to eliminate dual education in the South. The nation took notice and generally applauded the accomplishment. President John F. Kennedy sent personal congratulations to Atlanta leaders and pointed out the example to the rest of the South. *Newsweek* applauded "a proud city." The *Reporter* saw in it "hope for us all"; the *Journal* also complimented parents who "were able to enlist business leaders and elected officials," and Mayor William B. Hartsfield, who had made famous his slogan "Atlanta is 'a city too busy to hate'." *U.S. News and World Report* saw a "New Mood in the South on Mixed Schools." For the next several days, Atlantans were patting themselves on the back as the future of their town looked very good, indeed. But these accomplishments had occurred over a torturous road of legal and other resistance, and even hate, by white Atlantans and Georgians and a cautious, yet persistent, fight in the courts, the media, and other

Reprinted from The Journal of Negro History, Vol. LXXVI, Nos. 1-4, 1997, pp. 21-47, with the permission of The Journal of Negro History

vehicles of public opinion by black Atlantans.[2]

The legal attack on segregation in the Atlanta Public Schools began on January 11, 1958 when the Legal Defense Fund of the National Association for the Advancement of Colored People (NAACP) filed a suit in the U.S. District Court for the Northern District of Georgia on behalf of a group of black parents and their children in the city. The suit, known as *Calhoun vs. Latimer*, remained in federal courts, including the U.S. Supreme Court, for more than 15 years.[3]

The first decision in the case was rendered by judges in the Federal District Court in 1959. When U.S. District Judge Frank A. Hooper opened the trial in June, although he was prepared to announce a *prima facie* finding that the schools were unlawfully segregated, attorneys for the Atlanta Board of Education objected. Thus a full hearing, lasting over several days, had to be held. The eventual conclusion of the court, however, was still the same — Atlanta's public schools were operating in an unconstitutionally segregated manner. The court's findings were in line with the Supreme Court's decision in *Brown vs. Board of Education of Topeka, Kansas*, 1954, that is, that segregation meant that the schools were inherently unequal. But it was also clear that despite accelerated efforts in the 1950s to increase and improve black schools, the education of blacks in the city was inferior to that for whites. Indeed, as the Atlanta Urban League had put it, in the "postwar era . . . Atlanta schools [were] not only segregated but wholly lacking — even nominally — in equal education for Negro children. Such essentials as libraries, assembly rooms, cafeterias, and gymnasiums were considered a luxury by Negro children and parents." Yet the court did accede to the request of the Board of Education that the implementation of its desegregation order be delayed for at least one year. The School Board had, among other things, successfully argued that it faced an almost impossible task in view of laws enacted by the state of Georgia since 1954 which erected a posture of "massive resistance" to school desegregation. These acts included a plan for private schools and the closing of public ones, rather than desegregating them.[4]

Because of the sympathy which the District Court displayed for the plight of the Atlanta Board of Education and the caution of black leaders in pushing the matter, the effective implementing order for desegregation was not handed down until September 1960. It decreed that the School Board's desegregation plan was to take place with the opening of schools in the fall of 1961. Grades 11 and 12 were to be affected the first year, and in each subsequent year one additional grade would be desegregated until the process was completed. Under this arrangement it would require at least a decade to achieve full desegregation.[5]

The School Board's plan for the gradual desegregation of Atlanta's schools, which was approved over the objections of NAACP attorneys, was called a "Freedom of Choice" program. It stipulated that all school children were free to attend any public school in the city. Yet, because of a so-called pupil placement feature of the plan, which required transferring students to undergo "personality interviews" and aptitude and scholastic tests, the program "was not free" at all. Nevertheless, it was to form the basis of the first public school desegregation in Georgia, that is, if actions and events at the state capitol and elsewhere did not intercede.[6]

Many individuals and organizations in Atlanta were quite mindful of the challenges which faced their city at the beginning of the new decade of the 1960s. Among these was the powerful Atlanta Chamber of Commerce and the influential editors of the Atlanta newspapers. In January 1960 at its inaugural meeting for the year, the Chamber adopted a program of projected progress for the decade, in which was included a statement that "open schools" must be maintained. The clear implication was that this was to be done, even with some desegregation. Then, on January 5, 1961, the *Atlanta Constitution*, the South's "standard newspaper," recognized that the city's "critical year" was at hand. The *Constitution*'s editors, who included the Pulitzer Prize-winning racial liberal, Ralph McGill, expressed the hope "that the schools can be preserved and the children spared such experiences as we've witnessed in New Orleans." The newspaper also quoted Atlanta Mayor William B. Hartsfield as calling for "cool-headedness and common sense to solve our problems and to preserve the city's reputation." The alternative, he said, "to permitting Atlanta and other communities to handle their own problems is a bitter power struggle between federal and state authority with the children as pawns. In such a struggle the outcome is certain, as proved in Virginia, Little Rock and now New Orleans. Mobs, lawlessness, and terror won't change the courts." Similarly, Atlanta Board of Education President A. C. "Pete" Latimer said, "We are hopeful that the General Assembly will let us do what we have to do and that we will be able to go about it in an orderly, peaceful manner."[7]

These appeals for calm and statements of hope were made amid a campaign promise by Georgia Governor S. Ernest Vandiver to preserve segregation forever. The matter was also slated for priority consideration by the overwhelmingly segregationist, rural dominated

Georgia General Assembly, which convened in Atlanta shortly after New Year's Day of 1961. Heretofore, the only gesture which the legislature had made toward moderation over the issue was the creation of a commission on schools, commonly called the Sibley Commission. The group took its name from John A. Sibley, a venerable Atlanta lawyer who was also a board member of several of the city's leading businesses. The commission was charged with conducting a survey of public opinion around the state on the matter of "open" or desegregated schools as opposed to the state's present position, which called for the closing of any mixed school. After almost a year of hearings, the commission found a surprising degree of sentiment in the state for open schools, even with desegregation, but was to report that Georgians by a three-to-two margin still opposed the changing of their laws and customs on race.[8]

As Atlantans and other Georgians remained tense in the early days of the new year, thunder and lightning struck from a somewhat unexpected quarter. The question of desegregation at the state's revered university, the University of Georgia at Athens, had been decided more quickly than had been expected. On January 6, 1961, U.S. District Court Judge William A. Bootle at Macon ordered two young blacks admitted to the university. But Bootle, on January 9, granted a stay of his desegregation order pending an appeal by State Attorney General Eugene Cook to the Fifth U.S. Circuit Court of Appeals. This stay interrupted the plans of the blacks to register at the school immediately. The next day, at the request of the students' attorneys, Chief Judge Elbert P. Tuttle of the Court of Appeals set aside the stay. On January 10, the two blacks, Charlayne Hunter and Hamilton Holmes, both of Atlanta, enrolled at the University of Georgia — the first desegregation in public education in the state's history.

State laws already existed that prohibited appropriations to desegregated schools, and Governor Vandiver was now faced with the prospect of backing up his campaign promise that "no, not one" black would enter a white school in Georgia. As Vandiver remained noncommittal in the first hours of the desegregation, key legislators voiced their opposition to closing the University of Georgia. House floor leader Frank Twitty said, "I for one am not in favor of closing the University of Georgia under any circumstances." Senate President pro tempore Carl Sanders said it would be a "calamity" to close the school and asserted, "I believe that the General Assembly will do everything possible to keep the university open." And Lieutenant Governor Garland T. Byrd dismissed outright closing, but cautioned that "it poses a grave problem and most certainly calls for serious consideration by the General Assembly."[9]

Meanwhile, Judge Bootle had issued a permanent injunction prohibiting Vandiver and other state officials from implementing the state law that denied the payment of state funds to desegregated schools, and the two blacks, after two nights of rioting by whites at the university, had been suspended "for their own safety," then readmitted under court order, to the school. One thing which was certain in these uncertain days was that the clash between the state and the federal government over the University of Georgia would settle the legal and political status of desegregation of Atlanta's public schools. Understandably, then, Atlanta Mayor Hartsfield said, "Atlanta will watch the situation with great interest." Others were later to say that "the University of Georgia Crisis" saved the Atlanta public schools.[10]

Once Governor Vandiver decided to speak on the issue, he appeared, at first, to make contradictory declarations. At the opening session of the General Assembly on January 9, the governor had said that "we cannot abandon public education" and insisted that he had not halted any state aid for the University of Georgia. But on January 11, Vandiver said that he would deny state funds to any school that desegregated. He called on blacks and the National Association for the Advancement of Colored People to end legal actions to gain admission to white schools in order to avert a "head-on collision between federal and state sovereignty" and the probable closing of the schools. "But if they (blacks) persist," he warned, "we are going to resist...again and again. We are going to exhaust every legal means and remedy available to us."[11]

At the same time, sentiment both inside and outside the legislature was growing for a preservation of the University of Georgia and of public education, generally, even if desegregated. House floor leader Frank Twitty summed up a feeling of many legislators when he declared that there was "too much money and too many lives at stake to think of closing the University. The people I've come in contact with endorse almost unanimously the idea of keeping the University open." Lieutenant Governor Garland Byrd had also said, at the opening session of the legislature, that the state must "seek ways and means of continuing public education." Additionally, representatives and senators from 16 of the smaller counties of the state proposed a repeal of the segregation laws and an adoption of local option plans.[12]

On January 9, a petition was also adopted by the east and west districts of the Atlanta Methodist Church which favored "a continued uninterrupted operation of the University System and the public schools of Georgia." All of the 175 Greater Atlanta Methodist ministers who were present voted for the petition. A total of 200 delegates representing more than 60 Methodist churches in the Decatur-Oxford District unanimously adopted a similar resolution asking Governor Vandiver and the state legislature to keep Georgia's schools open. Meanwhile, the Athens Ministerial Association called upon Governor Vandiver and the General Assembly to enact such laws as would make possible the uninterrupted operation of all Georgia schools. And in Brunswick, the Glynn County Protestant Ministerial Association wired Governor Vandiver and state legislative leaders urging them to keep the University of Georgia and other schools open despite the desegregation orders. Also, at his installation as president of the Greater Atlanta Council of Churches, Dr. Arthur Vann Gibson, pastor of the city's Morningside Presbyterian Church, said that the role of ministers is "not promoting integration or segregation but creating an atmosphere in which men may think straight . . . The educational system must be preserved, and in doing so Christians must exercise great patience and love."[13]

Governor Vandiver sent his annual budget to the legislature on January 16. It was very significant that the appropriations bill left out the sections in the last appropriations act which provided that no funds could be spent on schools where the courts had ordered desegregation. This action came just one day after the United Churchwomen of Georgia, representing all faiths, adopted a resolution in Atlanta asking political leaders to keep the schools open by "making whatever changes necessary in the laws of Georgia."

One day after Vandiver's action, James S. Peters, Chairman of the State Board of Education, wrote in a letter published in the *Atlanta Journal-Constitution* that "some form of integration is inevitable, and the only question . . . is whether integration will be under the control of friends of segregation or the proponents of integration." He suggested that segregationist leaders should meet and seek a solution or face "defeat and the loss of our power and influence" in Georgia's state government. Peters warned fellow supporters of Senator Herman Talmadge, a rabid segregationist, that unless they compromised on segregation, Talmadge might be defeated in his upcoming bid for reelection and that the state's next governor might be former governor Ellis Arnall, who had said that if the schools were closed, he would campaign for high office on a pledge to reopen them. The practical wisdom of "Mr. Jim" Peters, especially as it reflected the views of those close to Senator Talmadge, was a compelling call to end massive resistance to desegregation in Georgia.

Until the "University Crisis," white ministers and churchwomen in the Atlanta Council on Human Relations and a group of moderate Atlanta professionals and housewives called HOPE (Help Our Public Education) had been the most vocal whites openly supporting public education even if desegregated. The Sibley Commission, in its hearings throughout Georgia, had discovered a sizeable minority of other such group and individual voices; but not until the crisis was at hand did powerful political, educational, and religious figures in the state face up to the realities of the situation. Once this was done change was imminent.[14]

On Wednesday night, January 18, Governor Vandiver went before an unusual joint session of the legislature and, in effect, asked the state to abandon its resistance to some desegregation. He called his program a formula designed to keep the schools open and in the hands of local officials. He emphasized that new laws were necessary to keep federal courts from seizing the schools. The four-point program included a pupil protection amendment which would write into the state constitution a provision that no child would be required to attend an integrated school; a tuition grant program which would authorize the issuance of funds to parents who wanted their children to attend private schools rather than public desegregated ones; a local referendum provision under which each community could vote to close its schools or to keep them open in the event they were ordered desegregated; and a classification of the system under which appeals could be made from local schools to the state Board of Education. Immediately after the Governor spoke, legislative leaders predicted passage of the bills "within a week." Vandiver himself had said that the opposition would come only from "a few" who would favor "unreconcilable conflict with superior armed forces." That conflict, he added, could end only in "abject defeat."[15]

Two days after Vandiver introduced his "save the schools" package to the Georgia General Assembly, James S. Peters, the chairman of the state Board of Education and an elder statesman of Georgia politics, said the plan was "fair to all parties." "It is now up to the local units to operate their schools with or without integration," he added. Following this lead, State School Superintendent Claude Purcell wrote local school officials to enlist their help in asking legislators to support the school bills. In Dalton, the Whitfield County Grand Jury praised its local state legislators for supporting the open schools bill. The grand jury said: "We support the position of local state legislators . . . in their announced views favoring continuation of the public school system in Georgia and recommend that they support legislation to abolish existing segregation laws and enact laws for a pupil-placement plan."[16] Meanwhile, the executive committee of the Atlanta Chamber of Commerce, at this point the only major business group in the state openly in favor of public education with desegregation, wired Vandiver congratulating him on his "excellent proposals."[17]

The Chamber of Commerce telegram may have served to break a long official silence on the desegregation question by the rest of Georgia's business persons. To be sure, men and women in business had expressed individual views on the school question. Some had served on the Sibley Commission and others had testified before the body in support of "open schools." But the Chamber's wire of January 20 was an open, group pronouncement which, when extended several days later, would place the business community squarely behind the movement for change in the midst of the crisis. In fact, the Atlanta Chamber members pledged to the Governor their "full cooperation in moving toward these new goals." The telegram was signed by Chamber President Ivan Allen, Jr., Vice Presidents E. D. Smith, Rawson Haverty, and Ben S. Gilmer; Treasurer Mills B. Lane, Jr., and immediate past president Edgar J. Forio. Allen was a multi-millionaire office furniture dealer and would soon be mayor of Atlanta; Smith and Lane were the presidents of the two largest banks in Georgia; Haverty was a wealthy furniture dealer; and Gilmer was president of one of the state's largest utilities. Some of the most influential white men in the state thus had endorsed limited desegregation on behalf of themselves and their business colleagues.[18]

Immediately following the Atlanta Chamber's call for "open schools," the businessmen of Georgia made their strongest and most forthright statement ever on desegregated education in the state. On Sunday, January 22, nearly a thousand of them called on Governor Vandiver and state legislators to keep the schools open, even with some desegregation. Some of the biggest names in the state's business community approved a resolution which said that "disruption of our public school system would have a calamitous effect on the economic climate of Georgia." The businessmen announced support of such legislation in the 1961 General Assembly "that may be necessary to effect the uninterrupted operation" of Georgia's public schools. "Immediate legislation," they added, "is urgently needed." They then voiced confidence that the Governor and legislature would act "to avoid the tragedy and unrest which several of our sister states have experienced." The authors of the resolution also expressed confidence that the legislation adopted would provide the maximum "freedom of choice."

The business resolution eventually contained almost 1,000 signatures, including that of John W. Dent of Cartersville, president of the Georgia Chamber of Commerce. All of the signatures were collected in a period of ten days.[19]

During the last five days of January 1961, the Georgia legislature, with the support of a substantial amount of the state's public opinion, officially abandoned massive resistance to school desegregation. On January 27 and 30, the General Assembly passed several bills which repealed six anti-integration laws; provided aid for pupils who chose to attend private, nonsectarian schools; permitted local boards of education to set academic, psychological, and other standards governing pupil transfers (this had formerly been a state function); authorized local elections on whether to close desegregated schools; and passed a constitutional amendment, to be voted on in 1962, that asserted that "freedom from compulsory association at all levels of public education shall be preserved inviolate." This amendment was to replace a constitutional requirement for "separate schools . . . for white and colored races." On January 31, 1961, Governor S. Ernest Vandiver signed the "open schools package" into law, commenting, "These are the four most important bills to be signed in this century in Georgia."[20]

The last 25 days of January 1961 had indeed been among the most momentous in the history of the state of Georgia. The University of Georgia crisis not only had opened the state's institutions of higher learning to blacks but had forced the state to abandon massive resistance to school desegregation at all levels. Since, at the time, only the Atlanta Public Schools were threatened with disruption due to desegregation, it is certainly no exaggeration to conclude, as others did at the time, that the university crisis saved the Atlanta public schools; for until that crisis erupted, Georgia's political leaders were adamant in their view that desegregation would be eternally resisted, even if public education had to be sacrificed. While these leaders spouted demagogic rhetoric, the business, religious, and educational leaders of the state remained, for the most part, silent. With the exception of (1) black advocates of desegregation, (2) the interracial Atlanta Council on Human Relations, (3) the group of white moderates known as HOPE and, (4) a scattering of other white Atlantans and Georgians, there were very few voices calling for the retention of public education with desegregation. Notable, however, among this group were the members of the Atlanta Chamber of Commerce. Of course, particularly with hindsight, it is clear that, in the end, the action of the General Assembly in January 1961 merely assured that the course of desegregation in the state would remain in the hands of the "friends of segregation"; for the federal courts were not likely to tolerate extended school closings as an impediment to desegregation. On the other hand, the January surrender did serve the useful purpose of forestalling any interruption of public education in the state.

The first major crack in the wall of massive resistance in Georgia, it must be said, was the report by the Sibley Commission. No one really expected that the group, in its survey of the state's ten congressional districts, would find a groundswell of support for integration. But the fact that two-fifths of those testifying and presenting resolutions suggested that they would tolerate some desegregation came as a real surprise to many. Excerpts from some of the televised hearings and the final commission report were a welcome weapon in the arsenals of the Council on Human Relations, HOPE, Organization Assisting Schools in September (OASIS), the blacks, and others who advocated compliance with federal laws. Once the state's major university was threatened, politicians were in the forefront of those admitting that changes in the state's centuries-old caste system must be made.[21]

Atlanta Mayor William B. Hartsfield had said in the early days of the university crisis that the city would watch the rapidly unfolding events with great interest. After January 31, he and most Atlantans could breathe a bit easier. The actions of the governor and the legislators, no matter how painful to them, had paved the way for the desegregation of Atlanta's public schools. Atlanta's political leaders, while not entirely "slaves" to the black bloc vote (as some segregationists charged), but certainly unable to ignore it, now set out to achieve the first peaceful desegregation of public schools in a major Deep South city. In this quest, they were supported by a substantial cross-section of Atlanta public opinion. Professional, religious, and even social groups seemed to be trying to outdo one another in adopting resolutions calling for peaceful desegregation. This time, the business community expressed an early eagerness "to get on with it," and the Atlanta newspapers, particularly the *Atlanta Constitution*, which had consistently lent its powerful voice to the movement for "open schools" and peaceful desegregation, were buoyed by these efforts and gave them a prominent place in their pages.[22]

In the face of these widespread efforts for peaceful desegregation, the extremist ravings of die-hard segregationists like restauranteur and mayoral candidate Lester Maddox were all but drowned out. Maddox was vehemently opposed to any desegregation and ridiculed white leaders for encouraging and "planning to invade every white high school in Atlanta, with negro [sic], students, in September this year. In the meantime, white race-mixers, working with negro [sic] children during the spring and summer, so that when school starts in September, the children will be sweethearts and friends — rather than strangers." "After a few years of this," Maddox predicted, "stories about young white girls being found in negro [sic] hotels will not even make the newspapers." While most of Maddox's charges and anxieties could be easily dismissed, it was true that the Atlanta Council on Human Relations, an interracial group, worked with black students helping to prepare them for the social and psychological traumas of desegregation, and while Maddox himself was not seen as a very serious threat, Atlanta police detectives were assigned to escort all of the black students to the newly desegregated schools. There were enough expressions of hate both within and without the city to warrant this precaution.[23]

As Atlanta school officials prepared to test more than a hundred black students for the limited desegregation scheduled for the fall, early in February, Atlanta's black college students began their second year of sit-ins and other protest demonstrations. The new protests deeply troubled many Atlantans, as they saw them jeopardizing the plans for peaceful school desegregation. Ironically, business leaders who were now in the forefront of the move for peaceful desegregation in the schools remained steadfast in their opposition to desegregation of their own lunch counters. Since the university crisis had just been met and there were uncertain days ahead in the fall, some business and political leaders viewed the new sit-ins as most untimely. They could only further inflame passions and make violence in September a likelihood. The white Atlanta newspapers adopted this view in their editorials and it was even supported by several black leaders, including the editor of the black *Daily World.*[24]

The view that peaceful school desegregation was the most important issue facing the community and that continued pressure for immediate lunch counter integration would threaten it was eventually accepted by most of the parties involved. On March 7, student and adult black leaders signed an agreement with downtown merchants which ended the sit-ins with a promise of lunch counter desegregation following school desegregation. The six months' delay was soon denounced by some younger blacks who threatened to renege on the pact and resume sit-ins. It took a personal plea from Martin Luther King, Jr., to convince them to accept the delay.[25]

With the postponement of the end of lunch counter discrimination until after the accomplishment of school desegregation, the last major obstacle to a process which had begun three years earlier was overcome. Thus, on August 30, the nine black students who had survived the rigorous testing and other procedures to qualify for transfers entered previously all-white high schools in each of Atlanta's four geographical quadrants without incident. Peaceful desegregation had become a reality in the capital of the New South.[26]

The events of the fall of 1961, however, were only the opening chapter in the long history of public school desegregation in Atlanta. The plan, under which the desegregation was to be accomplished, in itself, assured that the process would be a long one, as it allowed for more than a decade of piecemeal dismantling of the dual system of education. The pupil placement procedure also served as a deterrent to black transfers and a discouragement to black children. In a special report, during 1969, the National Educational Association aptly described the deterring qualities of pupil placement when it said:

> . . . 'freedom of choice' was not free — not under the rigors of a procedure that included interviews with . . . parents, personality interviews with . . . students, and the administration of scholastic and aptitude tests as a prerequisite for the approval of transfer; not under a procedure that resulted in the admission of only eight percent of transfer applicants to desegregating schools in 1961 and only 14 percent the succeeding year . . .

An Atlanta NAACP official commenting on the process said: "We've got a saying around here that it's easier to go to Yale than to transfer from one public school to another in Atlanta."[27]

Other policies and practices of the Atlanta School Board during these early years of desegregation also did not seem to be designed to increase the amount of or the pace of desegregation. For example, black students were continually transferred from extremely overcrowded to less overcrowded all-black schools, with no effort to place them in vacant classroom seats in all-white ones. Additionally at the elementary level (which had not yet been included in the desegregation program), some all-white schools were converted into all-black facilities. When the James L. Key School in the southern part of the city, a neighborhood of lower-middle to lower income white and black residents, was renamed Capitol Avenue School, it was designated an all-black facility. And whereas some white parents in the area sought additional white enrollments from outside the vicinity to boost the white attendance enough for the school to remain all-white, some black parents protested the board's action as a re-enforcement of segregation.[28]

As the desegregation began there were slightly more than 100,000 children attending the Atlanta Public Schools, 56 percent of whom were white and 40 percent black. Nine black students and 5,034 white ones were enrolled in the four desegregated high schools. During the next school year, 1962-63, there were six additional desegregated high schools; the number of black students in all of the schools had risen to only 44, while 10,945 whites attended multi-racial classes. Under these circumstances, the NAACP went back to the Federal District Court and accused the Atlanta Board of Education of "continuing to maintain and operate a segregated bi-racial school system." The group's attorneys asked the court to abandon the original desegregation plan, which would take more than a decade to accomplish, in favor of one which would bring total desegregation within five years. They also proposed that: (1) "the reassignment of all teachers, principals, and other professional personnel" be made on "the basis of qualifications and need, without regard to race"; (2) "all school-sponsored extra curricular activities" be desegregated; and (3) "freedom of choice" be replaced by "the establishment of zone lines for each school" and that all children living in the zone be assigned to school "without regard to race."[29]

On November 15, 1962, U.S. District Court Judge Frank A. Hooper denied the motions of the NAACP attorneys, citing, among other things, that "teacher assignment problems should be deferred until further progress had been made in desegregation of students." The lower court's decision was confirmed, upon appeal, by the U.S. Fifth Circuit Court of Appeals. That court said: "Gradualism in desegregation, if not the usual, is at least an accepted mode with the emphasis on getting the job done." The court did, however, warn against "discriminatory use of test scores criteria and personality interview results as a basis for acceptance or approval" of the applications of blacks for transfer to desegregated schools. The NAACP appealed the decision to the U.S. Supreme Court.[30]

Meanwhile, the Board of Education adopted a resolution detailing "new criteria" for student transfers, which included "choice of pupil or his parents, availability of facilities, and proximity of school to place of residence." In that school year, 1963-1964, grades nine through 12 in nine high schools were desegregated; 143 blacks and 10,488 whites attended multi-racial classes that year. With the blessings of the federal courts, Atlanta's desegregation was moving at a snail's pace.[31]

The Atlanta school case was argued before the U.S. Supreme Court in the 1963-1964 term. During the hearing, some of the justices seemed baffled by aspects of the litigation. A part of the confusion apparently stemmed from the fact that School Board Attorney A. C. "Pete" Latimer often discussed things that the board intended to do rather than what it had actually done. At any rate, the Supreme Court vacated the judgment of the Court of Appeals and sent the case back to the District Court for an examination of the contradictory claims of the parties concerning assignment and transfer policies."[32]

In February 1965 the U.S. District Court in Atlanta held the hearing mandated by the Supreme Court and in April ordered the complete desegregation of all grades in the Atlanta Public Schools by the 1967-1968 school year, under a continuation of the "freedom of choice" program. Specifically, it ordered that the original plan be amended so as to embrace the kindergarten and the first grade in the ensuing school year and then to move upward at the rate of two grades per year each year thereafter, thereby resulting in a five-year acceleration of the desegregation process. Several months before this decision, "in anticipation of" the decree, the Board of Education had already adopted a resolution stating "its willingness to proceed on this basis." Then, in June 1965, the Board moved ahead of the court order by voting to desegregate all grades under "freedom of choice" during the 1965-1966 school year. The court's decision and the Board action, ironically enough, resulted in the achievement of the same goals which the NAACP had sought in 1962.[33]

During the 1965-1966 school year, the first year of "total" desegregation under the freedom of choice program, there were still 100,000 children enrolled in the Atlanta Public Schools, but by this time black students outnumbered white ones 61,344 to 52,894. The early effects of "white flight" to the suburbs and private schools and away from the city schools and signs of resegregation were being manifested. While The School Board could report in January 1966 that 8,831 black students were attending desegregated schools, only 848, or less than two percent of the black elementary pupils and 1,416 or 11.3 percent, of black high school students were in schools where there was as much as ten percent desegregation. Of the white pupils, only four percent of the elementary ones, and 11.4 percent of high school students were in schools with ten percent or more desegregation. Using the then standard definition of "desegregated," i.e., more than ten percent of other race students enrolled, there were only six desegregated schools in the city during the 1965-1966 school year. At the same time, there were 62 schools in which the enrollment was over 90 percent black and 73 schools in which enrollment was more than 90 percent white. "Only four of the schools 90 percent or more black in 1965 had any white teachers."[34]

The following school year, 1966-1967, the number of desegregated schools in Atlanta increased by only two. Five years after the first desegregation 95 percent of all of the city's pupils were still attending segregated schools. In this period, the exodus of whites from the city, which had been continuing gradually since the mid-1950s, accelerated as did the transfer of whites from desegregating schools into all-white or overwhelmingly white ones. Also, by this time, two formerly all-white high schools and a like number of primary schools had become predominantly black. The erosion of desegregation was seen most dramatically at Kirkwood Elementary School, in a lower middle-income section of southeast Atlanta. Despite the efforts of moderate whites and blacks to stabilize desegregation there, in January 1965, Kirkwood went from an all-white to an almost all-black school almost overnight. As it turned out, this resegregation was aided by an action of School Superintendent John Letson who, while following the School Board's decision to allow black pupils to transfer into Kirkwood, also sent letters to white parents notifying them of the impending changes and "informing them [that] they could transfer elsewhere if they wished." On the day that approximately 500 blacks entered Kirkwood, all but six whites had left. The white teachers were removed with their white pupils. While this stunning action was "legal," in that elementary grades were not yet under a court order, it struck at the sincerity of the Atlanta school officials' commitment to desegregation and was viewed as "a breach of good faith" by many black parents.[35]

Other School Board actions, which were viewed as chicanery by some blacks, increased resentment in the black communities and eventually led to open protests. One such incident involved the conversion of a former vocational school to a junior high school where only black eighth graders would be enrolled. Several black parents picketed the new Central Junior High School, which was actually a renovated building, and boycotted classes for several days. School officials, however, assured the blacks that the school was only a temporary one and that a replacement would soon be constructed. Five years later the segregated school was still in operation.[36]

Also, in the first year of "total" school desegregation in Atlanta, enrollments at all of the black high schools exceeded capacity by as much as 240 percent, while six of the all-white or majority white high schools had vacant classroom seats. When it was decided that double sessions would have to be instituted at the C. L. Harper High School in northwest Atlanta, some parents there protested to the city school superintendent, John Letson, about the "school's overload." They sent him a telegram saying: "A half-day of education is not enough. We expect our children to receive a full day's education." These vigorous protests were continued at a later meeting of the Atlanta Board of Education. However, the *Atlanta Constitution* reproved the protesters in an editorial on the matter. The newspaper said: "Ultimatums, threats of boycotts, shouting matches and mass demonstrations are not going to solve the serious problem of overcrowded schools in Atlanta." But the paper then added:

> Parents of pupils at Harper and their spokesmen have suggested that the overcrowded condition there be alleviated by transferring pupils to other, less crowded schools. This proposal should be explored with the parents involved. They may or may not want their children spending an hour or two each day commuting rather than attending double sessions. It may or may not be a reasonable solution from the standpoint of the administrative problems and physical facilities involved.

Neither the protests of the black parents nor the *Constitution*'s editorials prodded the School Board into immediate action concerning the problem of overcrowded black schools. Although school construction had been continuous, financed by three multi-million dollar bond issues, during the 1960s, the increase in black school enrollment "continued to exceed the rate of school building effort."[37]

When Atlanta schools opened in 1967 every all-black high school in the city was on double or "extended day" sessions (as the School Board called them). But the School Board defended them, arguing that they "were educationally constructive, providing greater scheduling flexibility and permitting high school students to combine part-time jobs with schooling." The Board seemed not to take into consideration that there were also "extended day" sessions in many of the black elementary and junior high schools and that "often the children of working parents were forced to go to a home where no adult was present, or to the streets." At any rate, many angry black parents were not impressed by the School Board's defense. The matter subsequently became a central topic for discussion at a meeting of the Atlanta Summit Leadership Conference, the umbrella group of major civil rights and social welfare organizations in the black communities. The Conference resolved to end double sessions in the schools or "close [them] down." After an unsuccessful attempt to settle the problem in a meeting with the School Board, several black leaders then sat-in at the school administration building in downtown Atlanta. At the same time, the blacks presented the Board with a list of 12 demands. These included the immediate end of double sessions in black schools by transferring some blacks to available space in desegregated or all-white schools. Also, they asked that a black be named "first assistant" or "deputy superintendent" of the schools, and that, by January 1, 1968, "the Board name no fewer than two Negroes to head departments. In departments having associate heads," they demanded that blacks "be named at once to three of these positions." Furthermore, the blacks called for the appointment of black principals "to any schools where Negroes comprised 60 percent or more of the school enrollment," and the end of "permanent use of makeshift facilities." This latter demand referred to the continued use of Central Junior High School, which the School Board had promised would be open temporarily after its conversion to a black junior high school and to the more recent purchase of a church building in a "racially transitional area" to be used as a black school.[38]

As the dispute grew and further threatened to inflame racial tensions in the city, the Atlanta Community Relations Commission and the Atlanta Chamber of Commerce stepped in as mediators. This mediation produced a settlement which ended double sessions by the placement of portable classroom units at overcrowded black schools. Also, a black with "undefined" responsibilities was placed in the central administration; and the School Board announced that the "selection and promotion of personnel were without regard to race."[39]

This clearly compromised settlement was enough for some of the black leaders to urge an end to all demonstrations and protests against the School Board, but "the more militant black leadership" argued that it did not really solve the problems at all. They urged a boycott of the schools "until a more acceptable settlement could be reached." The division among the black leadership rendered the summit group asunder. The younger, impatient, and more aggressive blacks broke away and established the Metropolitan Atlanta Summit Leadership Congress as their vehicle for protest and action.[40]

In this era, black Atlantans were "not entirely alone" in their criticism of the Atlanta School Board's racial policies. White members of the Atlanta Council on Human Relations had been consistent critics and prodders. Another organization which began in two of Atlanta's white churches bolstered the claims of blacks that racial inequities persisted in the school system. Better Schools-Atlanta, as the group was called, issued its first major report in October 1968. It concluded, among other things, that students in Atlanta's black elementary schools attended larger first-grade classes, had fewer textbooks, had fewer speech therapy programs, had a lower proportionate value of buildings, furniture, and equipment, and a "smaller school site area per 1,000 pupils" than did students in white schools. Furthermore, 65 percent of the elementary schools were totally segregated, with 92.3 percent of the black elementary pupils being enrolled in all-black schools. Finally, the report cited the fact that by the time blacks reached the fourth grade, based upon 1966 median reading scores, in performance, they were more than one year behind pupils in white schools; by the eighth grade, the gap had widened to four years.[41]

The Better Schools Report, which highlighted what it called an "educational crisis in America's urban areas," angered some members of the School Board and its administration. An extreme response was that of School Board Attorney A. C. "Pete" Latimer, who "instructed school detectives to conduct a private inquiry of the president and other members" of Better Schools-Atlanta. Latimer defended the action on the ground that "many allegations similar to those contained in the Better Schools-Atlanta Report had been included in a recently filed petition in the continuing Atlanta school desegregation suit." Thus, according to Latimer, "the investigations, some of which had involved inquiries of the individuals' employees, were needed to defend the school district in court." Meanwhile, the new Metropolitan Atlanta Summit Leadership Congress, the organization of aggressive black dissidents, renewed its threat of a school boycott and called for the resignation of School Superintendent John Letson.

On February 10, 1969, the *Atlanta Journal* announced its pleasure that "at last the Atlanta Board of Education has agreed to discuss the report issued four months ago by Better Schools-Atlanta. This is progress far beyond surface appearance. This board heretofore has rigidly resented such public confrontation of the school system's failings."

The public meeting on the Better Schools Report was held in an auditorium at the Atlanta Area Technical School in southwest Atlanta on February 10. The meeting was attended by more than 800 persons. Superintendent Letson began by "detailing the achievements" of the school system in "school construction, educational improvement and innovation, and school desegregation." Among the "achievements" which he listed were the facts that 75 percent of bond moneys from the issues of 1963 and 1966 had been spent in and for predominantly black schools; that "as of September 1968, 95 percent of Atlanta's teachers were assigned to integrated faculties"; and that some black schools had higher academic performance levels than white ones.   Yet the superintendent admitted that "in general, schools enrolling all Negro pupils [had] a lower average achievement level than schools enrolling all white pupils." But, he added, "no school system had found a way to overcome easily or rapidly the effects of poverty and cultural deprivation. Through the many experimental programs in operation in Atlanta we think we have some leads but no final answers."[42]

The February meeting hardly resolved the conflict between the Board, which believed it was on a proper and progressive course, and those blacks and whites who saw the prevailing educational policies and practices regarding race as either conservative or reactionary. As a measure of their discontent, in October 1968, attorneys for black parents had already filed a request for reconsideration of the Atlanta "freedom of choice" program in view of the recent decision of the U.S. Supreme Court in *Green vs. County School Board of New Kent County, Virginia.* In the Green case, the Court had ruled that if "freedom of choice" plans failed to successfully desegregate a school system, other methods, such as zoning, must be tried. The plaintiffs contended that Atlanta was one city where "freedom of choice" had failed.[43]

Before the Federal District Court ruled on the new petition from Atlanta blacks, the U.S. Supreme Court had issued its opinion in the landmark case of *Alexander vs. Holmes County Board of Education, Mississippi.* In the Holmes case, the Court ruled that there could be no further delays in the orderly desegregation of schools, that the dictum of "all deliberate speed," established in 1955, was no longer "constitutionally permissible" and that desegregation must proceed "at once." At the time of this decision, in October 1969, 117 of Atlanta's schools were still segregated; only 34 were desegregated; and only 20,000 of the system's 100,000 children were in bi-racial classrooms. With these statistics in mind and with *Green* and *Holmes* now law, the U.S. District Court in Atlanta rendered two new decisions in the Atlanta case in January and February of 1970. On January 30, the court ordered the elimination of the segregation of teachers in the public schools by March. A quota system was approved wherein each school was to have the same racial composition in its faculty as there was for the system as a whole, i.e., 57 percent black, 43 percent white. Then on February 19, the same court ordered the School Board to provide free transportation for black children to the school of their choice, if the school from which the child was transferring was more than half black and the school which he or she wanted to attend was more than half white. This device became known as the "majority to minority" or "M and M" transfer plan."[44]

These new desegregation orders were effective during the 1970-1971 school year, when the number of students attending desegregated schools began to "level off." White flight from the school system continued apace and the percentage of black students in bi-racial classes surpassed the percentage of white students in such classes for the first time. An example of the startling effect of white flight can be seen in the instance of a private apartment complex in Atlanta which had been segregated before 1968. Shortly after an "open housing" policy was adopted in the complex, almost all of the whites moved out. The public school in the area had an enrollment of 500 prior to the housing desegregation, but when it opened in the following fall, schools there were only 200 white students left; then, by the close of the school year, it was all black."[45]

As Atlanta struggled with the goal of increased school desegregation amid the obstacles of white flight and what some considered a less than enthusiastic School Board policy, the U.S. Supreme Court issued another monumental ruling on the subject. On April 20, 1971, in the case of *Swann vs. Charlotte-McClenburg, North Carolina*, the Court ordered the use of "any technique of pupil assignment necessary" to desegregate the schools and remedy any "continuing effects" of previous discrimination. Specifically, the Court upheld transportation or busing as a "legitimate tool for desegregating schools" as long as it did not "jeopardize the health and education" of children. But in July of that same year, over the objections of attorneys for the NAACP, U.S. District Court Judges Sydney Smith and Albert Henderson, in Atlanta, declared that the Atlanta Public School System was a "unitary" one, i.e., had been sufficiently desegregated, and ordered the 12 year old case dismissed. The NAACP appealed the decision to the U.S. Court of Appeals for the Fifth Circuit."[46]

At the time that the Atlanta System was being declared "unitary," 103 of the 150 schools in the city were still segregated; only 33,000 of more than 103,000 students were in bi-racial classes, and less than ten percent of these were in schools with as much as five percent desegregation. The District Court had noted a "growing resegregation" of the schools due to white flight and suggested that the continuing problem lay in the "metropolitan area separation of races due to housing patterns," but concluded that these things were beyond its purview. But in October 1971, the U.S. Court of Appeals for the Fifth Circuit disagreed and sent the case back to the District Court for a re-examination, including the "metropolitan area aspects" of the litigation.[47]

As the once "closed," now reopened, Atlanta school case headed back to the Federal District Court, in the 1971-1972 school year, only 28,000 white students were left in the Public School System; two-thirds of these were in the 48 desegregated schools. But of the 71,000 black pupils, only 13,149 attended bi-racial classes. So, the NAACP argued, the matter demanded drastic and sweeping action; its attorneys, therefore, recommended the busing of some 30,000 pupils daily in order to achieve further desegregation. On June 28, 1972, the District Court rejected the NAACP's plan as "unreasonable," and, again, declared the Atlanta system a "unitary" one. The court did, however, suggest that the NAACP might seek further relief through its "metropolitan desegregation suit."[48]

Already, in 1968 and 1969, the NAACP had filed petitions for desegregation of the school systems in those portions of Fulton and DeKalb Counties which were outside of Atlanta. Then, on June 8, 1972, the American Civil Liberties Union (ACLU) filed a suit in the U.S. District Court for the Northern District of Georgia asking for a consolidation of the nine school systems in the metropolitan area or an order for their joint operation. In receiving the ACLU petition, the court ordered that the NAACP cases against the Atlanta, DeKalb, and Fulton systems be added to it. Together, then, Atlanta city, Marietta city, Decatur city, Buford city, DeKalb County, Cobb County, Clayton County, and Gwinett County schools were the targets of the court's scrutiny in the consolidated or metropolitan desegregation case. At the time, the four city systems had enrollments which were 69 percent black and 31 percent white, while the five county systems had only a seven percent black enrollment, with 93 percent white. Additionally, there were vast social, political, and economic differences between the areas. DeKalb County, a wealthy suburb just east of Atlanta, had a rather sizeable black population in the southern part of Decatur, its county seat. It was also the home of Emory University, one of the South's major institutions of higher learning. Buford, Marietta, the seat of Cobb County, and Gwinnett County were all to the north of Atlanta and were mostly white suburban enclaves. Clayton County, to the south of the city, was gradually becoming increasingly black, but had once been a stronghold of Ku Klux Klan type "rednecks." The Atlanta International Airport was located there. Except for the city of Atlanta, blacks had little or no political influence in the metropolitan area.[49]

At a joint hearing by a three-judge panel in the Atlanta Federal District Court, on September 22, 1972, the jurists postponed further action in the metropolitan suit until the U.S. Supreme Court decided a similar case in the Richmond, Virginia area.[50]

While Atlanta waited on Richmond, of the 324,000 students attending school in the nine school systems involved, 253,000 or almost 80 percent were in segregated schools. City schools were more desegregated than county ones. But the Buford, Decatur, and Marietta schools were the only systems in the entire metropolitan area with more than half of their students in bi-racial classes. These three systems, however, had a combined enrollment of only 10,192 students, only three percent of the area total. In the city of Atlanta itself, 28,484 of its 96,006 students, or 30 percent, were in desegregated schools in the 1972-1973 school year. At this time, the percentage of black students in the Atlanta system had reached almost 80 percent, with only slightly more than 20 percent of whites remaining. Of these, only 7,345 attended segregated schools, while more than 60,000 blacks were in such schools.[51]

Partly because of the gravity, at least in its eyes, of the rapidly increasing segregation in Atlanta, the ACLU had asked the U.S. Court not to wait for Richmond but to rule on the merits of its metropolitan case immediately. The court denied the request. But the U.S. Court of Appeals for the Fifth Circuit, on October 8, 1972, in the original Atlanta school case, agreed with the contentions of the NAACP that the Atlanta system was not a "unitary" one. Thus, the Appeals Court sent the case, again, back to the District Court so that it could order the "immediate desegregation" of all the public schools in the city. It said that the 20 "all or virtually all white" schools in the system "must receive special attention." The court also said that the desegregation could be devised in accordance with the guidelines it had established in Austin and Corpus Christi, Texas, where students of all races could attend various learning centers for part of the day, even if they had to be transported to these places.[52]

The sense of urgency of the ACLU, the NAACP, and the Court of Appeals not-withstanding, the Federal District Court ordered both sides to submit new proposals by February 15, 1973, the date of a new hearing on the 14 year-old case. While the new desegregation proposals were being drawn up by the Atlanta School Board and the NAACP, neither the picture of school desegregation itself or conditions in the all-black schools looked very bright. For example, in 1972-1973, 106 of the 153 schools were still segregated and 81 of these had never been desegregated; others had been resegregated. In the all-black elementary and secondary schools the average number of library books and textbooks per pupil were still less than for all-white or desegregated schools and the value of property, furniture, and equipment in the all-black elementary schools was still less than that in all-white ones. In the latter instance, a special committee from the National Education Association (NEA), based upon data for 1967-1968 and visits to schools all over the city, concluded that the "worst schools . . . were in the areas where children are poor and black and where there is little in either the community or classroom to motivate a child to learn." While the special committee conceded that "funds for textbooks, instructional supplies, and supplementary materials" were "currently allocated on an equal per-pupil basis to al schools in the city," some "inequity" remained. The "uniformity of current allocations," the committee said, "does not mean that the quality or quantity of instructional and supplementary materials is equal in each Atlanta school. If there are two groups of schools which have been treated unequally in the past, equal treatment now cannot make them leap forward to equality in the present . . . ."[53]

In compliance with the District Court's order, the NAACP submitted its latest desegregation plan in January 1973; the School Board plan followed a month later. Under the NAACP's proposal, the number of students attending desegregated schools would increase by 78 percent, from 27,239 in 1972-1973 to 48,555. On the other hand, the School Board's plan called for an increase of only 8,275 students, or 30 percent. The NAACP's plan provided that 53 percent of Atlanta's students would attend bi-racial classes, while the School Board's proposal would raise the number of such students in such classrooms from 30 to 44 percent. Of the 153 schools in the Atlanta system, at the time, the number of desegregated ones would rise from 47 to 90 under the NAACP proposal, as opposed to 64 with the School Board plan. The NAACP proposed to eliminate segregation in all of the all-white schools which the Appeals Court highlighted in its most recent decision, while the school board wanted to leave at least six of those schools segregated. Both plans called for the closing of some schools and the reassignment of pupils to aid the desegregation process.[54]

In the hearing, itself, lawyers for the two sides argued their plans, and numerous citizens, black and white, and groups, black, white, and interracial, were allowed to present oral and/or written testimony on the question of further desegregation. As was to be expected opinions varied widely, but cross-town busing to achieve desegregation was almost unanimously opposed by whites, while most blacks gave it endorsements ranging from lukewarm to enthusiastic. The court itself was clearly in a quandary. It had long exhibited a sympathy with slow, piecemeal desegregation and had only recently declared a largely segregated school system to be a "unitary" one. On the other hand, the Circuit Court of Appeals had disagreed and had strongly suggested some court ordered busing as a remedy for Atlanta's segregation ills. Thus, when the court saw signs that local blacks and whites might work things out for themselves, it gladly suspended its deliberations to give leaders of the various communities involved time to search for a solution.[55]

As the two sides — proponents of further sweeping desegregation, even with mandatory cross-town busing, and the advocates of gradualism or the status quo, virile opponents of cross-town busing — gathered, there were several realities, theories, philosophies, and myths which surrounded the decades-old problem and which undoubtedly entered the group's discussions. First, the School Board and its administration had consistently and correctly contended that "the establishment and maintenance of a racially balanced school system was virtually impossible" in the wake of rigid residential segregation within the city and the white flight or exodus to the suburbs. The major problem, they said, was not "so much desegregating a school," but "in keeping it desegregated." Since 1960, for example, 24 schools had gone from all-white to desegregated to all-black. Whites seemed simply intolerable of any school which became 30 percent or more black. When that "turning point" was reached, almost all, if not all, whites fled. The school system had no choice but to admit defeat in the face of this phenomenon. As one of its officials put it, "There is not much we can do if a person wants to sell his house to move to the suburbs. Whatever happens the school system is blamed. The school system is blamed for letting the black people in and the school system is blamed for not keeping the whites in." Similarly, the board's implementation of the "57-43" faculty desegregation quota could not succeed, as, in each year after its introduction, dozens of white teachers resigned and left the Atlanta system.[56]

On the other hand, critics argued, often correctly, that the Atlanta Board of Education and its administration had not done enough to promote desegregation. The system moved slowly and grudgingly, only with the prodding of blacks and the courts. It remained wedded to "freedom of choice," while attendance zones or formal school boundaries could have increased bi-racial classes. It continued to build segregated schools and convert other facilities which perpetuated segregation rather than seek creative ways — such as "learning centers" or "magnet schools" — to enhance desegregation.[57]

Finally, as the discussants met in 1973, there were two strong, prevailing myths that figured prominently in the debate. The first, largely promulgated by school officials, was that in recent years all inequalities had been removed from the schools. There may, indeed, still be some separate ones, but all were equal. The second, widely believed by both whites and blacks, was that all-black schools were inherently inferior. Reports from Better Schools-Atlanta and a special committee from the NEA had largely demolished the first myth for many by 1970. But it was the growing acceptance by blacks of the fallacy of the second that helped pave the way for the eventual solution to the long struggle over school desegregation in Atlanta.[58]

For a number of years, prior to the 1960s, blacks had exhibited a certain ambivalence in the matter of the inherent inferiority of their schools. On one hand, many boasted of quality education at the hands of black schoolmarms in both rural and urban all-black schoolhouses, and of the excellent training which the all-black colleges of the South had provided their leaders since Reconstruction. On the other hand, they argued in the U.S. Supreme Court for at least two decades that such schools could never be made equal to those for whites. In *Brown vs. Board of Education of Topeka, Kansas*, 1954, the Court accepted these arguments, concluding that the mere act of separation bred inequality and adversely affected the hearts and minds of black children in a way "unlikely ever to be undone."[59]

Perhaps a partial explanation of the ambivalence of many blacks on the question of equal schooling lay in the fact that in the past, "integration" was seen "as the only means of achieving equal educational opportunity for their children. This was not because the proximity of white children was so much to be desired but because experience had taught them" that separate facilities, in reality, were always unequal. All-white or majority white boards of education had simply not provided equal appropriations, equal supplies, equal buildings and furniture, and equal attention for and to schools in the black communities. By the 1970s, then, an increasing number of black Atlantans, including members of the leadership class, had come to believe that the greater issue was the achievement of "greater control over the educational decisions that [affected] their children in order to ensure improved education — whether in racially separate or integrated schools." Whereas some black parents would still bus their children to

Canada, if necessary, to achieve a quality education, others took the position that "we are tired of chasing white folks all over town just to sit next to them in a classroom." Another and significant mirror of the new attitude was reflected in the changing stance of Benjamin E. Mays, the venerable black educator, who, in 1970, became the first black person elected to head the Atlanta School Board. Mays, the former president of Atlanta's Morehouse College, had always been a staunch integrationist. But by 1970, he was ready to declare: "I don't believe it is necessary for a black child to have to sit next to a white child to get a good education." Indeed, at a higher level, he had proved this, himself, in his leadership at Morehouse College. As president there for 27 years, he helped make the all-black, all-male school one of the most prestigious small colleges in the nation, as its graduates won national, even international distinction in almost every field of endeavor [60]

Mays, the Atlanta Urban League's Lyndon Wade, the Atlanta NAACP's Lonnie King, Atlanta Life Insurance Company President Jesse Hill, and several other black leaders joined a group of white business and professional leaders in sessions at a downtown bank building during the early months of 1973. The blacks conceded the futility of total desegregation of the Atlanta Public School System. There "simply were not enough whites" left "to go around." They also decided to abandon the idea of mandatory cross-town or cross-jurisdictional busing, justifying this move on the basis of the great inconvenience and hazard for young children. They did insist that a number of specific schools, including several of the previously all-white ones, be desegregated, with at least an enrollment of 30 percent black. There would also be some pairings of black and white schools and some voluntary busing. They demanded, and whites agreed, that blacks must take administrative control of the now largely black school system. Specifically, there must be a black superintendent and at least 50 percent of all of the other top administrators must be black. This bargain, which became known as "the Compromise Plan of 1973," was sanctioned by the Federal District Court in Atlanta, and thus some 15 years after it was started, the Atlanta school desegregation case was, indeed, closed.[61]

While the national NAACP, some local black leaders, and some black parents objected to the "Compromise of 1973," there was no mass movement to undermine or undo it. Resegregation, then, had become the prevailing policy in Atlanta, and it had the endorsement of a federal court, influential members of the white power establishment, including the press, and influential members of the black power structure, including the black School Board president and the local president of the NAACP.[62]

In order to understand fully (1) how Atlantans succeeded in attaining peaceful school desegregation when so many other cities failed and (2) how, after only a decade of limited desegregation, blacks would sanction resegregation, one must begin with the six institutions of black higher education known as the Atlanta University Center. These schools and their products furnished the city with an unusually large group of educated middle-income blacks who joined with the masses to become, by 1949, an influential political force in the city. Additionally, these blacks generated a substantial part of the city's expendable income. On the one hand they were, because of their income and education, restless under the caste system, but on the other they were secure enough in their own right to be cautious and patient. This attitude, as much as anything else, delayed desegregation in Atlanta until 1961. The delay was perhaps fortunate, for had the crisis come in 1954 or 1957, chances of success would have been immeasurably diminished.

It was fortunate for Atlanta that for at least 25 years prior to the school desegregation, the city's political leadership had had very close ties to the city's business community. In fact Mayor William B. Hartsfield, who, in his last days in office, presided over the initial desegregation process, came out of that community, as did his successor, former Chamber of Commerce President Ivan Allen, Jr. The politicians and the businessmen, then, were often of one mind when it came to city policies.

Also, the fact that Atlanta was becoming the industrial, commercial, and transportation center of the South influenced its leaders to follow the course of moderation in the question of desegregation. Business would not locate or stay in places where there was turmoil or disruption of education. Violence in the streets would deter customers from shopping. It was, then, good business to be "too busy to hate."[63]

As historians of the South are fond of saying, "the railroads made Atlanta" the bustling metropolis it became. The railroads which brought Yankee goods and Yankee entrepreneurs to and through Atlanta were also soon to bring increasing numbers of unskilled blacks from rural Georgia and other parts of the agricultural South into the city. Equally important, however, they brought Northern white educators into the city to found black colleges and universities for the freedmen and to serve as teachers in these institutions. Within a generation of the Civil War's end, highly trained blacks were also coming into the city to take their places as teachers and administrators in black schools. For Black Atlanta and, indeed, for Black America, these developments proved to be of monumental significance. By 1929, when the six black colleges and universities began a program of affiliation, Atlanta had become the largest and best known center for the highest education of blacks in the world.[64]

The combination of the black academic elite was augmented by grammar school teachers and principals, preachers, a few other professional people, and black businessmen. By 1900, they constituted a highly visible black upper stratum, and by 1950, Atlanta had achieved national notoriety as a social and business capital for American blacks. These realities did not, however, loom very large in the minds of many white Atlantans. White Atlantans, like most white Southerners, believed in the inferiority of blacks, no matter how well educated or how wealthy, and generally upheld the sanctity of the caste system. When, as in the Atlanta Riot of 1906, they viewed black actions as a serious threat to the system, the more violent 'elements' among the whites lashed out equally at blacks of all classes.[65]

For educated middle-income black Atlantans, particularly, the inhumanity and illogic of the caste system was particularly acute, as they daily dwelled in a community which taught freedom of the mind, yet they themselves were virtually imprisoned in that community. From time to time members of this group would dare to speak out against the injustices which surrounded them. More often they would organize politically and urge their fellow blacks of every station to follow them in their quest to use the ballot to break down the racial barriers. These attitudes and practices served all of the black communities — and, indeed, all of Atlanta and the nation — well when it came time to meet the ordeal of desegregation of the schools in 1961.[66]

Whereas the way Atlanta achieved desegregation in 1961 brought the city much favorable publicity, praise, and laud, the resegregation agreement of 1973 brought such notoriety that some called it the "infamous compromise." The national NAACP said it could set back the cause of integration and, in fact, suspended its Atlanta branch because of it. Whatever the wisdom of the "compromise," it was abundantly clear in 1973 that many whites, perhaps a majority of them, in the city would go to extraordinary pains and expenses to prevent their children from attending substantially desegregated schools. While it is not certain that whites opposed housing desegregation more or less than school desegregation, the Atlanta experience, which was not unique in the nation, demonstrated that they apparently felt ill at ease with both. Flight from one affected the extent of desegregation in the other. The law could not stem white flight, and thus the courts were powerless to stabilize school desegregation within the city.[67]

As has been suggested, the policies and practices of the Atlanta School Board also undermined the desegregation effort in the city. Before *Calhoun vs. Latimer*, the only black member of the Atlanta Board of Education was Atlanta University President Rufus E. Clement. Clement, who was elected in 1953 and reelected for three terms thereafter, was a quiet-spoken, scholarly man. While he represented only the city's Third Ward, he became known as the Board member of all of Atlanta's blacks. No matter what part of Black Atlanta he appeared in, he was invariably introduced, particularly by whites, as "your board member." Yet he did very little in the segregation years to challenge the status quo. He did oppose the original "freedom of choice" desegregation plan, but voted for it in the interest of moving the process along. He won much respect among whites for his demeanor. On one occasion, School Board Superintendent Ira Jarrell, who presided over the closing days of segregation, praised Clement as one who had never uttered an unwise word. On the questions of school desegregation and racial equality, the fact of the matter is that Clement had hardly uttered any words at all. It was probably, then, quite a shock for Miss Jarrell and others when Clement testified for the plaintiffs in *Calhoun vs. Latimer*. He specifically rebutted the testimony of Miss Jarrell and others that there was equality in the Atlanta schools and that segregation there was a voluntary act on the part of both races. In the school administration itself, there had been a supervisor of black schools and several black program coordinators, but no top executives, at this time. So the policies and practices, with respect to the dismantling of the dual system of education, were decided by a preponderantly white School Board and implemented by an almost all-white administration.[68]

The School Board not only lacked a policy for desegregation, but it and the administration took several actions which actually impeded desegregation. Exemplary of the School Board's attitude was an incident during 1969. In April of that year, the Atlanta Community Relations Commission asked the Atlanta Board of Education to "call on the U.S. Office of Education for assistance in developing a school desegregation plan." The request was based upon Title IV of the 1964 Civil Rights Act, which provided for technical assistance to local school boards in "planning and instituting an integrated school system." But the Atlanta School Board was not interested in the Commission's suggestion. Board Attorney A. C. "Pete" Latimer said, "Bringing Office of Education people into Atlanta to help with integration would be like Rembrandt bringing in a housepainter . . . In my judgment the system you have now will produce the best results with far and away the most goodwill." Latimer concluded, "I don't think there is the crisis in the city . . . that you folks think there is . . . There is not too much difference between what the negro [sic] family wants and what the white family wants." Superintendent John Letson, successor to Ira Jarrell, complained that too much of a burden was being placed on the schools. He said, "The central community agencies have not contributed to the climate which is necessary to make it [desegregation] work . . . For example, there is not a single desegregated church in the area where we have worked so hard. The schools can work at it but the schools alone cannot make it work."[69]

Interestingly enough, the federal courts, including the U.S. Supreme Court, but especially the District Court for Northern Georgia, also retarded the pace of school desegregation in Atlanta. The Supreme Court's *dictum* of 1955 that desegregation should proceed "with all deliberate speed" remained the national policy until 1969. When it decreed "integration now" in *Alexander vs. Holmes*, the Atlanta School System had become almost two-thirds black. More importantly, in the "all deliberate speed" years, the Federal District Court in Atlanta, unlike many other District Courts and even its own Circuit Court of Appeals, adhered to the phrase slavishly. From the time that the presiding judge in Calhoun — Frank A. Hooper — announced in 1959 that he was ordering desegregation with personal reluctance, only because it was the "law of the land," until 1972 when the court declared a resegregated school system "desegregated" or "unitary," the U.S. District Court for the Northern District of Georgia aided and abetted the snail-like movements of the Atlanta School Board toward desegregation and, then, in 1973, gave its blessings to the compromise resegregation plan.[70]

But blacks themselves did nearly as much as other parties to bring about the resegregation of Atlanta's schools. Since the masses of Atlanta blacks were then largely inarticulate and allowed traditional leaders from the clergy, education, business, and the professions to speak and act in the name of all blacks, it is really the leadership class itself which bears much of the responsibility for the failure of school desegregation in Atlanta. Because in Atlanta, unlike most of the rest of the South, there was, even in the late nineteenth century, a number of quality, yet segregated, social and economic institutions, the "ironclad fist" of oppression did not always seem so awesome. The sizeable pocket of liberalism among whites from the universities, labor, and some of the churches helped to impress upon this class of blacks the possibilities of real racial harmony and goodwill. Concessions in race relations which the voting influence of blacks had brought from politicians and businessmen nurtured the idea of progress. Many of these white, liberal politicians and businessmen sought to convince the black leadership that a "go slow" attitude on racial change would reap the safest and most lasting benefits. For the most part, they were successful, as the black leadership cadre in Atlanta adopted a policy of cautious gradualism in its approach toward desegregation. This strategy was not visibly shaken until the student sit-ins of 1960-1961 and survived almost intact until the "Peyton Wall" housing crisis of 1962-1963. And although the black leadership demanded the "total desegregation" of Atlanta schools in 1963, it did not call for massive demonstrations or other forms of pressure on authorities, nor did it make the matter a major issue in the city elections of 1965. The protests and boycotts of 1967 were, at best, feeble and sporadic gestures and brought about an open split in the black leadership. Of course, by this time, white flight was also taking its toll on the desegregation effort.[71]

In 1965-1966, the school year in which the Federal District Court in Atlanta ordered the "complete desegregation" of the schools, there were some 46,000 white students and some 57,000 black students enrolled in the school system. "Complete desegregation," involving zoned attendance areas and extensive cross-town busing, but without the freedom of choice program, could possibly have been achieved at that time. But these "drastic" measures were not employed and the school year began with only 5,594 students attending eight desegregated schools. After 1965-1966, with the exacerbation and acceleration of white flight, the cause of school desegregation in Atlanta was lost. And while the federal courts, the School Board, and black leaders all contributed to the failure of school desegregation in Atlanta, in the end it may not have been the presence of hate, nor the absence of love, but it was certainly the persistence of white racism which turned the glorious days of the fall of 1961 into the admission of defeat, which the "compromise" represented in the winter of 1973. The crux of the matter may have been stated by a white woman at an anti-busing protest during a meeting of the Atlanta School Board on November 16, 1972, when she cried: "The white people will leave [Atlanta] and let the blacks have it . . . ."[72]

NOTES

[1] *Atlanta Constitution*, August 31, September 1, 1961; *Atlanta Journal*, August 30, 1961; Alton Hornsby, Jr., "A City That Was Too Busy to Hate" in Elizabeth Jacoway and David Colburn, eds., *Southern Businessmen and Desegregation* (Baton Rouge, 1982), p. 120, (Hereinafter cited as Hornsby, "A City Too Busy to Hate.")

[2] *Atlanta Constitution*, August 31, September 1, 1961; *Newsweek*, September 11, 1961, p. 31; *Reporter*, September 15, 1961, p. 14; *U.S. News and World Report*, September 11, 1961, p. 72; Hornsby, "A City Too Busy to Hate," p. 121; *Atlanta Daily World*, August 31, 1961.

[3] Research Atlanta, *School Desegregation in Metro Atlanta, 1954-1973* (Atlanta, 1973), p. 3. (Hereinafter cited as *School Desegregation in Metro Atlanta*); *Atlanta Daily World*, January 14, 1958.

[4] *School Desegregation in Metro Atlanta*, p. 13; National Education Association, "Central Issues Influencing School-Community Relations in Atlanta, Georgia," August, 1969, p. 18. (Hereinafter cited as NEA, "School-Community Relations"); *Atlanta Journal*, May 9, 1960; *Atlanta Daily World*, June 6, 1959; H. Mark Huie, "Factors Influencing the Desegregation Process in the Atlanta School System" (unpublished Ph.D. Dissertation, the University of Georgia, Athens, 1967), pp. 37-38, 82. (Hereinafter cited as Huie); *Minutes of The Board of Education of The City of Atlanta*, LII (January 4, 18, 1960) (Hereinafter cited as *Board of Education Minutes*); The Southern Center for Studies in Public Policy of Clark College, *Consensus Politics in Atlanta: School Board Decision Making, 1974-1978* (Atlanta, 1979), pp. 13-14 (Hereinafter cited as Clark College, *School Board Decision Making*).

[5] *School Desegregation in Metro Atlanta*, pp. 3, 13-14; NEA, "School-Community Relations," p. 18; *Atlanta Journal*, May 9, 1960; *Atlanta Daily World*, May 10, 1960; Huie, pp. 38-40, 82; Order of the United States District Court for the Northern District of Georgia in *Vivian Calhoun et al vs. Board of Education, City of Atlanta, et al*, Civil Action No. 6298, May 9, 1960.

[6] *School Desegregation in Metro Atlanta*, p. 4; NEA, "School-Community Relations," pp. 18-19; *Atlanta Journal*, December 13, 1959; *Board of Education Minutes*, LII (November 30, 1959), LII, January 4, 18, 1960; Huie, p. 82; Eliza K. Paschall, *It Must Have Rained* (Atlanta), pp. 22-28.

[7] Interview with Ivan Allen, Jr. by Marcellus C. Barksdale, September 25, 1979; *Atlanta Constitution*, January 5, 1961; Hornsby, "A City Too Busy to Hate," p. 125; NEA, "School-Community Relations," p. 19; Paschall, p. 21; Ivan Allen Jr. with Paul Hemphill, Mayor, *Notes on The Sixties* (New York, 1971), p. 32.

[8] The Sibley Commission received its name from its chairman, John Sibley, a venerable Atlanta Lawyer who, as a board member of several

businesses, had strong ties to the local and state business communities. Allen interview; Hornsby, "A City Too Busy to Hate," p. 126; Paschall, *ibid.*

[9] *Atlanta Constitution*, January 7-11, 1961; *Atlanta Journal*, January 10, 1961; Hornsby, *ibid.*

[10] *Atlanta Constitution*, January 7, 13, 1961; *Atlanta Journal*, January 7, 14, 1961; Hornsby, *ibid.*, p. 127.

[11] *Atlanta Constitution*, January 10, 12, 1961; *Atlanta Journal*, January 10, 12, 1961; Hornsby, *ibid.*

[12] *Atlanta Constitution*, January 9-11, 1961; *Atlanta Journal*, January 9-11, 1961; Hornsby, *ibid.*, p. 128.

[13] *Atlanta Constitution*, January 10-12, 1961; *Atlanta Journal*, January 10, 12, 1961; Hornsby, *ibid.*

[14] *Atlanta Constitution*, January 16-18, 1961; Hornsby, *ibid.*, p. 129; Paschall, p. 21.

[15] *Atlanta Constitution*, January 18, 19, 1961; Hornsby, *ibid.*, p. 130.

[16] *Atlanta Constitution*, January 19, 1961; Hornsby, *ibid.*

[17] *Atlanta Constitution*, January 21, 1961; Hornsby, *ibid.*

[18] Allen interview; *Atlanta Constitution*, January 21, 23, 1961; Hornsby, *ibid.*, p. 131.

[19] *Atlanta Constitution*, January 21, 23, 1961; *Atlanta Journal*, January 21-23, 1961; Hornsby, *ibid.*, p. 132.

[20] *Atlanta Constitution*, January 28-31, February 1, 1961; *Atlanta Journal*, January 28-31, February 1, 1961; Hornsby, *ibid.*, p. 133.

[21] Hornsby, *ibid.*, pp. 134-35; Paschall, pp. 21, 29.

[22] Interview with J. R. Wilson by Cynthia G. Fleming, September 7, 1978; Interview with Benjamin E. Mays by Cynthia G. Fleming, September 7, 1978; Interview with Robert Blark by Marcellus C. Barksdale, September 6, 1978; Hornsby, *ibid.*; Paschall, *ibid.*

[23] *Atlanta Constitution*, February 25, 1961; Hornsby, *ibid.*, p. 135.

[24] *Atlanta Constitution*, February 1, 20, 28, 1961; Hornsby, *ibid.*, p. 135; Allen, Mayor, pp. 39-40.

[25] *Atlanta Constitution*, March 8, 11, 1961; Hornsby, *ibid.* p. 136.

[26] Hornsby, *ibid.*

[27] NEA, "School Community Relations," p. 19; *School Desegregation in Metro Atlanta*, p. 4; *Atlanta Daily World*, May 3, 7, 1961; *Atlanta Constitution*, June 4, August 8, November 16, 1961; *Atlanta Journal*, June 3, August 18-20, November 15, 1961; Huie, p. 146; *Board of Education Minutes*, LVI (April 24, May 8, 23, July 6, 1961); Paschall, pp. 28, 31-32.

[28] NEA, "School-Community Relations," p. 20; *Atlanta Inquirer*, October 28, November 4, 1961.

[29] *School Desegregation in Metro Atlanta*, pp. 4, 14-15; NEA, "School-Community Relations," p. 20; Paschall, pp. 41-42.

[30] *School Desegregation in Metro Atlanta*, pp. 5, 15; NEA, "School-Community Relations," p. 20; *Board of Education Minutes*, LXIII (April 8, 13, 1964); Paschall, pp. 107-108.

[31] *School Desegregation in Metro Atlanta*, pp. 5, 15; NEA, "School-Community Relations," p. 20; *Board of Education Minutes*, LXII (June 12, July 8, 1963); Paschall, *ibid.*

[32] *School Desegregation in Metro Atlanta*, *ibid.*; NEA, "School-Community Relations," pp. 20-21; *Board of Education Minutes*, LXIII (April 8, 13, 1964); Paschall, *ibid.*

[33] *School Desegregation in Metro Atlanta*, pp. 5, 16-17; NEA, "School-Community Relations," p. 21.

[34] *School Desegregation in Metro Atlanta*, pp. 5, 17; NEA, "School-Community Relations," p. 21.

[35] *School Desegregation in Metro Atlanta*, *ibid.*; NEA, "School-Community Relations," pp. 21-22.

[36] NEA, "School-Community Relations," p. 22; Paschall, p. 109.

[37] NEA, "School-Community Relations," pp. 22-23; *Atlanta Constitution*, August 10, 1966; Paschall, pp. 120-21.

[38] NEA, "School-Community Relations," p. 23; *Atlanta Constitution*, September 27, November 9, 1967; *Atlanta Daily World*, September 22, 1967; *Atlanta Constitution*, October 3, 1967; *Board of Education Minutes*, LXXI (February 6, March 13, 1967), LXXII (September 25, October 9, 1967).

[39] NEA, "School-Community Relations," p. 24; *Atlanta Constitution*, *ibid.*; *Atlanta Daily World*, *ibid.*; *Board of Education Minutes*, LXXIII (February 12, 1968, April 11, June 10, July 8, 1968).

[40] NEA, *ibid.*; *Atlanta Daily World*, September 22, 1967.

[41] NEA, "School-Community Relations," pp. 24-25; Better Schools-Atlanta, "Student Achievement in Atlanta Public Schools: A Report" (Atlanta, 1968).

[42] NEA, "School-Community Relations," pp. 24-26; *Atlanta Journal*, February 10, 1969.

[43] *School Desegregation in Metro Atlanta*, p. 18; NEA, "School-Community Relations," p. 26.

[44] *School Desegregation in Metro Atlanta*, pp. 18-19; *Atlanta Constitution*, January 5, 10, 16, 21, 29, February 3, 18, March 12, April 25, 1970; *Atlanta Inquirer*, January 17, 24, 31, February 7, 28, March 14, 1970; Clark College, *School Board Decision Making*, p. 18; *Board of Education Minutes*, LXXV (July 14, August 11, 1969), LXXVII (July 13, 1970), LXXVI (January 9, February 9, 1970).

[45] *School Desegregation in Metro Atlanta*, pp. 6, 19; NEA, "School-Community Relations," p. 35, *Atlanta Constitution*, July 10, 1970; Board of Education Minutes, *ibid.*

[46] *School Desegregation in Metro Atlanta*, pp. 19-20; *Race Relations Law Survey*, I, No.5; (January, 1972), p. 167.

[47] *School Desegregation in Metro Atlanta*, pp. 20-21; *Calhoun Versus Cook*, F2d (Fifth Cir., October 21, 1971); *Race Relations Law Survey*, *ibid.*, p. 167.

[48] *School Desegregation in Metro Atlanta*, pp. 20-21; *Board of Education Minutes*, LXXIX (May 17, August 9, September 13, 1971; March 27,1972).

[49] *School Desegregation in Metro Atlanta*, pp. 9, 21.

[50] *School Desegregation in Metro Atlanta*, p. 21.

[51] *School Desegregation in Metro Atlanta*, pp. 21-22, 23-24.

[52] *School Desegregation in Metro Atlanta*, p. 22; *Atlanta Journal-Constitution*, November 14, 23, 26, 1972; *Atlanta Constitution*, November 21, 1972.

[53] NEA, "School-Community Relations," pp. 30-34; *Atlanta Journal-Constitution*, November 14, 23, 26, 1972; *Atlanta Constitution*, November 21, 1972.

[54] *School Desegregation in Metro Atlanta*, pp. 22, 53-63; *Atlanta Constitution*, December 2, 1972.

[55] *Atlanta Constitution*, November 21, 1972; January 23, 1973.

[56] NEA, "School-Community Relations," pp. 35-36; *Atlanta Constitution*, January 28, 1970; November 21, 1972; *Atlanta Daily World*, February 7, 1970; *Atlanta Inquirer*, February 7, 1970.

[57] NEA, "School-Community Relations," pp. 36-37; Clark College, *School Board Decision Making*, pp. 16-17.

[58] NEA, "School-Community Relations," pp. 27-29.

[59] NEA, "School-Community Relations," pp. 27-28.

[60] Interview with Benjamin E. Mays by Cynthia G. Fleming, September 7, 1978; NEA, "School-Community Relations," *ibid.*; Clark College, *School Board Decision Making*, pp. 16, 18.

[61] Clark College, *School Board Decision Making*, p. 18; *Atlanta Journal-Constitution*, March 18, 1973; January 27, 1974; *Atlanta Constitution*, January 23, 26, 1973, November 14, 16, 18, 21, 1972.

[62] Clark College, *ibid.*, *Atlanta Constitution*, November 13, 14, 21, December 2, 1972; *Atlanta Journal Constitution*, March 18, 1973; January 27, 1974.

[63] Hornsby, "A City Too Busy to Hate," p. 121.

[64] Hornsby, *ibid.*, p. 122; C. Vann Woodward, *Origins Of The New South, 1877-1913* (Baton Rouge, 1951), pp. 7, 34, 108, 144, passim; Alton Hornsby, Jr., "The Negro in Atlanta Politics," *Atlanta Historical Bulletin* (Hereinafter cited as *AHB*), XXI (Spring, 1977), pp. 7-8; C. T. Wright, "The Development of Public Schools for Blacks in Atlanta, 1879-1900" *AHB*, XXI (Spring, 1977), pp. 115-28; Myron W. Adams, *A History of Atlanta University* (Atlanta, 1930), pp. 1-38, Passim; Willard Range, *The Rise and Progress of Negro Colleges in Georgia, 1865-1949* (Athens, 1951), pp. 193-97, 224-27.

[65] Hornsby, "A City Too Busy to Hate," p. 122; Alexa Benson Henderson, "Alonzo F. Herndon and Black Insurance in Atlanta, 1904-1915," *AHB*, XXI (Spring, 1977), pp. 34-47; Robert Vowels, "Atlanta Negro Businesses and the New Black Bourgeoisie," *AHB*, XXI (Spring, 1977), pp. 48-63; August Meier and David Lewis, "History of the Negro Upper Class in Atlanta, Georgia, 1890-1958," *Journal of Negro Education*, XXVIII (Spring, 1959), pp. 128-39.

[66] Hornsby, "A City Too Busy to Hate," p. 123; Hornsby, "The Negro in Atlanta Politics," pp. 7-11; Clarence A. Bacote, "The Negro in Atlanta Politics, 1865-1948," *Phylon*, XVI (Winter, 1955), pp. 331-51.

[67] NEA, "School-Community Relations," pp. 21, 35-36.

[68] NEA, "School-Community Relations," pp. 18; Clark College, *School Board Decision Making*, pp. 19-21; Vivian Calhoun, et al v. *A. C. Latimer*, et al; Huie, pp. 37-38.

[69] NEA, "School-Community Relations," pp. 37-38; Clark College, *School Board Decision Making, Ibid.*

[70] *Atlanta Journal*, June 5, 1959; *Atlanta Constitution*, June 6, 1959; March 18, 1973; *Atlanta Daily World*, June 6, 1959.

[71] *Atlanta Constitution*, November 13, December 11, 1972; January 29, 1973. The "Peyton-Wall" housing crisis occurred after the city constructed a barricade at Peyton Rd. in Southwest Atlanta to deter "black encroachments" into all-white neighborhoods.

[72] *Atlanta Constitution*, November 17, 1972, December 11, 1972; January 29, 1973; *Atlanta Journal-Constitution*, March 18, 1973; January 27, 1974; *Atlanta Journal*, August 30, September 1, 1976; Robert C. Godfrey to editor, *Atlanta Constitution*, November 21, 1972.

POLITICS AND CIVIL RIGHTS

Chapter 11
Martin Luther King, Jr. and the
Civil Rights Movement in Atlanta, Georgia

As many of you know, Thomas Carlyle once said that those who would like to know history need only read the stories of the great men who have lived here. Although modern scholars tend to reject Carlyle's view as a much too simplistic notion of the meaning of history, many of us do concede the possibility that occasionally an individual — man or woman — can, largely through his or her own initiative, affect, for better or worse, the continuum of time. In these admittedly rare instances, the individual is most often a possessor of charisma, as evidenced through oratory or other personal skills, and he or she is also a genius, possessing unusual insight into problems and events. But Martin Luther King, Jr. refused to wholly accept the scholars' great man theory of history. He was more persuaded by the norm established by Jesus, when the savior told some of his disciples that "He who is greatest among you shall be your servant." On the basis of this definition, King felt that greatness need not be reserved for statesmen and military leaders, but that it could very well be extended to ordinary men and women. A cleaning woman, then, might achieve greatness over a King or a Drum Major might achieve it over a General.

If we were to assess Martin Luther King, Jr.'s own role in

Prepared for presentation at the King Week Celebration at Clemson University, Clemson, South Carolina, January 17, 1991

American history, in fairness to him, we should apply his own norm as well as the traditional great man theory. His leadership in the great campaigns for human rights at Montgomery, Albany, Chicago, Birmingham, Selma and Memphis would be the focus upon which the examination and conclusion would be based. But these events have been thoroughly covered by many prominent scholars; while his role in the civil rights activities in his own hometown, Atlanta, Georgia, is only now beginning to receive serious attention.

If, then, we were to take a microscopic view of King's role in American history, by examining his work in Atlanta, we should probably start with a brief summary of the patterns of race relations in the city.

Today, the City of Atlanta enjoys a reputation as a black Mecca in the United States, where race relations are unusually harmonious. But the city in which Martin Luther King, Jr., was born in 1929 was a premiere example of American racial bigotry and hatred. Much of this ignoble reputation stemmed directly from the infamous race riot which took place there in 1906. In that riot numerous blacks were killed and injured and several white persons were also injured. There was widespread property damage and a general breakdown of law and order. And it was all caused by racial mistrust, misunderstanding, and prejudice.

But, out of the Atlanta riot, at least one positive thing emerged — some of the city's white leaders — ministers, educators, politicians, and businessmen, who had been embarrassed by the turmoil, vowed that it should never happen again. They decided to open a dialogue with the leaders in the black communities and to try to develop greater tolerance and understanding between the races. Most of the blacks welcomed these overtures and a tradition of positive communications between the races emerged. Certainly it was because of this tradition that there has not been another race riot of that magnitude in the city since 1906.

The absence of mass violence, however, did not mean that there was complete racial peace and goodwill in the city in the years after 1906. Quite the contrary, during the youth of Martin Luther King, Jr., blacks continued to live in a state of separation, discrimination, and oppression. Young Martin, himself, was a victim of this system, even though his parents did all that they could to protect him from it. In its most severe form, the system was characterized by lynching or murder of innocent black men, women, and children and brutal treatment at the hands of law enforcement officers. In its milder forms, it exploited black labor and denied blacks equality in schooling, housing, voting and office-holding, and public accommodations. As a city, which participated in the system, both *de jure* and *de facto*, that is, in law and in practice, Atlanta was in congruence with the rest of the South, and, indeed, much of the North. But, even in the 1920s and 1930s, there was something different about Atlanta, which distinguished it from most of the South and much of the nation.

We have already alluded to the bi-racial communications, which were opened after the 1906 riot. These were continued and, as the years passed, increased and made meaningful. It was, then, not surprising that the Commission Interracial on Cooperation — the first south-wide group devoted to racial harmony — had its headquarters in Atlanta. But equally as important was the fact that, even before the Second World War, Atlanta had become a national center for black-owned and operated business and was the largest center for black higher education in the world.

The six colleges in the city and the black businesses were linkages in the development of one of the largest black middle class communities in the nation. The colleges attracted well-educated professors from all over the country, who in turn trained many other professional blacks. Many of these persons started their own businesses and professions or supported other businesses and professional concerns, which were operated by fellow blacks. By 1929, there were several black insurance and real estate companies in the city as well as a major black owned bank. This bank, incidentally, was so solid and efficient that it managed to stay open, even during the "Great Depression," when many other banks all over the nation were failing. And there was a healthy sprinkling of physicians, dentists, lawyers, and social workers.

The bi-racial communications, the black colleges, the black businesses and professions, and the large black middle class were, then, the distinctive elements that pointed to a better way of life for some black Atlantans and distinguished the city very early from most of its neighbors. Unfortunately, most black Atlantans did not possess the education and wealth of the middle class; many could not communicate with white persons with mutual respect; and all faced humiliating, and often debilitating laws, rules, regulations, and practices which bred separation, discrimination, inequality, and injustice.

And so, even as the Second World War ended and Martin Luther King, Jr. matriculated at Atlanta's Morehouse College, huge walls of bigotry and intolerance still divided much of the white side of Atlanta from the black side. But when King graduated from Morehouse in 1948, a major development had occurred which would profoundly affect the course of race relations in the city for generations yet to come. Indeed, it was a major crack in the walls which assigned blacks to almost total inferiority in their daily lives. For by 1948, Atlanta blacks had gained the right to vote freely in the city for the first time since the Reconstruction days. And they used their votes to demand new respect and new rights.

Prior to 1946, despite the 15th Amendment to the United States Constitution, which guaranteed all Americans the right to vote, Atlanta, Georgia, and most of the rest of the South, had developed and implemented numerous illegal and extra-legal devices to deny, restrict, or frustrate the right of blacks to participate in free elections. In Atlanta, qualified blacks could vote only in special and general elections. They could not vote in primary elections which, because of the one-party system which existed in the South at that time, were the only meaningful contests. As you know, the United States Supreme Court, in the Texas case of *Smith vs. Allwright*, 1944, first declared these denials of the right to vote unconstitutional. Then in 1946, in the case of *Chapman vs. King*, the same court ruled that blacks in Georgia must be allowed the right to vote freely in all elections. It was after this decision that black leaders in Atlanta galvanized other blacks to register and to vote. Their efforts were so successful that by 1948, a year before the next city elections, it was clear that the 30,000 blacks registered to vote would have a major influence on future political developments in Atlanta. One of the persons who knew this fact very clearly was the man who was then mayor of the city, William B. Hartsfield.

As an astute politician, Mayor Hartsfield realized that, because of common grievances and common interests, the black voters were likely to vote in the same manner or in a bloc. And, even though white voters still outnumbered the black ones, the black bloc votes, combined with only a few thousand whites, who were likely to vote the same way, could be the deciding margin between victory and defeat for local political candidates. After initially trying to fight this possibility or this eventuality, Hartsfield, wisely, decided to work with and for it. He also realized that those candidates who would seek to benefit from the black vote had to make concessions to it.

At that time, one of the principal concerns of the black communities was the relationship between them and the police. There had been repeated claims that many blacks had been both verbally and physically mistreated by local law enforcement officers. Black leaders believed that this situation could be remedied or rectified if there were black policemen to patrol the black communities. But before the emergence of the black vote as an influential factor in local politics, the concerns of the blacks were largely ignored. Then, in 1948, Mayor William B. Hartsfield conceded the right and the necessity of having black policemen in Atlanta. With his leadership, the first group of black officers were sworn into duty that same year. Although these policemen were segregated from their fellow white officers and could not arrest white persons, most blacks applauded and approved their appointments. The appearance of black policemen was not only a source of pride, but many felt that they would receive better and more courteous treatment from these officers.

The appointment of the black policemen endeared Mayor Hartsfield to the black communities and their leaders. Understandably, then, they voted heavily for him in the 1949 elections. These votes, together with those of a number of affluent and well-educated whites, were sufficient to give Mayor Hartsfield the victory in his bid for re-election. After 1949, this same coalition of blacks and affluent whites voted repeatedly for Mayor Hartsfield, thus keeping him in office as mayor of Atlanta until he retired in 1961. It became clear, in these years that no one could be elected mayor of the city without the combined support of the blacks and the affluent whites.

The political realities in Atlanta after 1949 dictated that all white candidates for citywide office should seek the votes of blacks as well as whites and most of the more successful ones did so. It was also understood that certain overtures of concessions would have to be made to the blacks in return for their votes. In these years, the concessions mostly took the form of some improvements in the segregated public facilities in the black communities, appointment of a few blacks to city boards and commissions, and increased communications, based upon mutual respect, between the two races. Still, however, schools, housing, and public accommodations were segregated and black ones were often inferior to those for whites; and no blacks held public office in the city.

Yet, there remained a noticeable atmosphere of racial tolerance and the mayor took the leadership in fostering this environment. And it was out of this environment that a black man, Dr. Rufus E. Clement, then president of Atlanta University, was elected as a member of the Atlanta Board of Education in 1953. He, thus, became the first black person to hold public office in the city since the days of Reconstruction. His election was made possible by the now invincible coalition of black and affluent white voters.

The election of Dr. Clement was reported widely and favorably in the national and international press, and Atlanta's reputation for good race relations was measurably enhanced. Interestingly enough, Dr.

Clement's election to the Atlanta School Board came just one year before the United States Supreme Court, in the monumental case of *Brown vs. the Board of Education of Topeka*, ruled that separate schools for blacks and whites were unconstitutional. This decision, as you know, ignited a stampede for racial equality in the United States and gave birth to what is called the Civil Rights Revolution or the modern Civil Rights Movement. After the famous bus boycott in Montgomery, Alabama in 1955-56, Martin Luther King, Jr., a native of Atlanta, Georgia, emerged as the single most influential leader in the Civil Rights Movement.

Keep in mind that it had been only seven years earlier that young King had left Morehouse College with his undergraduate degree. But, in these years, he had been well prepared for leadership. He had studied at Crozier Theological Seminary in Pennsylvania and Boston University in Massachusetts, receiving the Ph.D. degree for the latter. He had perfected his gift of oratory and he had become pastor of a leading black Baptist church in Montgomery, where he earned the respect of many in the black communities there. After his success in Montgomery, he was propelled into regional and national leadership.

Dr. King was a founder of the Southern Christian Leadership Conference (SCLC) in 1957. He saw it as an appropriate unit to coordinate the various direct action protests against racial injustices, particularly in the South. He soon realized that such an organization would be most effective if it were headquartered in a central location. Atlanta was the commercial and transportation center of the South and, thus, was the logical location for SCLC headquarters. Another important factor in the placing of SCLC offices in Atlanta was the city's well-known reputation for racial harmony. Whereas, already, there had been bombings, assaults, and other forms of racial violence in other Southern cities, including Montgomery, there had been no such incidents in Atlanta. And so, the city offered a favorable climate for leadership in civil rights activities.

Yet, it is both interesting and ironic that while Atlanta, as the home of the SCLC, the southeastern regional offices of the National Association for the Advancement of Colored People (NAACP), and the Student Nonviolent Coordination Committee (SNCC), became a national center of the Civil Rights Movement, the revolution had barely touched the city, itself.

In these early years of the movement, there were no efforts to desegregate the public schools, busses, or theaters, restaurants or other forms of public accommodations. The few efforts that were made were concentrated on colleges. There was also a successful move to desegregate golf courses, but very few blacks used these facilities.

When Martin Luther King, Jr. announced, late in 1959, that he was resigning the pastorate of Dexter Avenue Baptist Church in Montgomery to return to Atlanta to become co-pastor, with his father, of the Ebenezer Baptist Church and to occupy a full-time office in the SCLC headquarters there, the proposed move was greeted with mixed reaction in the city. Many blacks applauded it; many blacks and whites viewed it with apprehension and many whites and blacks opposed it. While the opposition on the part of some whites could be taken for granted, the motives of the opponents might seem baffling, particularly to us today. And, indeed, all of the attitudes of the black opponents have not been discerned by scholars. We do know, however, that by 1959 Atlanta already possessed an outstanding array of civil rights leaders, who had developed their own style of protest and reform, based largely on their substantial political influence. Some favored these methods over King's position or were concerned about what his position would do to their own. At any rate, some blacks apparently shared the fears of a former Morehouse College professor who declared that King would stir up trouble in Atlanta. There had, one must remember, been few, if any, major direct action protests in the city prior to this time.

It is unlikely that King was affected one way of the other by the concerns of his opponents in Atlanta, as he rarely allowed such attitudes to dissuade him from his missions. But he may well have conceded that the black leadership in the city, which included his own father, had things well under control, in their own way, and that he could best expend his efforts elsewhere. To be sure, much of Atlanta's reputation for good race relations, at the time, was more myth than fact, but conditions were far better there than in Birmingham, Montgomery, Jackson, and other areas of the urban and rural South. So Martin Luther King, Jr. did not play an active role in the movement for social change in Atlanta in the early days after his return to the city.

He was first brought into the movement in a major way in the spring of 1960. Students from the six colleges and universities comprising the Atlanta University Center had begun sit-ins, boycotts, marches, and other forms of direct action protest in February and March. On May 17th, the sixth anniversary of *Brown vs. the Board of Education*, student leaders planned a huge protest march on the state capitol. Segregationist Governor S. Ernest Vandiver vowed that they would not be allowed to set foot on the capitol grounds. So-called "Rednecks" and Klansmen were reportedly ready to assist in repelling the blacks. Atlanta University Center presidents were persuaded by the city's mayor and police chief that the safety of the students was endangered by the planned march. The best known of the presidents, a civil rights leader, himself, Benjamin E. Mays of Morehouse College, asked the students not to march. But after considerable confusion, hesitation, and anxiety, in the early afternoon of May 17th, several thousand Atlanta University Center students began to make their way toward the state capitol.

As the leaders of the march reached within a few blocks of the State House, Atlanta Police Chief Herbert Jenkins ordered them to retreat. There was division among the leaders at the head of the line, but the principal spokesman, Lonnie King, (no relationship to Martin) of Morehouse, ordered a diversion of the march to Wheat Street Baptist Church, which had been originally designated as a site of a post-march rally. Once the marchers reached Wheat Street, there were serious questions among both leaders and rank and file as to the wisdom of diverting the march. There was considerable rancor and discord. There were doubts about the courage and fortitude of those who had ordered retreat. And there was concern that the movement had been dealt a serious defeat. Some of the student leaders defended their actions; others disavowed them. But when Martin Luther King, Jr. entered the hall and said that "strategic retreats" were sometimes necessary in the struggle for civil rights, all but a few die-hard dissidents, left apparently pleased that the march had not been in vain.

Then, in October of 1960, Martin Luther King, Jr., for the first time, became directly involved in the Atlanta sit-in movement. Because of divided support from Atlanta's established black leadership and the adamant opposition of leaders of Rich's, the city's largest department store, by the fall of 1960, the Atlanta sit-ins had dragged on for more than eight months and negotiations to end them and to achieve desegregation of lunch counters and restaurants in the city were at a stalemate. In order to achieve greater unity in the movement and hopefully to break the stalemate, student leaders persuaded Martin Luther King, Jr. to reject his father's and other older black leaders advice and to join a sit-in on October 19th in a restaurant at Rich's Department Store. King and 51 other protesters were arrested and charged with violating the state's trespass law. Several of the demonstrators, including Dr. King refused to accept bond. But three days later, the city dropped the trespass charges and all of the demonstrators were freed, except King. Neighboring DeKalb County demanded that he be held on charges of violating a probated sentence for a September 1960 traffic offense. King was, then, transferred to the custody of DeKalb County and subsequently sentenced to six months in the state prison at Reidsville.

The injustice of the sentence aside, there were ominous fears for King's safety and well being at Georgia's maximum security prison. Among those expressing direct concern were the Democratic presidential candidate, John F. Kennedy and his campaign manager and brother, Robert F. Kennedy. The latter, in fact, intervened and persuaded a Georgia judge to order King's release on a $2,000 appeal bond on October 27.

As dramatic as King's arrest and incarceration had been, they did not immediately break the sit-in stalemate in Atlanta, where the chief executive of Rich's store, Frank Neely, had reportedly vowed that desegregation would occur only over his dead body. But the events had important national consequences, as many blacks, including Martin Luther King, Sr., publicly announced a switch of allegiance from the Republican candidate, Richard M. Nixon to the Democratic hopeful, John Kennedy. Some scholars and political analysts feel that many other blacks across the nation also made similar changes and that others, who were undecided or who were apathetic, decided to vote for Kennedy in appreciation for his campaign's concern for the welfare of Martin Luther King, Jr. In the close election of November 1960 these black votes may well have provided the margin of Kennedy's victory. Interestingly and ironically, however, Atlanta blacks still favored Richard Nixon, although by a rather narrow margin.

Finally, in March of 1961, an agreement was reached in Atlanta to end the sit-ins and to begin desegregation of restaurants and lunch counters in the fall of the year. The six months delay in implementing the agreement was a result of the insistence of white business and political leaders that lunch counter desegregation must follow school desegregation. Inasmuch as the Atlanta public schools were to be desegregated in late August, the earliest possible date for lunch counter desegregation would be September 1961. White leaders not only felt that school desegregation was a much more important matter than that of the restaurants, but they feared that any violence or backlash connected with any earlier desegregation of lunch counters could jeopardize the success of school desegregation. The black negotiators, particularly those who represented the established or older leadership in the city, accepted these arguments and persuaded the principal student negotiators to do likewise.

Among other student leaders and many of the rank and file, there were serious misgivings about accepting the six months delay in desegregating the lunch counters. Opponents argued that the Atlanta sit-in movement was already more than a year old and still without any concrete results. Now the blacks were being asked to accept another six months or more delay. Dissension and bitterness rose to such a peak that some threatened to disavow and disobey the accord and "rhetoricized" that the movement had gone "from sit-ins to sell outs."

Understandably, then, there was considerable tension on the evening of March 9, 1961 when students and others gathered at the Warren Methodist Church to hear the negotiators explain and defend the agreement. Student leaders were cursed and established leaders, including Martin Luther King, Sr. and Attorney A. T. Walden were hissed and booed. There was a real possibility that the negotiations would be discredited and that dissenters would resume the sit-ins. But when Martin Luther King, Jr. appeared in church, silence was attained. King said that as a leader of the movement, he, himself, could take an accusation that he had made a strategic mistake, but that he would be wounded by an accusation of "sell out" or other acts of disloyalty. He conceded that the sit-in agreement might not be a perfect one, but he urged its acceptance, at least for the moment. After Martin Luther King, Jr. spoke, the rebellion was stilled, at least for the moment. Peaceful school desegregation occurred in Atlanta in August of 1961 and the peaceful desegregation of many restaurants and lunch counters followed within a few weeks.

After the resolution of the Atlanta sit-in crisis, Martin Luther King, Jr. turned his attention to the great campaigns of Albany, Birmingham and Selma, and achieved a degree of immortality at the famous March on Washington in 1963. He did not participate directly in any further civil rights activities in his hometown.

King did, however, become embroiled in another racial controversy in the city in 1964. After receiving the Nobel Peace Prize, Atlanta's new mayor, Ivan Allen, Jr., who was elected on the strength of the black vote, and others, mostly black leaders, felt that King's achievement should be formally recognized in his native city. But Allen was shocked when major white business and professional leaders balked not only at the notion of honoring King, but of sitting down at a black-tie dinner with blacks. It took considerable arm-twisting from Allen and, especially, Paul Austin, President of the Coca-Cola Company, to entice the reluctant whites to support and attend the affair. In the end, some 1,500 persons of both races feted King at the dinner in a downtown hotel. It was the largest bi-racial affair of its kind ever held in the city to that time.

Finally, as we reflect on Martin Luther King, Jr's role in the Atlanta Civil Rights Movement, we see a rather different leader than the one who was visible at Montgomery, Birmingham, Selma, and other places. But in Atlanta King was an infrequent participant in direct action; only seldom the militant catalyst for change. There he was most often a peacemaker, counseling moderation, even retreats. The patterns of race relations which existed in Atlanta, at least since 1906, and his close ties to family and friends mitigated against him taking the dramatic stands which won him such notoriety elsewhere.

Yet, the event in which he did become involved in a major way, the Rich's department store sit-in, while not an impetus for ending lunch counter segregation in Atlanta, did affect a national presidential election in 1960. So, in terms of the Great Man Theory, his activities in the city probably helped to create a historical mutation. But more clearly, he would qualify for greatness under his own definition. In Atlanta and elsewhere, he did offer his life to serve others, and he was indeed, a Drum Major for righteousness, a Drum Major for Justice, and a Drum Major for peace.

Chapter 12
"Not Eaves Please": Race, Class, and Atlanta's First African-American Commissioner of Public Safety, 1974–1978

On March 30,1978, eight black men were sworn in as Atlanta's first black police officers. Although, the policemen were to be segregated and restricted in their arrest powers to blacks only, black Atlantans hailed the event as a major civil rights achievement. For it culminated a decade old campaign to achieve a fairer administration of justice in the city. For nearly a century, blacks had complained of abuse, both physical and verbal, and other unfair treatment at the hands of Atlanta's all white police force. Black officers patrolling black communities, they felt, could reduce, if not end, the "police terrorism" among them.[1]

In the late 1960s and early 1970s, one of the most strident voices of protest of alleged police brutality against blacks was Maynard Holbrook Jackson. Particularly during his tenure as vice mayor of the city, 1969-1973, Jackson had incurred the ire of many whites and the praise of many blacks for his vociferous demands that black citizens be respected by the police and that those suspected of abuse be made accountable.[2]

When blacks provided the margin of victory for Sam Massell, as

Prepared for delivery at the Association of Social and Behavioral Scientists Annual Meeting, Savannah (Pooler), GA, March 21-24, 2001

the city's first Jewish mayor, in 1969, they believed they had a white champion of their agenda, including an end to police brutality. But, Massell, incrementally, leaned more toward whites — even white conservative — interests; and by the end of his term had resorted to race baiting to try to win re-election. By 1973, then most African-American voters in Atlanta were convinced that their interests could best be protected and promoted by a black mayor. Largely because of his bold stands against police brutality, Maynard Jackson emerged as the most attractive candidate.[3]

Although, in the end, at least one of the major white daily newspapers in Atlanta endorsed Jackson for mayor and he garnered almost 20 percent of the white vote in the mayoral election, there was still considerable skepticism in white Atlanta about whether Jackson, indeed, would be a mayor of all the people. Would he, for example, hand most of the city's jobs to blacks? Did his militant stand against alleged police brutality mean that he would be "soft" on crime?[4]

But, even in his pre-inaugural planning, Jackson exercised care in seeing that whites were represented equally with blacks on all of his advisory boards. Indeed, some blacks complained that whites were over-represented on these bodies. In his inaugural address, Jackson, again, pledged bi-racialism and called for "a city of love." He promised to be tough on criminals, but *demanded* that policemen respect the citizens of Atlanta. This latter remark drew loud applause from the predominately black inaugural audience.[5]

True to his pledges, Jackson's administrative cabinet was evenly divided among whites and blacks, with whites holding the important positions of commissioners of the airport, the treasury and budget, and plug. The mayor's chief administrative officer was an imported Jew from New York. Still these moves did not placate many whites who charged that the overall scheme of reorganizing the city government into commissioners and directors, which the new city charter of 1973 permitted, was really designed to place a black man as head of the Atlanta's police department. On the other hand, blacks began to display impatience that the controversial white police chief, John Inman, had not already been removed, and began to doubt that Jackson would, in fact, appoint a black public safety commissioner. It seemed to them that there was too much white influence in what they conceived to be a black administration. The police department, then, was to become Jackson's "Achilles Heel." He had, on this issue, to walk with especial care.[6]

The animosity between Chief Inman and Maynard Jackson was long and deep. The chief had vehemently resented the former vice mayor's attacks on alleged police brutality. He had implied that Jackson was in sympathy with the aims and goals of groups like the Black Panthers. He had once said that Jackson was a major deterrent to "law and order" in Atlanta. Nevertheless, the outspoken chief, who had secured a binding eight-year contract with the city from former Mayor Massell, could not be easily dismissed. Thus, the only means of controlling him, it seemed, was to appoint a superior over him — a "super chief" as he came to be called.[7]

While Jackson began a national search for a "super chief," Inman began a legal attack to retain his power. In April 1974 he won a court order, which blocked any appointment of a public safety commissioner for several weeks and prohibited any interference with Inman's normal duties. The injunction, however, was lifted on May 3rd. Mayor Jackson promptly fired the chief. He named Captain Clinton Chafin, a *persona non grata* with Inman, acting chief of police. Chafin had earlier won favor with Jackson for siding with black officers who accused white policemen of a controversial knife-plant, in a recent case.[8]

The firing of Inman hit segments of white Atlanta like a thunder clap. The *Atlanta Constitution*, which had finally called for Inman's ouster, after he took the unusual step of suing the city, was not at all sure that the mayor had not acted with undue haste. Other whites, including the judge who lifted the injunction, shared this concern. Their reasoning seemed to have been that if Jackson had won the right to name his "super chief," why rub it in on Inman so hurriedly? Other whites lambasted the mayor. The firing of the chief proved that he was no friend of "law and order." He wanted, they claimed, a largely black police force. He had already shown his hand by advocating an "Atlanta residents only" police hiring policy. No matter that Jackson had purposefully chosen a white man to replace Inman, there was great anxiety among many whites for the future of "law and order" in Atlanta. In Black Atlanta, there was greater jubilation than at any time since the election of Mayor Jackson.[9]

The reactions to the Inman firing on the part of whites and blacks reflected the racial approach to the question of "law and order." To whites in Atlanta, and elsewhere, the reduction of crime, particularly black crime, had become the major issue confronting the community. Somehow the black criminals who threatened society, either with individual assaults or with "illegal" racial demonstrations against alleged injustices, had to be brought under control. Strong law enforcement, including the use of physical force, were seen as the best weapon against rising crime.   Blacks tended to see the matter differently.   They were by no means "soft" on "law and order," since they were not only the perpetrators, but, the victims of the most serious crimes — murders, assaults, rapes — and they suffered more than their proportionate share of burglaries.   Only in the case of armed robberies of major financial institutions, of which blacks had only three, were whites the major losers, statistically.   But the blacks spoke of something called "law and order with justice."   They were also mindful of the socio-economic deprivations, which underlay many of the crimes and of the often-abusive language and alleged excessive force, which policemen used in their communities.   One side, the whites, seemed ready to sacrifice compassion and justice on the altar of "law and order"; the other side, the blacks, wanted to make sure that respect accompanied the enforcement of the law.[10]

Yet the black jubilation and the white anger over Inman's dismissal were short-lived.   Three days after his firing, Inman had won reinstatement by a DeKalb County Court.[11]   (The DeKalb court assumed jurisdiction because a small portion of the city of Atlanta lies in that county)   While Fulton County Courts declined to intercede, calling instead for a "cooling off" period, the embattled police chief called on the DeKalb Courts again and again to keep him in power. When Black councilmen attempted to circumvent the courts' restraints, which prevented the mayor from moving against Inman again, by impeaching the chief, a DeKalb County Court again blocked the way. Finally that same court ruled the new city charter, under which the "super chief" was made possible, invalid.   It appeared that the city was in for another long, hot summer of racial tensions.   Blacks were in despair!   Whites had won again!   Their black government was powerless against a white police chief, backed by an all-white judiciary, issuing edicts from beyond the inner city.   Some blacks, under the leadership of the "wildman of Atlanta," Hosea Williams, took to the streets in protest.[12]

In facing his biggest crisis to date, Mayor Jackson acted calmly and with restraints.   He awaited an ultimate judgment from the Georgia State Supreme Court, where he was confident that his position would be vindicated.   He had called for a show of peaceful community support and patience.   At one "support-the-mayor" rally at city hall, black leaders and some lower echelon whites backed Jackson's actions. The top names in the white power structure stayed away in droves. There was much speculation that the upper echelon of the white elite did not fully side, if at all, with the mayor against Inman.   In fact, the mayor, himself, speculated that wealthy white businessmen were behind the chief, perhaps even with legal fees. Jackson charged that the matter had now gone far beyond any clash between the mayor and a defiant police chief. Influential whites, he suggested, were out to wreck the new city charter on which the foundations of the black government rested. Amid these tensions a black youth was killed by a black policeman. Hosea Williams took the occasion to return to the streets demanding the ouster of Chief John Inman.[13]

With both the mayor and the police chief out of the city, Atlanta policemen confronted black demonstrators in downtown Atlanta on June 23 and broke up their march with billy-clubs. It was the worse racial confrontation with police since the riots of 1966 and 1967. The city was becoming "a powder keg," as Jackson and the chief rushed back to assess the damage. The chief justified the force used against the demonstrators. The mayor termed it excessive. Then, Georgia Governor Jimmy Carter stepped up his efforts to get the police chief issue resolved. He met with, and had emissaries meet with Inman and his attorneys. He expressed the hope that the state's high court would expedite its definitive ruling. The *Atlanta Constitution* made the same plea to the court. Meanwhile, Jackson had by executive decree, allowed the protest marchers to continue, despite his opposition to them, and with police protection.[14]

Cries of catering to "law breakers" (the marchers had defied city laws requiring parade permits to march) were heard within the police department and among other whites, even from liberal-minded city council President Wyche Fowler. Fowler thought the city council might have something to say about the mayor's executive decrees, which had the effects of circumventing a local ordinance. Yet the mayor's action did serve to prevent further confrontations, while the governor and others sought a temporary solution, pending the ruling of the state Supreme Court.[15]

The police chief was confident of another victory in the state's highest court and, hence, rejected all talk of compromise. Meanwhile, the slaying of Mrs. Martin Luther King, Sr., the mother of the slain civil-rights leader in Atlanta on June 30, brought a momentary reconciliation between white and black in the city. Some of the top white political and civic leaders, including Chief Inman, were among those mourning Mrs. King. Hosea Williams, with some reluctance, called off his marches. Two days later, the Georgia Supreme Court, in a 5-2 decision, upheld the validity of Atlanta's new charter, authorized the appointment of a "super chief," and declared that Inman could be fired only after an impeachment trial. The chief, through his attorney, muttered something about further appeals and about the governor tampering with the courts, but all knew that John Inman had fought his last fight. It was possible that he might hold on to his job, but he would soon lose his powers. The search for a "super chief" suspended since the Inman litigation began, was now renewed. But, on account of the bitter court fights and the relatively low salary ($31,000 per year), all of the major candidates had withdrawn.[16]

Inman was now, in fact, vulnerable to dismissal. His removal, still a demand of much of black Atlanta, and the appointment of a black chief could remove some of the pressures for an immediate selection of a "super chief" who would under this reasoning be black, if the chief remained white. The impeachment process would, however, be a long and divisive one — white versus black, Inman men versus anti-Inman forces. To avoid such a spectacle, the mayor opted to allow Inman to remain where he was, provided he would capitulate, and to appoint the new public safety commissioner immediately.[17]

The Inman fight, which by the late summer of 1974 was nearing its end, had taught several valuable lessons: (1) whites were fearful for the public safety with a police department they did not control; (2) blacks did not trust a police department under white control; and (3) that an all white judiciary existed in Fulton and DeKalb Counties and at the state level which could reek havoc with the exercise of black political power in Atlanta. The episode also no doubt expelled any thoughts that the mayor might have had of maintaining white control of the Atlanta police department.

"Black militants are taking over Atlanta. They are changing the police department from white to black," cried an avowed racist candidate for Lieutenant Governor of Georgia in the August 1974 primary. Before that election was over, Mayor Jackson had nominated a college-mate and a top aide, A. Reginald "Reggie" Eaves as commissioner of public safety for Atlanta. If confirmed, Eaves would become the highest ranking, black law enforcement official in the South. The white Atlanta press had all but begged Jackson not to nominate Eaves, "not Eaves please" one of them pleaded. There was speculation that the nomination would influence the governor's race, causing a white backlash, which would put arch-segregationist Lester Maddox back in the state's highest office. Eaves was unqualified the white press roared. He had never even been a policeman (the closest he had come was commissioner of penal institutions in Boston), the opposition cried, "he was a crony" of the mayor. He could not exercise independent judgment. White councilpersons, including President Fowler and the liberal-minded Panke Bradley (who had previously supported most of the mayor's programs), decried the nominee's inexperience and the "cronyism" involved. "Not Eaves, please" rang throughout the white parts of town.[18]

But the city's nine black councilmen were reported ready, with some reservations, to support the Eaves nomination. White councilmen and the council president were said to be against confirmation. With the nomination in danger, an alleged bargain was struck by which police chief Inman would endorse Eaves and agree to take a subordinate role in police matters in return for a job guarantee of at least eight months — the time required for his pension to become effective. This alleged deal was supposed to give some white councilmen the "excuse" they needed to vote for Eaves. In any case, when the roll was called three white councilpersons joined the black bloc and Eaves was confirmed by a 12-6 margin. The three white council supporting Eaves, included Charles Helms of the second district — who had been elected from a predominantly black community.[19]

Meanwhile, as one Jackson-sponsored measure after another won council approval, cries of "rubber stamps" were raised in parts of white Atlanta and in the white press. The mayor was actually running the city single-handedly, some charged, because the legislature had no "back bone," and had forfeited its check and balancing functions. These developments exalted new fears that whites would be powerless in the political affairs of Atlanta during the ensuing four years.[20]

The confirmation of Commissioner Eaves was the "straw that broke the camel's back." It served to convince elements of the white power structure, including the white press, that the new city administration had anti-white tendencies. Eaves had moved quickly to demote and reassign members of the pro Inman clique in the Atlanta police department. Although white officers fell most often, since the Inman group was largely white and whites made up 75 percent of the police force, two whites were named along with two blacks to the top command. Nevertheless, there were whispers that the new commissioner was favoring blacks in its reorganization. There was renewed apprehension that the black government would be soft on crime. Members of the Georgia State Legislature called for hearings to determine whether or not the state should take over law enforcement in Atlanta — a suggestion made earlier by the now powerless Police Chief John Inman.[21]

Then in early October the text of a letter from members of the downtown power structure to the mayor was released. It cited fears and apprehensions on the part of some Atlanta businessmen. There were concerns about crime; about the continuing white exodus from Atlanta; and about a perception of an "anti-white" attitude on the part of the new city administration. Jackson's appointment of Eaves, an exponent of "law and order with justice" was another most compelling one.[22]

Amid these disputes, in 1974, Atlanta experienced 5,768 serious crimes for each 100,000 residents, one of the highest rates in the nation. Still, an Atlanta Regional Commission (ARC) Report showed nearly half of the city's crime went unreported. In Atlanta's more violent crimes, blacks were both perpetrators and victims. In all of the major categories of crime; murder, robbery, rape, aggravated assault, burglary, blacks were arrested two to three times more often than whites. The lone exception was auto theft where the races were charged in almost equal numbers. Although Mayor Jackson was acutely aware that social and economic ills lay behind the high crime statistics, he was determined to reduce them. And, despite the criticism from those who opposed the appointment of A. Reginald Eaves as "super chief" on the grounds that he had no police experience, Jackson challenged the new commissioner to aggressively fight crime. But Eaves faced several problems, in addition to white hostility, in carrying out his assignment. The predominantly white fraternal order of police, which represented more than a third of the 1,600 Atlanta policemen, complained about inadequate pay and other unfavorable working conditions. The all-black Afro-American patrolman's league reminded Eaves of past discrimination, which served to reduce the number of black patrolmen as well as superior officers. Eaves shared the belief held by many blacks over the years that an increase in the number of black officers could help reduce both crime and the allegations of police brutality. Since many of Atlanta's white police officers lived outside the city and the overall population within the city was largely black, Eaves, Jackson and other blacks reasoned that a residency requirement for public safety officers would help remedy the situation. Then, on June 3, 1976, the Public Safety Committee of the City Council approved, on a 5-2 vote, a measure, which would "mandate dismissal of any current employee who changes his residence but continues to live outside of Atlanta." White City Council President Wyche Fowler vehemently opposed the measure. He called it "near sightedness" and said it flew "in the face of state law, and it ain't going to work." The *Atlanta Constitution* also opposed the ordinance, editorializing that, "it also seems to us that you cannot require a person to live in a particular place as a requirement for employment." Meanwhile, the predominantly white Police Benevolent Association

(PBA) promised to fight the ordinance in court. Roger Norris, president of the PBA, claimed 892 members within the Atlanta police bureau, also predicted, "many officers will quit the police force as a result of the ordinance."[23]

Even before Eaves took over as commissioner of public safety, Jackson and council president Fowler had authored a proposal to create a civilian review board to investigate complaints of police brutality in Atlanta. But both men wanted to delay action on any such bill until the new public safety commissioner was hired, in order to get his views on the controversial matter. At two public hearings, both police Chief John Inman and the fraternal order of police, "hotly opposed" the proposal. Nevertheless, black councilman James Bond (Julian's brother) and white councilman Charles Helms who, (represented the majority of the black district), pushed the review measure before the full council in the spring of 1974. But on April 15, the council defeated the proposal by a vote of nine to seven. Three black councilmen, John Calhoun, Ira Jackson, and Q. V. Williamson voted against the measure, while two whites, Helms and George Cotsakis supported it.[24]

After the defeat of the police review plan, Eaves tried other measures to restrict excessive force by policemen. In October 1974, he ordered all Atlanta officers to carry their .38 caliber service revolvers as their primary weapons. Although the incident, which apparently precipitated the order was unrelated to race — a policewoman had allowed her boyfriend to carry one of her weapons while the two attended a local fair — it did give Eaves the opportunity to address the issue of excessive force in an indirect way. Many Atlanta officers, especially detectives, had preferred to use the higher caliber and more deadly 44 special and 9mm automatic weapons. The .44 caliber special, a detective revealed, "throws a chunk of lead as big as your thumb . . . as far as I'm concerned, the main objective is knocking him down. I want him stopped, and I don't want him [to get up]." Another officer on the largely white police force, who opposed Eaves' order, defended police shootings since "every time someone is shot, for the most part, they are either attacking an officer or a citizen."[25]

Despite the fact that he had not resolved all of his administrative, personnel, and public relations problems, Eaves did set out to reduce the crime rate in the city. Explaining that the police department might not have "sufficient manpower" to control such acts as prostitution, he concentrated his efforts on street crime. He sent large forces of police officers into high crime areas and often accompanied the men and women himself. City councilmen and ordinary citizens praised the effort. One woman, in a high crime area, exclaimed, "this is beautiful, this is wonderful. Bless your heart."[26]

Eaves' efforts appeared to bring quick and dramatic results in 1975, violent crimes in the city reportedly dropped almost ten percent "murders decreased from 248 to 185, burglaries dropped from 16,802 to 14,501, and armed robberies fell from 4,357 to 3,887." Some of the most startling reductions occurred in the 3.4 square-mile, 85 percent black, Model Cities area. In 1974, the police department had established a "cop shop" in an abandoned pool hall there. The unit, headed by black Police Captain Johnny Sparks, built a warm rapport with the citizens of the neighborhoods, which substantially aided their crime fighting efforts. By 1976, burglaries in the Model Cities area were down 42 percent, robberies were off 24 percent, and aggravated assaults were down by eight percent. The Model Cities unit had a crime solving or "cleanup" rate of 99 percent.[27]

The *Atlanta Constitution*, an opponent of Eaves' appointment as "super chief," lauded the reported decreases in crime. The newspaper's editors said that, "Commissioner Eaves and the officers of the Atlanta police department can feel proud of this improved record . . . Crime in the streets has become a frightening phrase. It is a cheerful note to find statistics on crime in Atlanta heading in the right direction, namely down." But the mostly white Atlanta chapter of the fraternal order of police charged that Eaves' administration had been "inaccurately reporting the ratio of arrests to actual solutions of crimes." And, while he denied any "overall attempt to conceal anything," Deputy Police Director Clinton Chafin said, "Several recent solution reports ["cleanups"] by police have been questioned." Also a group of Atlanta business leaders formed an organization in the summer of 1975, to "disseminate more accurate information about the city's crime data." The new citizens information committee aimed to dispel myths about crime in Atlanta as well as to build community support for policemen.[28]

Although the actual data on crime reductions and solutions might be questioned, and there were still serious doubts and misgivings about the Eaves-led police department, the conditions in the Model Cities area, FBI reports, and other indications seemed to show that progress was being made. Meanwhile, the Atlanta Police Bureau had been reinstated in the Georgia State Intelligence Network (GSIN) and reports of police brutality were decreasing. The newly constituted GSIN panel would not reveal the factors which led to its reinstatement of the Atlanta Bureau, just as it had not given the specific reason for the suspension of the unit. But Mayor Jackson welcomed the action, declaring that it had been "a most unfortunate and embarrassing episode in Atlanta's history, and . . . an entirely undeserved one. I am glad that it is over and we can look ahead now." The new attitudes and controls, which Eaves had instituted against excessive police force were so successful that by the summer of 1975, a black weekly newspaper was asking, "Whatever happened to police brutality?" In the first six months of the year, only three and one-half percent of citizen complaints had involved police brutality and only three persons had been killed by police — two who fired on officers while in the process of committing robberies and a third who pulled a gun on officers after a traffic accident. Yet the American Civil Liberties Union (ACLU) asked councilpersons Bond and Helms to renew their fight for a police review board. But black police Lieutenant C. J. Perry, head of the Bureau's Internal Investigation unit, felt that "with the way the commissioner is dealing with the department now, a civilian review board would be a mistake."[29]

Interestingly enough, the issue of crime came to play a role in Mayor Jackson's efforts to increase job opportunities for blacks within the city. During the summer of 1975, the Jackson administration proposed a new ordinance governing the hiring, promotion, and suspension of Atlanta's city employees. Among other things it sought to outlaw the use of written examinations for employees if "such measures adversely affect the hiring" of blacks and other minorities or "if the tests were not approved by Federal Civil Rights officials." It would also "ignore" criminal arrest records. The provision relating to ex-criminals provoked a storm of protest, particularly from whites. Council President Fowler, the Atlanta newspapers, and the fraternal order of police all opposed the proposed law. Fowler said the proposal would permit accused "murderers and kidnappers" to remain on the city payrolls. He revealed that his "phone has been ringing off the hook" as opponents called to protest the idea. Mayor Jackson called Fowler's reaction "hysterical," "silly," "juvenile," "wild," and "inflammatory." He insisted that his proposed ordinance made a "carefully drawn distinction" between those who had been arrested, but not convicted, and those who had actually been convicted. Gene Tharpe, an *Atlanta Constitution* columnist, humorously portrayed "Scarface" and "Babyface," remarking that "in Atlanta we could hold down a honest city job and while off duty we could hold up a few banks, maybe even shoot up a few folks . . ." Leaders of the FOP took their protests to the streets. They passed out handbills, which cautioned that, "Atlanta can be hazardous to your health," and claimed that the city was "hiring correctional officers to work in the Atlanta prison systems who have criminal records." While not admitting that he was bowing to these criticisms, Jackson revised, then withdrew the controversial measure.[30]

Among those minorities who Jackson hoped to hire in city government were policemen. In the fall of 1974, Public Safety Commissioner A. Reginald Eaves had promised to slash Atlanta's crime rate by ten percent if he could get $6.7 million in the 1975 general budget for the police bureau. This proposed allocation was a $3.9 million increase over the police budget for 1974. Eaves planned to use the additional money to grant pay increases totaling more than eight and one-half percent to policemen and firemen, to hike starting police salaries from $9,841 to $20,000 year and to hire 105 new officers. But the desire for additional police officers as well as other new city workers ran into difficulty, when council members and citizens discovered that all of Jackson's proposals in the 1975 budget would probably result in an increase in city taxes. Yet despite the projections of a $7 million deficit in the general budget, Jackson did not foresee a property tax increase as late as October 1974. But the next month key members of the Jackson administration recommended that the city lay off 175 of its workers and abolish 44 vacant positions in order to balance the 1975 budget without a tax increase.[31]

Mayor Maynard Holbrook Jackson returned to office by Atlanta voters on October 4, 1977, in a victory of near landslide proportions. Jackson captured 63.2 percent of the 85,978 votes, which were cast. It is estimated that he garnered 93.2 percent of the black votes, while almost 20 percent of white voters supported him. The white votes for Jackson was an increase of two percent from 1973. But about three percent less than that received in his 1969 race for vice mayor, despite all of the controversies over crime and police joint ventures, "racial politics," and annexation it was apparent that black voters stood almost solidly behind their first black mayor throughout his first term. But, in view of continuing white criticism, it was somewhat surprising that Jackson had increased his support among white voters. Yet, a number of the major controversial issues, which absorbed the Jackson administration's critics' attention during the first term had "simmered down" near the close of it. To be sure, there were still gigantic problems. Crime and the administration of justice remained a racially volatile issue.[32]

When Maynard Holbrook Jackson took the oath as the city's 47th and first black Mayor for the second time on January 3, 1978 he expressed pride in the accomplishments of his first term as the city's chief executive, but promised to "do even better than we have." He acknowledged that "unemployment, economic and racial discrimination, crime, inadequate housing and other challenges" would not permit his administration to rest on its "laurels." He denounced "unwarranted judicial interposition" in the affairs of the Atlanta Bureau of Police Services. Indeed, as Jackson began his second term, events were already unfolding in the police bureau which gave the Mayor his greatest challenge, thus far, and which threatened the tenuous threads upon which good racial relations hung in the city.[33]

The crisis began when a young black police officer, William M. Taylor and three other black policemen accused Public Safety Commissioner A. Reginald Eaves of authorizing Taylor to distribute test questions for a police promotions examination, in 1975, to a "select group of candidates," most of whom were black. The charges were first made to George Berry, Mayor Jackson's chief administrative officer, who was white on August 14, 1977. Taylor later made them public in an affidavit filed in a federal lawsuit in which white officers charged Eaves with "reverse discrimination."[34]

Mayor Jackson quietly ordered the city attorney to investigate the allegations of police cheating, and drafted a press release in which he "broadly hinted" that the accusations were "politically motivated." Two weeks later the *Atlanta Journal* published, for the first time, the four black officers' allegations. Commissioner Eaves denied them. On September 22nd, although he had not yet seen the city attorney's report on the cheating investigation, Jackson pledged to keep Eaves on the job if he, himself, were reelected in October. Following his re-election, Jackson named Felker Ward, Jr., a prominent black attorney, and Randolph Thrower, a reputable white lawyer, to conduct an "outside investigation" of the allegations. As a part of their probe, Ward and Thrower asked some of the principals in the case to take a lie detector test. Eaves took such a test on January 11, 1978. On February 20th, the Ward-Thrower Report was released. It concluded that widespread cheating had taken place on the police exams in 1975 and that Eaves, himself, authorized the cheating and attempted to "obstruct the investigation." The attorneys also charged that Eaves had "engaged in obvious efforts" to foil the lie detector machine and had later refused to take another test. Meanwhile, the embattled police commissioner entered Crawford Long Hospital for "a rest." Mayor Jackson delayed action on the Ward-Thrower Report until Eaves emerged from the hospital.[35]

Then, on March 7, the Mayor told a live television audience that while he had not yet made up his mind about Eaves' role in the cheating or his future, he was naming another city official, Calvin Carter to run the police department. Three days later Jackson suspended Eaves without pay until June 7.[36]

Commissioner Eaves consistently and persistently denied any involvement in the cheating scandal. In his most comprehensive response to the charges, he emphatically told a live television audience, on March 19, 1978, that he "did not authorize nor approve in any way the distribution to anyone of either advance copies of the promotional examination or the questions and answers on the examination." He denied that he had tried to obstruct the Ward-Thrower polygraph exam, claiming that his "slower than normal breathing" was a result of medication he had taken for hypertension. He said that the Ward-Thrower Report was "not factual, but a collection of unsupported opinions . . . derived from impression, gossip, and rumors of the worst kind." He added that there had always been rumors of cheating in the police bureau. Eaves further claimed that Mayor Jackson had "cleared" him of expressly authorizing any cheating on the police exams. And he declared that there was no animosity between him and the Mayor; that it was only a "battle for the truth." Nevertheless, on March 7, Eaves had submitted his resignation "as an act of good faith," but to avoid it "being interpreted as an admission of guilt," he had postponed the effective date to June 7.[37]

Mayor Jackson had actually said, during his televised speech on March 7, that he believed "Eaves either knew or should have known that cheating was occurring." And, in response to Eaves' defenses on March 19, Jackson said that the commissioner's statement had contained "some clear errors." The Mayor also chronicled his growing disenchantment with Eaves by revealing that the "super chief" broke a promise to deliver his resignation by noon on March 8, the day following Jackson's television address. Instead Eaves waited until 10 p.m. He also delayed the effective date of the resignation for the full 90 days. Although the two had agreed on a 60 to 90 day period, he even tried to retrieve his resignation letter. Finally, Eaves reneged on a promise to keep "a low profile" by answering questions put to him by the news media. All of these things, Jackson said, indicated "a lack of good faith." Consequently, the Mayor decided to both make Eaves' resignation public and to suspend him. There had been a serious "falling out" of the Morehouse classmates.[38]

Many in White Atlanta had sharply criticized Jackson's appointment of Eaves as public safety commissioner and, even though crime dipped in the city under his administration, continued their attacks on the running of the police bureau throughout the first term.

The cheating scandal seem to bring their greatest fears to fruition and to vindicate their skepticism and criticism. The White Press took aim at Mayor Jackson, particularly for his delays and dawdling during the affair. An *Atlanta Journal-Constitution* editor said flatly that Jackson "rightly" bore "his own share of blame for his police department's troubles," although "he started out with a messed up left field." An *Atlanta Constitution* editorial on March 3, entitled "Now is the time," said that Jackson's indecision was "difficult to accept," and the next day a cartoonist for the newspaper pictured the Mayor hiding under a desk, with the police cheating report on top of it, crying, "No damnit, not yet." Editorialists on two of Atlanta's major television stations, WSB and WAGA, also voiced repeated criticisms of Jackson's handling of the affair. Similarly, callers, who identified themselves as white, to local radio talk shows, many of them non-Atlantans, lambasted Eaves and the Mayor. On the other hand, the white business class, in contrast to the outcry against Eaves in 1975, mooted their criticisms. But one business leader, who had "worked hard in building bridges between downtown and city hall," declared that if Jackson tried to escape responsibility for the affair by blaming white racism or by using the old white power structure conspiracy trick, "then I'm just saying the hell with him." After the Mayor decided to suspend Eaves, white business leaders "predicted that Jackson's decision would help heal the city's image." Dan Sweat, President of Central Atlanta Progress said that the Eaves affair was "damaging," but the Mayor took the right action "to strengthen the city," and Thomas J. Kamill, Vice President of the Atlanta Chamber of Commerce, applauded the Mayor's decision as one which would "help to stabilize the morale in the Public Safety Department and in the city."[39]

Black Atlanta was sharply divided over the police creating scandal. While callers, who identified themselves as black, to the local radio talk shows overwhelmingly supported Eaves and voiced their suspicions of a white racist plot to discredit him and Jackson, the *Atlanta Constitution* found a majority favoring disciplining or even firing Eaves in a random poll of 14 blacks in February 1978. In another street poll following Jackson's suspension of Eaves, four of five blacks interviewed by the *Atlanta Journal Constitution* supported the Mayor's decision. The Reverend G. A. Roberts said the decision was for the "betterment of the city." Black public officials also reflected the division in black Atlanta. Some like State Representatives Julian Bond, Mildred Glover and Billy McKinney, and Councilmen James Bond and Jim Maddox publicly supported the Mayor. Indeed, Julian Bond,

James Bond, and Mildred Glover had been the only three black officials to ask for Eaves' resignation. But others, including State Representatives Douglas Dean and Hosea Williams and Councilmen James Howard and Arthur Langford staunchly and sometimes angrily defended Eaves. Representative Dean believed that the Mayor had made a mistake in suspending the commissioner and declared Eaves had "brought safety to this city." Former city Administrative Services Commissioner Emma Darnell called Eaves' ouster "a crucifixion" conducted by a mob including "the predominantly white fraternal order of white folks" — jealousy, greed, elitism, and classicism among blacks "had also gotten" Reginald Eaves, she declared. On March 13,1978 the pro-Eaves forces, led by Hosea Williams and Joe Boone, Executive Director of the Metro Atlanta Leadership Congress, confronted Jackson at City Hall. They told the Mayor that he had been pressured by the Atlanta Chamber of Commerce and Central Atlanta Progress to suspend Eaves and that he had not heeded the wishes of Black Atlanta, but Jackson concluded the emotional debate by declaring, "my decision [on Eaves] is the only one I can honestly make. That decision, I regret to tell you, my friends, is irrevocable."[40]

Even before Jackson publicly suspended Reginald Eaves, he had named his quiet-spoken Deputy Commissioner of Aviation, Calvin Carter to run the Atlanta police bureau "temporarily." And, he had also, with the support of then Commissioner Eaves, decided to move to abolish John Inman's post of director and recreate the position of police chief. By April 1978, both the Atlanta Civil Service Board and the Atlanta City Council had approved the new position of chief, after Mayor Jackson declared that the city had "an unusual situation" that required "an unusual remedy." But Jackson delayed this appointment until he could settle on a nominee for public safety commissioner, since he wanted the input of the new commissioner on the new chief.[41]

Finally, on April 17,1978, Atlanta got its new public safety commissioner. Lee Brown was unanimously confirmed by the Atlanta City Council. The new commissioner was a criminologist, the holder of a Ph.D. degree, but he had also had experience as a law enforcement officer. He came to Atlanta from Portland, Oregon where he had been a county sheriff and in county justice service. At the same time, the Council denied Reginald Eaves' request to appeal his dismissal before that body. Then in May, Jackson and Brown nominated another Ph.D. criminologist, Gorge Napper as the new police chief. Napper came to his position from a professorship at Spelman College. While he had not served as a policeman, he was director of the Mayor's crime analysis team.[42]

Still the disposition of the cases of others involved in the cheating scandal, hiring and promotion, racial tensions in the Bureau, and police pay remained as difficult and challenging issues for the new team of Brown and Napper. At the same time, crime rates were, again, rising in the city.

The continuing furor over the cheating scandal served to exacerbate racial tensions and mitigated against substantial improvements in police morale. The Ward-Thrower Report had recommended the firing or suspension of some 23 policemen, only one of whom was white, who allegedly participated in the cheating. At first, Mayor Jackson delayed action on the 23 officers, with ranks up to captain, while he made a decision on Commissioner Eaves. But then, he directed City Attorney Ferriss Mathews to draw up complaints against them (the highest ranking officer other than Eaves). Implicated in the matter, Mayor Claude Dixon had already been suspended. Following this order, Deputy Director Joe Amos began scheduling hearings before a police "trial board," composed of superior officers, for the 23 accused policemen. After five weeks, the panel had decided only six of the 23 cases. Those decisions were made in executive session and the recommendations were passed to Mayor Jackson, who indicated that he would make no final judgments until all of the cases had been heard. Finally, in June 1978 the trial board had sent its findings on 20 officers to Jackson (one officer had previously confessed and resigned; two others were exonerated). After consulting Commissioner Brown, Chief Administrative Officer Art Cumming and other advisors, Jackson fired four officers, including William Taylor, punished 13 others, and took no action on the remaining three cases. Although the matter still could not be put to rest; for six additional officers, who were named in the Ward-Thrower Report, had not been charged or tried and at least two of the fired policemen, Captain A. L. Cardell and Taylor, had appealed their dismissals in state and federal courts, as far as the Jackson administration was concerned, the cheating scandal had faded into history.[43]

In the end, the tenure of A. Reginald Eaves as Atlanta's and the New South's first public safety commissioner served to re-enforce prevailing notions of race, racism, and race relations in the United States. The attitudes and actions of whites concerning crime and race were conventional and would not merit substantial examination or re-examination, except for Atlanta's fabled reputation as a "city too busy to hate" and "an oasis of tolerance." But the Eaves affair demonstrated anew that Atlanta's white racism was little different from that of the rest of the South and the nation and that the "moderating influences," which were largely dictated by the power of the black vote, were not universal or consistent.

The role of "classcism" among blacks, during the Eaves affair, is the part of this study, which may be most illuminating and deserves even further examination. While Atlanta developed one of the largest black middle classes in the nation in the post-bellum period, class differences were often submerged under the all-embracing effects of Jim Crowism. The black political influence, which distinguished Atlanta after World War II and led to the election of Maynard Jackson as the New South's first African-American mayor, was achieved, and could only have been achieved, by an alliance of interest and organization among all classes of blacks. But, shortly after black political power triumphed in the city in 1973, distinctive class attitudes and issues became more apparent. While some middle and upper income blacks opposed Eaves' nomination as "super chief" and even more supported his ouster in the cheating scandal, more disadvantaged blacks tended to be more solid in their support of Eaves from beginning to end.

Although Eaves was a "Morehouse man," he had certain "rough edges" — he sometimes spoke ungrammatically and knew and spoke "the language of the streets." He had spent sometime in Boston, but he was not a "black Boston Brahman." Unlike Maynard Jackson and others, he was not even an Atlanta black Brahman. While Jackson and others, though largely opposed by the city's white power structure as "militant" and "radical"; they were politically astute enough to believe that they could not, in the end, govern effectively without some types of coalitions with whites, particularly the white business, commercial, and academic elite. On the other hand, Eaves and others, and particularly those in the black disadvantaged communities, seemed to believe in "race first," i.e., that the historical and continuing inequities of African-Americans could only be redressed by bold assertions of black power.

Notes

[1] Augustine A. Adair, "A Political History of the Negro in Atlanta, 1908-1953," MA Thesis, Atlanta University, 1955; Ivan Allen, Jr. with Paul Hemphill, *Mayor: Notes on the Sixties* (NY, 1971), Passion; *Atlanta Daily World*, July 10, 17, 23, 1947; November 26, December 2, 1947, January 7-9,

28, 1948, February 26, 1948; *Atlanta Constitution*, April 4, 1948; Atlanta *Daily World*, April 4, 1948; Clarence A. Bacote, "The Negro in Atlanta Politics," *Phylon*, 1955, passim

[2] *Atlanta Constitution* (hereinafter *AC*), September 5, 6, 1973; Alton Hornsby, Jr., "The Negro in Atlanta Politics, 1961-1973," *Atlanta Historical Bulletin*, Spring 1977, p. 29.

[3] *AC*, September 5, 1973; Hornsby, "The Negro in Atlanta Politics," *Passim*.

[4] Gary M. Pomerantz, *Where Peachtree Meets Sweet Auburn: The Saga of Two Families in the Making of Atlanta* (New York, 1996), Chap. 24; *AC*, May 24, 1975.

[5] *Ibid.*

[6] *Ibid.*

[7] Maynard Jackson, "State of the City Address," July 6, 1975; *AC*, May 4, 6, July 1, 4, 1974.

[8] *AC, Ibid.*; Pomerantz, *Where Peachtree Meets . . .*, Chaps. 24, 25.

[9] Pomerantz, *Where Peachtree Meets . . .*, Chap. 26.

[10] *Ibid.*

[11] *Ibid.*

[12] *AC*, June 24, 1974.

[13] *AC*, June 24, 25, 1974.

[14] Pomerantz, *Where Peachtree Meets . . .*, Chaps. 25, 26.

[15] *Ibid.*

[16] *Ibid.*

[17] *Ibid.*

[18] Pomerantz, *Where Peachtree Meets . . ., Ibid.*; Stone, *Regime Politics*.

[19] Pomerantz, *Where Peachtree Meets . . ., Ibid.*

[20] *Ibid.*

[21] "Three Mayors Speak of their Cities," *Ebony*, February 1974.

[22] *AC*, June 4, 1976.

[23] Pomerantz, *Where Peachtree Meets . . .*, Chaps. 25, 26.

[24] *AC*, October 1, 1974.

[25] *AC*, July 22, 1975.

[26] *AC*, July 7, 22, 1975, August 16, 1975.

[27] *AC*, August 22, 1975; *Atlanta Inquirer* (hereafter *AI*), August 22, 1975.

[28] *AC*, October 4, November 5, 6, 1974.

[29] "Bacote Analysis of the Municipal Elections," October 6, 1977; *AC*, January 5, 1978; *Atlanta Journal* (hereafter *AJ*), October 16, 1978.

[30] *AC*, January 4, 1978.

[31] *Atlanta Journal-Constitution*, (hereinafter *AJC*), March 18, 1978.

[32] *AC*, September 29, 1977; *AJ*, August 23, 1977; *AJC*, March 12, 1978.

[33] *AC*, March 20, 1978; Julian Bond, "A Difficult Decision," *Atlanta Gazette*, March 17, 1978.

[34] *AC*, March 20, 21, 1978; *AJC*, March 12, 1978; Bond, *Ibid.*

[35] *AC*, February 27, 1978, March 3, 4, 11, 1978; Bond, *Ibid.*

[36] *AC*, February 22, 1978, March 11-14, 1978; *AI*, March 18, 1978; Bond, *Ibid.*

[37] *AC*, February 13, 15, 1978, March 18, 1978; Bond, *Ibid.*

[38] *AC*, March 30, 1978, April 12, 14, 17-18, 1978, May 10, 11, 14, 16, 1978; April 12, 18, 1978; Bond, *Ibid.*

[39] *AC*, April 18, 1978, May 10, 11, 14, 16, 1978; *AI*, 12, 18, 1978.

[40] *AC*, February 9, 10, 27, 28, 1978; March 3, 1978, April 2, 16, 1978; *AJC*, June 17, 25, 27, 1978.

[41] *Ibid.*

[42] *Ibid.*

[43] *Ibid.*

ECONOMICS

Chapter 13
Roots of Rural Poverty since 1914

As you know, and as I am sure you will hear again and again during this conference, there are approximately 50 million people in the United States who are "poor," i.e., they do not have enough money to buy an adequate living for themselves and have little or no opportunity to better themselves. We also know, for the most part, who the poor are and where they live. For example, almost 30 percent, or 19 million, of the poor are young people, under 18 years of age. Nearly half of the poor, about 40 percent, are old people. The rest of us fall in between.[1]

The poor live in both rural and urban areas, but the rural poor has been described as the poorest of the poor or, as one scholar put it, "the poorest, lowest, and meanest in the nation." The rural poor include farm laborers and migratory workers, retired farmers and retired coal miners, unemployed timber workers and Indians on reservations. Of this group, the migratory farm workers, who move from place to place and from season to season seeking work, are the worse off. They make less money, they are generally in poorer health, and they have less education. A recent estimate concluded that one and one-half million rural farm families live on less than $250 a month; almost three million rural non-farm families have no more than $80 a month to pay for all that they need to live. The relationship between poverty and education is also clearly indicated by the fact that a half-million rural youth

Prepared for presentation at the Fort Valley Conference on Rural Poverty, Fort Valley State College, March 24, 1978

between the ages of 14 and 24 have never finished elementary school.[2]

We also know that a disproportionate number of the poor come from ethnic minorities — blacks, Puerto Ricans and other Spanish-surnamed Americans, and the American Indians. The old saying of the "last hired and the first fired" applies well to these groups. It might also be added that even when working they are paid less. The brunt of minority poverty is felt by blacks, by virtue of the fact that they are the only group which is not technically defined as Caucasian or white and by virtue of the fact that blacks constitute the largest minority group in the country. Nearly half the total black population in the United States — almost ten million people — are poor. They number one-fifth of the total poor in the country. Generally speaking, wages for non-whites are lower than for white workers, even when they do the same jobs or have the same jobs. Black college graduates, for example, can expect to earn only about as much in a lifetime as a white worker who only completed the eighth grade. White workers in their lifetime earn 50 percent more than blacks and Puerto Ricans and one-third more than Spanish-surnamed Americans. Of the one-half million American Indians, more than one-third or nearly 400,000 are mired in poverty.[3]

So we do have a good idea as to who the poor are and where they live. But the larger part of my assignment is to help uncover the roots of their poverty. Professor Grant has enlightened us on the period up to the First World War. Let us now try to complete the story since that time.

During and after World War I, the roots of rural poverty in America were pretty much the same as they had been before the war. Hereditary environment played a small part, i.e., the descendants of the poor continued largely to constitute the lower income group. Education, or the lack of it, continued as a prime cause of poverty. Poor education and poor incomes generally matched on a one-to-one basis. Ethnic discrimination, particularly against blacks, continued to rank as a principal root of rural poverty.[4]

In the main, blacks ever since the end of the Civil War had been tillers of the soil. Some became and remained self-sufficient farmers owning their property and sometimes employing fellow blacks to work sizable acreages. But the great majority were either tenants, sharecroppers, or wage or day laborers; often they worked on cotton or other plantations, as they had before the Civil War. After 1900, particularly in the Progressive Era, the black farmer remained largely trapped in the unprofitable tenant system or continued as a subsistence laborer. The coming of the First World War gave many rural whites and blacks what they thought was a golden opportunity to break the chains of poverty; blacks, seeing also a chance to escape segregation, discrimination, and lynching in the South seized the opportunity eagerly.[5]

During the period 1916-1918 alone about a half-million blacks suddenly moved from the South to Northern states. As we said earlier, blacks, like whites, were motivated to migrate by economic causes. They were seeking a better living. For example, in the period just preceding 1914, wages of blacks in the South varied from 75 cents a day on the farm to a high of $1.75 a day on certain jobs in the city. After the outbreak of World War I, the wages rose, but the cost of living also rose. The net effect of this was that the black worker was no better off than he had been before the war.[6]

A black preacher in Alabama aptly described the situation which existed at the time. He said: "The Negro farm hand gets for his (pay) hardly more than the mule he plows; that is, his board and shelter. Some mules fare better than blacks . . . High rents and low wages have driven the Negro off the farms. They have no encouragement to work. Only here and there you will find a tenant who is getting a square deal and the proper encouragement."[7]

Even some white Southerners recognized the serious economic plight of blacks and understood why they were leaving the South. An editorial in the Montgomery, Alabama *Advertiser* said: "Why hunt for a cause when it's plain as the noonday sun the Negro is leaving this country for higher wages? He doesn't want to leave here but he knows if he stays here he will starve. They have made no crops, they have nothing to eat, no clothes, no shoes, and they can't get any work to do, and they are leaving just as fast as they can get away . . . If the Negro race could get work at 50 cents per day he would stay here. He don't want to go. He is easily satisfied and will live on half rations and never complain."[8]

Adding to the woe of farmers, black and white, in 1915 and 1916 was the boll weevil. This cotton pest ravaged large sections of the South and thousands of farmers faced economic ruin. Cotton crops were lost, and the farmers were forced to change from cotton to food products. The growing of cotton requires about 30 times as many farm hands as food products. As a result many blacks were thrown out of work.[9]

Poor black workers were keenly aware of the close relationship between poor schools and poverty. In 1915, 33 percent, or 225,000 Southern blacks, ten years of age and over, could not read or write, as compared to only eight percent of the white population. But illiteracy among poor, rural whites was also high, 77 percent. Yet rural black illiteracy was the greatest of all — 79 percent. There was, of course, discrimination against blacks in every area of school life — from books and equipment to standards and salaries for teachers. All of these factors helped to drive rural blacks from the agricultural South to the industrial North.[10]

The wartime boom in American industries and the better wages pulled blacks to the North. Wages for unskilled work in the North in 1916 and 1917 ranged from three dollars to eight dollars a day. There were shorter hours of work and opportunity for overtime and bonuses. In addition, the immigration of foreign labor to the country was cut off by the war and thousands of aliens were returned to their mother country. Since those immigrants had done most of the unskilled work in the North, employers were, thus, forced to look to the South and to blacks.[11]

Blacks were also drawn by better housing opportunities. Although houses available for blacks in the North were unfit and unsanitary by white standards, they were still better than the crude plantation cabins of the South.[12]

Finally, black migrants were impressed by the prospects for better education for their children in the desegregated schools of the North.[13]

A clear picture of the dramatic shift of the black population from the South to the North can be seen from the fact that every one of the Southern states had a tremendous net outflow, i.e., more blacks leaving than coming in, of black population for every decade between 1910 and 1960.[14]

The black migration has, for the most part, been an urban one. In 1960, 96 percent of all Northern blacks lived in the cities. Even in the South, blacks who remained moved in droves to the cities, so that in 1960, more than 75 percent of all blacks North and South, are city dwellers. Thus the black population today is more urbanized than the white one.[15]

As you know, although the Southern black migrants to the North found some material improvements in their lives, the North did not prove to be the "Promised Land." First of all, the migration had a disruptive influence on black family life. Some black men had to leave their families behind as they went north seeking a new life. The understanding, of course, was that they would send for the families when they were able to do so. Many did find a new life and soon were joined by their families. Others found their increased wages eaten up by higher living costs in the North and were never able to send for their relatives. In these tragic cases, the father lived in marginal poverty in the North while his wife and family remained in dire poverty in the South.[16]

To be sure, Northern schools provided better education than Southern ones and by 1965, more than 62 percent of black adults had at least gone to high school. Illiteracy was almost non-existent. Yet blacks found that their education in the North was increasingly in schools attended only by blacks and was, for the most part, inferior to that of whites. Inferior education in the North, like inferior education in the South, placed one at a terrific disadvantage in the job market. Even blacks with degrees from places like Fort Valley State, Tuskegee, and Morehouse found the better paying jobs of the North closed to them solely because of their race.[17]

Thus restricted by inferior education and racial discrimination, blacks were confined to the poorest paying jobs and the poorest living conditions. Many whites, although not burdened by the disadvantage of race, heredity environment and poor education have also placed them in a similar position to almost half of the black population. These, then, are the roots of our poverty, rural as well as urban.

Notes

[1] Louis A. Ferman, et al., *Poverty in America*, Rev. ed., (Ann Arbor, 1969), pp. 134-136.

[2] *Ibid.*

[3] *Ibid.*

[4] *Ibid.*

[5] Alton Hornsby, Jr., *In the Cage: Eyewitness Accounts of the Freed Negro in Southern Society, 1877-1929* (Chicago, 1971), p. 83.

[6] John H. Bracey, Jr., et al., *The Rise of the Ghetto* (Belmont, California, 1970), pp. 44-46.

[7] *Ibid.*, p. 46.

[8] *Ibid.*

[9] *Ibid.*, p. 47.

[10] *Ibid.*, pp. 47-48.

[11] *Ibid.*, pp. 49-50.

[12] *Ibid.*, p. 50.

[13] *Ibid.*

[14] Andrew Billingsley, *Black Families in White America* (Englewood Cliffs, New Jersey, 1968), p. 73.

[15] *Ibid.*

[16] *Ibid.*, p. 78.

[17] *Ibid.*, pp. 79-82.

Chapter 14
Historical Discrimination in Atlanta's Marketplace

Ante-Bellum to Reconstruction

The economic activities of blacks in Atlanta and Fulton County prior to Reconstruction were divided between a small number of slaves and an even smaller group of so-called quasi-free blacks. By 1860, there were only about 30 of the latter group living in the County, with 25 of this number residing in the City of Atlanta. "The comparative lateness in the creation of Fulton County, a scarcity of economic opportunities, and the hostile attitude of Atlanta's city fathers" help to account for the small number of free blacks in the area.[1]

Throughout the State of Georgia, proscriptions placed on free blacks, both by law and custom, inhibited their achievement of full "economic stability and independence." These proscriptions included restrictions to certain occupations as well as limitations on those who could call upon them for goods and services. "A pervasive feeling that free black people were fundamentally inferior, shiftless, and improvident served to exclude them from many professions." Hence, many were "unable to provide themselves with their economic needs," and were forced "to depend on the beneficence of whites."[2]

Despite restrictions in law and custom, a few blacks, through

A Research Project for the Minority Business Enterprise Legal Defense and Education Fund, Inc. (MBELDEF), October 31, 1989

extraordinary industry and thrift, did manage to achieve a degree of "comparative affluence," although none ever reached levels comparable to upper-income whites. And, the "great majority" were "to be found near the bottom of the economic scale."[3]

Illustrative of the economic restrictions placed on the free black population during this period was a state law passed in 1845, which denied free black mechanics or masons the right to make contracts for the erection of or for the repair of buildings. This act was prompted by "fear that they might injure whites as business competitors or as artisans." Also, while blacks could work as laborers in drug stores, "they could not compound or dispense" prescriptions. Fear of competition was also the apparent motivation for white complaints, in 1859, against Dr. Roderick Badger, a black Atlanta dentist. Badger allegedly served a clientele of both black and white citizens. This interracial practice was suspended, however, after white dentists and others told the Atlanta City Council that they were "highly aggrieved" because the Council tolerated a black dentist in their midst."[4]

Also, during the ante-bellum period, the City of Atlanta prohibited free blacks from operating "eating or boarding houses or shops for the sale of small articles of food." Neither could they work as salespersons in Atlanta stores or sell "'beer, cake, fruit or confectionery in the streets or alleys' of the city." Yet, despite these restrictions on access to the marketplace, free blacks were taxed "on both their persons and property" at rates equal to those for whites.[5]

The proscribed economic position of free blacks in Atlanta in the ante-bellum period can best be seen in the Census of 1860. Of the 25 blacks in this class who resided in the city, only nine were listed as employed. Five of those were washer people, four women and one man. There were two black "laborers" and two "train hands."[6]

Reconstruction to the New Deal

Following the close of the Civil War and the constitutional liberation of black slaves, new arrangements were required to govern the political, social, and economic relationships among all blacks and the white population. Immediately, "the efficiency of Negro free labor" in Georgia "was unquestionably demonstrated by increased production of Southern commodities." But many whites also "began a program of ruthless, merciless exploitation of ignorant Negro labor." Between 1869 and 1870, for example, the standard wage for unskilled farm laborers was only $60 per year. In 1898, the average wage of black agricultural laborers was only seven dollars per month. By 1902, it had only climbed to eight dollars per month and, even, in 1937, the black agricultural worker in Georgia rarely earned more than ten dollars or $12 per month. Meanwhile, many proprietors attempted unsuccessfully to import immigrant white laborers who generally demanded higher wages than blacks. Blacks were normally retained, however, because of the reluctance of the proprietors to increase wages.[7]

Beginning also in the Reconstruction Era, black artisans and other semi-skilled and skilled laborers in Georgia began to face increasing competition from whites. Because of the widespread poverty which the Civil War left among many whites, ideas and concepts of labor among them changed to a remarkable degree. More whites were now more willing to seek and accept occupations which required the use of their hands. Blacks, then, were forced to abandon their virtual monopolies on such trades as blacksmithing. The typical white attitude was that blacks should be relegated to only the most undesirable manual labor. To assure a lack of competition in the skilled trades, white "workmen refused to take Negroes as apprentices and refused to admit" them to their growing unions or to work with them if the employers should venture to hire them."[8]

Restrictions on skilled occupations available to blacks both in unionized and non-union trades served to exclude blacks from many occupations while relegating them to the lowest paying positions in others. For example, in the construction industry, many white contractors refused to employ skilled black workmen if they had to "pay them standard wages," especially if they could find available whites. The "average white contractor" also generally preferred "to hire white skilled workmen" and employed blacks "as helpers only." These policies and practices often lead to high unemployment rates among black men, especially. Thus, black women, in much greater numbers than white ones, had to seek employment outside of their home and many black men "abandoned" their families in order to migrate to the North, seeking better economic opportunities.[9]

Although black women entered the labor market in large numbers after the Civil War, their occupations were overwhelmingly manual or domestic and their wages often lower than even the unskilled black male laborer. Indeed, one scholar has described these wages for black women as "ridiculously low." "In many instances cooks and maids" worked for their board and from one to three dollars per week."[10]

Discrimination by law and custom effectively served to keep black men and women away from the most lucrative semi-skilled and skilled jobs in the post-bellum period in Atlanta and the rest of the state. Opportunities for the accumulation of significant capital would, then, be largely confined to the business and professional sectors of the economy.   But, as has been shown, both legal and extra-legal proscriptions militated against black advancement.   Some of these, however, were lifted, unenforced, or ignored after the Civil War. Yet, the legacy of discrimination persisted and new restrictive policies and practices developed.   In the former category, the virtually total exclusion of blacks from merchandising, finance, and manufacturing in the ante-bellum period denied them opportunities "to learn business or accumulate capital to engage in it." It is, therefore, not surprising that post-bellum black businesses in Atlanta and elsewhere show a predominance toward areas of merchandise and service, mostly connected with food, and semi-skilled or skilled positions related to the slave experience.[11]

Largely because of studies by the Sociology Department at Atlanta University, we are able to reconstruct the status of black businesses in Atlanta at the turn of the last century.   At the time, the city had a black population of about 28,000 people.   The Atlanta University study identified, as late as 1899, 61 black "business enterprises of sufficient size to be noticed."

These included:

> 22 Grocery Stores
> 5 General Merchandise Stores
> 6 Woodyards
> 6 [Large] Barber Shops
> 7 Markets
> 2 Restaurants
> 2 Undertakers
> 2 Blacksmiths and Wheelwrights, with stock
> 2 Saloons
> 1 Tailor, with stock
> 1 Drug Store
> 1 Creamery
> 1 Pool and Billiard Parlor
> 1 Loan and Investment Company
> 1 Carriage and Wagon Builder
> 1 Real Estate Dealer[12]

Among the black businesses in Atlanta by 1899, only two were capitalized in excess of $10,000. One of these was a barber shop and the other an undertaker. The oldest business was 29 years old. The average age of the enterprises was about ten years. Regardless of their age, almost all of the black businesses in the city depended "primarily on Negro patronage." Of the 25 firms "especially studied in 1898, none depended wholly on white trade, the rest depended wholly on Negro trade, except nine which had considerable white trade, and two had some white patronage." Some businesses, such as restaurants and barber shops had to "draw the color line without exception and either serve all whites or all Negroes." Black undertakers could serve blacks only. "All of these considerations" made for "a vast difference between white and Negro business men." A black undertaker in Atlanta served a population of 35,000 people, "chiefly of the laboring class"; while a white undertaker had "a constituency of perhaps 80,000 largely well-to-do merchants and artisans." The white grocer had "not only the advantage of training and capital, but also of a constituency three times as rich as his Negro competitor." Moreover, 75 percent of the black firms were "compelled by custom to do business largely on a credit basis," and had "fewer means of compelling payment." Finally, the black merchants "as a class" were "poorly trained" for their work. Of the 25 "especially studied" in 1898, only one had "college training," while nine had attended "Common School," 12 could "read and write only," and three had "no education."[13]

In addition to the Atlanta University sociology class studies, the Atlanta Conferences on Negro Business had, in 1899 and 1912, also assessed the status of black businesses in Atlanta and other parts of the state. They found among other things, that black businesses suffered from the lack of prior experience and the poor training of their proprietors as well as their failure to advertise. They were also adversely affected by a belief on the part of some fellow blacks "in the superiority of the white race and the inherent inferiority of their own people." Hence, they tended to "mistrust and envy their business men." Even some "Negro professional men and so-called race leaders" patronized white business in preference to Negro concerns. But the study concluded that "the ugliest and the most serious handicap of Negro businesses" was "race prejudice."[14]

With some few exceptions, like the Atlanta *Daily World* newspaper, the Atlanta Life Insurance Company, and the Citizens Trust Bank, black-owned enterprises in Atlanta remained small and marginally profitable, if at all, from the Reconstruction period to the New Deal. Several factors impeded success; but the most obvious and persistent one was racial discrimination, based upon both law and custom.[15]

The economic conditions of the professional class of Atlanta blacks in the post-bellum period were similar to those of the black business community. The group was a very small one which was proscribed by discriminatory policies and practices to serve a primarily black constituency. Professor Asa Gordon, in *The Georgia Negro*, described the plight of Georgia's black physicians:

> The masses of the Negro physicians were very poor directly after the war. Since the Negro physician was largely barred by prejudice from serving the white people, regardless of his efficiency, he had to depend upon his own people entirely. His prices could not compete with his white competitors, who could afford to serve the poor colored people at lower rates and make it up by higher charges to their more affluent white patrons, which was in accordance with the well established traditions of the medical profession...[16]

Discriminatory policies and practices also restricted the patronage of black pharmacists, black hospitals, and black lawyers. Rarely, if ever, did white physicians prescribe drugs with black druggists; but black physicians sometimes sent their patients to white pharmacists. Hospital facilities, even those supported by tax dollars, were segregated by both law and custom. The black hospitals and wards were invariably smaller and more poorly equipped than the white ones. The noted NAACP leader Walter White even suggested that his father's death was affected by his summary transfer to the black ward of Atlanta's Grady Hospital, after it was discovered that the light complexioned man was actually a Negro. Interestingly and ironically, black nurses were gradually employed by all types of black hospitals and wards, but black physicians were barred from both black and white facilities. On the other hand, although blacks frequently engaged the services of white attorneys, Atlanta's seven black lawyers were restricted by custom and prejudice to an almost entirely black clientele. Blacks, themselves, often preferred white attorneys in Atlanta because of the perception that all-white juries would convict them more readily if they were represented by a black. They also were well aware of the prejudice and discrimination directed toward black attorneys by judges and other court officials. Oft-times the black lawyers were addressed as "boy" or "nigger," and faced contempt simply for vigorously defending their black clients.[17]

Except for the ministry, the largest category of professional blacks in post-bellum Atlanta was that of teaching. Several blacks acquired teaching positions in the city's six black colleges immediately after the close of the Civil War. But large numbers of whites also taught in these schools. Yet, neither public nor private white colleges and universities would employ black professors, and it was not until 1878, six years later after the establishment of a public school system for blacks, that the first black elementary teachers were hired in Atlanta. The justification

> most commonly given for not hiring black teachers was that a sufficient number of competent blacks had not been trained to staff an entire school. Another consideration was the fear that whites might lose control over the black race. School officials also thought it was unfair to dismiss white teachers to hire black ones...[18]

Although the black faculty in the Atlanta public schools "were subjected to the same rules and regulations as white" teachers, they were not paid equal salaries. By 1894, for example, the annual pay for a black principal was $650, while only one of the 13 white principals received an identical amount, and "the majority of others were paid over $1,200." Black teachers, at the time, were paid between $350 and $400 annually, while the lowest paid white teacher received $500 per year. This "pattern of discriminatory compensation" continued until 1948, when it was struck down by a Federal Court.[19]

New Deal to the Era of Civil Rights

During the Great Depression of the 1930s, blacks in the city of Atlanta, "even though increasing at a larger percentage than whites, lost in the proportion of gainfully employed while white workers gained in numbers employed . . . Persons working in managerial classifications in Atlanta were overwhelmingly of the white race." And workers "engaged at clerical, sales and kindred jobs" were also predominantly white in Atlanta between 1930 and 1940.[20]

As in the post-bellum period, blacks continued to be the greater proportion of unskilled workers in Atlanta after 1930. Indeed, "this occupational category, as the clerical category is to white workers" became "a haven for Negro workers male and female alike." Weekly wage trends among black and white workers also showed that blacks received a lower average weekly wage than white workers." Since white employers still clung "to the archaic philosophy" that blacks responded "more readily to white supervisors than to Negro supervision," Atlanta's black workers remained "at the bottom" of the occupational structure. "Certain traditional [menial, manual, and domestic] occupations [were] earmarked for the bulk of Negro workers while the white workers [found] province in the higher occupational classifications."[21]

Discrimination in the trade unions also continued to effect adversely the employability of blacks in the Atlanta area. The Atlanta Bricklayers locals, for example, were segregated until 1961, and there were no black bricklayers apprentices until 1965. "The very low percentage of Negroes in apprenticeship programs seems to have resulted in misdirection and malpreparation of Negroes for skilled occupation." "Because of past discrimination," black youths could not call upon "skilled Negroes to give [them] guidance and encouragement."[22]

The lack of skilled craftsmen among Atlanta blacks resulted in a scarcity of "relatively high wage earners in the community which limited the buying power of the community." It also left "a large portion of the population in low-paying, marginal occupations."[23]

It was not until the coming of the New Deal following the election of President Franklin D. Roosevelt in 1932 and the outbreak of the Second World War in 1939 that optimistic forecasts for economic renewal in Black America seemed plausible. The President had promised that all would share in his programs of reform and recovery. But much of the implementation of the New Deal programs was left in the hands of the states or to native federal officials in the state. In the South, these practices resulted in discriminatory applications of New Deal projects. Whereas in the Depression, blacks had been "the last hired and first fired," in the New Deal, they were still often poorly employed or not employed at all. By 1941, national black leaders had threatened a "March on Washington" to protest discriminatory employment in war related industries. The "March" was suspended when President Roosevelt issued an Executive Order creating a Fair Employment Practices Committee (FEPC) to insure non-discriminatory hiring in defense related businesses. Meanwhile blacks in several cities, including Atlanta, supported "Don't Buy Where You Can't Work" Campaigns.[24]

During World War II, in Atlanta and elsewhere, FEPC offices received hundreds of complaints of job discrimination from black citizens. Several of the complaints were directed at the Firestone Rubber and Tire Company's Atlanta Aircraft Division. At least one was received against a U.S. Army Warehouse in the city. During the course of these investigations, an employer at the A&P Bakery in

Atlanta freely admitted that she "did not hire colored women" as trainees. In other instances, employers were found who omitted advertising for certain skilled jobs in "the colored section" of the local newspapers "want-ad" columns, while including the positions in the white ones.[25]

Beginning in the 1950s, demographic factors, often with racial appendages, began "to create problems in neighborhood commercial areas" throughout Atlanta. There was a

> substantial increase in population and income in the suburbs, creating a potential for rapid growth and commercial expansion in those areas . . . As anchor stores relocated and entrepreneurial talent left the central City for the suburbs, the smaller stores remaining suffered from the loss of traffic which had been generated by the larger stores . . . [F]ewer goods and services were offered, often at lower quality and higher prices.[26]

Most of the demographic changes after 1950 occurred among white Atlantans, many of whom (especially after 1954) took "flight" from the city in the wake of increased residential desegregation and the impending desegregation of the city's public schools. But a number of middle-income blacks, seeking better housing and schools, also began to move to the suburbs of neighboring counties.[27]

Overall the City of Atlanta, after 1950, experienced "a significant loss" in such businesses as drug stores, groceries, restaurants, service stations and hardware stores. Between 1958 and 1977 alone, "the number of convenience goods stores declined 28 percent and the decline for all other was 26 percent." Yet, these "convenience goods stores" constituted the bulk of neighborhood commercial enterprises in the city's black communities. Before 1950, as with housing, these stores and shops had been restricted to a largely black clientele both by law and custom. Then, at the very moment restrictive legal and other impediments were being removed, the city began to lose a large percentage of both its white and black middle-income occupants.[28]

The outward migration of middle-income residents from Atlanta after 1950 affected many black professionals in a manner similar to that of the black business class. As white-owned enterprises and professional services abandoned inner city areas, black professionals could, at least, break beyond their previous barriers on Auburn Avenue on the near east side of town and Hunter Street on the near west side of the city. But by the time black physicians and attorneys could claim office suites in the central downtown area, many former residents relocated their trade to their previous servers in the suburbs. Other whites continued the custom of ignoring black professionals, and many blacks continued to do likewise. The latter group maintaining an attitude that they could not be best served by members of their own race.[29]

The Civil Rights Era to the Inauguration of the First Black Mayor

A U.S. Bureau of Labor Statistics (BLS) comparison of white and black family incomes in Atlanta in 1960 revealed that the average annual income of black families in the city was $3,307, or only 48 percent of the average of an Atlanta white family, $6,894. Local black leaders continued to insist that "discrimination barriers" in the hiring and promotion of "workers in all types of employment" helped largely to account for these discrepancies. Even some major white Atlanta employers who claimed they had "eliminated racially discriminatory hiring practices" admitted that blacks still had difficulty "in getting or advancing to better jobs and higher pay" because they had "received vocational training in segregated schools." Thus, they often either failed to pass or failed to score as well on aptitude tests as white applicants.[30]

Federally sponsored programs to increase black employment often did little to alleviate the heritage of discrimination, while both overt and subtle discriminatory practices continued to persist. For example, in March of 1961, just a few weeks after taking office, President John F. Kennedy issued an Executive Order (No. 10925) which gave the President's Committee on Equal Employment Opportunity the power to require government contractors "to eliminate discrimination in hiring and promotions." The "key aspects of the plans, as the Program's supporters pointed out, were the 'voluntary' and 'affirmative' points of the documents." The program became known as the "Plans for Progress."[31]

In the summer of 1961, representatives of nine large corporations, "each of them a defense contractor, affixed their names to the first Plans for Progress, pledging their voluntary support for equal employment opportunities." They pledged that "they would work affirmatively . . . toward elimination of job discrimination in all of their branches, plants, and divisions."[32]

More than a year after Plans for Progress had been in effect in

Atlanta, the Southern Regional Council (SRC) conducted a survey of 24 Atlanta firms to "determine what increase there had been in the number of Negro employees hired since the firms signed up under the program." Since, however, there were no such figures available, the Report was drawn from interviews with Atlanta regional executives of the following firms:

> American Machine and Foundry
> Burroughs Corporation
> Chrysler Corporation
> Collins Radio
> Continental Motors
> Ford Motor
> Garrett Corporation
> General Dynamics
> General Electric
> General Motors
> Goodyear Tire and Rubber
> Hercules Powder
> International Business Machines
> International Harvester
> Kaiser Industries
> Lockheed Aircraft
> Minneapolis-Honeywell Regulator
> Pan American World Airways, Inc.
> Philco Corporation (a division of Ford)
> Raytheon Corporation
> Thompson Ramo-Wooldridge
> Western Electric
> Westinghouse[33]

These firms employed, or had regional jurisdiction over, about 26,000 persons. The largest employer in the group was Lockheed Aircraft in nearby Marietta, with 14,500 workers. General Motors assembly plants were second with 6,490; Ford had 2,000. All had at least one year in which "to take affirmative and voluntary action toward elimination of job discrimination." But, the results of the survey clearly indicated that, "except for a handful of the companies, the Plans for Progress were, for the regional office[s] in Atlanta, largely meaningless." Only seven of the firms interviewed produced evidence of affirmative compliance with their pledges. The remaining 17 firms had paid "varying degrees of attention to Plans for Progress, ranging from ignorance to indifference."[34]

By 1972, one of the Plans for Progress firms, Lockheed Aircraft, had been sued for "alleged discrimination in hiring, pay, promotion and training of black employees." One of the plaintiffs, Theodore Ramsey, contended that at least six white persons in his department had been promoted over him, although "they had less experience in the department." He also cited four whites "on the same level" who received higher salaries.[35]

Several months earlier, U.S. District Court Judge Sidney O. Smith had signed a decree in which the Georgia Power Company, also a major regional employer, had agreed to notify 20 black job applicants that they would be offered the "first available jobs" for which they were qualified. The 20 had been found to be victims of discrimination in a class action suit brought against the company by the U.S. Justice Department.[36]

Even after Atlanta had come under the control of a black dominated government, another federally sponsored program failed appreciably to erase the vestiges of past discrimination. In the first two years (1974-1976) of the Comprehensive Employment Training Act (CETA), unemployment in Atlanta "had differentially affected the population with blacks even more vulnerable than usual. The general relationship of the black unemployment rate as twice that of the whites was exceeded for males. During 1975 and 1976, the rate for black males was closer to three times that for white males. Nearly one of five black males were unemployed." Also, in the CETA program larger proportions of blacks held craft and laboring jobs (18 percent) compared to whites (six percent), and larger proportions of whites held professional jobs (20 percent) compared to blacks (ten percent). In the end, the CETA public sector jobs program "did not enroll the educationally disadvantaged, but creamed for the better educated." Thus, it "seriously compromised the objective of serving the disadvantaged."[37]

With respect to workers actually employed by the City of Atlanta, it was not until after the election of Ivan Allen, Jr., as mayor in 1961 that the names of all qualified applicants, black and white, were "placed on the same registers in rank order of attained grades." Prior to this time, most positions were established accordingly "as either a black or white register." After January 1, 1963, blacks made up approximately 13 percent of "the total persons placed on eligible registers for classes of positions not traditionally held by Negroes." Blacks also constituted about eight percent of the persons actually employed from these registers. "In actual numbers," only 93 blacks were "employed in jobs which were not generally open to them prior to 1963."[38]

The integration of the registers did not result in "and was not expected to result in any dramatic or radical change of the employment picture in the city government." The city's Personnel Department blamed a low turnover rate in "upper level positions" and the absence of a "large pool of Negroes qualified and/or interested in the technical fields" as reasons for the lack of "dramatic change."[39]

By 1970, the proportion of the work force employed in government increased in the city, "but the greatest percentage of growth by far" was "in the professional and managerial black areas of West Atlanta." At least partly this may have been a reflection of "changing civil rights attitudes and affirmative action regulations."[40]

Also, by 1970, Atlanta was still perceived as a city where black business enterprises had "a better than average chance for survival and growth." But "at times," the city appeared "hostile to black business development." For example, even after blacks gained control of City Hall in 1974, the city's Commission of Administrative Services pointed out

> that of $4.7 million in construction contracts, minority-owned firms were awarded only about 4 percent of the total. These firms fared even worse in non-construction contracts, sharing a miniscule 0.007 percent of the $6.9 million awarded. All this is despite Atlanta's purchasing director's opinion that minority firms have a 10 percent participating capacity in construction contracts and a 15 percent or more participation capacity in non-construction contracts.[41]

In addition to problems of government contracts, improvements in the status of black businesses in Atlanta were "directly related to improvements in overall economic and social conditions of the black community." And, even in the 1970s, social indicators substantiated "the inner city and the Bankhead-Marietta wedge as the poverty zone," characterized by "crowded domiciles," female-headed households, "and areas of housing deterioration." There were, at the time, "at least ten black low income neighborhoods in comparison to only three white low income neighborhoods." The "consolidation of unemployment" in 1970 was "toward the central core and the Bankhead-Marietta wedge." This pattern corresponded "with the poverty black areas."[42]

Summary

Atlanta's small black population, slave and quasi-free, emerged from the Civil War in a state of legal freedom. But it was soon proscribed by some of the same laws and customs which had restricted it, socially, politically and economically in ante-bellum times. Specific acts restrained the types of enterprises and services in which blacks could engage and the race of the clientele they could serve. Discriminatory policies and practices on the part of employers, including the city government, and labor unions, combined with separate and unequal education hampered their employment and advancement in skilled jobs. And laws and customs imposed disadvantages on the professional class of blacks by restricting their businesses to certain areas of the city and reducing the size and buying power of their potential clientele.[43]

Although the Civil Rights Act of 1964 and various executive orders of U.S. Presidents, extending back to Franklin D. Roosevelt in 1941, prohibited economic discrimination against black Americans and, indeed, sought to promote affirmative, often voluntary, action to redress past discriminations, both overt and subtle bias persisted into the 1970s (the termination period of this historical summary).

In the end, historical systemic and institutionalized discrimination against blacks in Atlanta, which has severely restricted their access to sources of wealth and power, emerges as the major factor accounting for their marginal economic position in the area's business population.

Notes

[1] *Statistical View of the United States. Being a Compendium of the Seventh Census* (Washington, 1854), p. 63; *Eighth Census of the United States, 1860: Statistics of Population* (Washington, 1860-1864), pp. 70-71; *Eighth Census of the United States, 1860*, Schedule 1, "Enumeration of Free Inhabitants," for Fulton County and Atlanta, unpublished, Georgia Department of Archives and History: Edward F. Sweat, "Free Blacks in Ante-bellum Atlanta," *The Atlanta Historical Bulletin* (Spring, 1977), p. 64.

[2] Sweat, *Ibid.*, p. 65

[3] *Ibid.*

[4] Oliver H. Prince, ed., *A Digest of the Laws of the State of Georgia* (Athens, 1837, pp. 788-789; *Acts of the General Assembly of the State of Georgia*, 1859, pp. 67-70 (hereafter cited as *Georgia Acts*); *Georgia Acts*, 1845, p. 49; *Georgia Acts*, 1835, pp. 268-269; *Atlanta City Council Minutes*, Book 3, p. 230, Atlanta Historical Society Archives; Sweat, "Free Blacks," p. 65.

[5] *Atlanta Ordinance Book A, 1851-1860*: Sweat, "Free Blacks," p. 66.

[6] *Eighth Census of the United States, 1860*: Sweat, "Free Blacks," p. 66.

[7] Asa Gordon, *The Georgia Negro*, pp. 69-70.

[8] W. E. B. DuBois and Augustus Granville Dill, "The Negro American Artisan," *The Atlanta University Publications*, No. 17, (Atlanta, 1912), pp. 56, 129; Leonard Hammock James, "The Policies of Organized Labor in Relation to Negro Workers in Atlanta, 1869-1937," Unpublished Masters Thesis, Atlanta University, 1937, pp. 6-7, 14-16; Gordon, *The Georgia Negro*, p. 72; Herman D. Bloch, "A Circle of Discrimination Against Negroes, 1625-1960," *The Crisis* (May, 1964), pp. 296-299.

[9] James, *Ibid.*; Bloch, *Ibid.*; Gordon, *Ibid.*, pp. 72-74, 79-82, 83-84.

[10] Gordon, *The Georgia Negro*, pp. 74-75.

[11] Gordon, *Ibid.*, pp. 248-253.

[12] *Ibid.*, p. 254.

[13] *Ibid.*, pp. 254-257.

[14] *Ibid.*, pp. 260-263.

[15] Alexa Benson Henderson, "Alonzo F. Herndon and Black Insurance in Atlanta; 1904-1915," *Atlanta Historical Bulletin*, (Spring, 1977), pp. 34-44: Edward R. Carter, *The Black Side: A Partial History of the Business, Religious and Educational Side of the Negro in Atlanta, Ga.* (Atlanta, 1894), pp. 246-250: William E. B. DuBois, ed., *Economics Co-Operation Among Negro Americans*, Atlanta University Publications, No. 12 (Atlanta, 1907), pp. 106-107: William E. B. DuBois, ed., *The Negro in Business*, Atlanta University Publications, No. 4 (Atlanta, 1899), p. 57; Gordon, *The Georgia Negro*, p. 267-268.

[16] Gordon, *The Georgia Negro*, pp. 276-280.

[17] *Ibid.*, pp. 282-284.

[18] *Atlanta City Council Minutes, May 5, 1871*, Atlanta Historical Society Archives: *Annual Report of the Atlanta Board of Education* (Atlanta, 1874), p. 18 (hereafter cited as *Board of Education Report*): *City Council Minutes, May 5, 1871*: *Board of Education Report*, 1873, pp. 34-35: *Atlanta Board of Education Minutes*, July 26, 1877; August 22, 1878.

[19] *Board of Education Report*, 1981, pp. 7-11; C.T. Wright, "The Development of Public Schools for Blacks in Atlanta, 1872-1900, *"The Atlanta Historical Bulletin"* (Spring, 1977), p. 126.

[20] Kenneth E. Barton, "A Comparative Study by Race of Occupational Changes and Gainfully Employed Atlanta Workers from 1930 to 1940; and Statistically Treated Occupational Information on Employment Patterns in Twenty-Five Atlanta Business Firms from 1941 to April, 1948," Unpublished Masters Thesis, Atlanta University, June, 1948, p. 82.

[21] *Ibid.*, pp. 83-84.

[22] Ples Earl McIntyre, Jr., "The Effects of Discrimination in Apprenticeship Programs on the Employability of Negro Youth: An Atlanta Study." Unpublished Masters Thesis, Atlanta University, May, 1967, pp. 32, 36, 46.

[23] *Ibid.*, pp. 46-47.

[24] Bloch, "A Circle of Discrimination Against Negroes, 1625-1960," pp. 299, 304-305.

[25] Amos Ryce, Jr. to Bruce Hunt, April 12, 1944, Regional Federal Archives, East Point, Ga.: War Man Power Commission, U.S. Employment Service, "Report of Discriminatory Hiring Practices, August 5, 1944, Regional Federal Archives, East Point, Ga.: United States of America, Before the President's Committee on Fair Employment Practice, December 31, 1944, Case Number 7-GR-44, Regional Federal Archives, East Point, Ga.: *The Atlanta Constitution*, April 12, 1945; John Hope, III to Witherspoon Dodge, March 3, 1945, Regional Federal Archives, East Point, Ga.: War Man Power Commission, U.S. Employment Service, "Report of Discriminatory Hiring Practices," September 12, 1944, Regional Federal Archives, East Point, Ga.: United States of America, Before the President's Committee on Fair Employment Practice, July 7, 1944, Case Number 7-BR-412, Regional Federal Archives, East Point, Ga.: *The Atlanta Journal*, April 6, 1944.

[26] Paul E. Hemmann, *Commercial Growth and Decline in the Atlanta SMSA, 1950-1980*, p. 4.

[27] Alton Hornsby, Jr., "The Negro in Atlanta Politics, 1961-1973," *The Atlanta Historical Bulletin*, (Spring, 1977), pp. 14-16, 29; Charles E. Silberman, *Crisis in Black and White* (New York, 1964), pp. 16-18, 202-203; *Atlanta Journal*, September 20, 1972; *Atlanta Constitution*, September 21, 1972.

[28] Hemmann, *Commercial Growth and Decline*, p. 14.

[29] Clarence N. Stone, *Regime Politics: Governing Atlanta, 1946-1988* (Lawrence, Kansas, 1989), p. 39: Hemmann, *Commercial Growth and Decline*, pp. 3-14; Malcolm A. Murray, *Atlas of Atlanta, The 1970s* (University of Alabama, 1974), pp. x, xi, xii.

[30] *Atlanta Constitution*, December 14, 1962.

[31] "Plans for Progress: Atlanta Survey, " The Southern Regional Council, January, 1963, p. 1.

[32] *Ibid.*

[33] *Ibid.*, pp. 7-8.

[34] *Ibid.* pp. 8-9.

[35] *The Atlanta Journal*, January 4, 1972.

[36] *The Atlanta Constitution*, January 29, 1971.

[37] Gretchen MacLachlan, "Making CETA-PSE Work: A Case Study of Public Service Employment Under Atlanta's CETA Program," The Southern Center for Studies in Public Policy (Atlanta, 1978), pp. 51-52, 55-57, 66, 70.

[38] *Atlanta Personnel Board Annual Reports, 1954-1965*, p. 2.

[39] *Ibid.*

[40] Murray, *Atlas of Atlanta*, xii.

[41] Robert J. Yancy, *Federal Government Policy and Black Business Enterprise* (Cambridge, Mass., 1974), p. 108: Robert C. Vowels, "Atlanta Negro Business and the New Black Bourgeoisie," *The Atlanta Historical Bulletin* (Spring, 1977), p. 51.

[42] Murray, *Atlas of Atlanta*, xi-xii.

[43] DuBois and Dill, "The Negro American Artisan"; p. 129: McIntyre, "The Effects of Discrimination in Apprenticeship Programs," pp. 36-39, 45-47; *Atlanta Code Supplement of 1936*, pp. 247-248; *Charter, Related Laws and Code of General Ordinances of Atlanta, Georgia, 1953*, Secs. 55.91, 55.51, 36.64, 38.31, 56.15, p. 731: Bloch, "A Circle of Discrimination," pp. 296-306: *A Salute to Atlanta's Black Heritage*, *The Atlanta Historical Bulletin* (Spring, 1977), pp. 7-142: Stone, *Regime Politics*, pp. 11-12, 16-21, 32-50, 56-60, 67, 80, 85-91.

INDIVIDUALS

Chapter 15
The Legacy of Grace Towns Hamilton
to the Development of the City of Atlanta

As many of you know, historians and other scholars continue to debate the significance of and the degree of the impact that any single individual can have on historical events. There are those who believe that because of the awesome power of natural and social forces that men and women can be little more than pawns on the chessboard of history or at best eventful persons who appear at the right time and place and seem to exert an extraordinary influence on major developments of their time. But thy exponents of the so-called Great Man Theory and others strongly contend that a few, select individuals with rare insights and skills can and do impact major developments of certain eras, largely through their own initiatives. Whether or not one subscribes to one or the other of these theories or to neither, I would suggest that it will be instructive in discussing the legacy of Grace Towns Hamilton to the development of the City of Atlanta to examine not only her personal characteristics, but also the milieu in which she emerged as a woman and as a leader. Such an examination might also tell us some valuable things about the evolution of present-day Atlanta.

If one undertakes such a probe as we are suggesting, particularly as it relates to the life and works of Grace Towns Hamilton, we might begin with the post-Reconstruction Era between 1877 and the 1900s.

Prepared for delivery at the Annual Grace Towns Hamilton Lecture, Emory University, Atlanta, Georgia, April 19, 1990

During this period, Atlanta was like much of the rest of the South, particularly in its politics and in its social mores. Conservative, upper income white men, who normally voted democratic statewide and nationally, ran the city.   White women and all blacks were disfranchised for much of the period, except in special and general elections.   From time to time, even a number of white males were denied access to the franchise because of barriers of property, poll taxes, literacy and understanding tests and other requirements.   For African-Americans, especially, it was a time of great tension motivated largely by the emergence of legal and extra-legal repression through laws mandating separation of the races in public places.   Any equality promised by such segregation statutes rapidly disappeared under the weight of both law and custom.   One of the most disastrous results of the tension and hate nurtured by the caste system was the Atlanta Race Riot of 1906, in which scores of both races were killed or injured, and hundreds, mostly blacks, fled the city.   These manifestations of hate soon spread beyond blacks to Jews, communists, liberals, and others who did not conform to color, ethnic, religious, and political standards set by the Anglo-Saxon majority.   In one instance, Leo Frank, a Jew, became the victim.   In another, it was a black communist, Angelo Herndon.

Yet, amid all of the similarities between Atlanta and the rest of the South in the post-Reconstruction Era, there were always some significant differences, which astute observers, even from afar, could discern.   And so, by the early 1900s travelers like Ray Stannard Baker, Julian Street, and Jan and Cora Gordon reported on Atlanta as Southern, but not quite so Southern; conservative in attitudes and mores, but with a touch of progressivism.   Quite often those who drew a distinction between Atlanta and the rest of the South pointed to its newness or its modernity (the city was only 30 years old at the close of the Civil War).   They also cited its booming economy, based more on commercialism than agriculture and fed by its location as the transportation (meaning railroads) center of the region.   The city did in fact many believed resemble Henry Grady's New South.   But observers invariably noted what was perhaps the most unique feature of all — the city was the site of the largest center of higher education for blacks in the world, and it had, even in the earliest days after the Civil War developed not only a black intellectual community, but a prosperous group of black entrepreneurs and professionals.   The size and influence of the business and professional class had, in fact, grown so large that Forbes Magazine, by 1928, could call its main thoroughfare, Auburn

Avenue, "the richest Negro street in the world."

At the major anchor for the economic and educational, indeed all aspects of the early development of the African-American community in Atlanta stood the black church. Several of the city's black colleges were founded in such institutions and all of them were closely affiliated with specific denominations or individual congregations. For example, Spelman and Morehouse Colleges were closely linked to the Friendship Baptist Church, Morris Brown College to the Bethel AME Church, and Atlanta University to the First Congregational Church. The churches were also, early on, the first source for the social welfare of the African-American community in Atlanta and a major base of economic investment and security. They attended to the social and financial needs of the indigent, cared for the sick, and brought solace and support to widows and orphans. They established burial societies and similar functions to bury the dead and sustain their survivors. It was out of such church-sponsored activities that major black insurance companies like Standard Life and Atlanta Life had their roots.

The presence of the Atlanta University complex of colleges, of independent black entrepreneurs, and of large community centered churches spawned a black bourgeoisie which, while generally accommodating itself to the racial caste system, grew restless and chafed under the proscriptions of Jim Crow. Amid the legal restrictions and the physical dangers of open rebellion against their oppression, they continuously insisted on equal facilities, treatment, and conditions, particularly in publicly supported enterprises and public accommodations. While discrimination in public transportation, in housing, and in law enforcement variously drew their attention and protest, they were more consistently concerned with equal education for their children and unfettered access to the franchise.

It was, then, in this environment that Grace Towns was born to George Alexander and Mary Coates Towns in 1907. George Towns was the son of an ex-slave, Luke Jr., and his wife, Mary Coates. Luke's father was a half-brother of Georgia Governor George W. Towns. George Alexander earned bachelors degrees at Atlanta and Harvard Universities, and in 1900, began a long teaching career at Atlanta. In the nearly 40 years that he spent on the Atlanta University campus, he became known as the "grand ole man" of the institution. He was certainly one of the most versatile personalities, serving as a teacher in several disciplines, a performer and fundraiser for the university quartet, coach of the debating team, alumni representative, editor of the Alumni magazine, secretary for W. E. B. Dubois' Atlanta University conferences, and coach of the baseball and football teams.

Among other things, nevertheless, he found time and energy to oppose inequalities in the Atlanta Public School System, disfranchisement, and other discriminations against blacks. He was a prominent member of the Georgia Equal Rights Convention, an anti-disfranchisement group, and a founding member and officer of the Atlanta NAACP. He expressed his own personal revulsion toward Jim Crowism by riding a bicycle to downtown Atlanta rather than board the segregated streetcars and buses.

George Towns' social and political consciousness was not atypical of the activities and attitudes of the black leadership class in Atlanta. At the turn of the century, almost all of the ministers of the large churches, First Congregational, Wheat Street, Ebenezer, and Friendship Baptist, and Bethel A.M.E were leaders in causes of social and political ameliorations for African-Americans. Pioneer businessmen like Heman Perry, founder of the first black business empire in the city, also supported such causes; as did John and Lugenia Hope of Morehouse College and others from the academic community. Persons like Towns and the Hopes were products of the often defamed "mulatto elite" in African-American history and folklore, but men and women of other hues were generously represented in the leadership cadre. Regardless of hue, the elite constituted a distinct, separate class in the African-American community of Atlanta and in their lifestyles and social mores they displayed their distinctiveness from the masses of poorly educated, low-income blacks in the city. But despite the existence of a few who decried the shiftlessness and criminality of their uncouth, disadvantaged brethren and sisters and who appealed for special status and recognition, even among whites, as the so called "talented tenth," the large majority realized that their own civil conditions, particularly, were inextricably bound with all other African-Americans.

Growing up on the Atlanta University campus and educated in its laboratory school and the university, itself, Grace Towns was an eyewitness to all that members of the black elite could attain in education and in material comforts. But she also saw the limitations, which the caste system placed on their aspirations and, indeed, their freedoms. Thus, through both word and deed, she could see and understand, too, the struggle for equality and justice, which her father and other black elites led. The minimal, but often significant results of their agitation and protests — the hiring of black teachers for black schools, the attainment of a black high school, an additional street light or paved roadway here and there, a balance of power in some special elections — and she could see how much more remained to be done.

Significantly also, young Grace grew up in one of the only really desegregated communities in the city, the Atlanta University complex, where many white administrators, faculty members, and their children often interacted with blacks as intellectual and social equals.

While social equality among the races in Atlanta was largely confined, at the time, to the black college campuses, since the Atlanta Race Riot of 1906 interracial associations at high levels had taken on more formal characteristics. In the wake of the riot, some of Atlanta's leading white clergymen deplored the immorality of the violence, while some of the city's white businessmen recognized the threat which the events posed to the city's contemporary as well as long range economic and social health. Those expressing concern and commitment to action included the president and secretary of the Atlanta Chamber of Commerce. A strategy adopted by the traders, at that time, served as a model for handling racial crises, which threatened the public peace in Atlanta for more than half a century. The white leadership enlisted the support of prominent members of the black leadership (mostly ministers) in seeking to restore order and build the foundations for peace. This type of communication later became known in the words of the late Mayor William B. Hartsfield as "liaison," that is, liaison between the races. It was also a part of what some of us have characterized as "the Atlanta style" of race relations.

In reality these early interracial associations were borne more out of economic necessity than from legal, moral, or ethical concerns. But other groups, including anti-lynching organizations, human rights councils, including those in the YMCAs and YWCAs, and the region-wide Committee on Interracial Cooperation (a forerunner of the Southern Regional Council), which was based in Atlanta, brought blacks and whites together over issues of legal equality, justice, and morality. Preachers, professors, church women, and students predominated these groups.

In view of Grace Towns' background, it is not surprising that, as a young woman, her interests quickly turned to matters of education, social uplift, and interracial relations. After her graduation from Atlanta University in 1927, and while still working on a masters degree at Ohio State University, she took a job as girls work secretary for the Columbus, Ohio YWCA. After receiving her degree two years later and marrying another member of the so-called mulatto elite, Henry Cooke Hamilton, she held college and community positions with the national YWCA in New York City. She interrupted YWCA work between 1928 and 1930 to teach social work and psychology at Atlanta University and Clark College, respectively, in her hometown; but returned to it from 1930 to 1934, after the family moved to Memphis, Tennessee.

By 1943, when Henry Cooke "Cookie" Hamilton became principal at the Atlanta University Laboratory School, Grace Hamilton had become well prepared by virtue of interest, training, and experience for the position which would soon propel her into the highest ranks of African-American leadership in Atlanta and eventually place her among the most successful and influential women in the United States. This ascendancy began in 1943 when Grace Hamilton was appointed executive director of the Atlanta Urban League, reached an apex when she became the first black woman ever elected to the Georgia General Assembly in 1965, and began to wane only a few years before her defeat for re-election in 1984. In these 40 years, more than any other single woman, and more than many women, Grace Hamilton made significant and lasting impacts on the development of the city of Atlanta and particularly its African-American community. Her work led to alterations and ameliorations in almost every area of black life in the city, including education, employment, housing, health care, civil rights, and race relations.

In the few minutes that we have left, a brief examination of Mrs. Hamilton's work in education, civil rights and race relations, and health services should suffice to illuminate the legacy which this one woman, a descendent of a Georgia governor and an ex-slave, has left on her native city as well as her state and nation.

As we mentioned earlier, black Atlantans had always placed equal opportunities and conditions for the education of their children among their top priorities. In 1913, the Women's Civic And Social Improvement Committee, led by Mrs. Lugenia Burns Hope, enlisted the support of influential white women in the city in a campaign to "better the conditions of the Negro public schools of Atlanta." An inspection of 12 black schools in the city had revealed deplorable sanitary conditions, poor lighting and ventilation, and double sessions with the same teacher instructing both of them. Real remediation, however, came only after blacks helped defeat a school bond issue in a special election in 1919. As a result, by 1923, the city built four new elementary schools for blacks and the massive Booker T. Washington Junior-Senior High School. Despite these minimal improvements, double sessions in black schools continued to persist and only two percent of the black student population received a full day's schooling in the 1920s. The Atlanta School Board, however, refused to take any further action to enhance the quantity and quality of the black schools.

Instead they focused on upgrading white schools. To this end, after World War II, the School Board proposed another bond issue which earmarked $10 million for the white schools and only one million dollars for the black ones. The proposal outraged many black Atlantans.

One result of the black anger was the formation of a research committee in the Atlanta Urban League to undertake a new study of the actual conditions in the city's black schools. The organizer of the committee, Grace Hamilton, appointed a team of "experts," who included the director of the school of education at Atlanta University, the president of the Black Georgia State Teachers Association, the associate director of the Southern Regional Council, and another staff member of the Atlanta Urban League. The committee's report, issued in 1944, indicted the Atlanta School Board for making little or no progress since 1922, when a team of investigators from Columbia University revealed "shocking discrepancies" in educational facilities provided for white and black children in the city. The new Urban League Report charged that the black school children in Atlanta were still markedly disadvantaged in comparison to white children. In order to promote equality, the League recommended reductions in pupil-teacher ratios, elimination of double sessions for blacks, and improvements in the physical conditions of existing facilities as well as the construction of several additional buildings.

The League followed up on its Report by conducting a town meeting to decide what action to take in view of its findings. Although legal and political courses of action were suggested, the League voted in favor of a campaign of public education on the report, which had been suggested by Grace Hamilton. The public education campaign, which Mrs. Hamilton also directed, included lectures, leaflets, pamphlets, and more public meetings. Grace Hamilton sought and got favorable press reactions to the campaign from the local black and white press, as well as respected national black weeklies like the *Pittsburgh Courier*. Most of these not only praised the report and urged attention to it, but they also lauded the efforts of Grace Towns Hamilton.

The report also resulted in some tangible improvements for the segregated black schools. The first publicly supported black kindergartens were opened in 1945; black secretaries were employed in African-American schools, and plans were drawn for the first vocational high school for blacks. The School Board also revised its current bond proposal to increase the amount slated for black schools from one to almost four million dollars, more than 40 percent of the entire bond package. In recognition of Mrs. Hamilton's role in these efforts, the black Omega Phi Fraternity named her Atlanta's "most useful citizen for 1945."

Still the achievements of 1945 and early 1946 were only incomplete ones. By 1950, the School Board had spent only about a half of the school bond money issued in 1946 for black school buildings, while the amount spent on white schools had exceeded the budget. In a new study, that same year (1950), the Atlanta Urban League charged that pupil expenditures per white child were in fact exceeding those for black children by a margin of two to one. These new revelations came to the attention of the Fulton County Grand Jury which in May 1950, directed the Atlanta Board of Education to release the balance of the bond funds due the black schools.

As we have seen, because of the disfranchising white primary in Georgia, Atlanta blacks, who met other qualifications, could vote only in certain general and special elections. But the difficulties in registering and the prospects of economic and other intimidations discouraged many from attempting to qualify. Yet, these mostly middle-income blacks who did regularly participate in the political process, even under restricted circumstances, occasionally gained a victory which encouraged them and inspired others. Such victories as those in the bond elections of 1919 and 1921, where the victories actually arose from the defeats of the measures, and the special recall election of 1932, where hundreds of black voters tilted the scale against the recall of three-term Mayor James L. Key, were illustrative. The black voter influence in the Key recall election was actually related directly to a movement begun earlier in the year to educate and register more black voters. Black professionals, including university professors and lawyers organized the voter registration campaign and conducted so called Citizenship Schools to teach civics and give instructions on how to register and vote. For the short term, they placed their sights on the general and special elections, which were open to qualified blacks, but in the long run they voiced optimism for a U.S. Supreme Court decision which would outlaw the white primary.

The crack of the dawn for black political influence in Atlanta first broke in 1943, with the inauguration of Ellis Arnall as the first moderator on racial matters to occupy the governor's office since Reconstruction. He convinced the Georgia State legislature to repeal the disfranchising poll tax and lower the voting age to 18. Almost immediately black voter registration in Atlanta doubled from 15,000 to 30,000 persons. While these votes still could be cast only in special and general elections, the days of the white primary all over the South had been surely numbered by the United States Supreme Court's decision in *Smith vs. Allwright* in 1944. In that case the court struck down the disfranchising primary in Texas.

The rejuvenated black electorate in Atlanta got another unexpected chance to flex their muscles in a special election called in February 1946 to fill the un-expired term of Fifth District Congressman Robert Ramspeck, who resigned his office. Nearly 7,000 blacks qualified to vote in the contest; the black registration having doubled in one year due to the efforts of the NAACP, the newly formed Atlanta Civic And Political League, the *Atlanta Daily World* newspaper, black ministers, and other groups. Nineteen candidates sought Ramspeck's seat, but only six campaigned openly for the black vote. Of these, blacks favored Helen Douglas Mankin, who had earned a reputation for fairness to blacks as a state legislator. On Election Day, blacks cast their votes solidly for Mrs. Mankin, thus giving her a narrow victory over her nearest rival, Tom Camp. Black ballots sent Helen Mankin to Congress.

Then, on April 1, 1946, the United States Supreme Court, in the case of *Chapman vs. King*, declared, as expected, that the white Primary in Georgia was unconstitutional. Armed with this victory and aware that the rabid white supremacist Eugene Talmadge was vying for the Governor's office, Atlanta's African-American leadership again sprang into action. An All Citizens Registration Committee was formed, lead by university professors, businessmen, Robert Thompson and Grace Hamilton from the Atlanta Urban League. The organization was technically under the auspices of the local branch of the NAACP, but its activities were supervised and directed by Robert Thompson and Grace Hamilton. The goal of the project was to expand the black electorate beyond its middle-income base and, indeed, to register all black citizens and guide them in the wise exercise of the franchise.

Thompson and Mrs. Hamilton were ideally suited to provide the population analysis and census tracking to locate each of the predominantly or all-black neighborhoods in the city. They identified 1,150 such blocks in Atlanta. These were canvassed and visited by a force of nearly 900 volunteers. The door-to-door campaign was augmented and supplemented by leaflets, stickers, pamphlets, the voice of the *Atlanta Daily World,* and the messages of black ministers. When the registration books closed for the 1946 elections, and after only a campaign of less than 60 days, the black voter registrants in the city of Atlanta had been tripled from 7,000 to more than 21,000. These votes, even when added to those of other blacks in the state, were not nearly enough to keep Eugene Talmadge out of the Governor's office, but they established the Atlanta black electorate as a major force in local politics. In the immediate future, no white candidate for local office could sensibly ignore the black voter and the needs and aspirations of the African-American community. Within less than a decade, starting with the election of Atlanta University President Rufus E. Clement to the Atlanta School Board in 1953, the events of 1946 led to the election of blacks, themselves, to important political offices in the city and Fulton County, as well. It is interesting and ironic, perhaps sweetly ironic, that Grace Towns Hamilton, one of the architects of the All Citizens Registration Campaign, would be one of the pioneer group. Her election to the Georgia House in 1965 distinguished her as not only the first black woman to sit in the Georgia Legislature, but one of the first blacks of any gender since Reconstruction days.

It should be clear, however, that Grace Hamilton and her Urban League colleagues, especially, conducted All Citizens Registration Campaign in the same unobtrusive way that they pushed for better schools for blacks. It was foremostly an educational campaign, not designed ostensibly to support or oppose any candidate, but to educate blacks in their civic responsibilities, including the right and the obligation to vote. Hamilton and the Urban League were particularly sensitive to and vulnerable to any charges of politicking or political agitation. The Urban League, nationally and locally, had slowly won the confidence of important persons in white corporate America, many of whom served on its national, regional, or local boards of directors. The League had also won, in many places, membership in and financial endorsements from the Community Chest (forerunner to the United Appeal). And even though most Urban Leaguers were seen as patriotic, sound, and conservative, some more rabid whites viewed their interracial memberships and advocacy of social uplift as a threat to the status quo. In these misguided minds, the league was composed of race mixers and Communists.

On the other hand, the Urban League experience fit hand and glove with the character, training and experience of Grace Hamilton. It offered her an opportunity to work for social uplift and social and political change through education rather than confrontation, always hoping in the process to improve race relations. This approach was extremely valuable in her famous campaign to gain a hospital for non-indigent blacks in Atlanta as well as a training facility for black physicians. These and other efforts also aided in her election to the Georgia House in 1965, but by the 1970s the path of moderation had lost considerable ground in the face of changing circumstances and changing black expectations all over the country.

But, in the matter of health services, even as late as World War II, Atlanta trailed several other American cities, including Chicago, New York, Washington, D.C., Nashville, Tennessee, and Tuskegee, Alabama in the facilities it provided for black patients as well as the opportunities for training black medical personnel. The woeful crowding in the black wards of the city's charity hospital, Henry Grady Memorial, seemed to have an effect on the high infant and adult mortality in the city. The crowded conditions at Grady were exacerbated by the lack of sufficient beds or facilities, even for black patients who were able and willing to pay. Grace Hamilton and others in the city's black leadership class believed that a separate facility for the black non-indigent and training opportunities in the black wards of Grady would have a most salutary effect on what they called the deplorable state of black health care in Atlanta. Mrs. Hamilton first led a successful fight to secure an African-American health center on the city's west side. This facility, which was opened in September 1944, was the first public health center for blacks in the state.

At the same time, the Atlanta Urban League joined with churches, schools, clubs, the *Atlanta Daily World*, and other social agencies in winning a major treatment center for venereal disease in the black community.

But the health center and the venereal disease treatment center still did not address the major issues of a hospital for non-indigents and a training facility for black medical personnel. Thus, in 1947, the Urban League, again, attempted to educate the city as to the seriousness of the remaining health problems among black Atlantans. In the "report on hospital care for the Negro population of Atlanta, Georgia," the League cited a severe shortage of beds for the black population and a severe shortage of black physicians. It also warned that ill health among blacks in Atlanta could lead to health problems for all Atlantans. The report concluded that the city direly needed a hospital for non-indigent blacks as well as opportunities for medical training there and at Grady Hospital.

With data in hand, Grace Hamilton used her interracial contacts to attack the problems head on. She approached Hughes Spalding, one of the city's most influential white lawyers and chairman of the Fulton-DeKalb Hospital Authority, which ran the mammoth Grady facility. Once Spalding was convinced to embrace the idea of a hospital for non-indigent black patients, he enlisted other influential whites "in this cause of humanity," but cautioned that the plan must always be presented so as not to endanger social customs or to give prejudiced people an opportunity to oppose it.

While, at first glance, the bi-racial advisory board of trustees, of which Mrs. Hamilton was a member, for the proposed hospital might have appeared to offend social customs, in the end, the new facility would be under the administrative control of the all-white Fulton-DeKalb Hospital Authority. So, with wide support in powerful white circles, including the Atlanta newspapers and Emory University, which operated the teaching program for physicians at Grady, and solid backing among the city's black bourgeoisie, the new hospital was dedicated on May 29, 1952. It was named the Hughes Spalding Pavilion (that is, pavilion of Grady Hospital), after Hughes Spalding, whom Grace Hamilton said had the "greatest single influence" in its establishment and who had also, in the process, grown in knowledge and understanding.

Yet, sadly, neither Spalding's growth in knowledge and understanding or that of other influential white Atlantans, including leaders of the Emory University medical community, were sufficient enough to attain teaching opportunities for African-Americans at Grady Hospital. Grace Hamilton's own tolerance was tested by the procrastination and apparent deceit. For example, on Emory's claim that it could not proceed with the training because of inadequate funds, Mrs. Hamilton declared: "I cannot believe that Emory's reluctance to assume the leadership and the responsibility for the program is based solely on financial inadequacy." Still she did not point the finger of racism at Emory or any other institution or person. She simply dug in and continued the fight through gentle persuasion. It, however, took student protest demonstrations and a federal court order to get black physicians and trainees into Grady Hospital, in the 1960s.

The direct protests, which helped to achieve first-class training opportunities for black physicians in Atlanta, were a method of achieving social change, which Grace Hamilton had consistently opposed. She, like other older black leaders were wedded to the Atlanta style of handling racial problems. From the white side, the Atlanta style sought racial harmony through interracial association or liaison with a chosen group of black elites. They would concede gradual gains in civil rights, particularly under court orders. On the black side, leaders were flattered by the attention they received from influential whites and saw themselves as equals at the bargain table. These meetings also gave the blacks an opportunity to help whites grow, that is, to become more tolerant in their racial attitudes. For white assistance in maintaining racial peace, blacks conceded to gradualism in attacking Jim Crow. While these approaches succeeded in sparing Atlanta much of the hate and violence, which bloodied the streets of many other American cities, North and South during the Civil Rights Era, critics charged that they delayed unnecessarily the dismantling of the apartheid system in the city.

After 1960, proponents of the Atlanta style, including Mrs. Hamilton, came under increasing criticisms not only for past attitudes and practices, but also for their continuing devotion to gradualism and their faith in white redemption. While on one hand, Mrs. Hamilton's relationships with and influences on men like former Mayor Ivan Allen, Jr. and House Speaker Tom Murphy might bolster the cause of redemption; many observers saw these as only a continuation of the same patterns of paternalism, particularly to members of the so-called mulatto elite, that extended back at least to Reconstruction days.

Whatever the legitimacies of the criticisms of Grace Hamilton, they rarely included accusations of a lack of civility and gentility. The approbation she received in the Georgia Legislature as "the lady from Fulton" spoke not only of the county of which she represented, but also of her attitude and demeanor. Besides this, in the periods of her greatest contributions to the development of Atlanta, she and others in the black leadership cadre acted within the constraints of a legally established caste system bolstered by economic intimidation and violence. Furthermore, in these early days, many African-Americans throughout the country had not developed the sense of self-esteem and the personal security to advocate or support aggressive, confrontational protests. On the other hand, Hamilton and others who might be perceived as reactionary or at least conservative by today's standards were often attacked, in their own day, as revolutionaries as they campaigned for a better life for black Atlantans, even within the caste system. In the case of Hamilton, she also overcame, in the same quiescent manner, huge barriers erected against her gender.

A political leader who changes his stances to fit the times is oft-times called a politician, in the dirty sense of the word. One who refuses to change, who remains with her life long ideals, is often called reactionary and stubborn. But such a person may also be seen as possessing both honesty and integrity. It is, then, because of this latter possibility or probability that we remember and honor the legacy of Grace Towns Hamilton to the city of Atlanta today.

Chapter 16
Andrew Jackson Young:
Mayor of Atlanta, 1982–1990

Two days after the beginning of the New Year, 1989, Atlanta Mayor Andrew Jackson Young stood before a background of polished green granite in the new $31 million City Hall Annex to deliver his final State of the City address. The mayor outlined his accomplishments after seven years in office and "sketched his vision of the city's future."[1]

Young declared that the city had undergone an economic revival during his two terms in office, and he seemed determined to cite every office tower, hotel complex, and housing unit built or renovated in the city since he took office. He boasted about the soon-to-be opened Underground Atlanta, a $142 million entertainment and shopping complex in the heart of downtown Atlanta, the construction of two new major hotels in the central city, the extended Atlanta Apparel Mart, the expansion of the city's rapid transit rail system, and many other projects.[2]

"When I was elected, I felt as though an era were coming to an end," the mayor said. "We have seen a diminishing of government funds. Yet we've been able to find a way to reach many of our goals. I contend that that was not an accident." Young said that his administration was able to accomplish so many of his goals through

Reprinted from The Journal of Negro History, LXXVII, No. 3, Summer, 1992, with the permission of The Journal of Negro History

what he called "public purpose capitalism." This concept involved the participation of private businesses in projects "in the public interest." The achievement was made possible because of the city's "open-door policy" toward business owners. Young said that his administration "sent a signal to the world that we know how to do business . . . I averaged about 200 business visits a year, in my office. The idea was to get across that this government was accessible to business."[3]

The only disappointments in the mayor's assessment of his administration were in the areas of housing and crime. Yet Young claimed that the struggle to find "affordable housing for all of our citizens" had been a valiant one. But he conceded that the city would still need 70,000 new housing units by the year 2005.[4]

Young preceded his wide ranging summary by declaring that his two terms as the city's mayor were, "the seven most exciting years of my life."[5]

Both Young's supporters and opponents no doubt agreed that there were, indeed, exciting moments during the mayor's tenure. But not all would agree with his list of successes and that his only failures were in crime and housing. In fact, as Young began his final State of the City address, he thanked a rebellious City Council, with whom he had often sparred, particularly toward the end of his term.[6]

But Andrew Young came to the mayor's office in 1982 under extremely favorable circumstances. Although the mayoral campaign of 1981 had been a racially polarized one, Young garnered only ten percent of the white vote in the decisive run-off election, but maintained a solid lock on the massive black vote. After assuming office, he quickly implemented his campaign promise to counsel closely with the predominately white business leadership and to promote economic growth. These pledges and positions understandably won the support of the white power structure, including the white press. Thus, immediately, Young avoided a problem that had plagued the city's first black mayor, Maynard H. Jackson, a perception that the city government was anti-business.[7]

While Jackson's pro-neighborhood and historic preservation stances had riled many white business leaders during his eight years in office, he had directed the successful completion of the nation's largest airport and the opening of the city's rapid transit network. Much of the criticism, then, from white leaders stemmed from his dogged insistence on affirmative action in employment and in city contracts and his reduction of the influence of those leaders in Atlanta's decision-making.[8]

Andrew Young's avidly pro-business posture certainly helped

smooth his entry into office, but the pioneering efforts of the city's first black mayor, Maynard Jackson, were also of enormous benefit. Although Jackson, particularly in his first term, had a stormy relationship with white business leaders and the white press, as well as state and local political and civic leaders, he weathered the storm and left office more popular than when he entered. And after eight years of a black administration, much of the novelty of a black mayor had worn thin.[9]

Since, by law, Atlanta's city budgets must be balanced each year, Jackson also, perforce, left his predecessor a debt-free city — a major feat for urban governments (as well as state and federal ones) during this period. But the budget deficit prohibition also assured that each yearly budget would be a very tight one and that, in the absence of tremendous economic growth and/or continued tax increases, many city services could not be met.[10]

Even though, as he prepared to leave office, Mayor Young could boast that property taxes had dropped from 14.95 mills in 1982, when he submitted his first budget, to 11.99 mills in 1988, most property tax bills went up, nevertheless, because of reassessments. Still, the Young administration was confident that it would leave the city with lower taxes than when it came into office. To accomplish this feat, however, Young had to sacrifice his plans for much-needed raises for city employees and had to continue to neglect pressing infrastructure needs.[11]

In the fall of 1988, it was estimated that sewage and drainage, road and bridge repairs, and other infrastructure requirements would cost the city nearly one billion dollars. The city had failed in two recent attempts, one a bond referendum in May and the other constitutional amendments in November, to achieve funding for these needs. The $158 million bond referendum was soundly defeated by Atlanta voters, even though an additional $150 million was also offered for local schools. Mayor Young and other city officials did not campaign hard for the passage of the referendum and, thus, according to some, contributed to its defeat. Similarly, top Atlanta officials did little to push statewide constitutional amendments in the November general elections, which would have increased the city's bonding capacity from $4 million to $12 million without having to conduct a referendum. Although passage of these amendments required a statewide vote, they were even defeated in Fulton County, where the benefits would have accrued, with 63.8 percent of the voters opposing them.[12]

Through his 1989 (final) budget, Mayor Young managed to avoid serious difficulties with the city employees' labor unions without granting their wishes for a substantial wage increase. Young had hoped to give each employee a salary increase averaging $1,000. But the final budget contained only a small increase designed to offset rising health insurance costs. These advances and money for other projects were made possible when the mayor shifted $8 million from various other city funds.[13]

While Young had expressed confidence that he could persuade the voters to accept a small tax increase to meet the city's pressing needs, the Atlanta City Council was overwhelmingly opposed to any such increase in an election year. Thus, in August 1988, they convinced the mayor to sign a resolution pledging to submit a budget with no property tax increase.[14]

Mayor Young's final budget was still the largest in the city's history — $310 million. Most of this money, about 70 percent, was earmarked for city employees' salaries. The mayor submitted the budget without enthusiasm and cautioned that important city needs would not be met. In addition, several city officials warned that a tax increase could not be avoided in the near future.[15]

Next to assuring the financial well being of the city, Mayor Young's most important responsibilities during his two terms in office were in the area of public safety. And in this area, by his own admission, his record was not an enviable one. Like most large major urban areas in the 1980s, Atlanta was plagued with serious problems of crime against persons and property. But Atlanta managed to remain at or near the top of all major American cities, particularly in violent crimes. Incidence of forcible rape in the city averaged 157 per 100,000 population per year, five times the national average. Aggravated assault averaged 1,573 per 100,000 population; robbery 1,099 per 100,000; and murder eight per 100,000. In recent years the problems were exacerbated by the growing trade in illicit drugs, especially crack cocaine.[16]

By the end of 1988, court dockets and jail cells in Fulton County were so full with drug offenders that cases of possession with intent to distribute often drew only a probated sentence. State law required that the sentence in such cases be from five to 30 years in prison. Many of those cramming the city's jails were young people. In the first nine months of 1988 alone, Atlanta police arrested 171 offenders younger than 17 years of age, almost three times as many as during the same period in 1986.[17]

The drug crisis in the city was so overwhelming that the Atlanta Public Safety Commissioner, George Napper, while promising to be "aggressive and visible," admitted that "there's nothing that I can see over the next five or ten years to make me confident that we can turn this thing around." But as part of his "aggressive," "visible," and "caring" policy, Napper did create a special "Red Dog Squad" in April 1988 "to get crack cocaine dealers off the streets." In its first seven months of operation, the elite "Red Dog Squad" was responsible for 721 felony drug cases.[18]

The formation of the "Red Dog Squad" was partially in response to the complaints of citizens and the media that the Atlanta Police Department was not doing enough to stem the tide of drugs in the city and to combat other crimes. In this instance, unlike other questions of public safety, black citizens seemed more outraged than white ones. For example, in March 1988, a group of residents in a lower-income section of southeast Atlanta personally confronted Commissioner Napper and other police officials to complain that the police were not doing enough to combat the "devastating drug problem" in their community. One resident, former state Senator Douglas Dean, told the policemen, "You need to send a message to the thugs and hoodlums that you're going to get tough."[19]

Getting tough on crime had previously been an issue that divided many Atlantans along racial lines. Frequently whites, both residents and suburbanites, accused both black administrations, the Young as well as the Jackson, of being "soft on crime." Their perception of unsafe streets in downtown Atlanta is what caused many of them not to visit the area for shopping, dining, or recreation, they contended. But many blacks, including city officials, countered that the problem of violent crime in downtown Atlanta, except for an occasional well-publicized occurrence, was, in fact, only a perception. The real crime problem in Atlanta, they said, was in the poorer neighborhoods of the city, particularly the public housing projects. But black attitudes on controlling this crime were often affected by the city's long history of police abuse of black citizens.[20]

A fall 1987 incident in the all-black George Washington Carver housing project in southeast Atlanta can serve well to illustrate the racial polarization over the issue of law enforcement in Atlanta. On September 10, 1987, a white police officer, Michael H. Long, killed a black, 240-pound Vietnam War veteran, Eddie Lee Callahan, whom he says was wrestling a revolver away from his partner, another white officer, Ridley A. Watson. Callahan died from six wounds, five in the back, at close range. Long and Watson insisted that their lives were endangered by Callahan's attempt to gain control of the officer's gun, but several Carver Homes residents who witnessed the altercation claimed that Callahan was subdued on the ground when Long fired point blank and repeatedly into his back. Both a Fulton County Jury and an internal police panel cleared Long of any wrongdoing in the slaying. But Watson, who was not indicted in the incident, was subsequently fired. Public Safety Commissioner George Napper said the dismissal resulted from "8 or 10" citizen complaints against the officer over the three years he had been on the police force. Long was removed from street duty and assigned to a desk job in the basement of police headquarters.[21]

In the days immediately following the Callahan shooting, residents of Carver Homes were joined by other blacks, including Atlanta City Councilman Hosea Williams, in daily protests. They asserted that the white police officers had "murdered" a subdued, even handcuffed, black man and that Mayor Young and Commissioner Napper refused to punish them. Even after the internal police panel and a Fulton County jury acquitted the officers, the protests continued both in the neighborhood and at City Hall. Mayor Young tried to stabilize the situation, even going into Carver Homes itself, to urge the residents to calm themselves and allow the due processes of law to determine what exactly happened and who should or should not be punished. The mayor's attitude was rewarded by hisses and boos from some of the residents and a personal, political attack from Councilman Williams, a former ally in the Civil Rights Movement.[22]

Despite the mayor's impassioned approach to the Callahan case, some whites accused the city administration of "tying" the police's hands. Many white police officers denounced the firing of Watson and the "punishment" of Long. And Dick Williams, conservative white columnist for the *Atlanta Journal-Constitution*, charged that the Young administration's treatment of the acquitted Long and Watson had made Atlanta cops "afraid to use their weapons." This experiment in "New Age Sociology," he said, both threatened the police force and the city. Atlanta, he continued, was already a city "of hidden fears," because of its serious crime problems. But their cure seemed "beyond the grasp" of Mayor Young.[23]

Whatever the perception of crime and punishment by both races in Atlanta, the issue has taken on its greatest urgency in the lives of the residents of the city's public housing projects. Since 1937, when Secretary of the Interior Harold Ickles came to Atlanta to dedicate the University Homes, 40 other massive housing projects have been constructed in black neighborhoods in the city. At least two others, originally constructed for whites, have become predominately black.[24]

Despite what he termed a valiant struggle, Mayor Young admitted, after seven years, the failure of his administration to meet the city's demand for affordable housing. But he gave somewhat less emphasis to the failure to meet the social and economic needs of those thousands of Atlantans, mainly black, already housed in the city's decaying public housing projects. Ironically, some of the worst conditions have developed and festered in one of the "newer" complexes, the Bankhead Courts in northwest Atlanta.[25]

The Bankhead Courts apartments were built on a dump site in 1970 at a cost of almost $10 million. By the end of 1988, the 500 units housed 1,703 tenants, 1,025 of them younger than 19 years of age; 81 of the units were vacant. Only 42 of the tenants were employed in 1988; they had an average annual family income of $3,500. Residents paid an average monthly rent of $79. Almost all of the households, 98, were headed by women, many of them teen-aged mothers and young grandmothers.[26]

Even at the end of 1988, "not a single social program" or other organized activity was functioning in the Bankhead Courts projects. Tenants complained of serious management problems. City officials blamed slovenliness and vandalism on the part of residents. But the Atlanta Housing Authority's (AHA) Deputy Director Bettye Davis acknowledged serious sewage and plumbing problems caused by the location of the apartments. And while the AHA had spent more than $2 million on repairs between 1984 and 1988, it would cost another $1.8 million to renovate the 81 vacant apartments existing at that time. These vacant units had been the source of criticism from both tenants and public officials, because they were often used by drug dealers and other criminals at the same time that there was a housing shortage in the city. But in the end, the project "never should have been built," Deputy Director Davis believed. And she said, "We would tear it down and relocate everybody . . . if we had authorization from the Department of Housing and Urban Development (HUD) in Washington."[27]

Subsequent to a temporary suspension and reduction of public services in Bankhead Courts, several black public officials and civic leaders, including Fulton County Commission Chairman Michael Lomax (also a mayoral candidate in the 1989 city elections), State Senator Arthur Langford, and City Councilman Archie Byron, held what they called an "educational vigil" in the "drug-ridden" apartments. The vigil, however, was cut short when gunfire was heard in the area on Christmas Eve night. Lomax, who called the project a "Drug Supermarket," returned shortly, as did other officials, including Mayor Young and black U.S. Congressman John Lewis. The political and civic leaders sought to learn first-hand from the residents the nature of the drug crisis, as well as other social and economic problems, and to assure the tenants of their interest and concern. As Congressman Lewis moved through the housing project, a woman resident warned him "to shake his overcoat to make sure no cockroaches had settled in it..."[28]

Cockroaches and other non-drug related concerns could not be solved by "educational vigils," black Councilman Robb Pitts offered. Instead, he, Councilman Thomas Cuffie, and others called for a comprehensive improvement plan. They suggested that, in the short run, abandoned units could be boarded up and new grass planted. But over the long term, existing governmental resources of housing, health care, schools, and jobs must be employed to "clean up" all of the city's housing projects one at a time.[29]

Central to the "clean up" of the city's housing projects, almost all admitted, was the need for managerial changes or improvement at the Atlanta Housing Authority. Although the editors of the *Atlanta Constitution* had thought they sensed a "new mood at [the] Housing Authority" in the Summer of 1988, when its executive directors issued an ultimatum to the staff to renovate more than 320 vacant apartments by the end of June or face possible termination, radical reform was still a long way away. Thus, at the end of the year the editors were demanding that "the AHA . . . make sure its project managers are strong, active administrators who get out of the office, mingle with residents, and keep abreast of what is going on in the complex." At the time hundreds of families still remained on the waiting list for apartments and hundreds of unrenovated units remained vacant — some having been empty since 1984, one of the highest vacancy rates in the country.[30]

Although Andrew Young was cognizant of and sympathetic to the housing and social woes of inner city projects like Bankhead Courts and demonstrated continuing concern for the plight of the estimated 10,000 homeless persons in his city, he seemed more preoccupied with the development of "upscale" housing in the central city. One such project, City Scape, envisioned 192 apartments on the fringe of downtown in the northeastern part of the city. At the groundbreaking ceremonies for the $10 million dollar project, Mayor Young exclaimed: "The jobs are coming and the people are coming and for good jobs they need good housing." City Scape, which was scheduled for completion early in 1989, was slated to consist of seven three-story buildings with rentals ranging from $535 to $825 per month. Clearly, in the mayor's thinking, good jobs and good housing were important links in his master plan for the economic development of downtown Atlanta. But at times his policies ran counter to his goals, as in the instance when the city allowed a proposed agreement with the Metropolitan Atlanta Rapid Transit Authority (MARTA) that would have encouraged downtown housing "to fall through." The mayor's Commissioner of Community Development persuaded him that the $13.5 million site purchase price was too expensive and that the project "would have eaten up" too much of the Community Development staff's time. While the city's failure to act did not kill the prospects of housing on the downtown site near the Atlanta Civic Center, the opportunity was "substantially diminished."[31]

Development of upscale downtown housing, while a key to downtown revitalization, was also seen as a stimulus to gentrification — the relocation of suburban whites into the central city. Perhaps because of the concern that many blacks had that gentrification would dilute black voting strength and, hence, black political control of the city, the mayor rarely spoke of these issues in racial terms. But on the other hand, those people who were already in the city and most in need of "affordable housing" were black lower income residents — one of the mayor's core constituents. Throughout his two terms in office, the mayor had to perilously walk this delicate political tightrope.[32]

If Mayor Young did not include transportation along with crime and housing among his administration's failures, it was probably because as his term neared its end, the new Atlanta Airport was among the busiest in the world, the rapid rail system had been extended further into northeast Atlanta and to the airport, and the downtown freeway was being expanded from six to ten lanes. But the mayor had not succeeded in adding additional sorely needed runways at the airport, the northern white suburbs still resisted a link-up with MARTA, north Atlanta neighborhoods were still choked with traffic, and Young had not been able to build a wide-lane parkway to the library of his former boss, President Jimmy Carter.

Since the completion of the new Atlanta Airport terminal in 1981, the city has vied yearly — and often monthly — with Chicago for claim to the title of "world's busiest airport." Despite the addition of two new runways since 1981, the facility quickly outgrew them. Soon city officials acknowledged that new runways were needed not only to compete successfully with Chicago, but to prevent additional, long passenger delays in both takeoffs and landings. These delays had already helped to promote the development of new Southern air transportation hubs in Charlotte, North Carolina and Nashville, Tennessee. But many Clayton County (the actual site of the airport) residents and their officials remained steadfastly opposed to any new runway expansion. Their opposition was based on the increased noise pollution that expansion would bring, as well as adverse effects on property and other investments. Some Clayton citizens accused Atlanta officials of supporting runway expansion simply for the "prestige" of outdistancing Chicago as the world's busiest airport. And the chairman of the Clayton County Commission threatened to impose an additional sales tax on the airlines flying out of the airport if they supported the city's runway expansion plans. At the time of his final state of the city address, Mayor Young had not been able to overcome these objections.[33]

When the creation of MARTA was proposed in a referendum in 1971, four of metropolitan Atlanta's seven counties were asked to approve the rapid rail system. But only two, Fulton and its eastern neighbor, DeKalb, voted for the system. The referendum was narrowly approved by a margin of only 400 votes. Black voters provided the margin of victory. In return for their support of MARTA, which had been defeated in an earlier vote, black leaders extracted, among other things, guarantees that 20 percent of the design, engineering, and construction work on the project would be awarded to minority firms and that bus and rail fares would be reduced from 50 to 15 cents for up to seven years.[34]

Although the 15 cent fares barely lasted for the seven year period and have risen on an almost annual basis since, the transportation agency has continued to operate at or near a deficit. In 1988, despite opposition from many black residents and public officials, the fare climbed again, to a new high of 85 cents. The 85-cent rate was a compromise between those who wanted little or no increase and those championing the higher fare of one dollar. An additional concession to fair hike opponents was that the new fare would be frozen for a period of three years. Yet by the end of the year, the 85-cent fare was already in jeopardy as MARTA estimated that it would need to find an additional $7.5-$10 million by June 1989 or the system would be forced to make substantial cuts in bus services. To maintain the freeze over the entire three year period, transit officials said they needed a total of $20 million.[35]

In the absence of dwindling state and federal support, one of the keys to the financial health of MARTA was increased ridership. The new and prosperous line to the Atlanta Airport had buttressed this argument. But the extension of MARTA buses and trains into the affluent, largely white suburbs of North Fulton, Cobb, and Gwinnett Counties was an ingredient that could infuse much needed blood into MARTA. Persistently, however, most residents and many officials in these places have resisted becoming a part of the MARTA network. The bases of the opposition, according to some, are increased traffic in residential areas, the fear that "lovely properties" would be converted into MARTA parking lots, and the disturbances that the rails would bring to nearby schools. Others cite the fear of "crime" and the intrusion of "undesirables" as reasons for their opposition to MARTA in the suburbs. While few openly declare that these are code words denoting fear of Atlanta blacks, almost all of Atlanta's black officials suggest that white racism remains the major impediment to new MARTA ridership. Such racism, many also claim, often permeates the MARTA Board of Directors itself.[36]

By the end of 1988, as throughout most of its history, the majority of MARTA's ridership was made up of lower-income blacks, yet only six of the 11 MARTA directors in that year were black. And at the time, none of the nine chairmen of the MARTA board who had served since 1972 were black. But the MARTA Board, in an election in December 1988, again passed up an opportunity to elevate a black person to its top leadership position.[37]

The leading black candidate was Dr. Joseph E. Lowery, a lieutenant of Martin Luther King, Jr. in the Civil Rights Movement and chairman of the Southern Christian Leadership Conference. In addition to his administrative experiences, Lowery, the most persistent champion of low fares for MARTA's riders, had served on the MARTA Board for 13 years "with distinction." Yet the Board selected as its tenth chairman a white retired Atlanta developer, George H. Ivey, Jr. At the time of his election, Ivey had been on the MARTA Board for only three years. The vote to select Ivey proceeded strictly along racial lines, as he gained all of the votes of white board members and Lowery received all of the votes of black board members.[38]

Nevertheless, white board members denied that race was an issue in the election of the MARTA chairman. Former Atlanta Mayor Sam Massell, a member of the nomination committee, expressed the hope that "we're beyond that [racism] by now." Other board members pointed to Lowery's "poor" attendance record at meetings. In 1988, he had missed almost half of the 23 board meetings held prior to the election of the chairman. George Ivey, Jr., a retiree, on the other hand, had maintained perfect attendance. A few whites offered that Lowery's election would make it more difficult to persuade white suburbanites to join MARTA. This, however, they suggested was not racism, but pragmatism. But Lowery and Atlanta's black public officials clearly believed that white racism led to his defeat. He said he lost to "sophisticated racism in the suites." And black Fulton County Commissioner Michael Lomax insisted that there was no other explanation "but racial" for Lowery's failure to gain the chairmanship.

This view was supported by the editors of the *Atlanta Constitution* who declared that "their claims to the contrary aside, MARTA's white board members bowed to racism . . . when they voted to snub Dr. Joseph Lowery as MARTA's" tenth chairman.[39]

There were two other transportation issues with very few racial overtones or implications which frustrated Andrew Young throughout most of his term as Atlanta's mayor. Ever since Jimmy Carter left the White House and selected Atlanta as the site of his Presidential Library, Young, the former president's ambassador to the United Nations supported the so-called Presidential Parkway project, but leaders of neighborhood groups in northeast Atlanta that would be destroyed or divided by the thoroughfare staunchly opposed its construction. They used non-violent protests, including the blocking of construction equipment, political lobbying, and legal action at the federal and state levels, to press their demands that the road not be built.[40]

In recent days, the Parkway foes picked up a powerful ally in Washington, U.S. Representative John Lewis of Atlanta, who had also been an official in the Carter administration. In November 1988, Lewis tried unsuccessfully to get the U.S. Department of Transportation to suspend federal funding for the Parkway. After this failure, he urged the House Public Works and Transportation Committee to ban the use of federal money for the road. That appeal also was likely to fail. So as Andrew Young prepared to leave office, the Presidential Parkway had not been constructed, but many of the obstacles to it, both political and legal, had apparently been removed. Young remained confident that the road would become a reality. In anticipation of its construction, he began negotiations with Soviet sculptor, Zurab Tzereteli to carve a 30-foot, 300-ton statue to tower over the parkway.[41]

The other controversial road project involved the proposed extension of a state highway, Georgia 400, through the affluent north Atlanta Buckhead neighborhood to connect with the city's freeways. In 1986 the Atlanta City Council approved the planning process for the roadway, but not the actual construction, with a provision that the state Department of Transportation (DOT) come back to the body for final approval. While business and development interests applauded the proposed toll road, neighborhood activists immediately decried its potentially destructive impact on their communities. On October 19, 1988, these groups filed a suit in Fulton Superior Court requesting that the state be enjoined from working on the road because construction had not been approved by the Atlanta City Council. At the same time the Atlanta City Council passed a resolution banning all toll roads, including the proposed extension of Georgia 400, in the city.[42]

Four days after the City Council prohibited toll roads in Atlanta and only two days after neighborhood groups filed suit against the construction of Georgia 400, Mayor Andrew Young vetoed the toll roads ban. Young said the collection of tolls was "a necessary component" of the construction of Georgia 400, an "important transportation artery." The banning of tolls, he added, was "an impediment for the city and state in our efforts to complete this much needed freeway."[43]

Following the mayor's veto, pro-neighborhood councilmen, led by D. L. "Buddy" Fowkles, began a move to override Young's action, and business and real estate development interests launched "an unprecedented lobbying campaign" to prevent an override of the veto. The pro-road groups and Mayor Young argued that the continuing traffic problems in north Atlanta, if unrelieved, would strangle commerce in the area. Anti-road protesters, however, countered that the future transportation needs of the area could be met by the proposed extension of a MARTA rail line, which would allow the preservation of neighborhoods.[44]

The "freeing" of the freeways and other important roadways in the city were essential elements of Andrew Young's program of economic development. Already, the Atlanta Airport, at times "the world's busiest," and the MARTA rail system had aided in the city's reputation as one of the best places to do business in the country. Indeed, since the 1960s, when the Atlanta Chamber of Commerce launched its "Forward Atlanta" campaign, Atlanta had been one of the nation's "boomtowns." But the spread of economic success had been uneven. North Atlanta, particularly affluent Buckhead, and the northern suburbs, particularly Gwinnett County, were so successful that their infrastructure needs were bursting at the seams. Employment in these areas met or exceeded the national average. But the economic boom, except for conventions and tourism, was far less dramatic in downtown Atlanta, in its southern, largely black business and residential areas, and in the suburbs south of the airport.[45]

Atlanta has been called "a perfect example" of what is sometimes called the "split level South." While the metropolitan area has had a population growth of more than 22 percent since 1980 and job growth of 43 percent, the majority black inner city has grown by a mere one percent in population, with an unemployment rate that is 2.3 times higher for blacks than for whites. Auburn Avenue, once called "the richest street in Black America," "remains a ragged island in a sea of affluence." The only modern and prosperous enterprises on the once thriving thoroughfare are those catering mostly to tourists, including the Martin Luther King, Jr. Center for Non-Violent Social Change.[46]

Apparently much of the economic recession in parts of Atlanta, particularly lower income and black ones, has resulted from the failure of the city's financial institutions to make substantial loans to homeowners and business people in these areas. In May 1988, the *Atlanta Journal-Constitution* published a series of articles documenting discrimination in mortgage lending and the "poor relationships between Atlanta banks and the black community." Indeed, the series, called "The Color of Money," accused almost every major bank in the city, except the two black owned ones, of the nefarious and illegal practice of "redlining." The report prompted the launching of several investigations by both local and federal agencies.[47]

Even though Atlanta bankers refused to concede that they had practiced "redlining," several took almost immediate steps to increase their activities in south Atlanta. A consortium of banks created a $65 million loan fund, with reduced interest and a major suburban developer teamed up with the non-profit Cabbagetown Restoration and Future Trust (CRAFT) to renovate 25 homes to be sold at low interest rates to poor and middle-income persons in the largely white southeast community known as "Cabbagetown." Concurrently, although not ostensibly linked, city officials approved the sale of the Candler Warehouse property in southwest Atlanta for $2.2 million. The city had tried unsuccessfully since 1984 to promote the revitalization of this property as a gateway to economic development in the area.[48]

Before these new actions in southside economic development were taken, the city's showcase program for black and other minority enterprise was its "widely lauded" Minority Business Enterprise (MBE) program. That program, which was one of the outstanding legacies of the Maynard Jackson administration, required that 35 percent of all city contracts be signed with minority businesses. During the seven years since Andrew Young took office, 500 minority owned and operated firms have done nearly $200 million worth of business in the public sector. In 1988 alone, the city awarded 36.7 percent of its work, worth $29.4 million, to minority companies. But even this highly successful venture has been criticized, because the vast majority of minority contracts repeatedly go to a relatively small group of black owned businesses.[49]

The first major expansion of the city's efforts to increase minority and poor economic conditions occurred in July 1988 when the Atlanta City Council voted unanimously to require private firms doing work with the city to hire 50 percent of all extra, unskilled help from a list of the city's "down and out" workers. The "First Source List" program, which took effect on January 1, 1989, lasted for three years. It was uncertain, however, whether only a handful or as many as 1,500 unemployed laborers would qualify for the "First Source List." Also, some contractors were "apprehensive" about the concept, and many were uncertain that it would work. Still, the editors of the *Atlanta Constitution* believed that "the idea of helping the chronically unemployed capture a bit of the prosperity the rest of the city has enjoyed is commendable."[50]

Whatever the prospects of the "First Source List" program, both Mayor Andrew Young and the Atlanta Chamber of Commerce were keenly aware that neither it nor public sector employment could meet all of Atlanta's immediate and future job needs, particularly for unskilled and semi-skilled laborers. The Chamber had projected that 50,000 new jobs would be needed by the end of the 1980s and pledged to work toward that goal. Young wanted to continue to boost the already successful convention and tourist industry while promoting new investments, particularly from foreign countries.[51]

In his quest to become the "businessman's mayor," Young championed new downtown development with such fervor that he riled the city's historic preservationists, and his dozens of trips around the country and abroad seeking new investments led to him being dubbed "the globetrotting mayor."[52]

The Atlanta Urban Design Commission (AUDC) sparred with Mayor Young for most of his terms in office. Repeatedly as the AUDC sought to preserve historic edifices, especially in the downtown area, the mayor overruled its decisions and authorized demolitions in favor of new hotels, office buildings, or other developments. He often argued that it was unfair to restrict property owners from disposing of their property as they wished. And he seemed to take the position that history must yield to the present and the future, especially where economic development was concerned. Preservationists particularly sprang into action after the mayor called one of the city's oldest structures "a hunk of junk." Then at the annual awards program of the AUDC in the Spring of 1986, both the white executive director and the black chairman of the AUDC lectured the mayor on the importance of historic structures to the life and culture of a city. And international travel writer Arthur Frommer also joined the fray, warning that "you can't attract people just with hotels and not life." He predicted that unless downtown Atlanta became "more livable," there would be a serious "downturn" in the city's convention and tourism industry. "What's pitiful," he said, is that "the mayor of Atlanta is not sympathetic to this."[53]

But Mayor Young did appear to grow somewhat more realistic, if not "sympathetic," toward historic preservation following the 1986 AUDC awards program. He lent his support to a comprehensive review of historical landmarks in the city and eventually supported a compromise plan for listing and protecting some of these structures. While this program gave substantial assurances of the preservation of the landmarks, it also sought to protect the economic interests of property owners and developers.[54]

As a "globetrotter" and "salesman" for Atlanta's economic development, Andrew Young attracted both national and international attention to the city and general praise for himself. Phoenix, Arizona Mayor Terry Goddard, President of the National League of Cities, declared in 1988 that "the success of Atlanta is fabled and known to us all . . . Mayor Young gets a lot of credit for that." But while appreciative of the mayor's efforts, others, particularly in Atlanta, hoped that Young could spend more time in the city helping it "over the rough spots." City Councilwoman Barbara Asher even suggested that there were "some things on the home front" that were being neglected by the mayor. Young tossed such criticisms aside, saying that his travels produced investors and that investors produced jobs. Indeed, his activities had proved a key to Atlanta's growth at a time when most other cities were suffering.[55]

Although new investments and projects, national and international, were a cornerstone of Andrew Young's plans to increase the economic vitality of his city, the retention and improvement of the thriving convention and tourist trade were also highly significant features. Thus, when the city's professional football franchise threatened to leave the city in 1986, both business and governmental leaders reacted with alarm.

The seldom-do-well Atlanta Falcons had brought professional football to the new Atlanta-Fulton County stadium in 1967, the first National Football League team to play in the Deep South. But by the 1980s, the 60,000 seat stadium, which was also shared by the Atlanta Braves National League Baseball team, had become one of the smallest facilities of its kind in the nation and had what players called "the worst" playing surface in major league sports.[56]

Despite several renovations, the stadium still remained inadequate and as early as the summer of 1984, there were discussions among city leaders about replacing it. But because of the huge costs associated with such a project, there was procrastination and even insistence that the present stadium could be further renovated and reconfigured to make it an acceptable facility. These ideas were dashed, however, when Rankin Smith, owner of the Atlanta Falcons, flatly declared in December 1986 that, under no circumstances, would he field his team in the Atlanta Fulton County Stadium after the expiration of the current lease in 1990. Two years later, the Atlanta Braves baseball team made similar threats.   The Falcons had as an alternative an attractive relocation offer from Jacksonville, Florida, while the Braves began relocation negotiations with neighboring suburban counties.[57]

While some city councilpersons and residents clamored about a certain tax increase, increased public indebtedness, and destruction of neighborhoods if a new stadium were built, Atlanta Mayor Andrew Young continued to flip-flop on the issue.   Sometimes the mayor seemed to favor the existing stadium, sometimes a new stadium, and at other times two new stadiums.   Exacerbating the matter was Rankin Smith's insistence that any new stadium be a huge, domed edifice.[58]

Eventually, additional encumbrances, other than the cost factor, were added as impediments to the construction of the new stadium. As the 1989 city elections approached, the City Council became acutely sensitive to the concerns of the lower income black neighborhood in which the proposed domed stadium would be located. Houses would be destroyed, churches would have to be relocated or inconvenienced, and neighborhood commerce would be interrupted, critics charged. They said some sort of housing relocation guarantees were essential, as well as assurances on the future of affected churches. Finally, in a city with a majority black population as well as electorate, some guarantees of minority participation in the construction and operation of the facility ought to be attained.[59]

After the organization representing a private group of investors and the city reached an impasse in their negotiations for the construction of the new stadium, the project was saved at an eleventh hour through the intervention of Georgia Governor Joe Frank Harris. Harris developed a plan by which the state would provide land near the Georgia World Congress Center, the state's largest convention facility, as the site of the stadium.   The $152 million stadium, increasingly dubbed "the Dome," could augment the state-owned Congress Center as a convention exhibit and entertainment complex. Harris also suggested that additional construction and operating costs, other than those provided by private investors, could be attained if the state permitted the city of Atlanta and Fulton County to increase their sales taxes by up to two cents on the dollar. He pledged to push such a measure in the Georgia General Assembly during its 1989 session.[60]

Both the Atlanta City Council and the Fulton County Commission gave tentative approval to the state-backed proposals, but added conditions that provoked another impasse. Atlanta and Fulton insisted on a $10 million housing trust fund for displaced families in neighborhoods adjacent to the proposed Dome, some financial consideration for affected churches, a guarantee of a 35 percent minority participation goal in the stadium's design and construction, and representation on the governing board of the Georgia World Congress Center, the group that, under the governor's proposal, would oversee the construction and operation of the Dome. When the private investors as well as state officials balked at these demands, the Dome again was put on hold. Nevertheless, in yet another eleventh hour in the life of professional sports in Atlanta, Mayor Young remained forever optimistic and predicted that a solution would be found.[61]

While the proposed construction of the Dome continued to frustrate city and state officials, the mayor could rightfully boast of two other successes in his local revitalization program. In September 1988, the city reached a tentative agreement with MCA, an entertainment corporation, to build a multi-million dollar, 18,000-seat amphitheater on the site of the old Lakewood Fairgrounds on the city's southside. The project was expected to provide hundreds of jobs in the area and thousands of dollars in annual taxes on the city's investment of only $1 million. More importantly, it would be a key ingredient in Atlanta's long, often frustrating, desire to reinvigorate the depressed southside of the city.[62]

But the "crowning jewel" in Andrew Young's blueprint for economic development in downtown Atlanta was the $142 million new Underground Atlanta project. The old Underground, a popular entertainment-retail complex during the 1970s, had fallen victim to crime and perceptions of crime shortly before Young entered office. But he quickly envisioned its revival as a necessary ingredient in his development plans. Underground, he said, could spur new downtown hotels, new downtown housing, business and job growth, and, hence, new taxes. Skeptics both in and out of government worried that the fear of crime that had doomed the old Underground would deter too many tourists and white suburbanites, the latter group seen as the critical mass in the equation, to allow the project to succeed. The indomitable mayor was undeterred, however. He convinced a group of important Atlanta businessmen to "stake out" $15 million in "seed money" for the project and the City Council to contract with the nationally respected Rouse Company, an urban development firm, to develop designs. The key to Young's persuasive abilities in this instance was his promise that the new Underground would be saturated with security and the project would embrace 150 businesses, providing

3,000 new jobs and producing $5 million a year in new tax revenue.[63]

Still, the new Underground Atlanta, which was scheduled to open in the summer of 1989, was one of Young's biggest gambles as mayor. Hundreds of police and other security officers could increase safety, but could not absolutely assure it. One or two major incidents could send customers running forever. Or, no matter what the security precautions, could the fear that white suburbanites had of downtown Atlanta and its mostly black pedestrians, particularly in the evenings, be overcome? If Young's Underground failed, the city would inherit a huge debt and the mayor's future political career and his place in the nation's political history would suffer tremendous damage.[64]

The mayor was already painfully aware of political and other problems that adverse publicity at a tourist facility could cause. In 1984 the American Association of Zoological Parks and Aquariums (AAZPA) withdrew the accreditation of the Atlanta Zoo, and in a survey of the nation's zoos, the American Humane Society called Atlanta's "the worst." The zoo's woes received national attention when officials could not account for a sick elephant who had allegedly been sent to a traveling circus "to die," and when reports surfaced that one of the keepers had eaten some of the smaller animals from the children's petting zoo. As news of the zoo's deterioration spread, attendance in 1984 dropped to a new modern low of 279,805 persons.[65]

The responsibility for the zoo's decline was laid at the feet of Dr. Emmett Ashley, chief veterinarian at the southeast Atlanta facility. Ashley, who had personally cared for Mayor Andrew Young's dogs for 15 years, was the first black person to head the Atlanta Zoo. Some citizens and officials accused Ashley of incompetence and insensitivity. They surmised that "niggers can't even run a zoo," which bolstered the conclusion of some of Young's critics that blacks also could not run a city. For his part Mayor Young sympathized with Ashley's claim that he, as the first black department head at the zoo, was a victim of white racism and pointed out that his own animals had always received competent and caring treatment from the veterinarian. But after the Atlanta City Attorney's office and a Fulton County Grand Jury exonerated Ashley of any culpability in animal deaths, the city of Atlanta paid him $7,000 as a settlement for leaving his position. Following Ashley's departure, a white man, Dr. Terry Maple, was placed in charge of the zoo. The park quickly rebounded, regained its accreditation, and by 1988 was attracting nearly 800,000 visitors each year.[66]

The fostering of a good image for visitors and tourists at the zoo and elsewhere was crucial to the claim of Mayor Young and others that

Atlanta was "the world's next great city." The most important event in this regard during Young's tenure was the hosting of the 1988 National Democratic Convention.

When it became clear that the Democrats favored a Southern site for their 1988 party convention, Atlanta's chances to win the selection increased markedly. In the end, the city had only two real rivals in the South, New Orleans and Houston, both of which had or would have convention hall facilities superior to that of Atlanta. But Atlanta held the edge in transportation and in the number of hotel rooms. And Atlanta was the official home of the last Democratic President, Jimmy Carter, and the city was led by one of the party's leaders, former U.N. Ambassador Andrew J. Young. Under the leadership of Young and Georgia Governor Joe Frank Harris, a business-government partnership was formed under an umbrella group known as "Atlanta 88." Members of this organization traveled to New York, Washington, and elsewhere, wooing Democratic National Committee (DNC) site selection committee members, particularly Democratic National Party Chairman Paul Kirk, and lavishing them with "Southern hospitality" during their visits to Atlanta. Eventually only the relatively small size of the 15,000-seat Omni Arena stood between Atlanta and the Democrats. But the DNC came to believe that ingenious architectural configurations could ease, if not solve, the difficulty, and Atlanta was awarded its first national political convention.[67]

Even if the Democratic Party leadership could overcome its reservations about the Omni Convention Hall, "Yankee" journalists, who descended on the city for an inspection tour shortly after the convention site was announced, could not and did not. Several leading periodicals, including *Newsweek*, *U.S. News and World Report*, and the *Wall Street Journal*, published unflattering stories about the Omni and Atlanta right up to the eve of the Democrats' arrival. They found the Omni small, cramped, crowded, and ugly. While the city had sufficient hotel capacity, too many of the rooms, including those assigned to some journalists and some delegations, were miles away from the Omni, even in adjoining cities and counties. The city's infrastructure, including the freeway system, was in disrepair, and so was the city itself. Finally, the city lacked important cultural sites and was drab and deserted at night. And at the time, some local officials were even threatening to shut down the nude dancing bars. Atlanta, the journalists claimed, was not ready for "prime time."[68]

State and city officials were visibly angered by the journalists' assaults. After all, the Atlanta 88 group had spent millions of dollars in public and private funds to prepare for the Democrats and particularly for the 15,000 media representatives from throughout the world. In fact, it was this latter group, even more than the delegates, on which Atlanta wanted to make a favorable impression. For, although the delegates and others would leave behind approximately $70 million after the four-day convention, pictures and words of a vibrant, dynamic, international city would be worth billions of dollars in the years to come. Seemingly undaunted by the naysayers, Mayor Young announced that Atlanta would be ready for the Democrats in July and continued to plant new trees and flowers, clean the streets and hang banners. Meanwhile, a Fulton Superior Court Judge ruled the county could not ban nude dancing in the city's bars.[69]

After spending a sizzling July week in Atlanta, some Democrats complained about the heat and the cramped and crowded Omni Arena, where on the last two nights of the convention the fire marshal locked several of them out of the building. Many journalists, particularly in the print media, claimed that their pre-convention complaints had been justified and fretted about the heat. But most people apparently left the city with a very favorable impression of Atlanta's progress and its potential. Although much of this aura was achieved by an unprecedented outpouring of courtesy, civility, and hospitality, it nevertheless had a distinct imprint of genuineness. For example, U.S. Senator Bob Graham of Florida wrote: "Atlanta showed the world what Southern hospitality is all about . . . Atlanta's triumph is a tribute to the leadership of Mayor Andrew Young and Governor Joe Frank Harris." Mike Sullivan, the governor of Wyoming commented: "Atlanta established a new standard [of hospitality] during the . . . Democratic National Convention. It was a marvelous effort . . . You have every reason to be proud of your city, your people . . ." And, Donald G. Ward, Director of Special Markets of the Greater Houston Convention and Visitors Bureau, who had tried to wrest the convention site from Atlanta, wrote that Houston wanted to "'tip its hat' to Atlanta for its outstanding success in hosting" the Democrats. He said: "The 1988 convention in Atlanta had to be one of the most outstanding successes in political party history."[70]

Atlantans themselves also adjudged the convention a great success and gave themselves a collective "pat on the back." But the person most responsible for the achievement, according to the city's leading developer, John Portman, was Mayor Andrew Young. Portman declared:

> All Atlantans can feel proud of Mayor Andrew Young as he graciously hosted the most important convention of the city's history.

What made his contribution particularly special? It is his leadership. Leadership in helping the convention come to Atlanta in the first place. Leadership demonstrated by his diplomatic handling of civil disobedience. Leadership in helping beautify Atlanta with the Trees Atlanta and Peachtree Planters program . . . And finally leadership in helping our visitors from all over the world feel at home . . . At a time when Atlanta is working hard to become 'the next great international city,' Andrew Young helped make the city a little more personal and a little more friendly than any other city in the world. And that's something [of] which all Atlantans can be proud.[71]

With the successful Democratic Convention only a few weeks behind him, Mayor Young took the leadership of a campaign to bring the 1996 Olympic Games to Atlanta. He was continuing to work hard to make Atlanta, in Portman's words, "the next great international City."[72]

It was, then, one of those recurring ironies of history that the same Andrew Young who emerged as a hero of the 1988 Democratic National Convention almost spoiled the occurrence for both himself and his city with a single phone call. The intriguing series of episodes began on March 19, 1987 when Mrs. Alice Bond, the wife of former State Senator Julian Bond, walked into a police precinct near her home and told a group of white police officers that her husband was abusing cocaine. Mrs. Bond had been earlier provoked by an alleged attack on her with a shoe by Carmen Lopez Butler, the ex-senator's alleged girlfriend. The affair catapulted from a domestic one to a political one when, during her interview with police, Alice Bond suggested that Dr. Walter Young, the mayor's brother, and other prominent Atlantans were drug users and/or dealers. She was also quoted as saying that she had been told that Mayor Young himself had used drugs.[73]

During the early course of the police investigation, which was soon curtailed as a result of actions by Atlanta Police Chief Morris Redding and Public Safety Commissioner George Napper, Mayor Young learned some of the details of Mrs. Bond's reports. He called Mrs. Bond out of what he called "concern" for the couple, his longtime personal friends. But U.S. Attorney Robert Barr believed the call may have amounted to interference with an ongoing criminal investigation (The FBI had already entered the probe). Some of Young's supporters accused Barr, a white Republican "with political aspirations," of joining a racist conspiracy to undermine the credibility of black elected officials and of conspiring to undermine or embarrass the Democratic National Convention in Atlanta.[74]

Local, state, and national Democratic Party officials were clearly disturbed about the ramifications of the mayor's call of concern to Mrs. Bond. Could the Democratic Convention be held at all in a city where the mayor, a prominent national party leader, was under a cloud of suspicion or under indictment? If it were held, particularly since one of the leading contenders for the nomination was also a prominent black politician, might not there be considerable racial antagonism and political embarrassment? Yet throughout the affair, Mayor Young insisted that he had only made an innocent, humanitarian gesture in calling Mrs. Bond and had not in any way attempted to interfere with the investigation resulting from her accusations. DNC Chairman Paul Kirk — at least publicly — continued to voice unequivocal support for Young and for Atlanta as the site of the 1988 convention. Those white politicians and business leaders, including Governor Joe Frank Harris, who dared to voice an opinion on the matter, affirmed their belief in Young's innocence. Former U.S. Attorney General Griffin Bell was selected to head Young's defense team. But shortly after Young testified before a Federal Grand Jury and Alice Bond told the same jury that Young had not interfered, U.S. Attorney Barr announced that there was insufficient evidence to prove that Young had broken any laws. National Democratic leaders undoubtedly joined Young, at least figuratively, as he wiped his brow and breathed a sign of relief at a news conference immediately following the report of his exoneration.[75]

Other events during and immediately following the 1988 Democratic Convention in Atlanta also threatened to smear the favorable image for which Mayor Young and other city fathers had worked so hard. Although developer John Portman praised the mayor's handling of convention protestors, many others, including some inside City Hall, decried actions taken against demonstrators before and after the main festivities.

The first major altercation occurred on the Sunday afternoon preceding the first day of the convention. A legally authorized protest by a small group of white supremacists, led by Richard Barrett of Mississippi, attempted to march from the State Capitol to near the convention hall. They were attacked by a group of 500 counter demonstrators under the banner of anti-Ku-Kluxers. The anti-Klan mob overwhelmed the small contingent of state and local police who had sought to protect the marchers. With the approval of Mayor Young, Public Safety Commissioner George Napper halted the supremacist march and ordered it canceled. While defending the cancellation, Young rebuked the anti-Klan counter demonstrators for their "liberal tyranny." But Gene Guerrero, Executive Director of the American Civil Liberties Union of Georgia, tossed a strong dose of criticism at the Young administration. He said: "To let a small group of a few hundred counter protesters interrupt freedom of speech is shameful . . . ."[76]

The mayor came in for even stronger condemnation for his administration's handling of a wave of anti-abortion demonstrations that began during the convention, but were continued throughout the rest of the year. The anti-abortion protestors, composed primarily of white middle-aged, middle-class, religious fundamentalists, descended upon Atlanta from all over the country during the Democratic Convention. In their first two weeks in the city, they surrounded a select group of abortion clinics in an attempt either to shut down the facilities or to make it difficult for patients to enter. In these first two weeks more than 100 were arrested. Almost all of them refused to give their correct names. Instead, they adopted the names, "Baby John" or "Baby Jane Doe." This strategy prevented the courts from granting them bail.[77]

By August 17, the number of anti-abortion arrests in Atlanta had risen to 563. And although some demonstrators reportedly "charged the police line and even took swipes at officers," the police carried out their duties without employing force, gingerly lifting limp protestors and carrying them to patrol wagons. Indeed, the patience of police officers "amazed" some observers as well as activists and even drew praise from fundamentalist leader Jerry Falwell. But in the wake of continuing and more aggressive demonstrations and a large outpouring of public hostility toward the protests, the police tactics suddenly changed and Atlanta's reputation for tolerance came increasingly into disrepute.[78]

The break first appeared during the first week of October 1988 when a new wave of anti-abortion demonstrators re-enforced the Atlanta group to conduct the so-called "siege of Atlanta." Scores of protestors were arrested by police officers who used neck holds, pressure holds, arm twists, and finger holds to forcibly remove them. At least one demonstrator was kicked by a police major. In a meeting with Atlanta Police Chief Morris Redding on October 11, several members of the Atlanta City Council sharply criticized the police actions and demanded an investigation. Councilman Dozier Smith said that "it was a sad day for the city of Atlanta," and he "chastised" Mayor Andrew Young for remaining silent during the protests. Councilman Hosea Williams compared the city's intolerance of peaceful protests to the tactics of Adolph Hitler.[79]

Several observers underscored the "tragic irony" of examples of intolerance toward civil disobedience demonstrators on the part of

Atlanta officials since many of them, including Mayor Young, had been leaders of similar protests during the Civil Rights Movement. The city itself had become known as a "city too busy to hate" and "an oasis of tolerance" at the height of that Movement. But Mayor Young stuck to a positon he had held at the beginning of the protests. In response to a plea from 44 members of the U.S. House of Representatives in August, he had said, "I don't think I'm required in any way to be involved in these demonstrations." The protestors, the mayor pointed out, could be freed if they simply gave their real names. But Councilman Hosea Williams, also a veteran of the Civil Rights Movement, announced in November that he would sue the mayor and the city, if necessary, to prevent the police from denying anti-abortion demonstrators the right to exercise their "First Amendment right of free speech."[80]

Mayor Young's stand on the anti-abortion protests in Atlanta, while seemingly contradictory to his strong credentials as a civil libertarian, in many ways reflected his schizophrenic approach to governance in the city. The central theme of the liberal mayor's two terms in office was economic development. He became as "accommodating of business needs" as even few white mayors had been. Conservative business leaders, even some Republicans, emerged among his strongest supporters. And although he always claimed that the fruits of a healthy business community would "trickle down" in the form of jobs to even the most disadvantaged of his citizens, very little of this occurred during his eight years in office. Near the end of his tenure, poor blacks began to express increasingly public discontent with the mayor's performance. Susie LaBord, president of the Grady Homes housing project tenant association, blamed the mayor's high rate of absenteeism from the city as one of the factors causing dissatisfaction among his poorer constituents. "So, many times, things happen and we can't find him," she said. "If he is concerned, you'd never know it. This city hasn't moved forward. There ain't no better jobs and they are getting harder and harder to get. He should be doing more."[81]

Other critics, including political scientist Tobe Johnson and economist Robert L. Woodson, suggested that Young's "trickle down" theory and focus on jobs have been misplaced. The mayor, Woodson believed, failed "to understand the difference between jobs and wealth. No matter how good one's job, a job is not something one can leave to one's children. Homes, businesses, and other capital assets represent wealth that can, in turn, create jobs . . . ."[82]

To be sure, Mayor Young did energetically pursue the city's model affirmative action program for black businesses, but, in the end, the program mostly benefited a few dozen large black firms. As one critic put it, "it made the rich richer." Generally, there was little growth in major black businesses in the city, and many smaller black-owned groceries, restaurants, and other service institutions fell into Asian hands. As the prize-winning Atlanta newspapers series, "The Color of Money" revealed, much of the capital needed for the development of black business in the city was withheld from that community by white banks. But it was not until after the appearance of the newspaper articles that Mayor Young and other black political and civic leaders applied strong pressures on the bankers to reform.[83]

Mortgage-lending practices in the city also had some effect on the ability of lower and middle-income families to secure affordable housing. The high cost of property in the city also dissuaded many developers from considering low rent projects. Yet the mayor seemed more preoccupied with the development of "upscale" housing downtown, which would promote gentrification, than pushing for "affordable" units for lower income families. And the Atlanta Housing Authority (AHA), which ran the city's public projects, seemed immune to demands for reform from the mayor or anyone else. Meanwhile, the city's homeless shelters were overflowing.[84]

In a city with the second highest poverty rate in the nation, a large homeless population, and a high — but declining — high school drop-out rate, a significant problem with crime is virtually assured. In the midst of a nationwide crack cocaine drug crisis, Atlanta perhaps should not be singled out for its top ranking among the nation's leaders in major crimes. But many, particularly white suburbanites, have contended that the amount of crime in the city can be attributed to the failure of the city's leaders. They have not backed the police in their efforts to aggressively enforce the law. On the other hand, aggressive law enforcement in the past had led to repeated complaints by black residents of police brutality. Thus, when the mayor tried to reduce the perception that the city officials were "soft on crime" by such measures as stronger firearms and more lethal bullets for the police, he aroused black critics. And when he tried to address the perception of police brutality by urging more black officers for "racial balance" and punishing errant officers, he was greeted by a chorus of discord from white critics.[85]

In the end, it would not be correct to say that the only remaining problems in Atlanta after eight years of the mayoralty of Andrew J. Young are crime and housing. While the city is in sound financial condition, many of its pressing physical and human needs have gone unmet. While its mid-town and northern sections have experience true "boom town" economic growth, the largely black south side remains mostly depressed. While its transportation system is one of the finest in the country, much needed expansions are being blocked by racist and other opposition from surrounding suburbs. While the city is aggressively seeking international status, it is straining to convince local white citizens to visit downtown.

Like any good politician, Mayor Young perhaps overstated his accomplishments in his last state of the city address. There have been failures, both real and perceived. Nevertheless, it is clear that he left office with high marks for his leadership in economic growth, as an international ambassador for the city, and as a charismatic broker in Atlanta's delicate balance of race relations.

When Atlanta's last white mayor, Sam Massell, was engaged in a desperate struggle to retain his office in the elections of 1973, he hinted that the city would die under black leadership. Atlanta's first black mayor, Maynard H. Jackson, proved that the prophecy was wrong. Andrew Young, while differing in style and in some substance from Jackson, inherited a strong and vibrant city from his predecessor. Has the city of Atlanta moved forward under Mayor Andrew Young? In 1988 43 percent of white Atlantans said "yes," 43 percent of black Atlantans said "yes"![86]

NOTES

[1] *Atlanta Constitution*, January 4, 1989; City of Atlanta: State of the City Address, January 3, 1989.

[2] *Atlanta Constitution*, January 4, 1989; City of Atlanta: State of the City Address, January 3, 1989, pp. 6-11.

[3] *Atlanta Constitution*, January 4, 1989; City of Atlanta: State of the City Address, January 3, 1989, pp. 4-5; Robert E. Johnson, "Andy Young's Bold Plans for Atlanta," *Jet* (December 3, 1981), pp. 12-14.

[4] *Atlanta Constitution*, January 4, 1989.

[5] *Ibid.* January 4, 1989; State of the City Address, January 3, 1989, p. 1.

[6] *Atlanta Constitution*, December 6, 1988, January 4, 1989; *Atlanta Journal-Constitution*, September 24, 1988; Minutes of the Atlanta City Council, November 7, 1988; State of the City Address, January 3, 1989, p. 1.

[7] *Atlanta Constitution*, October 28, 1983; Charles H. King, Jr., "Unlike Jackson's, Young's Style Invites Challenge," *Atlanta Journal-Constitution*, October 7, 1984, February 20, 1983; *New York Times*, October 21, 1973; Johnson, "Andy Young's Bold Plans," p. 13.

[8] *Atlanta Constitution*, October 28, 1983, August 12, 1987; Charles H. King, "Unlike Jackson," pp. 1, 7, E; *Atlanta Journal-Constitution*, February 20, 1983; State of the City Address, January 3, 1989, pp. 2-3.

[9] *Atlanta Constitution*, October 28, 1983; King, "Unlike Jackson," pp. 1, 7, E; *Atlanta Journal-Constitution*, February 20, 1983; *New York Times*, October 21, 1973.

[10] *Atlanta Journal-Constitution*, September 4, 1988; State of the City Address, January 3, 1989, p. 41.

[11] *Atlanta Journal-Constitution*, September 4, 1988; *Atlanta Constitution*, February 19, 1988; State of the City Address, January 3, 1989, p. 39-40.

[12] Alida C. Silverman to Editor, *Atlanta Constitution*, August 10, 1988; *Ibid.*, March 18, May 5, December 30, 1988; Cynthia Tucker, "Bond Issue That Sticks to Basics Has Better Odds," *Ibid.*, March 19, 1988; *Atlanta Journal-Constitution*, November 6, December 4, 1988; Minutes of the Atlanta City Council, April 18, 1988, December 19, 1988; State of the City Address, January 3, 1989, p. 41. Atlanta is the seat of and the largest city in Fulton County.

[13] *Atlanta Constitution*, December 14, 1988; Minutes of the Atlanta City Council, December 19, 1988.

[14] *Atlanta Journal-Constitution*, December 4, 20, 1988.

[15] *Atlanta Journal-Constitution*, December 4, 1988; *Atlanta Constitution*, December 31, 1987, December 14, 1988; Minutes of the Atlanta City Council, December 19, 1988. The Mayor had proposed a budget of $293,914,251 in 1988. *Atlanta Constitution*, December 31, 1987.

[16] Olav H. Alvig to Editor, *Atlanta Constitution*, June 3, 1988; *Atlanta Journal-Constitution*, May 8, 1988; *Atlanta Constitution*, February 10, 1983, October 15, 1985; State of the City Address, January 3, 1989, pp. 24-26.

[17] *Atlanta Journal-Constitution*, October 14, November 27, 1988; State of the City Address, January 3, 1989, pp. 24-26.

[18] *Atlanta Journal-Constitution*, May 8, November 27, 1988; State of the City Address, January 3, 1989, pp. 24-26.

[19] *Atlanta Constitution*, March 17, 1988.

[20] C.W. Diercke, Jr. to Editor, *Atlanta Constitution*, April 1, August 19, 1988; Olav H. Alvig to Editor, *Ibid.*, June 3, 1988; *Atlanta Journal-Constitution*, June 4, 1983, August 4, 5, 12, 13, 1984, August 24, 1985, *Atlanta Constitution*, July 20, 1983, August 14, 1985; State of the City Address, January 3, 1989, pp. 23-26.

[21] *Atlanta Journal-Constitution*, September 10, 1988.

[22] *Atlanta Constitution*, September 11, 14, 1987.

[23] Dick Williams, "City Fathers are Tying the Hands of Atlanta's Finest," *Atlanta Journal-Constitution*, January 7, 1989; *Ibid.*, September 10, 1988.

[24] *Atlanta Constitution*, September 23, 1983; *Intown Extra* of the *Atlanta Journal-Constitution*, August 7, 1986.

[25] State of the City Address, January 3, 1988, pp. 26, 30, 40; *Atlanta Constitution*, September 23, 1983; *Atlanta Journal-Constitution*, September 15, 1985, *Intown Extra* of *Ibid.*, August 7, 1986.

[26] *Atlanta Journal-Constitution*, December 25, 1988.

[27] *Atlanta Journal-Constitution*, December 25, 1988; Minutes of the Atlanta City Council, July 5, 1988.

[28] *Atlanta Journal-Constitution*, December 16, 26, 1988; *Atlanta Constitution*, December 31, 1988, January 24, 1989; Minutes of the Atlanta City Council, December 19, 1988; State of the City Address, January 3, 1989, pp. 25-26; *Wall Street Journal*, January 4, 1989.

[29] *Atlanta Constitution*, December 28, 1988; Minutes of the Atlanta City Council, December 19, 1988, January 17, 1989.

[30] *Atlanta Constitution*, June 22, 1988; Minutes of the Atlanta City Council, December 19, 1988, January 17, 1989.

[31] *Intown Extra* of the *Atlanta Constitution*, November 31, 1988; *Ibid.*, Dec 15, 16, 1988; Minutes of the Atlanta City Council, November 19, 21, 1988; State of the City Address, January 3, 1989, pp. 26-30; *Atlanta Journal-Constitution*, August 10, November 28, 1985, The State of the City: The Honorable Andrew Young, Mayor of Atlanta, January 4, 1988, p. 13.

[32] *Intown Extra* of the *Atlanta Constitution*, August 18, 1988; State of the City Address, January 4, 1988, pp. 11, 12-13.

[33] Jim Jenkins to Editor, *Atlanta Constitution*, November 15, 1988; Editorial, "Don't Delay Fourth Runway;" *Ibid.*, February 25, 1985; *Ibid.*, February 18, 1986, September 29, 1988; *Atlanta Journal-Constitution*, December 4, 1988.

[34] *Atlanta Constitution*, December 20, 1988, March 12, 1989.

[35] *Ibid.*, December 20, 1988.

[36] David J. Levy, Lucinda J. Levy to Editor, *Atlanta Constitution*, December 14, 1988; *Ibid.*, August 8, 1985; Bill Shipp, "It's Time to Shape Atlanta's Future," *Atlanta Journal-Constitution*, February 26, 1983.

[37] *Atlanta Constitution*, December 9, 12, 1988; Adrienne Howard Houston to Editor, *Ibid.*, January 4, 1985.

[38] *Ibid.*, December 13, 1988.

[39] *Ibid.*, December 9, 13, 15, 1988.

[40] Robert Evans to Editor, *Atlanta Journal Constitution*, September 24, 1988; *Atlanta Constitution*, April 2, 1983, June 1, 1983, March 7, 1985, April 24, 1985, May 16, 1985, June 7, 1985, September 5, 17, 18, 27, 28, 1985, October 9, 13, 21, 1985.

[41] *Atlanta Constitution*, November 15, 1988; *Atlanta Journal-Constitution*, November 10, 1988.

[42] *Atlanta Journal-Constitution*, January 19, 1985, December 4, 1988; *Atlanta Constitution*, December 15, 1982, August 20, 1983, October 22, 1984, September 15, 1986; Minutes of the Atlanta City Council, April 8, 1988,

August 15, 1988, December 19, 1988, State of the City Address, January 3, 1989, p. 8.

[43] *Atlanta Constitution*, May 17, 1983, October 20, 21, 1988; *Atlanta Journal-Constitution*, May 24, 1986; Minutes of the Atlanta City Council, November 7, 1988; Andrew Young to Marvin S. Arrington, October 20, 1988, Clerk of the Atlanta City Council Files.

[44] Ed Siler to Editor, *Atlanta Constitution*, November 3, 1988.

[45] *Atlanta Journal-Constitution*, October 17, 1984, August 4, 1985, March 12, 1989; *Atlanta Constitution*, August 17, 1984, August 10, 12, 1987; Thomas Oliver, "Atlanta: The Unequal North and South of it," *Black Slate Digest* (May, 1985), pp. 1-2.

[46] Robert L. Woodson, "Building a New Base for Black Prosperity," *Atlanta Journal-Constitution*, July 31, 1988; *Ibid.*, August 12, 1984, October 17, 26, 1984, August 4, 1985; *Atlanta Constitution*, October 21, 1983, July 31, 1985, August 10, 12, 1987, December 5, 1988, January 3, 1989, "Atlanta: The Urban Dilemma," *Black Slate Digest* (May 1985), pp. 1-2.

[47] *Atlanta Constitution*, May 9, 12, 13, 1988.

[48] *Atlanta Journal-Constitution*, September 28, 1985, November 15, December 16, 31, 1988; *Atlanta Constitution*, October 7, 22, 31, 1984, May 12, 13, 1988; Minutes of the Finance Committee of the Atlanta City Council, December 15, 1988.

[49] Andrew Young, "Fairness Formula Has Been Crucial to Atlanta's Success," *Atlanta Journal-Constitution*, March 12, 1989: *Atlanta Constitution*, October 19, 1984, January 24, 1989.

[50] *Atlanta Constitution*, August 10, 1988, Minutes of the Atlanta City Council, July 25, 1988.

[51] *Atlanta Journal-Constitution*, December 19, 1982, December 2, 1983, August 21, 1988.

[52] *Atlanta Constitution*, August 10, 1987, December 6, 1988; *Atlanta Journal-Constitution*, October 30, December 2, 1983.

[53] *Atlanta Journal-Constitution*, October 30, 1983, January 11, June 19, 1986, November 5, 1988; Thomas C. Coffin to Editor, *Ibid.*, May 18, 1986; *Intown Extra* of the *Atlanta Constitution*, July 18, 24, 1986; Minutes, Atlanta Urban Design Commission, March 13, 1985.

[54] *Atlanta Journal-Constitution*, January 11, 1986; Thomas C. Coffin to Editor, *Ibid.*, May 18, 1986; Andrew Young, "Atlanta has a commitment to historic preservation — and the future," *Ibid.*, August 1, 1986, *Atlanta Constitution*, June 19, 1986; Minutes of the Atlanta City Council, August 1, 1988; Minutes of the Atlanta City Council, December 19, 1988.

[55] *Atlanta Constitution*, December 6, 1988; *Atlanta Journal-Constitution*, December 2, 1983; Johnson, "Andy Young's Bold Plans," pp. 13-15.

[56] Jim Auchmutey, "Saving the Falcons: Is It Love, Profit or Civic Insecurity," *Atlanta Journal-Constitution*, October 9, 1988; *Ibid.*, May 29,

1988; *Atlanta Constitution*, August 12, 1987; Bruce Galphin, "Two Terms of Endearment," *Atlanta Weekly*, June 14, 1984.

[57] *Atlanta Constitution*, October 28, 30, 1985, July 3, December 3, 8, 12, 1988, July 4, 1989, *Atlanta Journal-Constitution*, May 29, 1988.

[58] *Atlanta Journal-Constitution*, July 3, December 24, 1988; Tom Borsum to Editor and Paul D. Coverdell, "Don't Force Dome Plan on Public," *Ibid.*, October 9, 1988; R. B. Patterson to Editor, *Atlanta Constitution*, August 9, 1988.

[59] *Atlanta Constitution*, August 12, 1987, July 29, August 2, 3, 1988; *Atlanta Journal-Constitution*, August 8, 1987.

[60] *Atlanta Constitution*, August 12, 1987, August 3, September 12, 1988; *Atlanta Journal-Constitution*, January 7, 1989.

[61] *Atlanta Constitution*, August 2, 3, 18, 1988.

[62] *Atlanta Constitution*, September 29, 1988; State of the City Address, January 3, 1989, p. 10; Minutes of the Budget Commission of the City of Atlanta, December 15, 1978; Minutes of the Finance Committee of the Atlanta City Council, December 15, 1988.

[63] *Atlanta Journal-Constitution*, January 19, 1985, December 4, 1988; *Atlanta Constitution*, December 15, 1982, August 20, 1983, October 22, 1984; September 15, 1986; Minutes of the Atlanta City Council, April 8, August 15, December 19, 1988; State of the City Address, January 3, 1989, p. 8.

[64] *Atlanta Journal-Constitution*, October 7, 1984, December 4, 1988; Minutes of the Atlanta City Council, December 19, 1988.

[65] *Atlanta Constitution*, July 11, October 22, 1984, June 30, 1988, February 2, 1989, Jean Jandel Bombach to Editor, *Ibid.*, July 12, 1984; *Atlanta Journal-Constitution*, June 10, July 4, 1984; State of the City Address, January 3, 1989, p. 34.

[66] *Atlanta Constitution*, June 10, 1974, August 1, 1975, July 11, October 22, 1984, June 30, September 24, 1988, February 2, 1989, Jean Jandel Bombach to Editor, *Ibid.*, July 12, 1984; Author's Interview with W. Lewis Williams, July 18, 1984; Author's Interview with Larry Carter, Atlanta, Georgia, July 19, 1984; *Atlanta Journal-Constitution*, July 4, 8, 1984; State of the City Address, January 3, 1989, p. 34.

[67] *Atlanta Journal-Constitution*, August 31, 1985, July 19, 20, 1986; *Atlanta Constitution*, July 17, 1986, February 6, December 15, 1987; The State of the City: The Honorable Andrew Young, Mayor of Atlanta, January 4, 1988, p. 2.

[68] *Atlanta Constitution*, June 23, 25, 29, July 24, 1988; *Wall Street Journal*, February 29, 1988.

[69] *Atlanta Constitution*, June 23, 25, July 11, 24, 1988.

[70] *Atlanta Journal-Constitution*, July 23, 1988; *Atlanta Constitution*, July 24, August 10, 1988.

[71] *Atlanta Constitution*, August 10, 1988; State of the City Address, January 3, 1989, pp. 42-43.

[72] *Atlanta Constitution*, August 10, September 12, 1988; State of the City Address, January 3, 1989, pp. 41-42.

[73] *Atlanta Journal-Constitution*, January 28, March 19, 1989.

[74] *Ibid.*, August 8, 9, 1987, March 19, 1988.

[75] *Ibid.*, March 19, 1988.

[76] *Atlanta Constitution*, July 18, August 10, 1988.

[77] *Ibid.*, July 20, August 10, 1988.

[78] *Atlanta Constitution*, August 10, 17, 1988; Carol Wienstein to Editor, Nisha Sumama to Editor, Robert Frost to Editor, Betty Burton to Editor, M. Sullivan to Editor, Cathy A. Snapp to Editor, *Ibid.*, August 18, 1988; Cynthia Tucker, "Protesters Have Little Sympathy for Struggles of Life Outside Womb," *Ibid.*, August 18, 1988.

[79] *Ibid.*, August 18, October 6, 12, 1988.

[80] Don McKee, "Have Atlanta's Leaders Forgotten the Right to Engage in Civil Disobedience?" *Atlanta Journal-Constitution*, October 19, 1988; *Ibid.*, November 12, 1988.

[81] Michael McQueen, "Dream Deferred: Despite Their Wider Influence, Black Leaders Find Goals for Black Poor Elusive," *Wall Street Journal*, July 30, 1987; Jim Minter, "Andy Young, Atlanta's Preacher and Healer," *Atlanta Journal-Constitution*, January 9, February 20, July 24, 1983, State of the City Address, p. 15; *Atlanta Constitution*, February 23, May 23, 1987; King, "Unlike Jackson."

[82] *Atlanta Constitution*, May 23, 1988; Woodson, "Building a New Base for Black Prosperity," *Atlanta Journal-Constitution*, July 31, 1988; State of the City Address, January 3, 1989, p. 15

[83] *Atlanta Journal-Constitution*, May 15, 1988: State of the City Address, January 3, 1989, pp. 13-15.

[84] *Atlanta Constitution*, November 15, 1988; *Intown Extra* of *Ibid.*, August 18, 1988; *Wall Street Journal*, February 9, 1983.

[85] Dick Williams, "City Fathers are Tying the Hands of Atlanta's Finest," *Atlanta Journal-Constitution*, January 7, 1989; William Ellis to Editor, May 7, 1988; *Ibid.*, February 19, 1983, August 31, 1985, September 24, 1988; Graham Brett to Editor, *Atlanta Constitution*, April 4, 1985; *Ibid.*, June 4, 1983, June 26, 28, October 26, 1984, August 1, 1985.

[86] *Atlanta Constitution*, August 10, 1987, May 23, 1988; King, "Unlike Jackson," *New York Times*, October 21, 1973.

Chapter 17
Martin Luther King, Jr.:
The Man and His Philosophy

As you know, scholars and others spend a lot of thought and a lot of ink speculating on the environmental and personal influences which affect the attitudes, programs, ideals, and philosophies of outstanding individuals in history. Sometimes, the more foolish, or should we say less wise, search for a single incident, event, institution or individual which or who had the decisive impact in shaping the direction which a certain important or great life took. Obviously, this is a rather fruitless enterprise, for it is rare, if not impossible, that one can cite a single act, institution, or program that accounts solely for the thought and action of any individual. Certainly, several influences converge, beginning in childhood, to finally make the man or woman what he or she becomes and the value decisions that he or she will make in their lives.

In the example of the subject whom we treat today, Martin Luther King, Jr., one might argue narrowly that his birth and rearing in the city of Atlanta, Georgia was decisive in determining what he later became; or one might argue that his education at Morehouse and/or at Crozier and Boston were central to his philosophy; or one might argue that his early location at Montgomery was the pivotal factor in his path to greatness. Such a view would suggest that had he been born in Chicago, had he attended Southern Illinois and/or Yale and Howard, or had he first took up a pastorate in Miami, his life and our lives would

Presented at Southern Illinois University at Carbondale, January 14, 1982

have been much different. While as suggested, this may be a narrow view, in that it emphasizes several single influences, one cannot discount the cumulative effects of environment, institutions, and personalities on the ultimate lifestyle, ideas, and ideals of any of us. Thus, it is more than simply an heuristic exercise to examine the origins, growth, and development of an individual and particularly a notable individual, like Martin Luther King, Jr. In fact, such an examination, when viewed cumulatively, rather than singularly, can, perhaps, aid in the understanding of the person and his or her philosophy. And so, one might ask of Martin Luther King, Jr., what manner of man?

In terms of his early environment, we do not and possibly cannot know whether King's birth in Atlanta, Georgia on January 15, 1929 forecast for him a different role in society than had he been born in Chicago, Illinois. We do know that birth and rearing in Atlanta was apparently pivotal in the eventual career of Walter White and that DuBois' tenure in the South, largely in Atlanta, helped to shape much of his thought and action. These men have told us as much. So, perhaps, we should look briefly at the city of Atlanta during the formative years of Martin Luther King, Jr. to see if we might discover any significant guideposts which may have left lasting impressions upon him.

Today, when we view the city of Atlanta, we often picture it as a "Black Mecca" — a city whose political life is effectively controlled by blacks and which boasts one of the most prosperous and most visible black middle classes in the nation. But, when Martin Luther King, Jr. was born in that city in 1929, it was still a capital of white supremacy. The prescribed life of black Atlantans was typical of that in all parts of the Southern caste system. The horrendous Atlanta Race Riot of 1906, in which dozens of blacks had been wantonly killed or injured, showed clearly the precariousness of life for blacks in the city. It was during that riot that young Walter White, although blond of hair and blue of eyes, cast his lot with the Negro race, after standing at a window with his father, gun in hand, as a white mob approached his home. Yet, in 1929, Atlanta was also rather unique in the life it offered some black Americans. It was, even then, the largest center for the higher education of blacks in the world, with four colleges, a seminary, and a graduate university. It already boasted a black bank, which would keep its doors open, even during the Great Depression, and numerous other businesses, including, at the time, the wealthiest black life insurance company in the nation. There were handsome black homes on the east side of the city, where the black population was heaviest, and on the near west side, in the vicinity of the black university complex. While black voters were excluded from the white primary contests, which were tantamount to election, they could vote in general and special elections. They demonstrated, very early, a high degree of political sophistication when, in the 1920s they cast their votes solidly when they could in special and general elections. In one such special election, they bargained with the white power structure, offering their crucial support in a bond election, only if a long sought black high school was constructed in the city. Such inter-racial contacts and negotiations had been made possible after many white leaders expressed revulsion over the Atlanta Riot of 1906 and particularly its negative effect on the city's image as capital of the New South and the concurrent negative impact on the growth of business.

As can be seen, however, the positive images of black life in the youth of Martin Luther King, Jr. could be experienced mainly by members of the middle class — preachers, teachers, business persons. Yet, because of segregated housing, poor black folk often lived within a stone's throw of their more fortunate neighbors. So, although young Martin was the son of a prosperous and influential minister in the city, who had attained much of his prosperity and influence by marrying the daughter of a prosperous and influential minister, his matriculation at the David T. Howard School assured that he would have classmates and playmates of lower as well as middle socio-economic levels. Of course, the worshippers in his father's church also contained such a mixture. Only when he transferred to the Laboratory School of Atlanta University could he find a relatively homogenous student body. But, even here, King could not escape the environs which were dominated by two housing projects for low-income blacks and the notorious Beaver's Slide slums. Yet, the Atlanta University School did provide another ingredient that was unique in King's educational experience, white teachers, mainly from the North who were Classicists in their secular instruction and rigid and orthodox in their social, moral, and religious training. This atypically black educational scene was broken for King when he moved to the Booker T. Washington High School, a public school, for the last two years of his pre-collegiate training. Lab high school ended at the tenth grade. At Booker T. Washington, King returned to a heterogeneous class environment and an all-black faculty. But, he apparently suffered little, if any, in terms of the quality of the educational experience he received.

Black Atlantans had dreamed of and agitated for a high school for their race at least since the beginning of the new century. It was, however, only after they bargained their votes in a special bond election that the Booker T. Washington High School was erected in 1923. It immediately became a source of great pride for black Atlantans and exercised influence among them, second only to the local churches. The first corps of teachers, as well as subsequent ones, were often more highly and, perhaps, better trained than their white colleagues. Because professional opportunities for blacks were so narrowly limited, blacks crowded into teaching, even though many of them possessed advanced degrees, and because they could not study in the South, many of them were possessors of graduate degrees from the best Northern universities. But, perhaps, the single greatest influence at Washington High School during these years was the principal, Professor C. L. Harper. Harper was a man of considerable intelligence and a proponent of the same type of strict social and moral deportment that King had experienced at lab school. Yet he was also a "Race Man" — a militant advocate of black pride, voting, and civil rights, and equal, even if separate, educational opportunity. His influence was clearly felt throughout the school, and as President of the local NAACP throughout the city and state. Some pupils, like Martin Luther King, Jr., were apparently affected by him to a greater degree than others, for King's family had close personal ties with Professor Harper.

After Washington High School it was on to Morehouse College for young King, and it was, indeed, young King, for as a result of several accelerations in his pupilage, he was only 15 as a college freshman. Morehouse was a natural destination for King, in that his grandfather had been an ardent supporter of the school, his father was a graduate and supporter, and his mother and sister had attended the school's sister institution, Spelman College. It, importantly, at least to the Kings, had a heritage of affiliation with the Baptist Church, and it had a reputation for excellent leadership under a series of staunch Baptist intellectuals, particularly John Hope, one of the earliest challengers of the philosophy of Booker T. Washington, and the current President Benjamin E. Mays.

It was probably the inspiration of Mays and Professor George Kelsey of the School of Religion which helped pull King away from Medicine or Law and into Theology, something of course his family had wanted all along. These learned, but spirited, men were catalysts in convincing the young King that black ministers could be more than exhorters, but could actually mesh the worldly and the other-worldly in a scholarly, yet meaningful way. Mays, for example, in his religious practices, sought a middle ground between those black churches characterized by "whooping and hollering" and those which were inordinately stiff and formal. This was also the middle ground that young Martin Luther King, Jr. was seeking. Outside of this, Mays stressed excellence in life and in work and challenged Morehouse men to defy mediocrity, rising, even above segregation and discrimination, to demonstrate their worthiness. He rejected segregation, even amid segregation; always insisting on a multi-racial and multi-national faculty.

Possibly because he had skipped several grades in his pre-collegiate career and because he was well known and popular at Morehouse, King's tenure there was not exceptional. It was at Crozier and Boston that King, now more mature and separated from Atlanta, seemed to drink more fully at the fountain of knowledge. He listened to scholars like George Davis, Morton Einslin, Doc Brightman, and Harold DeWolf. He pondered the words of activists like the Socialist-Pacifist, A. J. Muste. He delved into question and discussion with faculty and classmates. He read Mays on the black church, Walter Rauschenbusch on the social implications of religion, and Reinhold Niebuhr on passivism and non-resistance.

King's first biographer, Lawrence Reddick, describes these years as a groping for a philosophy of life. King was apparently seeking self-fulfillment as well as a way to meet what he viewed as his social obligation. His courtship and marriage of Coretta Scott, while a student at Boston, set him on a course toward the type of stable family life he sought. In terms of other features of his ideals, a major influence came from Dr. Mordecai Johnson who spoke in Philadelphia, near Crozier Seminary, in 1950. Johnson had, particularly since his recent trip to India, embraced the teachings of Mahatma Gandhi in his struggles against British Imperialism. Gandhism, as Johnson interpreted it, stressed simplicity, intellectualism, social equality, and the redemptive power of love as a vehicle for non-violent social action. This message, particularly as delivered by the President of Howard University, a fellow Morehouse graduate, and a family friend, seemed to hit home in the mind of Martin Luther King, Jr. He had not fully accepted Niehbur's non-resistance, nor Muste's pacifism, but he had rejected violent force as an appropriate means for social reform. Thus, in non-violent resistance, idealistic pacifism as well as violence could be supplanted by love which became the preeminent force for social change. It appeared that such a philosophy had wrought significant changes in India, it might well be, at least to Martin Luther King, Jr., a rationale for personal fulfillment and for social obligation.

The most immediate concern facing King as well as any other

socially conscious black American at the time was the plight of the black race in America. Since King entered Morehouse in 1944, the white primary had been outlawed; blacks were voting uninhibited in his native city of Atlanta; black policemen patrolled black Atlanta streets; the federal courts had ordered the doors of some all-white colleges in the South open to blacks; and the Supreme Court was preparing to rule segregation in the lower schools unconstitutional. These were, indeed, momentous changes. But, for the most part, devious and illegal devices still kept most Southern blacks away from the polls and out of elective office; legalized segregation persisted, despite recent and imminent court rulings, and humiliating segregation and discrimination in public accommodations and in transportation continued throughout almost all of the South as well as many parts of the rest of the country. Any astute observer, then, could conclude that the black race had come a fairly long way, at least or certainly from slavery, but had a long way to go.

So it might be said that in 1955 the forces of the past — segregation, discrimination, white supremacy, white privilege, white arrogance and the forces of the present and future — black literacy, an articulate and economically secure black middle class, increased black political participation, increased legal assaults on the caste system, and black pride converged at Montgomery, Alabama in the arrest of Rosa Parks for defying Southern law and custom by refusing to give up her seat to a white man on a local bus. The desirability, the demand for action on the part of the black community was clear. But it needed a mode, direction, a philosophy, and a leader. Martin Luther King, Jr. was excellently prepared and situated to provide the strategy, the leadership, and the ideals. As a relative newcomer to Montgomery, he was not deeply entrenched in community factionalism. This probably enhanced his opportunity. But there were other qualities, many possibly influenced by the environment of his formative and early adult years, which immeasurably aided his ascension to leadership. He was a son of the black church — the most important social institution in the black community. And while he rejected the more emotional aspects of that church, he could understand the spiritual and practical needs of worshippers of every class and rank. He had received an excellent education, from kindergarten to college and university. He had been reared in a loving and caring family and aspired to have a similar one, himself. Although, comfortably middle class all of his life, he was intimately acquainted with the life of the poor. Although his family shielded him from the harshest aspects of segregation and discrimination at Atlanta, he lived and moved in a segregated society,

where degradation could not be avoided. These broad experiences, combined with his gift for oratory, enwrapped him with the necessary charisma to inspire confidence in himself and in others and to attract a legion of followers. As he became a national leader, he could build upon his earlier experiences and his recent experiences at Montgomery to forge a succinct philosophy of non-violent resistance to segregation and discrimination. He portrayed the philosophy eloquently in his "Letter From the Birmingham Jail," in his other books, and in numerous orations across the country. In that the Kingsian philosophy evolved from the internal dynamics of the black community, including the central role of the church and the cultural milieu of a laboring and poorly educated people, combined with Niebuhrism, Rauschenbusenism, and Gandhism, as well as the tenets of the American creed, it can be called a new social-intellectual system. But, it was also pragmatic, for although King showed signs of growing weary of American systemic imperfections toward the end of his life, he never publicly advocated radical social reform. He was probably wise enough to know that he who seeks radical reform in America also seeks suicide. And although, J. Edgar Hoover's FBI apparently tried to encourage him, King was not suicidal. Instead of overturning Capitalist-Democracy, King simply asked America to live up to the creed it professed.

In employing confrontation with oppressive forces as his major strategy, Martin Luther King, Jr. was an exponent of force in social change, but in submitting to arrest and assault, he used love, not violence as the instrument of his force. Yet, most agree, that he achieved as much without firing a shot as some who have employed tanks and grenades. In the Carlylian sense, he took the charisma and genius which he possessed and led a movement which wrought a manipulation in the prevailing contours of history, thus qualifying for greatness. And, in the Judaeo-Christian context, he gave his life serving humanity, again qualifying for greatness. Most of us will not qualify for greatness in any sense and so I think it is in recognition of the unique character of this son of the South who did so much for humanity and the human spirit while he was among us that we gather here today and that similar gatherings are occurring all over the country. Finally, I suggest that since he gave up his preferences for a pastorate and for a professorship, gave up his passion to be an ideal father and husband, and ultimately gave up his life for others, we might not only pause once a year in his memory, but also remember and study his life, his works, and his dreams, and build upon these for the sake of our nation, ourselves, and our posterity.

INDEX

ABOUT THE AUTHOR

Alton Hornsby, Jr., a native of Atlanta, Georgia, is Fuller E. Calloway
Professor of History at Morehouse College and former editor of the
Journal of Negro History. His previous works include: *Chronology of
African American History* (two editions), *Milestones in Twentieth
Century African American History,* and *A Short History of Black
Atlanta, 1847-1990.*